WOMEN AND WORK

WOMEN AND WORK

Problems and Perspectives

RACHEL KAHN-HUT
San Francisco State University

ARLENE KAPLAN DANIELS
Northwestern University

RICHARD COLVARD
Southern Oregon State College

New York   Oxford
OXFORD UNIVERSITY PRESS
1982

Library of Congress Cataloging in Publication Data
Main entry under title:
Women and work.
Bibliography: p.   Includes index.
1. Women—Employment—Addresses, essays, lectures.
2. Industrial sociology—Addresses, essays, lectures.
I. Kahn-Hut, Rachel.   II. Daniels, Arlene Kaplan.
III. Colvard, Richard.
HD6053.W638   305.4'3   81-14025
ISBN 0-19-503033-8   AACR2
ISBN 0-19-503034-6 (pbk.)

Printing (last digit): 9 8 7 6 5 4 3 2 1
Printed in the United States of America

Preface

A common image of the work that women do and the work that men do is that women manage the home and child care while men earn the family income. Although this image is inaccurate even in the United States, many find such a division of labor so natural and inevitable that they deplore any deviation from it. But why does such a stereotype seem so natural? In this set of sociological and feminist articles about women and work from recent issues of *Social Problems,* historical and contemporary explanations are presented and critically evaluated.

Once we can see that even a very familiar division of labor is socially constructed rather than eternal and inevitable, we can consider a whole new set of questions. What kinds of work do women actually do? Who does and who does not benefit from patterned differences between men's and women's work? Is it desirable to change these patterned differences—in work both within and outside the home? If so, what are some of the main obstacles to and opportunities for change?

Not everyone—not even every sociologist—agrees on how to answer these questions. The articles in this book draw on a number of perspectives—micro and macro, liberal and radical—with different emphases and policy implications. All offer important ideas and necessary information about the variety of work experiences women have and the consequences of this patterning for men and for women, as well as for the social institutions of family and economy. Several authors suggest that we can find answers to our questions only when we develop a new understanding of "work" in society: given conventional social and academic definitions, much of the work women do in society remains invisible. In addition, while past studies of the division of labor have separated the spheres of women's and men's work in both description and analysis, the new theory developed by feminists suggests this separation is artificial and limits our understanding. We present neither a final explanation of why things are as they are nor a recipe for what to do about them. But we do provide both theories and facts that students can use to develop their own explanations and make their own decisions. We think this book is valuable for those studying the worlds of work as well as those concerned about the position of women in contemporary American society.

The variety of readings presented here under the titles *Women and Work: Problems and Perspectives* is an interrelated collection and the book is itself a collective effort—not just involving the three editors. Seven of the edited readings were selected either from the April 1975 issue of *Social Problems* dedicated to the memory of Caroline Rose or the April 1976 issue on feminist perspectives guest-edited by Lillian Rubin. The remaining ten were selected from other *Social Problems* issues in recent years. Our own efforts as editors were strongly supported financially and administratively by the Society for the Study of Social Problems, publisher of *Social Problems*. Special thanks are owed SSSP's executive officers, Herbert and Rebecca Aurbach of the State University College, Buffalo, New York for their support and encouragement.

All royalties will go to SSSP, which was organized in 1951 by sociologists who felt the traditional concern of sociologists for the study of social issues was lost in the growing absorption in abstract theoretical problems. Since then, SSSP has addressed many social issues and been in the forefront of those in sociology taking account of changing roles for women. It is also a leader in sociology in electing women to its highest offices. So it is not surprising to find many strong articles with a feminist perspective in its journal.

Actually constructing the book involved the efforts of many other people. Mrs. Sybil Bolotin from the staff of the Program on Women, Northwestern University, was especially helpful in assembling the references from newspapers used extensively in the Introduction; and Mrs. Ellen Poole and Mrs. June Weatherly, from Northwestern's Sociology Department, worked unstintingly on drafts of several sections. Lori Biever, Cindi Poling, Lorraine Osborn, Joette Bowden, Gayle Corns, Elizabeth Wilson and D'Anne Iler, all of Southern Oregon State College, assisted in many aspects of the production of the manuscript. Chris Colvard, then assistant to the editor of *Social Problems*, typed several drafts several times, often on short notice, and did much "invisible work" essential to a book with contributions from twenty-three authors and three editors.

Great appreciation goes to colleagues who read drafts and helped sharpen the focus of introductory and interstitial sections. Most particularly we wish to thank Professors Nona Glazer, Barbara Laslett, Val Lorwin, Myra Strober, and Gaye Tuchman.

San Francisco   R.K-H.
Evanston   A.K.D.
Ashland   R.C.
September 1981

Contents

WOMEN AND WORK

Introduction: The Work Women Do

Changing Images, Unchanging Institutions

What do we already know about the work women do? A common stock of knowledge comes from what we hear, see, and read in the mass media. In this introduction we deliberately begin with that source of common knowledge available to us all. Today the popular news media present an increasing number of stories about "women at work." Often the emphasis is on women evolving new life-styles such as commuter marriages or defying tradition by taking leadership positions in crafts and unions, business and professions, art and politics. The press also gives coverage to lawsuits claiming sex discrimination on the job, to pending legislation and administrative correction of inequities. And the press covers coalitions of interest groups— as when labor unions and women's rights groups work together for the Equal Rights Amendment or labor law reform.

Many of these stories include reminders that these events occur at a time when more than half the adult female population in this country works for pay. Leslie Bennetts' articles in *The New York Times* over the past two to three years provide good examples of how this background information is worked into current news. These stories sometimes include speculations by social scientists (e.g., Smith et al., 1979) that some 52 million women may be salaried or seeking paid work by 1990, and that this group will include two-thirds of all married women under fifty-five and over half of all mothers with children under six years of age. They work for a variety of reasons. The number of single women (never married, or divorced) is rising (Smith et al., 1979:14; Weiss, 1979), and these women work to support themselves. With continuing inflation, more households require two wage earners. In 1950, two-thirds of middle-income families had only one earner. By 1972, the typical middle-class family had at least two earners. And many had working children as well, a pattern historically more common in working-class families (Vickery in Smith et al., 1979:165).

The media report this information as part of the news because it raises questions about common images of the way we live. The most likely changes in life patterns and expectations, particularly when more workers are married mothers, are not yet understood. If women are to be equal participants in the paid work force, must social expectations about work and the family change? How drastic will the changes be? Will they superficially alter or radically transform basic relationships between employer and employee, husband and wife, parents and children? (Lloyd and Niemi, 1975, 1980, have projected how changes in the economy will affect women's place in society.) What happens to the intimate relationship between husband and wife if both do the same kinds of work at home and in the paid labor force? Who will rear the children?

While this book of readings cannot answer these questions, it does present some new ways of examining them. For example, we question the conventional definition of "real work" as paid work, usually done by men. We argue that women have always worked in society but that their unpaid contributions have frequently been devalued and remained unnoticed. When they do work for pay, women face many of the same problems of social and economic devaluation. We show how women's typical paid work is related less to their individual characteristics and more to the conditions of the occupational world and the place assigned to women in that world. While a greater variety and number of women have entered the labor force, their opportunities are limited by stereotypes of what women want and can do. Dependence on these stereotypes distracts our attention from the increasing numbers of women who now work outside the home while retaining responsibilities for managing the home and family: 51 percent of all women who work for pay are married, according to the report compiled by FEW (1980). This dual set of responsibilities results in a new style, tone, and tempo of family life, but each woman and each family makes whatever individual adjustment to competing demands and interests that their resources and imagination permit.

As economic and social changes push more women into the labor force, the common assumption that women's "traditional" commitment is to be wives and mothers is being reexamined. There is now greater realization that many women have *always* worked outside the home (Kessler-Harris, 1981; Roby, 1975). When Sojourner Truth spoke in 1851 at the Akron Convention on women's suffrage, she reminded listeners in her speech "Ain't I a Woman?" that oppressed women of all races have always worked as hard and as long as any man. (Her speech is reprinted in Rossi, 1973: 426–429.) The sheltered lady who stayed at home to create a genteel atmosphere in which the children could be reared was an ideal created for the European upper and middle class and exported to their white urban counterparts in the United States (see the article by Epstein, this volume). Yet, it is from the economically privileged group that organized women's movements emerged. These women questioned the advantages of their own sheltered lives and demanded attention for the needs and rights of all women, particularly those working outside the home with no protection.

The ideology of today's women's movement still provides an impetus for relatively privileged women to join with working women in pressing for equality and opportunity in the work force. Doing paid work in addition to work at home is a burden for many who must support families, but many middle- and upper-class women now emphasize a broader need to work outside the home. In a society like ours, inclined to judge individuals by their occupations and pay, middle-class women are now less willing to limit themselves to the homemaker role, to identify themselves as "only a housewife" (Lopata, 1971). Women with the same educational advantages as men are reluctant to accept a subordinate role after college graduation. In *The Feminine Mystique* (1963), Betty Friedan initiated a new phase in the women's movement. She crystallized the growing discontent of college-educated women in the phrase "the problem without a name." The problem was that these women wanted opportunities for self-expression and individual recognition outside the home. They felt frustrated when required to restrict all personal ambition to family and volunteer community service.

Discussion of this problem was made possible by changes in family life. With the transition from an agricultural economy to a capitalist urban-industrial economy, the production of goods and the provision of education, health care, and other services moved from the home to the market. In the process, both wives and children did less that counted visibly and financially as economic work. Children were no longer an economic advantage but a responsibility. Most families were dependent on regular wage work and could afford to give only a few children the care, training, and possessions deemed necessary for social and economic success in a class-stratified society. At the same time, adults were encouraged by family and friends, as well as by the mass media, to evaluate their own worth by how well they cared for their children; these pressures, combined with new and more effective birth control methods, caused a continuing decline in the birthrate. At the same time, opportunities for adults to spend money on their own interests have increased. And many would-be parents see these interests in potential competition with those of a family. In consequence (as Ryder argues in this volume), whatever the fate of abortion legislation, couples will probably continue to limit family size.

All these changes have been recognized and commented on—either as independent or connected trends in our society. Social critics argue, for example, about how much responsibility society should assume for children left unsupervised when both parents work. But the great and even drastic changes in social arrangements that will inevitably occur are unforeseen. Will the institutions of marriage and family continue as we now know them? Some representatives at the White House Conference on the Family in 1980 still clung to the old idealized magazine-cover picture of the American family: a youngish couple with two—and a fraction—children in a relatively affluent white suburb (from which the husband commutes and in which the wife spends her day in housework and child care). Yet only a small minority fit this picture: 7 percent of American families have a working father, dependent mother, and two children (FEW, 1980).

One *minor* adaptation to the changing patterns of work inside and outside the home is the slowly growing formal acceptance of women's right to equal pay for equal work. It is more than fifteen years since Congress declared it illegal to discriminate against women because of their gender by paying them lower wages than men for the same or nearly the same work in the same establishment. To protect women's rights, we have the Equal Pay Act of 1963 and Title VII of the 1964 Civil Rights Act. As yet, however, serious enforcement of this legislation is scarcely envisioned: Equal pay for equal work is still a goal, not an accomplishment. Women still earn far less than men, even when they do similar work. For example, for every salesman's dollar earned, a saleswoman earns 40 cents (FEW, 1980).

In addition, there are affirmative action regulations and legislation for businesses, educational establishments, government agencies, and even voluntary associations to minimize occupational segregation by sex. But disparities in earned income rest on separation of the work force into "ghettos" based on race and sex (Gross, 1968; Reich, Gordon and Edwards, 1973; Williams, 1975). Today, 97.6 percent of all secretaries are female, for example (FEW, 1980). In a historic pattern, job classifications in which females predominate have commanded lower wages, resulting in wide disparities between the average earnings for male and female full-time, year-round employees. "On the average, women currently earn 59 cents for every dollar earned by men—a figure that hasn't changed in 40 years," according to the U.S. Labor Department (Leslie Bennetts, *The New York Times*, Dec. 15, 1979). Accordingly, as long as the work force is segregated as it has been in the past, equal pay for equal work is not a concept that can be used to redress all wrongs. Today a new concept is gaining attention: the idea of equal pay for work of comparable worth. The argument is that in a society where reward is ideally based on skill, jobs should be evaluated in terms of the skills and responsibilities required, whatever the work and whoever does it: A registered nurse is highly skilled and should not be paid less than a janitor or a truckdriver, for example. Yet, in 1980, nurses with 14.2 years of education earned 5.8 percent less than deliverymen; secretaries with 13.2 years of education earned 38 percent less than truck drivers with 9.0 years of education (FEW, 1980). Assessment methods are required to decide what jobs have equal value or comparable worth so that their pay can be equalized (Celarier, 1981; Perlman and Ennis, 1980).

Assessments of comparable work highlight the fact that discrepancy between men's and women's wages does not occur because women are less well educated or trained; women are disproportionately in low-paid service and clerical jobs. More than half of all employed women work in such jobs with limited opportunity and reward (Ross and Sawhill, 1975). Even where women do rise to more prestigious jobs, they inhabit the lower echelons of business, industry, and the professions. Despite the brave new promise of the increasing number of women in the traditionally male professional schools, few women are rising to the key positions of power (Brown, 1979). According to Scientific Manpower Commission reports, only 2 percent of the executives earning more than $25,000 a year are women, and only 1 percent of women hold top jobs (FEW, 1980). Even women graduates of the Harvard Business School earn from $6,000 to $12,000 less than male graduates (*The Chicago Tribune,* Jan. 8, 1978, p. 4). These disparities appear and continue even in fields in which equality between men and women in training and experience is unchallenged. The difficulty of recognizing disparities increases when comparisons between men's and women's salaries are not easily made because so few persons of the opposite sex are present. Thus, an assessment of comparable worth becomes necessary when so many women are concentrated in female occupational ghettos such as nursing and secretarial work.

The large numbers of women flooding the labor market exacerbate the effect of occupational segregation, turning formerly mixed as well as entirely new fields into female occupations. (Valerie Oppenheimer, 1970, traces the long history of this trend.) Typists and secretaries, once male, are now virtually all female (Benét, 1972). Bank tellers (Jackall, 1978) are now almost all females. These clerical positions do not lead to higher-ranking jobs, as they did when men predominated in them. Gissing (1977, originally 1893) suggested, through his novel, *The Odd Women*, that secretarial work could provide independence and opportunity for women otherwise limited to a wretched subsistence as governesses, companions, or shop assistants. But this opportunity has not been the boon that Gissing prophesied, and secretarial work provides little opportunity for women today. Often, previously segregated jobs are opened to women once improved technology has made the work routine. With the reduced skill required, the work becomes dull, low-paid, and unattractive to men (see Braverman, 1974; see also the Glenn-Feldberg and Hacker articles in this volume).

What must happen before working women can participate fully in the occupational hierarchy? Obviously, in the short run, more equitable treatment of women would be very expensive to capitalists: Raising wages reduces profits. It will also raise the costs of public services. The potential disruption of assumptions about reasonable costs are noted in the case brought by nurses against the city and county of Denver for sex discrimination: Tree trimmers, sign painters, and parking meter repairmen, among others, were all paid more than nurses. In ruling against them, the judge said, "This is a case which is pregnant with the possibility of disrupting the entire economic system of the U.S." But comparable-worth advocates say that the financial burden of eliminating pay discrimination is not a valid reason for the courts to reject the principle. "I'm not prepared to put a price tag on correcting discrimination in compensation, and discrimination should not be justified on the basis of the cost to correct it," said a union representative (*The New York Times,* Oct. 26, 1979).

Another concern of those pressing for the rights of working women is sexual harassment on the job. Activists have argued that this problem must be brought into the open for discussion and control if women are to have equal opportunity at work. Expectations about equal salary and fair reward for competence are meaningless unless women are assured a work setting where they will not be openly bullied or indirectly intimidated out of work opportunities by sexual behavior from those with the power to hire, promote, and fire.

Another problem women often face in work both inside and outside the home is the widespread lack of support structures to help with child care or housework (Vanek, 1980; Walker and Woods, 1976). There are very few day-care arrangements that many working women can afford; 84 percent of the children with working mothers have no government-licensed day-care facilities (FEW, 1980). Furthermore, the quality of existing arrangements is not always acceptable, even to those who can find and afford them. In addition, many women face problems getting to and from paid work; this issue is still not acknowledged by politicians. Mass transit is not only a general social problem but a specific one for working women who must take their children to and from school or day-care facilities, return home in time to care for children after school, and arrange transportation for children when they themselves are not available. (Lopata, 1980, analyzes the problems facing women in one metropolitan area.) As Ericksen (1977) points out, the problem is exacerbated for minority women in the inner city who must travel long distances to work. Similarly, there are no widespread, easily available arrangements for paid home care and housework to help women meet many responsibilities still considered primarily theirs. The visions of communal care, presented by early feminists and socialist thinkers like Charlotte Perkins Gilman in *Herland* (1979), have remained utopian. Each family or living unit must manage on its own. This becomes particularly difficult for mothers who work outside the home and, in this group, even more difficult for mothers who are single parents and heads of households (Glazer et al., 1979).

A woman is likely to *feel* defensive about leaving her children. Our society still approves most strongly of the mother who supervises and cares for her children (see Coser and Rokoff, this volume). It is not recognized that many families do not fit the "ideal" pattern: Fathers are absent or unable to support the family adequately; women work to feed and clothe their children in addition to providing traditional mothering. Although they have a dual role, women are encouraged to feel guilty about not remaining home as full-time mothers. This attitude appears in social policy: The state is unwilling to pay the social costs—of child care, for example. And this increases the psychological and emotional burdens of the working mother. Thus social pressures upon the family to care for its own children are increased by the lack of institutional supports for those who cannot meet the ideal standards for parents (see Hunt and Hunt, this volume).

The stigma attached to welfare programs such as Aid to Families with Dependent Children suggests how grudgingly the state meets even the direst need. Since preservation of the family is represented as crucial in much U.S. political ideology (see Coser, this volume) and protection of the family is seen as an individual rather than a societal matter, welfare mothers, like mothers in the paid labor force, are personally blamed for deviating from the idealized family pattern. Whether they work to keep their family off the welfare roles or work at home, caring for their children at the subsistence level of welfare, these women are not meeting pervasive societal expectations.

The larger issue underlying these specific issues is that of equal opportunity for men and women—in paid work and in the home. How can it best be realized? What structural and value changes are necessary? What institutional supports must be provided to give women equal opportunity in the work force? Or to give men the freedom to stay home as the major homemaker and nurturing parent? While some may disagree, the image presented in this reader is not one of optimism about rapid change in such directions.

Some have argued that women like things as they are. One business leader explained the wage differential by pointing out that women leave the labor force for years at a time to raise families. In his view, they thus lose seniority and avoid higher-paying professions in placing family demands over job continuity (*The Chicago Sun Times,* Apr. 29, 1980, p. 24). A study by the National Bureau of Economic Research concludes, "The research indicates that the longer the hiatus in a woman's career the greater the impact on her future earnings" (Clearinghouse International Newsletter, December, 1980). However involuntary this "hiatus" is for many women, employers can interpret it as "what women themselves want." Such reasoning, which also ignores the irrationality of considering the skills and experience involved in raising a family as of no value in later paid work, is evident in a recent statement by representatives of the Business Round Table (an association of executives from nearly 200 of the largest U.S. corporations), denying the existence of wage discrimination against women (*The New York Times,* May 4, 1980, p. 28).

Such a stereotyped view of women's preferences is bolstered in some social science theories focusing on socialization—early learning of values and roles—as *the* barrier to equality (Weitzman, 1979a, b). While there still is what Coser and Rokoff (this volume) call a "cultural mandate" for women to "put family first," an emphasis on socialization as the source of the problem provides a rationale for ignoring current structural arrangements and interactional processes that establish and maintain such mandates. We should not forget that these arrangements benefit owners, employers—and men generally—while discouraging women from trying to attain the better positions in the labor force. Some women lack interest in advancement because the pressures from employers, supervisors, and peers (male and female) make advancement seem too difficult. If we ignore these continuing social pressures against women, we fall into the intellectual trap of "blaming the victim." Those who use this explanation can then disclaim responsibility for the plight of those who are dominated or mistreated even when they themselves are the oppressors (Ryan, 1972).

Other explanations of the ways in which women can be kept down focus on present conditions. One sociological view stresses the familial division of labor by gender: Whether women want it or not, they still carry major responsibility for the home and for integrating the family into the community and the larger society. Men may give the family its status in the community (Parsons et al., 1955), but women provide the liaison with community institutions such as the school, church, and neighborhood, mediating relationships between the family and the larger society (Hess and Handel, 1959). Attached to their husbands, women take what work they can get near their homes. Or, separated from their husbands and supporting themselves and their children, they take what work they can while still maintaining their responsibilities at home (Weiss, 1979). Whether sole or joint parents, women bear the brunt of the work necessary to introduce children to others outside the home. And (as Coser points out in this volume) it is women who are expected to prepare the child's "presentation of self" (Goffman, 1959) in such matters as clothing, lunches, lessons and special recreation.

When this less visible woman's work is acknowledged, as it is in the writings of scholars such as Dorothy Smith (1975–76), as ways women reproduce social class relations, it becomes hard to assume that growing labor force participation by women means progress toward equity. When women work in the labor force, they have two jobs instead of one. Irrespective of how activists feel, it may be a long time before classes and interest groups with the most influence on social policy face all the consequences involved. There is little shared history or sense of common cause for women and other members of the working class to help create real change. Employers have traditionally been successful at using women, minorities, and children to deskill crafts, break strikes, and lower wages. In this competitive labor market, men could not earn enough to support families. In response, unions fought for the right to a family wage for each white male worker (see Huber, this volume). The consequent segregation of jobs between blacks and whites, men and women, has usually been supported by skilled craftsmen who want to minimize competition when it threatens their privileged positions (Bergmann, 1974). The consequences of struggles between workers and owners thus appeared to be conflicts within the working class (Braverman, 1974).

Some social movements both inside and outside unions have worked against this trend in the labor movement. For example, the AFL-CIO may undertake a major drive to organize women workers (*The New York Times*, Dec. 6, 1979). Recognition of their importance to the labor movement has spurred recruiting efforts (*The New York Times*, Dec. 25, 1980). Interest in the rights of women is also seen in the belated union support, beginning in 1975, for the Equal Rights Amendment (*The Chicago Tribune*, May 8, 1980). Much of this activity has been spurred by women already in the union movement, some of whom have organized their own pressure group within unions (Coalition of Labor Union Women) to demand that unions represent the interests of women members and organize all women workers. However, these efforts have not as yet been very successful.

The short-run costs of equity to employers and owners, and the conflicts among workers, are not the only social forces working against equal opportunity for women workers. There is also the value system in a male-dominated society that permits men to bring their work into the home but penalizes women who take their family responsibilities into the outside world. Males of high status, as Coser and Rokoff (this volume) indicate, can have special exceptions when they wish to help their wives manage child and home care; but women are seen by their employers as "insufficiently committed" to their work role if they ask for special arrangements in order to meet the demands of their household. Women are likely to be punished when they cannot successfully maintain the separation of "work" and "home" expected of *them*, even though men in similar positions may be rewarded for their zeal when they permit work to encroach on family time.

To the extent that male work values dominate, women who wish to succeed must accept male definitions and expectations about work commitments. But women are not likely to have the support and assistance at home that male colleagues traditionally have expected from their wives. Working women must bear the burden of two jobs—paid worker and homemaker (see Hunt and Hunt, this volume). Even their coping strategies are seen as a personal rather than a societal problem. Accordingly, women learn not to "bother" their superiors or peers with the problems of child care or other family arrangements, although they are still part of a *woman*'s principal responsibilities (see Bourne and Wikler, this volume). Nona Glazer (1980) shows how articles in the mass media implicitly tell women to develop individual solutions (working more efficiently, planning timesaving schemes) to the problems of combining paid work and home work.

Popular magazines for working women promote the picture of women as modified men. They seldom suggest that the principles of society should be changed or that demands made on women workers are unfair or impossible. Instead, they stress such issues as how to dress for success, how to get ahead while still maintaining a feminine identity, and how to impress colleagues and superiors with one's efficiency and alacrity at work.

All of the customs separating work and home, men's work and women's work, public life and personal life, have become so habitual that they seem inevitable, even natural. When changes in customary patterns do occur, they may seem both random and deviant from the norm. They are individual adaptations to be deplored or admired, according to personal beliefs. Because so many policy makers perceive these changes as idiosyncratic, scattered, or deviant, they see no pressing need for social policy to make institutional adaptations.

New Approaches to Understanding the Problems

Some social critics have tried to show why these changes are not random and how new adaptations might be developed. One product of feminist research and criticism on work is the reexamination of male values (see Hochschild, 1975). The widespread belief, canonized in sociology textbooks, that bureaucrats act rationally and efficiently is questioned, and the importance of feminine values such as affection and emotionality in organizations is advanced by Hochschild (in Millman and Kanter, 1975). More and more feminists now criticize aggressiveness and competitiveness because of their consequences—increased heart attacks and tobacco and alcohol addiction, for example. As women's lives grow more like men's, the gaps between the sexes in alcoholism, suicide, and even auto accidents narrow (Jo Ann S. Lublin, *The Wall Street Journal,* Jan. 14, 1980). Success in business is costly to anyone who strives for it (*The New York Times,* Jan. 6, 1980). Do women really wish to be more like men if successful men have these problems?

Feminist critics also question the costs and benefits of ambition and commitment to work and how they might be divided between men and women. Pleck and also Hunt and Hunt (this volume) wonder whether it is reasonable to expect women to make all the sacrifices, to make superhuman efforts to be competent at work and at home. Should women have to choose between career and family when men do not? If women can't have both, what will happen to society if more and more women forego marriage and childbearing in order to pursue careers? And what will happen to men's lives?

Other critics question the costs and benefits of equality. Some writers feel threatened by what might happen to male-female relationships if the economic dependence of women upon men were removed. How would the relations between men and women, parents and children, be modified in a society which paid more than lip service to the notion of equality between the sexes? A change in the traditional balance of power may leave some men at a loss. Some men complain, for example, that they find successful women sexually intimidating. And many women are likely to demand more of a voice in family decisions when they contribute to family income (Bahr,

1974). Changes in decision-making power can affect who is assigned grubby or tedious tasks, responsibility for shopping and cleaning, choice of recreation and household location. Thus far, restructuring has caused relatively little inconvenience to men. Older children can pick up the slack, and housekeeping standards are relaxed when women juggle home and job (see Lorber, 1975). What if egalitarian principles permit some women to emerge dominant in the family? Can we accept role reversal should the husband wish to be subordinate to his wife?

One position is that any such changes are not possible under capitalism. This system is based on keeping labor as cheap as possible—in part by dividing the work force and drawing on a "reserve army" of the unemployed that includes women and minorities. But some wonder whether any industrial society is flexible enough to provide equal opportunity through work rearrangements even more drastic than job sharing and part-time appointments—shortened work days and lengthy parental leaves, for example.

Such reexaminations also question the criteria for progress and the priorities of modern societies. Who is progress for? Is it for both men and women? Does it follow that what is good for the rich is also good for the middle classes, professionals, and working classes? Who decides that we need more technology rather than development of services? These are hard questions to answer. They are still open for much discussion, but it is clear that the desirability of technological change and the possibility of social mobility (for women as well as men) have been taken for granted more often in the past than today.

These questions are part of a general reevaluation of established thought about women. In historical studies, attention is now paid to women's and children's roles and to domestic and daily life, in comparison to the former emphases on government, royalty, and war (Bridenthal and Koonz, 1977; Tilly and Scott, 1978). In other social sciences, the feminist perspective leads to questioning the naturalness or functionality of gender roles by revealing how the cultural values and social structures women live with are based not only in classes and interest groups but also in a constraining sexual system (Chodorow, 1976; Reiter, 1975). It is increasingly evident that the many limits on women's work exist within a broader system of patriarchy (Hartmann, 1981), in which women are kept subservient to men.

Analytical Questions and Sociological Perspectives in the Readings

Thus far, we have discussed some of the shifting images and realities of women at work today, the continuing institutional resistance to major changes, and some of the questions raised by the pressures for—and resistances to—change. Next, we briefly consider some of the analytical questions raised in the readings, explain their presentation and ordering, and identify the sociological perspectives they represent.

Guiding Analytical Questions

Why do women tend to work at home or to give home work roles the highest priority? When they do work outside the home, why do women almost always have the jobs offering less prestige and pay than men? What are some of the main obstacles to more satisfying work lives for women, especially the growing number who do both home work and market work?

Order of the Readings

Answers to these and other questions are suggested by all our authors, although many unresolved problems are also discussed briefly in our final chapter. The introductions and the contributors' readings are organized as follows:

WOMEN AND THE DIVISION OF LABOR: LIMITING ASSUMPTIONS

This section analyzes the origins of common assumptions about the division of labor in our society—for instance, that it is natural and generally beneficial for women. The readings show the many negative consequences of such assumptions—for women, for society, and for our efforts to understand the work women do.

HOME WORK AND MARKET WORK: SYSTEMATIC SEGREGATION

These articles explain how cultural expectations, often based on class and male dominance, still strongly segregate men's and women's roles. Such mandates still limit the socioeconomic statuses women may achieve, whether at home or in the marketplace.

INVISIBLE WORK: UNACKNOWLEDGED CONTRIBUTIONS

These readings emphasize the need to recognize, redefine, and reward many kinds of work women still typically do for others—in the home, the community, the market, and society in general. In our capitalist society, many such efforts are often not even acknowledged as "real" work.

WOMEN AND THE DUAL ECONOMY: CONTINUING DISCRIMINATION

The final set of articles identifies persisting social, economic, and technological barriers to women who wish to leave occupational ghettos. It is the less skilled, less organized, more competitive sector of the market in which women still typically work.

Each section of readings has an analytical introduction, an overview of the articles, and a set of study questions. Generally, the first article has a historical component showing some of the *origins* of the processes and issues considered. The second identifies in detail the *present expectations* for women's work. The third emphasizes typical *consequences* of some of these expectations in actual work situations. The fourth highlights *implications*—for understanding and for individual or collective action to improve work life, especially for women.

Analytical Perspectives: Feminist and Sociological
All of our authors are sympathetic to feminist desires for more satisfying, effective work for women and more reasonable, humane societies for all people. Interactionist, functionalist, and conflict sociological perspectives are most frequently represented. While many contributions are not confined to one school of thought or style of work, some articles do focus on one of these perspectives. In the first set of readings, for example, Huber analyzes how both men's and women's movements have responded to various stages in U.S. industrialization. Her emphases on who benefits economically from technological change (in family and factory) and on ideologies (of child care and equal opportunity) identify her approach as a variation of conflict sociology (see, e.g., Zeitlin, 1973:103–138). Coser and Rokoff's stress on the cultural mandate for women to put family first and their analysis of status articulation systems are indebted to the structural-functional analysis developed by Robert K. Merton and his followers (see Merton, 1968). Levinson's analyses of how employers interpreted the meaning of the job ads they had placed in their local newspapers identify his approach as one influenced by the symbolic interactionist perspective (see Blumer, 1969). Each of these approaches is represented—in varying degrees—not only in the other readings sections but also in the introductory and interstitial sections. Our final section, "Unresolved Questions," summarizes three distinct feminist perspectives—liberal, Marxist, and radical (or cultural)—that are also interwoven in the preceding sections.

Much of the evidence collected by our authors is part of the reader's everyday experience. The articles are framed theoretically, but the studies included and our efforts to interrelate them should encourage readers to examine their own lives and societies, and to make their own independent assessments of the evidence and how it is interpreted. They can then develop their own perspectives on women and work today.

I

Women and the Division of Labor: Limiting Assumptions

Why do women tend to work at home, taking care of the domestic tasks and rearing children, while men have occupations and earn income away from home? How natural or necessary is such a division of labor? In considering these questions, we should realize that the image of the family they assume and the men's and women's roles they refer to are familiar modern constructions, not eternal or biologically fixed patterns. Until the Industrial Revolution in Europe, all work was centered in the household, and labor for domestic use and for market trade was shared by all household members. Adults, children—as soon as they were capable—and servants provided goods both for the family and for exchange. Men and women had different responsibilities, but their domestic and productive or private and public specialties were not distinguished by gender. And these responsibilities did not mark men as main providers for the family, women as dependents. In preindustrial Europe, marriage did not mean total economic dependence for women or total economic responsibility for men. Both spouses were responsible for economic maintenance and child rearing. They also shared responsibility for providing the surplus needed for trade or cash. Adult females did what we today call "work," and women's work was necessary.

The shift from an economy centered on household work to an economy based on work in the marketplace took hundreds of years. In the Middle Ages, women helped to earn cash as money became important for household maintenance. Although often excluded from formal apprenticeships, women could become members through marriage and entered in crafts and guilds as men's helpers (Tilly and Scott, 1978).

The household was the center of craft production, where the product, quality, and amount to produce were decided. At first, merchants accepted whatever artisans wanted to make; later, merchants began to specify the products they were willing to purchase. They assigned work to households through a system called "putting out." In consequence, artisans no longer had control over what they produced. Yet as long as people worked in their own cottages, they could control the pace and organization of work and thus integrate market with domestic productivity, including reproduction and child care. Thus women remained full participants.

Industrialization changed this pattern. Household and market production were separated when manufacturers wanted more reliable workers in centralized locations. The locus of work changed from the home to the factory. At first, industrialization did not radically change women's work or the amount of time they devoted to productive labor for the market. Some women did go to the factories—particularly single women and the wives of unskilled or itinerant workers—but most women remained in homes as servants, farm family workers, or garment workers doing piecework. While single women helped to support the family or attempted to maintain themselves by factory work, married women tried to combine wage earning with domestic work. Some women took in boarders; others became peddlers, laundresses, or innkeepers. However women tried to integrate their work, the importance given to women's wages cannot be ignored. Many women worked away from the home only when they had small children. The family needed extra income, and so women left home to earn it. As the children grew and contributed to the family income, women were more able to concentrate on domestic tasks (Tilly and Scott, 1978).

The important change was that more women were earning wages for formerly unpaid household work (when they became servants to the more wealthy), while men were earning wages for a new kind of work in factories. Thus both men and women were still participating in the market to earn the family wage, but spatial segregation now sent them in different directions (Tilly and Scott, 1978). One result of this separation was that women became solely responsible for child care and domestic tasks. Men and older children, away from the household for most of the day, could no longer participate (Kessler-Harris, 1981). In time, if family wages improved, women relinquished all income-producing activity and specialized in managing the household for the family members who worked for wages.

In preindustrial Europe, a family pattern of economic interdependence included a set of values legitimating women's economic role. This pattern is illustrated in Pinchbeck (1930:1–2): "You cannot expect to marry in such a manner as neither of you shall have occasion to work, and none but a fool will take a wife whose bread must be earned solely by his labour and who will contribute nothing toward it herself."

With industrialization, the role of women was drastically altered. As new expectations arose, history was rewritten; we have almost forgotten that other patterns ever existed. It is now taken for granted that men fulfill their familial responsibilities by earning money in the public arena and women fulfill theirs by caring for the family's private—or domestic—affairs.

Many men are—or believe they are—evaluated by how well they provide for their families; a major responsibility of husbands and fathers is to earn an adequate living. Conversely, many women believe that their major responsibility as a wife and mother is to maintain the home as a retreat from the stress of the outside world. Yet this rigid division between men and women and between family and work is less than 200 years old—hardly a natural division of labor.

Still, much of the organization of our occupational and family life today presupposes our understanding and acceptance of this norm. This acceptance extends to our concept of capitalism as the natural form of economy. We often take it for granted that this system grows out of and reflects an inherent human desire for profit, competition, and technological development. However, Max Weber, who wrote *The Protestant Ethic and the Spirit of Capitalism* (1930, originally 1907), described the special circumstances required for the rise of such an economic system. One condition is that economic enterprise and family must be separated. Because work is evaluated largely on the basis of capital accumulation, the worker must adapt to what owners and managers define as occupational needs rather than the needs of family or self. Thus we have swing and "graveyard" shifts in many industries requiring some workers to change living patterns drastically because "it does not pay" (the owners) to shut the machinery down at night. Normal daily patterns of life give way before the demands of technology and profit.

In this economic system, employers deal with women as if they all conform to a stereotype in which domestic responsibility comes first. In this oversimplified view, women will not or cannot put paid work demands first. Market work and family are, in fact, often in conflict for men; but ideologically, the two systems are better integrated for men through expectations of the appropriate male role in the family (see Pleck, this volume). Supposedly, men are spurred on by the need to provide for their families and by the expectation that their wives will help by managing the home. The occupational world is still organized on the increasingly arbitrary assumption that all workers have someone who can help them be efficient paid workers by managing their nonoccupational lives.

Some occupations—notably the professions—are even more demanding. A forty-hour work week is insufficient for adequate, much less outstanding, performance; a sixty-hour week might be more typical—especially early in one's career—exactly when the demands of young children are greatest. But if one does not devote effort and time to produce the signs of "commitment," rewards are limited. To succeed, one must begin a career immediately after college or professional school and never change direction or take time out for other interests. Arlie Hochschild calls this lockstep the "clockwork" of professional careers. Using academia as an example, she shows how this clockwork excludes women:

> The academic career is founded on some peculiar assumptions about the relation between doing work and competing with others, competing with others and getting credit for work, getting credit and building a reputation, building a reputation and doing it while you're young, doing it while you're young and hoarding scarce time, hoarding scarce time and minimizing family life, minimizing family life and leaving it to your wife—the chain of experiences that seems to anchor the traditional academic career. Even if the meritocracy worked perfectly, even if women did not cool themselves out, I suspect there would remain in a system that defines careers this way only a handful of women at the top. (1971: 49)

As Hochschild argues, this clockwork is progressively entrapping. A worker is formed through these experiences and soon sees no way— and no reason—to change. This pattern, while limiting to men, largely excludes family women even from participation.

If we now reconsider why women are so often in the home, we see that this division of labor is far from natural and requires a complex system of economic and social supports to make it function (Brown, 1970). It is particularly difficult for many women and men who do not have such a support system to meet the standards. Those without supports are handicapped not because they lack ability but because of invisible (and often unrecognized) social demands. It is incorrect to assume that the current division of labor between men and women is natural—if we really want to understand where, how, and why women work today.

We must also recognize that in this division of labor, some workers are seen as less important than others. The dominant imagery in our society is shaped by the capitalist model. In this model, priority is given to idealized economic values—efficiency, productivity, and profit. In such a society, only work for income—associated with productivity for profit—brings widespread recognition and respect.

Crucial to the capitalist economy is the centrality of the market. Families, friends, and communities once provided many services that we now purchase. All family members who do not produce income can readily see—through purchase of these products and services—their own dependence on those who do. And so, men gain status and power not so much through their unique, individual attributes as from the fact that they do the paid "productive" and respected work and control the means—money—of giving others in the family necessary goods and services.

Thus the domestic arena, where efficiency and profit do not have first priority, is automatically devalued—not a part of the "real world." Nor are the people associated with it as important as those in the real world. Although women are presumably honored and respected as wives and mothers, such honor is empty when their skills are not seen as useful outside the home (Clearinghouse International Newsletter, 1980). Years at home are defined as years out of the labor force, with no experience to list on a job application. Nor does experience as an adult worker gain homemakers credibility in politics or in developing public policy. As Boulding (1976) notes, when some women do gain social importance, it is based not on their domestic competence but on their class position and prerogatives in the outside world. It is not surprising that women take on paid work more readily than men accept household work. As long as home work is seen as a service to the family rather than as a valued accomplishment, it will be hard to give recognition and a sense of purpose to those who do it. Familiar distinctions between men's and women's roles are fading because more women are working in the market, not because more men are working at home (Hartmann, 1981).

Even men who realize that they are seizing the opportunities provided by their wives are usually unwilling to provide them with the same advantages if it means that they themselves must assume more domestic responsibilities. S. M. Miller describes his own difficulty in recognizing that household chores could ever be as important as occupational tasks:

> It is not that I object in principle to housekeeping and childrearing. I don't find such work demeaning or unmasculine—just a drain on my time which could be devoted to other, "more rewarding" things. . . . My energies are poised to help me work on my professional, political concerns, and I resist "wasting time" on other pursuits, even those basic to managing a day-to-day existence. [He recognized that his wife, a professional woman, has paid the costs in her own

career.] I have always felt guilty about her not achieving more, so I have nagged her to publish, though I have not provided the circumstances and climate that would make serious work much easier. I have had the benefit of feeling relieved that I was "motivating" her by my emphasis on her doing more, but I have not suffered the demands on my time and emotions that making more useful time available to her would have required. (1971: 37)

Although recognizing the costs to his wife's career, Miller was unwilling to assume more domestic responsibilities to help her; he feared the cost to his own career.

The first set of readings in "Women and the Division of Labor" continues this critical reconsideration of persistent present assumptions. Each author's perspective is sociologically distinct, but all the analyses illuminate important aspects of the origins, consequences, or implications of current common expectations about women's work. Each author shows specific constraints imposed by the current sexual division of labor: Women face the strain of conflicting demands and lack of respect; men face the pressures of economic responsibility and lack of family participation. In her analysis of why women have not entered the paid labor force in large numbers, Huber relates developments in technology, fertility patterns, and responsibility for child care. She also identifies many obstacles to the contemporary women's movement. Huber's attention to the societal problem of caring for and training children appears in later readings as well, but her article also provides historical background on the cultural mandates from which many of our present expectations are derived. According to predominant cultural beliefs, women are unqualified for prestigious, demanding jobs because their allegiance is owed to their family. Once we make this assumption, we too easily interpret all women's behavior in paid work as signs of a supposed lack of commitment to their job or professional responsibilities.

Drawing on the structural-functional interest in maintaining shared values, Coser and Rokoff show how the cultural mandate for women to "put family first" is perpetuated. Levinson adds a third aspect— social pressure—to those of history and culture. He shows how the segregated division of labor is maintained through the process of sex-role stereotyping in the occupational world. People who do not accept these familiar stereotypes as guides for their own behavior are not allowed to demonstrate the viability of other possibilities. Each denial of a job interview to someone of the "wrong" sex reaffirms familiar, if outmoded and even illegal, gender expectations. We have here a strong example of the way cultural mandates are maintained and solidified in everyday interaction.

Finally, we see the consequences of history and culture on social science research. Feldberg and Glenn show that some key analyses of work by male sociologists are biased, for they unwittingly accept the cultural views of women and men. Such biases limit our discoveries and cloud our vision with assumptions about what is happening. Feldberg and Glenn ask us to redirect our questions, refocus our vision, without accepting cultural givens as descriptions of reality unless they are supported by empirical evidence. They also show how new models for studying work help us to understand how the chance to get a job, the various jobs and promotion possibilities, opportunities for training and experience, and interactions of men and women at work all affect gender differences in work behavior and attitudes. We need both accurate concepts and systematic evidence if we are ever to understand how job structures and sexual expectations work, independently and in interaction, to create different work opportunities and obligations for women and men.

Toward a Sociotechnological Theory of the Women's Movement

JOAN HUBER
University of Illinois, Urbana-Champaign

1. Origins. Some argue that the sexual division of labor rests on the fact that women bear the children. On this biological fact, a whole system of sexual categorization has been constructed which assigns women the primary role in parenting. Little attention is given to the fact that industrialization and the declining birthrate have made parenting a less time-consuming part of women's lives. Women can now move in growing numbers into the paid work force, even if their primary responsibility for the home remains unchanged. Huber argues that what distinguishes the current women's movement from earlier ones is the recognition that the social position of women will not change until we accept both fathers and mothers as capable of child rearing.

How has technological change affected the work responsibilities of men and women today? Some say that women add to their burdens when they take a job; others see the opportunity to work as liberating women from what were once their major alternatives—marriage or the cloistered life. What do you think?

The most recent women's movement, which I shall refer to in capitals as the Women's Movement to distinguish it from earlier forms, emerged in the political turmoil of the late sixties. In the early sixties, many college students had been idealistically attracted to the Black Movement, but when blacks took over their own movement, white youths were ejected. They soon found another cause. The escalating Viet Nam War—and the rising draft calls on the campus—stimulated many college students to join loosely with New Left radicals and other groups in a vigorous egalitarian movement. When young radical women found that the total transformation of society was to stop short at the kitchen door, they began to meet in small groups to engage in consciousness raising, collectively identifying the social mechanisms that kept women down. At the same time, older professional women, aware of their continuing second-class status, attempted to remove legal restrictions on women's work (Freeman, 1975). In time, the two streams tended to coalesce.

One basic theme pervades feminist literature: Women are kept in their place by their responsibility for child care and domestic work. This proposition implies that the problem is not only women's invisibility in market and political institutions but also men's invisibility in the home. Many men still see only one side of the problem: desegregating the world of work, hard as that may be. The other side may be even harder: bringing men back in—to the kitchen, to the bathroom when it is time to scour the kiddies, and to the utility room which contains a fancy, many-dialed machine that many men have not mastered. The most intractable issue is child care—a problem of equality in parental responsibility that has hardly been addressed (Lorber, 1975). Institutions that would support shared childcare are almost nonexistent. Hence even those couples who favor equality for women find it almost impossible to incorporate their convictions into their life-styles.

The purpose of this paper is to analyze the factors responsible for the emergence of the Women's Movement in order to assess its prospects for the future. The task is difficult for researchers in any one discipline because the data must come from all of the social sciences; furthermore, until recently, women's work was almost ignored.[1] In this paper, I argue that the decline in fertility and the shift of productive work from home to factory in the past two centuries has upset the equilibrium of sex stratification in industrial societies. The basic theoretical premise is that the right to distribute and exchange valued goods and services to those not in a person's domestic unit confers power and prestige in all societies. This leads to the hypothesis that male dominance results from the frequency with which men control extra-domestic distribution (Friedl, 1975: 8). With industrialization, fertility rates dropped, women were less often pregnant, and whether because of fewer pregnancies or because of a technology that separated feeding from lactation, time spent in lactation was reduced dramatically. Production of household goods was transferred to the factory, but women's work there was controlled in response to the ebb and flow of demand for male labor. Women's entry into white-collar work was regulated differently, but the result was similar: They were crowded into occupational ghettos. The situation seemed more equitable before 1940, when the typical woman worker who was young and unmarried entered the labor force only briefly until she married and returned to tend to home and children. After 1940, when the female work force was increasingly composed of married women with children, women workers were more likely to be aware of their permanent second-class status and their double burden of domestic work. In the egalitarian climate of the sixties, women's awareness that the ideology of equal opportunity did not apply to them helped to precipitate the Women's Movement.

Technology and Biology

Although a substantial literature supports the belief that the basic cause of sex stratification is biological, examination of the biological differences relevant to the division of labor shows that all but one are of degree rather than kind. Physiologically, men tend to be larger and stronger; women tend to be more durable (Bayo and Glanz, 1965; Madigan, 1957). The extent to which psychological differences result from biology or socialization is open to question; recent research emphasizes socialization (Maccoby and Jacklin, 1974; Whiting and Edwards, 1973). Whatever the cause, the overlap is too great to assign such factors much, if any, importance.

Only one biological difference categorically separates women and men: No man can bear a child. Yet technology permits humans to transcend biological characteristics. This commonsense observation—people can fly, although no one is born with wings—is made only because it is so often forgotten in discussions of women's place. That women can bear children is, to date, a fact of nature, but that women are assigned the responsibility of rearing children is a man-made fact subject to change. Even though no man has a womb, it is now technologically possible for men to share equally in the important and dedicated work of socializing the next generation. How did this come about?

The Decline in Fertility

Two quantum changes have given men equal opportunity for child rearing. The first is the long-term fall in fertility rates. I speak of this decline as long-term to stress that it has been going on for more than 200 years and is now apparently a permanent characteristic of industrial societies.

The primary reason for the decline apparently was the perception that children were no longer economic assets; by the second half of the nineteenth century, this perception became increasingly common in Western Europe (United Nations, 1973: 89). The primary demographic source of the fall in fertility was the decline in mean completed parity of married women from about seven children to less than three, achieved by cessation of childbearing at progressively earlier marital durations (United Nations, 1973: 68). The principal method by which the decline was achieved was coitus interruptus—historically the principal male contraceptive technique; the female method was abortion (Tietze, 1968: 383). These are still the chief methods of birth control worldwide, increasingly replaced by newer methods only since 1960 (Kirk, 1968: 344).[2]

However much the fertility decline might have been desired by the individuals who brought it about, it made governments nervous when they finally perceived what was happening. The emergence, in the 1930s, of demography as a science reflected those governmental concerns about decreasing fertility. Governments feared that low or negative growth rates would yield too few military personnel. Also, they thought that population increase was necessary for economic growth—a view supported by some demographers today (Sauvy, 1961: 355). It was those concerns that, at least partly, motivated efforts to make motherhood more attractive and underlaid governmental support of restrictive and protective legislation for women in the work force.

While such movements had little or no effect on the declining birth rate before World War II (for when the majority of a population wants to control family size, it apparently acts without regard for official policy or law [Eldridge, 1968: 387]), the feminists of the era were caught in a difficult bind. The reality of the industrial work world was a horror for *all* who worked in its factories—men as well as women and children. Under those conditions, to argue against protective legislation or to oppose any movement that showed hope of getting women and children out of the factories was difficult, indeed. A long-term perspective was necessary to make that argument comprehensible, as well as an understanding of the connection between women's social status and their relationship to the distributive and productive forces of the society. Feminists in the 1920s, as I will show later, split on the issue of whether motherhood was the essence of womanhood, and its corollary—the demand that women be removed and/or protected from full participation in the public, productive sphere— was an issue on which the movement of that era eventually foundered.

By the 1950s, however, owing to rapid progress in controlling deaths without a compensating decrease in the birth rate after World War II, scholarly worry about decreasing fertility reversed. Public opinion paralleled scholarly views. Since then, approval for measures to restrict fertility has increased sharply—birth control services for teenage females who request them, birth control education in public high schools (Blake, 1973a), and abortion (Jones and Westoff, 1973; but see Blake 1973b). Concern with the environment also rose sharply from 1965 to 1970 (Erskine, 1972: 120), with some scholars now arguing that high fertility rates positively affect the rate of environmental degradation (Preston, 1975).

It is important that governments as well as individuals now apparently view low fertility rates as desirable because it implies less support for policies to improve women's maternal status at the expense of their social status. It is reasonable to speculate that low fertility rates will continue (barring atomic holocaust and the reemergence of hunting and gathering societies, if we are lucky) on a wide scale. Meanwhile, the question emerges with increasing clarity: If the average woman is only briefly incapacitated for paid work, and if she is expected to work for an increasing portion of her adult life, on what grounds can we rationally assign the major burden of parenthood to women?

Lactation

The second change that makes it possible for men to rear children as effectively as women is the improvement in methods of infant feeding that became widespread after the early years of the twentieth century. The fact that a baby's survival in its first years no longer depends on the ability of its mother to breast-feed it cannot be overemphasized. Techniques of food sterilization have shattered the ancient dependency of a baby on a lactating woman. The lack of such techniques in the nineteenth century, coupled with higher birth rates, was doubtless a reason why, even to feminists, the woman issue seemed so intractable. Early feminist issues focused mainly on activities like voting, owning property, and access to higher education—issues that were less affected by pregnancy and lactation than was the household division of labor. The separation of childbearing and child rearing, like the separation of ownership and management, was a possibility only dimly seen at the time.

While industrialization was transforming children from economic assets to economic liabilities, it also was creating the modern labor market. Landless peasants became urban industrial workers. Women became a low-wage reserve. In a broad sense, the labor force participation of working-class women was regulated in the nineteenth century; that of middle-class women, in the twentieth century. The results are visible today.

Regulating Women Blue-Collar Workers

During industrialization, populations were urbanized and a modern labor market emerged—a literate work force, geographically and occupationally mobile. Nonmonetized work performed on the basis of status became paid employment performed (more or less) on the basis of contract. Everywhere the ideology of equal opportunity emerged and came to justify inequality of reward. The most efficient way to motivate workers to perform industrial jobs is, after all, to make individuals feel responsible for their own fates (Ossowski, 1963). While the importance of this pervasive ideology cannot be overemphasized, it is not foolproof. For whenever sizable groups with some political clout discover that, despite their best efforts they are not getting a fair share, social movements emerge. In the nineteenth century, male industrial workers, struggling for better wages and more control over their work, persistently threatened the stability of governments. Until recently, no one noticed that all the great worker movements of the nineteenth century were men's movements.

Women were almost invisible in labor movements in the nineteenth century, although their labor force participation never was and is not now in doubt. The question has always been how to regulate the quantity and locus of their participation. Regulating the employment of working-class women was not difficult because those who might have been their natural sex allies—middle-class women—and their class allies—working-class men—saw such regulation as a primary goal. Under the guise of humanitarian concerns for women and children, and resting the movement on the primacy of maternal duties for women, they joined together to limit women's participation in the world of work.

The industrial revolution affected working- and middle-class women differently. Early in industrialization women were excluded from learning skills, leaving working-class women unfit for anything but household work and low-wage jobs (Abbott, 1913: 254; Clark, 1919: 300; Holcombe, 1973: 174), a situation with parallels in the industrializing world today (Boserup, 1970). In contrast, wives of the prosperous bourgeoisie were idled and assumed mainly ornamental and child bearing functions, while their productive activities were assigned to male employees. The children of middle-class women were reared by working-class women. Nineteenth-century feminists, economically unproductive and dependent on men, attacked women's exclusion from the perquisites of upper- and middle-class men—education for the professions and civil service, control of property, extension of the vote—and supported measures to reduce the hours women could work in factories.

Working-class men and their leaders were primarily concerned with reducing women's hours of work for four reasons. First, although they depended on their wives' earnings, they wanted to be masters in their own homes (Rowbotham, 1974). A complaint early in industrialization was that women could find work when men could not, undermining the authority of the family (Smelser, 1959: ch. 9).

Second, many radicals and reformers were ambivalent about birth control. Factory owners had used Malthusian analysis to justify lower wages; higher wages were thought to inspire higher fertility, which would, in turn, only reduce the level of subsistence. Because of the conservative implication of Malthusian theory, radicals rejected the idea that poverty was caused by overpopulation. Socialists tended to identify contraceptives as an upper-class device foisted on the lower classes to avoid basic social change. In the 1820s, this belief surfaced in Britain—a belief that troubled English radicals then and that still troubles socialists a century later (Rowbotham, 1974).

Third, socialists assumed that capitalism was the root cause of the woman issue. Engels, Bebel, and Lenin understood what domestic drudgery did to women, but they expected that under socialism the state would assume women's domestic functions; the family would wither away. Radical and reform feminists in the United States at the turn of the century also thought that capitalism caused women's problems (Rossi, 1973: 474). The fact that working women bear a double burden in both socialist and nonsocialist countries casts doubt on this assumption. By 1964, for example, only 5 percent of household work was performed by state employees in the Soviet Union (Geiger, 1968: 184). But the tendency of radicals and laborites to attribute women's position to capitalism persists.

Fourth, and most important, was the fact that women were used as a reserve labor force which, ultimately, served to drive male wages down. As soon as they could organize to drive out these low-wage competitors, male workers did so. Early in industrialization, there was little opposition to women and child workers because working-class families had little choice. As male wages were reduced again and again, only the earnings of the entire family enabled it to subsist (Fuller, 1944: 415), a situation similar to that of migrant agricultural workers today. But such a situation becomes a self-perpetuating vicious circle. Since women and child workers were typically supplementary earners, they could be induced to work for ever lower wages, thus aiding in the further depression of the wages of their husbands and fathers.

Thus, the wage threat was real. In the United States in the mid-nineteenth century, women's wages were about half of men's (Woody, 1929: 494). Children in the cotton factories performed many kinds of work "better than adults" and cost only one-third as much (Adams, 1875: 124). The first *Annual Report* of the United States Commissioner for Labor for 1885 and the *Dewey Report* for 1890 noted that the wages of adult women were somewhat less than three-fifths and those of children and youth somewhat more than one-third the wages of adult males (Long, 1960: 104).

Under such circumstances, those workers who can, organize to bargain collectively with management for rules that exclude their low-wage competitors. Whenever unemployment was high, which was fairly often in the nineteenth century, working men agitated to eliminate women's and children's competition. By the turn of the century, women, blacks, Orientals, other ethnics, and children had been largely removed from competition for high-wage jobs (Aronowitz, 1973; Hill, 1967, 1973). I will next briefly discuss how children were eliminated from the labor market and what effect that had on women.

Compulsory Education

The employment of children in mills and mines was a horror of industrialization. Humanitarian agitation to control or eliminate child labor began early in the nineteenth century and increased through time. Agitation for public education began a little later. It is difficult to assess the impact of humanitarian reformers. But the fact is that as industries became more capital-intensive, children were not hired because they could no longer be profitably employed and because male workers in those industries could organize to keep them out. In the twentieth century, children were employed only in low-wage, nonunionized industries.

The children extruded from the mills, the mines, the farms, and the streets were embraced by the public schools. By the 1880s public education was compulsory in almost all industrial countries. Why? The received view in the United States is that it was motivated by the belief that republican ideals and democratic equality could be promoted only by general education at the public expense. But the received view is questioned (Cremin, 1965: 45). Dobbs (1969: 152) suggests that unoccupied youth in growing cities posed a sufficient threat to social order to alarm the taxpayers. Katz (1971) suggests that the middle class wanted to educate its children at public expense.

Whatever the reasons for its success, public education stimulated the idea, paradoxically, that mothers belonged at home to give the children a hearty breakfast and see that they looked respectable when they went off to learn how to be upwardly mobile. Over time the birth rate fell, the school year lengthened, and the required years of attendance increased. But the mother's free time did not increase because a rapidly rising standard of living meant that the children had to be better dressed and odor-free in order to keep up with other children. Instead of producing goods, mothers spent more time chasing dirt. Mothers with very high aspirations for their children had to haul them to the right museums and expose them to symphony concerts, lest they be flummoxed by a question on Renoir or Beethoven when they took their college entrance examinations. By the middle of the twentieth century, women's investment in their children's human capital seemed so natural that most people forgot it was a comparatively recent development (Rossi, 1964). Forgotten, too, was the fact that this particular brand of motherhood was, first, a product of women's exclusion from the productive work force and, second, an ideal that could be only very imperfectly realized by most women in most families. For most working-class families of America—in the present era or in the recent past—have had to rely on the wife's working outside the home for at least some period during the marriage.

Labor Unions
The history of women's exclusion from high-wage industrial jobs goes back almost a century and deals with unions' refusal to admit women to membership or to organize them and with the development of labor legislation designed to protect their maternal status. By the 1880s the frontier had closed, recurrent depressions made agriculture risky, and factory jobs were, therefore, more attractive to men than earlier in the century. European immigration was heavy. Massive unemployment plagued urban areas. Skilled workers had ample reason to eliminate low-wage competi-

tors. Women were just one of a number of groups that unions excluded from high-wage jobs.

The idea that women were *excluded* from high-wage jobs does not represent the dominant view of labor leaders or students of the labor movement. Most labor history is written from the vantage point of workmen's interests, a legacy of nineteenth-century class politics. Since women were viewed as auxiliary earners whose problems stemmed from an exploitive industrial system, their interests vis-à-vis those of men are underplayed. In 1903, John Mitchell (1973: 131) stated the mainstream view succinctly: "If trade unionism had rendered no other service to humanity, it would have justified its existence by its efforts on behalf of working women and children." Because it represents a minority view, the literature dealing with unions' exclusion of women is slender. In an annotated bibliography on women in American labor history from 1925 to 1935 (Soltow, Forché, and Massre, 1972: 22–49), only 12 of the 112 items listed under "Trade Unions" depart from the mainstream view.

Chafe (1974: ch. 3) states that to some extent, women's low participation in the labor movement reflected the work they did: low-wage jobs in candy factories, textile mills, and laundries. But fundamentally, women failed to become part of the trade union movement because they were not invited in until the late 1930s. The American Federation of Labor (AFL) treated women workers with open hostility and did almost nothing to organize them. Both Gompers and his successor, William Green, attacked the presence of married women in the work force and asserted that women should marry and care for families. When a group accused the Executive Council of the AFL of prejudice, Gompers replied that the AFL discriminated against any nonassimilable race. Even when women organized themselves, they were denied recognition.

Because it organized workers by industry rather than skill, the formation of the Congress of Industrial Organizations (CIO) improved the situation of workers excluded by the skill-apprenticeship system of the AFL. Yet sex inequality continued to pervade organized labor even in the most "progressive" unions.[3] For example, half the members of the Amalgamated Clothing Workers were women, but the union sanctioned lower wages for women than for men and granted women only token recognition as officers (Chafe, 1974: 87).

Protective Labor Legislation

The movement for labor legislation stemmed from workers' desire to exact higher wages and better working conditions from management. The movement for *protective* labor legislation stemmed from the desire of male workers to restrict the competition of women and children and from the humanitarian impulses of middle- and working-class reformers to protect women and children from the worst features of the industrial system.

Protective legislation appeared much earlier in Britain than in the United States. Beginning in 1802, statutes progressively limited the working hours first of children, then of women, until by 1847 the ten-hour day was standard in British factories. Because factories needed uniform work schedules, the hours of men were also reduced (Tolles, 1968: 419).

In the United States, because the employee's right to bargain with the employer was held unconstitutional, protective legislation arrived much later, but the British pattern was repeated: women and children first. Until 1932, liberals tried to protect women, conservatives to keep them free. By 1896, only thirteen states restricted women's working hours (the easiest way to exclude women from high-wage jobs), and the constitutionality of these laws was doubtful (Brandeis, 1935). In 1908, however, the Supreme Court unanimously established the constitutionality of legislation on women's health, exempting women from the freedom-of-contract doctrine because they needed special protection. Feminists who objected to women's being singled out were accused of antilabor sentiments. The result of the 1908 decision was a spate of legislation between 1909 and 1917, a peak year when the Court passed almost all the labor legislation that came before it. A conservative trend followed, peaking in 1923, when Justice Sutherland held that the nineteenth (voting) Amendment established sex equality; hence special legislation for women was unconstitutional. Labor leaders deplored the decision.

The issue of protective legislation split the women's movement in the 1920s. In 1923, the National Women's Party (NWP) proposed an Equal Rights Amendment to eliminate special legislation for women. It was opposed by the League of Women Voters (LWV), descendant of the National American Women's Suffrage Association. What separated the two groups was the issue of whether women's maternal functions preceded all others, since the argument for protection stemmed from employed women's double burden. The NWP claimed that protective legislation merely excluded women from high-wage jobs; the LWV, that it eased the burden of women workers. Both the NWP and the LWV were composed primarily of middle-class women, many of them strong supporters of the labor movement. The issue was whether women were to be primarily productive workers or primarily child caretakers. Unlike many nineteenth-century feminists, the NWP clearly saw the implications of this issue.

The issue of special women's legislation tended to disappear in the Roosevelt era, which brought legislation giving American workers benefits long taken for granted elsewhere. Whether New Deal legislation discriminated by sex has never been systematically investigated. Certainly some of it was discriminatory. In four NIRA codes, women were permitted to receive lower wages than men; the industries affected were those that employed the largest proportions of women (Chafe, 1974: 85).

How effective was protective legislation, either in easing women's burdens or in excluding them from high-wage jobs? The evidence is unclear because most of the literature is deductive argument, devoid of evidence. Persons associated with unions or the Department of Labor tended to think such legislation improved women's lot.[4] A rare empirical study held that it did not. Baker (1925) investigated protective legislation's effects in New York State. Examination of specific jobs in specific industries showed that within a few years after it took effect, women were virtually excluded from high-wage jobs. Laws would restrict women's working hours; then unions would require workers to take the night shift for a specified period of time to acquire seniority. Since women were prohibited to do night work, they were excluded from the seniority system. The law penalized skilled women most, but the result was felt by all women workers because it automatically threw them back into already overcrowded occupations, into competition with less skilled women (Baker, 1925: 427, 433).

Whatever protective legislation's actual effects, labor unions have supported it. The AFL-CIO failed to support the ERA (which would nullify such legislation) until October 1973, and it still shows ambivalence, apparent in the California ERA fight (Miller and Linker, 1974).[5] A rare opinion study on measures to restrict women's work found working women most opposed and men employed in manufacturing least opposed to such restrictions (Duncan and Evers, 1975).

Thus women's opportunities for skilled work respond to the ebb and flow of demand for male workers.[6] Women became skilled manual workers before, during, and immediately after World War I but were driven out during the Depression. Again in World War II women became skilled workers, but only today do they form as high a proportion of skilled workers in the United States as in 1920. Currently, women blue-collar workers are crowded into the underclass of dirty service workers and into nondurable goods manufacturing (Bibb and Form, 1977).

Regulating Women White-Collar Workers

In the twentieth century, the blue-collar proportion of the work force changed little, but the white-collar proportion mushroomed. Despite the enormous growth of that sector of the work force, women were crowded into the low-salary white-collar occupations. The mechanisms were less formal than those that were applied to blue-collar women because white-collar males, typically unorganized, lacked a handy organizational weapon.

Socialization for child-care responsibility affected women in three ways. First, it made them ambivalent about the relation of work and family roles whether in the United States (Mason and Bumpass, 1975), the Soviet Union (Wilensky, 1968: 243), or Eastern Europe (Matejko, 1974: 215). Public opinion, including women's, generally holds that a woman's first duty is to her family. In 1900, disapproval of unmarried women's working was confined to the upper classes (Smuts, 1971: 137), but disapproval of married women's working was apparently widespread (Oppenheimer, 1970: 42). As late as 1968, only 47 percent of United States women thought that married women should contribute to family income (Erskine, 1971). A recent analysis based on a "patchwork" quilt of sample surveys shows, however, that the proportion of women supporting the traditional division of labor has declined from 1964 to 1974 and the proportion supporting women's rights in the labor market has increased (Mason, Czajka, and Arber, 1975).

Second, socialization predisposes women to train for and seek nonladder jobs. Little girls when their aspirations are high want to be school teachers. Little boys want to be business executives.[7]

Third, socialization encourages women to adopt behavior patterns poorly suited for the job world (Chafetz, 1974; Henshel, 1973; Weitzman, 1975). Adolescent boys want to master a subject; girls are concerned with the impression they make (Rosenberg and Simmons, 1975).

More directly, women have been excluded from high level white-collar training and employment by refusal to admit or hire them.[8] Often their numbers in colleges and professional schools are restricted by quota systems and requirements of higher performance scores for women than for men. Women are still underrepresented in colleges and professional schools all over the world (Zimmer, 1975). Whether this is the result of prior socialization or direct exclusions is unknown, but both work powerfully to reinforce one another. The informal practices which isolate women from major communication networks and, consequently, exclude them from high-salary occupations have recently been well documented (Epstein, 1970a, 1970b; Rossi and Calderwood, 1973).

Women have reason to be discontented with current patterns of sex stratification. Because they can bear children and are expected to rear them, they occupy second-class status in the job world, the main arena for status and prestige in industrial societies (Tsuchigane and Dodge, 1974: 105). But why did the most broadly based women's movement to date emerge in the late sixties rather than earlier? Persistent discrimination against any group is not sufficient to provoke a collective response. What is needed is the perception of an unfair situation coupled with the conviction that something can be done about it. The answer lies in the rapid increase in women's labor force participation after 1940.

Women's Employment Since 1940

From 1870 to 1950, women's labor force participation increased gradually. In 1900, 20 percent of women between the ages of 18 and 64 worked. Mostly young and unmarried, they would work for a few years, marry, and leave the labor force, never to return. By 1940 their participation had increased only to 30 percent, and the life-cycle pattern was about the same. After 1940, however, married women formed an increasingly large proportion of women workers, owing to a number of factors, such as the expansion of clerical occupations, a decrease in the supply of young unmarried women, and the increase in college attendance, which gave rise to the need for added family income when children approached college age (Oppenheimer, 1970, 1973, 1974).

Working for pay is becoming normative for married women, even for those with children (Land and Pampel, 1980; Spitze, 1979). The employed woman is no longer deviant, obliged to explain why she works. In turn, women are less defensive about being employed; hence they increasingly ask why the ideology of equal opportunity does not apply to them. The answers increase their discontent.

Earnings differentials by sex persist. All over the industrialized world, women earn half to two-thirds the earnings of men (Lydall, 1968: 55). Wage differentials in the United States, well documented (Ferber and Lowry, 1976b), are increasing (Blau, 1978).

Yet women need their earnings as much or more than men do. The divorce rate continues to rise (U.S. Bureau of the Census, 1979), hardly surprising in view of women's options to become well-educated, employed, and to limit family size (Glick, 1979). Since child support payments are small—in 1975 about three-fifths of women receiving them averaged less than $1,500 in total (U.S. Bureau of the Census, 1979), and since the majority of employed women are single, widowed, divorced, separated, or are married to husbands whose earnings are low (Pearce, 1979), the idea that women are only supplementary wage earners is inaccurate.

Whether they are employed or not, women still bear the brunt of domestic work and child care in the United States (Walker and Woods, 1976) and even in such supposedly egalitarian societies as the Soviet Union (Lapidus, 1978); a comparison of urban Soviet workers' time budgets showed little change in the allocation of domestic work by sex between 1920 and 1960 (Sacks, 1976). Contrary to popular belief, improvements in household technology do not cause a decline in the amount of housework (Robinson, 1980). Nor is there evidence that government-supported childcare facilities will increase in the near future (Kamerman and Kahn, 1979). An added handicap for employed mothers is the fact that schools are located in residential areas while jobs are downtown, making it hard to mix jobs and child care (Friedl, 1975: 137).

Will the Women's Movement Fade?

I have argued that the secular decline in fertility and the shift of productive work from home to factory resulted in men's monopolizing the exchange of valued goods and services while, owing to their child rearing responsibility, women monopolize increasingly trivialized domestic work and second-class jobs. Current sex stratification patterns are better adapted to an age when fertility could not easily be controlled. On the assumption that stratification systems adapt to the range of possibilities determined by the level of technology (Lenski and Lenski, 1973), it seems likely that women will continue to press for equality in child rearing responsibility, since such equality is now technologically feasible. Historically, fertility levels fell when individual families defined children as economic liabilities. Will fertility rates drop still further if women define children as a personal liability? What kind of support patterns would make childbearing sufficiently attractive (but not too attractive) to maintain "desired" fertility rates? The thrust of the Women's Movement poses this basic question.[9]

Unlike earlier women's movements, which focused on a narrower range of rights, the current movement includes all human activity in its scope. The problem is dual: bringing women into the world of work and bringing men into the "world" of the home. In the absence of children, this is no problem. Any adult can easily learn to clean up its own daily mess. But what if, as seems probable, men do not want an equal share of child rearing? Then pressure for extra-familial agencies will increase. Whether this will improve matters for children is also unknown. Perhaps the results are mixed.

Technological change brings many unanticipated consequences. The Women's Movement is the unplanned result of the change in what traditionally has been defined as women's work—child care and domestic chores. But unless these changes be undone, the Women's Movement is here to stay.

Notes

1. The history of the U.S. family has been neglected (Bailyn, 1960: 76), and changes affecting women's work and family lives in the nineteenth and twentieth centuries are unexplored (Scott and Tilly, 1975: 640); a comprehensive history of the U.S. colonial economy has yet to be written (Cremin, 1970: 638). Women have been invisible in anthropology (Friedl, 1975: 6), economics (Bell, 1974), history (Stern, 1944: 443; Tilly, 1975), and sociology (Millman and Kanter, 1975).

2. Considering the importance of the problem, the bibliography on the way humans give life or refuse to give it is astonishingly meager (Sauvy, 1961: 55). Himes, *Medical History of Contraception,* (1970), first published in 1936, is the only large-scale effort to document the attempt to control fertility from prehistory to modern times (Tietze, 1969: VII).

3. The situation is much the same. Women's proportion of union membership rose from 18 percent in 1952 to 22 percent in 1972. Women are still almost absent from high national offices (Bergquist, 1974: 5,7).

4. A Women's Bureau study (U.S. Department of Labor, 1928) and a later government report (Pidgeon, 1937) concluded that restrictions on women's hours had not increased the substitution of men for women or prevented women's promotion to supervisory positions. The National Manpower Council (1957: 333) also concluded that the restrictive consequences were slight, but this conclusion is based on a misinterpretation of Baker's (1925) research. A small minority of women laborites held that restrictions ensured that women's low wages would be even lower (Breckinridge, 1906), but others claimed that the arguments favoring restriction of men's hours applied a hundredfold to women (Goldmark, 1905).

5. Most unions and the Department of Labor continue to show little interest in women workers. The Department of Labor has seen little need for affirmative action for women (Hedges and Bemis, 1974). The Coalition of Labor Union Women formed in 1974 received no financial aid from the AFL-CIO, nor is it formally recognized by them, in contrast to the UAW, which funds a director for its women's department (Raphael, 1974: 32).

6. Blumberg (1976, 1977) notes the importance of fluctuations in the supply of male labor in accounting for occupational segregation. Her suggestive analysis (Blumberg, 1976) shows that, despite a formally egalitarian ideology, women were gradually excluded from the more productive jobs in the kibbutz. Although the kibbutz collectivized child care and domestic service to free women for more productive work, no men were assigned to child care and no mechanisms ensured equal participation of the sexes in domestic services. An important factor was the arrival of young male immigrants that the kibbutz was committed to absorb; they gradually replaced women in agricultural work. Eventually, service work absorbed 90 percent of kibbutz women.

7. Women college graduates are less able than men graduates to capitalize on their education investment (Spaeth, 1975). Czech women university graduates receive the same wages as working men who completed the ninth grade (Scott, 1974: 6). U.S. women college graduates working full time, year round receive the same wages as men who have not completed high school (U.S. Bureau of the Census, 1973: 1, 242).

8. The study of economic discrimination dates only from 1957; economists have been reluctant to interpret systematic group differentials as exploitation (Becker, 1968: 208). Most theories fail to show how economic variables in the model interact with the event to be explained (Berk, 1980; Marshall, 1974: 861).

9. Other references on this topic include: Armytage (1970), Bernard (1974), Boyd (1974), Carden (1974), Dodge (1966), Ferree (1974), Form (1973), Lemons (1973), Lopata (1971), Meissner et al. (1975), Preston and Richards (1975), Sacks (1975), Safilios-Rothschild (1974), Suter and Waite (1976), Tilly (1978), Tilly et al. (1976), U.S. Department of Labor (1974), and Westoff (1978).

Women in the Occupational World: Social Disruption and Conflict

ROSE LAUB COSER AND GERALD ROKOFF
State University of New York, Stony Brook

2. Current Expectations. Coser and Rokoff take Huber's argument one step further—that women's roles as wives and mothers influence the expectations people hold of them as workers. They argue that a conflict of allegiance exists for women with children who enter the work force, but not for men with children. Through paid employment men fulfill their family responsibilities, while "career and family life are presented as mutually exclusive alternatives for women." The irony is that women are allowed to work most readily in those jobs that provide the least flexibility to balance conflicting demands; most women work at uninteresting jobs with rigid time schedules. In professions where there is more flexibility in time use, women are poorly represented. But professional ideologies depict such work as a "calling" that requires round-the-clock devotion to work. The commitment required by this devotion is a primary allegiance that conflicts with the cultural mandate of women's primary responsibility to family. Yet the daily work schedules of professionals are often easier to integrate with family duties than are those of the lower-status jobs women most often hold. Clearly, there is more than rational organization of occupational and familial demands at issue here. What do you see as the disadvantages of the "status articulation mechanisms" Coser and Rokoff identify? Where do "cultural mandates" come from? How might they be changed?

Conflicts of allegiance between the family and other activity systems are not a uniquely modern phenomenon. Economic, political, or religious systems often compete with the family for the allegiance of its members. There always is some tension between society's need for the family as a transmitter of status and values to the next generation and society's claim on its members for extra-family commitments.

In some societies or organizations that can be called "greedy" because they claim the total allegiance of their members, the importance of the

39

family is played down or denied. It is in this way that we must understand the fact that the Catholic Church has prescribed celibacy for its priests, monks, and nuns. And, paradoxical as this may seem, some Bolsheviks tried to obtain the total allegiance of committed members through an opposite sexual pattern, that is, by extolling the virtues of "free love" and thereby preventing permanent unions. Similarly, in many utopian communities, prescriptions of either sexual abstinence or sexual promiscuity helped prevent permanent unions and thus served to have the energies of their members concentrated on the well-being of the "community" or the furthering of the "cause" (L. Coser, 1974; Kanter, 1968).

In modern society, total allegiance to one or the other activity system is rarely expected. Modern life is to a significantly greater extent than primitive or medieval life characterized by the individuals' ability to segment their roles. The modern person involves some attributes in some roles, other attributes in others. The most salient roles in modern American society are those of family and work.

Normative priorities for involvement are often assigned through prescribed separation of activities by time and place. Modern capitalism, as Max Weber has been one of the first to show, owes much of its tremendously rapid and forceful development to the fact that the place of work became separated from the home (Henderson and Parsons, 1947). This has made possible the exclusion of personal needs and desires, of affective attractions and distractions, from the rational pursuit of the efficient enterprise.

The fact that the place of work is separated from the home makes it possible for the two role sets, that of the family and that of work, not to overlap; if they accidentally do, as when an associate on the job is also a neighbor, they overlap less than would be the case if the two realms were not separated. This separation of the different role sets makes possible the operation of mechanisms that facilitate and, more important, routinize status articulation, that is, the decision a person must make as to which of the role sets he or she will give priority. This is not to say that individuals will never experience contradictory demands in their different roles, but that they will face fewer of them than if these mechanisms were not at work.

We do not have to go far to investigate the mechanisms that facilitate status articulation. They are the same as those outlined by Merton in regard to role articulation, that is, in regard to the decision persons must make about the multiple expectations facing them in the single role they will give priority. Merton (1968: 425 ff) shows that the fact that an individual is not in the presence of all the role partners at the same time helps reduce the burden of their incompatible or conflicting expectations; and so does the fact that the various role partners have a different amount or type of power over the status occupant, as well as a different type of interest in the latter's activities.

Here Weber's observation about the importance of the separation between home and work gains salience. Through the territorial and temporal separation of activities, the mechanisms of *insulation from observability, differential authority over,* and *differential interest* in the status occupant on the part of the various role partners operate more efficiently than if these activities were merged. In this arrangement the individual is not only insulated from the observability but also from the authority and the interest of the role partners in the other set. A woman is not expected to tell her husband how to behave on the job, nor can his employer tell him how to behave at home. The fact that in both cases it can be said that "it is none of their business to care" bears witness to the normative limits of interest in the status occupant's behavior in the other system. If it will be objected that frequently men try to tell their wives how to behave on the job, this confirms the point we are making: her being separated from him when she is at work makes the exercise of his authority less likely, if at all possible, in the occupational realm.[1]

The important fact about the operation of these mechanisms is that they reinforce the normative pattern of priorities which helps remove from individuals the burden of making their own decisions anew in most situations. Thus expectations concerning everyday behavior become largely routinized. Children learn early that there is no choice in the matter of leaving the home in the morning for school; no decision has to be made as to whether or not father is to go to work. This routinization accounts for the fact that the various activity systems operate relatively smoothly even as they demand crisscrossing allegiances from their participants.

It would seem that the mechanisms for dealing with multiple allegiances operate in the same way for men and women. Yet, this is not always the case. These mechanisms are a necessary but not a sufficient condition for routinizing status articulation. They are likely to eliminate the conflict only when they help status articulation become routinized, and this happens only under conditions of normative consensus about priorities. It is only because the expectations that father be at work during the day and children at school is shared by all that no decision has to be made about whether and when to take up these activities. Where normative consensus is lacking, or where there is normative ambiguity, the routine is likely to break down occasionally. Such is the case, among others, in emergency situations.

Emergency situations are a convenient example for showing the difference in normative priorities for men and women; these situations highlight the fact that the mechanisms for routinizing status articulation fail to operate for women the way they do for men.

The Failure of Routines and Status Articulation

An emergency can be said to occur in the routinized distribution of activities when one activity system claims the time and effort that is normatively assigned to the other, as when a mother or father has to stay home from work to care for a sick child or has to work on a weekend instead of being available to the family. In such instances of unanticipated demands, i.e., when the demands cannot be dealt with through ordinary normative regulation, an individual has to articulate his or her status anew by making a decision about which of the role sets will be given priority.

However, such a choice is not between equally weighted alternatives. In fact, the examples of mother or father staying home for a sick child, or working overtime on weekends, are hypothetical. In all likelihood it will be mother (and *not* father) who will stay home for the sick child, and it will be father (and *not* mother) who would give to the job the weekend time that is usually assigned to the family. Even where there is a choice to be made between two activity systems, it follows a preferential cultural pattern. The woman has the cultural mandate to give priority to the family. The fact that, even when working she is expected to be committed to her family first, her work second, helps prevent disruptions within the family.

Nonroutinized status articulation, even if it does not violate the norm, is potentially subversive. The working woman's expected commitment to her family is a source of disruption in the occupational sphere because "those involved in the role set have their own patterned activities disturbed when [the status occupant] does not live up to . . . role-obligations" (Merton 1968, p. 436). This is likely to happen even if the mechanisms operate, or are being manipulated, to maximize the status occupant's insulation from the observability of the role partners and from the exercise of their authority and interest. Incompatible expectations force the individual to articulate the status anew, to give priority to some normative demands at the expense of others. The woman who remains absent from work in order to care for a sick child creates a disruption in her place of work; the father who cannot come home for dinner because of some emergency at work creates a disruption at home. *Implicit in the act of articulating one's status beyond the routine is a disruption within one role set, whether or not the disruption is considered legitimate.*

Merton's distinction between role articulation and status articulation becomes useful for examining the significance of social disruption as a result of contradictory expectations. Status articulation involves the temporary abandonment of one role. Role articulation, in contrast, usually is aimed at better performance of the role, even if it implies some disappointment for some role partners within one role set. And the sanctions for such disappointments are more easily avoided than if one role has been abandoned altogether.

Role articulation tends to be less disruptive than status articulation because the latter is more likely to involve a choice between two geographically distinct places at the same time. It therefore involves a whole separate role set being abandoned if a person decides to turn to the other set. Moreover, manipulation in this case may be more difficult.[2] As a matter of fact, the separation between home and work does not give a woman the same advantage it gives a man because if she works outside the home, she is still not freed from the cultural mandate of being devoted to her family first. The separation forces her to articulate her status and prevents her from combining her gainful work with her household activities, and thus to alternate between the two, and "cheat" the one or the other in turn without this being noticed much by the role partners. Just because the two systems are separated in time and place, it is harder to live up to demands emanating from both at the same time.

Status articulation is, therefore, both easier and harder to achieve than role articulation. It is easier because the mechanisms of insulation and of differential authority and interest favor the routinization of activities in the two activity systems. This happens when the cultural mandate concerning priorities is unequivocal. If, however, the cultural mandate is equivocal, that is, if a person is expected to give priority to the place of work at the same time as having to be committed to the family, routinization breaks down, and the separation between the two activity systems makes status articulation most difficult.

It follows as a consequence that the act of status articulation, when it is not routinized, produces role conflict. This is because individuals anticipate the disruptions they might create in situations that would demand repeated status articulation. The conflict about priorities and about whether or how to manipulate the mechanisms for status articulation is structural not only in the sense that it stems from incompatible or contradictory demands but in the sense that individuals anticipate that status articulation will create some disruption for someone in the role set. The conflict is not merely their own. It is between two activity systems that have legitimate demands on the actors' allegiance.

The social anxiety created by the anticipation of such structural role conflict helps activity systems remain protected from disruptions. There is a fit between the perceived need of potential recruits to occupations to minimize the conflicts that would ensue from repeated demands for status articulation, and the perceived need of occupations and professions to minimize disturbances resulting from such status articulation. Hence, women tend to limit their options by "wanting to do what they have to do," and occupations narrow women's access to opportunities.

The Cultural Mandate

If women were to press for admission to medical schools and law schools and academic disciplines the way Jews used to, they would crash the gates. They do not even though their numbers in professional schools have been rising steadily. And even when they become practicing professionals, their careers are circumscribed (see Bourne and Wikler, this volume). This is because they accept the cultural mandate in defining their own priorities as belonging to the family. The reason for this lies in the most familiar of all facts: that almost every woman is married, or hopes to be married to a man. The family is the locus of consensus regarding the cultural mandate.

The most salient value pertaining to women's cultural mandate is that they ought to expect men to be providers of economic means and of prestige.[3] All through their early lives at home and in school, and later in college, women learn that their value commitments differ from those of men,[4] and that the basic principle underlying these commitments is that women are not to have social prestige of their own. The woman is to be the caretaker of the family, whose prestige is determined by a man.[5]

Sex segregation in school in regard to physical activities and emphasis on masculine prowess are perhaps not as symbolically important in teaching women their "proper place" as the fact that it is the boys who will give public prestige to the school through their performance in games, and that the girls are to act as cheerleaders.[6] This is the general image of women's role: they are to cheer men on, i.e., they are to help men in *their* achievements.

There is a negative connotation to the term "career woman." No such derogatory term exists for men, since their careers are taken for granted. It is acceptable, even commendable, if middle-class women take jobs to help their husbands advance their careers while going to school, or to help children go to college. Their caring in this way for members of the family is seen as part of their cultural mandate. Their occasional working is even acceptable if it is to buy some extras for themselves, or for Christmas presents, just as children are encouraged to engage in character building by earning their own Christmas money. Just as for children, women's work is not meant to give them prestige. At best, it will earn recognition for being a good sport.

As a corollary, women are available to pick up the slack at times and places where an occupational system gets overloaded, when it does not want to allocate resources that are considered too costly for an activity that nevertheless has to be carried out. Women's availability for such jobs stems, of course, from the fact that home and family to which they are assigned do not need all the time at their disposal. They can fill in as a saleswoman (typically called sales*girls* no matter what their age because of the low status of the activity) at Christmas time; be invited on the spur of the moment to teach introductory courses where an unexpectedly high number of freshmen enter a class; be called upon when a college department has to give service by teaching what is defined as "unessential" courses—say, sociology to students in nursing, engineering, or business; or be volunteers in understaffed hospitals, where they are supposed to make up for the lack of nurturing services—implying that nurturing is an unessential activity which is nice when you can get it but to which we cannot afford to allocate time that is considered "valuable," namely, that has to be paid for. Paradoxical as it may seem, women's time is considered cheap just because they live up to the highly prized cultural mandate. This is because, it will be remembered, it is the occupational role that gives prestige, and prestige-seeking is assigned to men.

What is at stake is that in their talents and achievements women are not supposed to be equal, much less superior, to men. The mass media often show women to be "smarter," but if they are really "smart," they will manipulate the situation so as to make men believe that they, and not the women, have ultimate control.

Girls learn this practice in college when they tend to underplay their academic achievements in the presence of boys, as when they underreport their grades to their dates and boy friends (Komarovsky, 1946). While in the privacy of the household a woman's superiority can sometimes be tolerated or even command deference, what is important is that her achievements not be made public, as they would be if she were to gain her own occupational status.[7] As a consequence, most educated and talented women do not even attempt to enter high-status professions or train for them.

Career and family life are presented as mutually exclusive alternatives for women. It would seem as if modern women were not capable, as modern men are, of segmenting their various roles and statuses. The American family appears as a "greedy institution" which demands total allegiance of women. Those who choose permanent careers are expected to be likely to remain celibate, like Catholic priests.

As a consequence, women are hard put to avail themselves to the extent that men do of the mechanisms of status articulation which make up the fabric of modern society. Status articulation between two activity systems is rarely routinized for working women with children because the family too often claims time and energy from them that should be assigned to work. The normative priorities for working women who have a family are ambiguous: if they live up to the normative requirement of caring for their families in situations of unexpected demands (such as illness), they introduce a disruption in their place of work; if they do not live up to this normative requirement, they introduce a disruption in the family.

The anticipation of conflict which this creates in women is integrated with the desire on the part of occupations to prevent disruptions as they are socially defined. These two factors account in large part for the widespread absence of women in high-status positions and in the professions.

Replaceability and Commitment

The replaceability on jobs where women are or feel readily admitted, as well as the commitment to and individual control over work in which they are or feel unwelcome, are, to be sure, normatively defined rather than necessarily inherent in the nature of work. That we deal here with *social definitions* of replaceability and commitment rather than with actual task requirements can be shown with two examples: the social definition of replaceability in school teaching, which is mainly done by women, and the social definition of individual control over patients in a hospital by the predominantly male house staff.

In schools, there is an institutionalized mechanism for allowing absenteeism. The prediction that there will be a high rate of absenteeism among its predominantly women teachers has led to the practice of substitute teaching. This is so patterned that in many states a special diploma is needed to perform this task. Everyone knows, however, that substitute teaching is a poor substitute for teaching. Notoriously, the students are hostile to substitutes, and their hostility is patterned, in that it is tolerated by adults and expected by peers; and nobody expects that pupils will learn much while "their" teacher is off the job. Surely, if we examine the nature of teaching, we recognize that a grade-school teacher is as much in control over the class as a college teacher, and should, therefore, be as irreplaceable as the latter. Yet, what seems to be important is to prevent disruption in the system which would occur if pupils were left unattended or if the already overloaded classrooms were required to "double up." Substituting in teaching does not serve to replace performance as much as it serves to avoid disruption.

Let us consider, in contrast, a higher-status profession like medicine. Here, the work is defined as personal service to the patient. Although, as far as the nature of work is concerned, interns and residents on a hospital service could replace one another because they usually know one another's patients, the male or the still uncommon female intern or resident will not make use of this *de facto* replaceability by giving priority to the demands of the family. The house staff is supposed to learn during training the importance of individual responsibility for and control over individual patients, with all the commitment this entails. This explains at least in part the disproportionate demands made on the trainees' time and energies in teaching hospitals. Here, absences due to anything other than illness or death in the immediate family would not be tolerated. In this normative system, the ethos is that there be no priority of commitment to the family on the part of man *or* woman. Consequently, there are still few women in this profession.

Occupations differ in the measure of commitment, i.e., internal involvement they claim from their members; and this measure is directly related to prestige in the stratification system. The distinction Merton (1959) makes between behavioral and attitudinal conformity can be usefully applied here. He speaks of *behavioral* conformity when, whatever the individuals' dispositions, they *act* according to normative prescriptions; and of *attitudinal* conformity when individuals grant legitimacy to institutional values and norms (cf. R. Coser, 1961). In routinized occupations, performance requires mainly *behavioral* conformity to detailed prescriptions and little involvement of internal dispositions. In contrast, professionals are to be guided by *attitudes* and internal dispositions, and there exists leeway concerning behavioral details (R. Coser, 1966). Individual decisions regarding courses of action are to be made; and if these are to conform to standards, they must be informed by internalized values on which to rest individual judgment. "Sanctions . . . do not attach to particular acts . . . but only to very general principles and attitudes" (Parsons, 1937: 323). Between the two extreme expectations of pure behavioral and pure attitudinal conformity there is a continuum of relative emphasis on either type, determined by the measure of routinization and the measure of individualization of judgment and control that allegedly are involved in the practice of a particular occupation. For example, grade-school teaching or nursing should require attitudinal involvement; yet to the extent that these occupations are socially defined as being routinized, there is less expectation of internal involvement and the practitioners are considered to be replaceable in their work.

Commitment can be defined as the positive involvement of internal dispositions, but we must make a second distinction, namely, between commitment to one's *work* and commitment to *other persons* engaged in the same work. Craftspeople who have pride in their work can be said to be committed to it. But what distinguishes a craftsperson from a professional is that the latter is expected to be committed to *colleagues.*

In high-status occupations, commitment is expected to be not only to work but to one another. It is not only important that the work be done, but that it be done with the approval of colleagues with whom one shares basic values. Long years of training not only serve to teach technical skills but to instill the necessary attitudes and professional values (Merton, 1957). The future commitment and the strength of the bonds of solidarity with co-professionals are to be commensurate with the investment of time, energy, and affect that such long years of intensive training require. Co-professionals are to become a most meaningful reference group toward whom the practitioners' internal dispositions will be oriented. All through their training, "the theme is mutual commitment, reinforced by students' auxiliaries sponsored by the professional associations, and by the use of such terms as 'student-physician,' which stress that the student is already in the professional family. One owes allegiance for life to a family" (Hughes, 1963).

And thus allegiances are sex-typed: a man owes to his profession what a woman owes to her family. An occupation that requires the involvement of internal dispositions demands the kind of absorption of the mind that the family claims from mothers and wives. As the writer Marya Mannes (1963) rightly says, pointing to a woman's deep involvement, "No woman with any heart can compose a paragraph when her child is in trouble or her husband ill: forever they take precedence over the companions of her mind."

The type of commitment that is ideally expected of the professional implies selflessness and devotion to a calling. Since women are expected to give this kind of commitment to their families, they tend to be restricted to the type of work that is defined as requiring a larger measure of behavioral conformity and a smaller measure of attitudinal involvement; this designates them mainly for the type of employment where they are replaceable in case of disruption caused by their normative family commitment.

As a result, professions that are sex-typed as feminine will be accorded less prestige. A corollary of the principle of replaceability is that a profession in which women predominate will be defined as requiring less commitment, whether or not task performance could profit from it. Although grade-school teaching or nursing could be defined as needing much attitudinal involvement, the premise of the cultural mandate depresses the commitment value of these occupations and hence depresses their prestige.[8]

The distinction between routinized tasks and professions also applies to the stratification system. The lower the status, the more it is associated with expectations for behavioral conformity; the higher the status, the more it is said to require the involvement of internal dispositions, and the less it is defined as being replaceable.

It would seem that strong commitments are held to be incompatible with disruption of activities. Yet it will be objected that professionals and other high-status occupants cause disruptions when their commitments take them away from their place of work. This raises the more general problem of legitimate and illegitimate disruptions.

Legitimate Disruptions, Role Flexibility, and the "Self-Fulfilling Prophecy"

In high-status positions there exist provisions for disruptions and for flexibility of role performance. These provisions are not equally available to men and women.

If high-status occupants were to stay put at their desks, they would resemble employees at the lower levels of bureaucratic structure. These, however, are defined as being replaceable. In actual fact, high status is associated with demands emanating from many places. A chief of a teaching hospital, for example, has to go to meetings all over the city or region, participate in regional, national, and sometimes international meetings, not counting trips to Washington and elsewhere in the country. Professors travel to hold lectures elsewhere, take part in meetings and conferences, give consultations, and ever so often take a leave of absence for a semester or a year. These absences create disruptions in their organizations. The hospital's chief is absent from rounds, staff meetings, and case conferences. A professor may have to cancel classes, or be away for a year; advanced students may be left without a thesis advisor.

With rise in status, the number and diversity of obligations as well as the number of role partners tend to increase, and this multiplies the number of expectations. Correlatively, the more complex the role set, the more territory it covers; and this augments the demands for being in many places. For it will be remembered that commitment of professionals is not only to their work but to one another, and colleagues are scattered all over the country, if not all over the world. Consequently, the higher the status, the more likely that all obligations cannot be met. The rule enunciated earlier, that the *higher the status, the less is the position defined as being replaceable* must be supplemented with another rule: *the higher the status, the more frequently will demands upon its occupant cause disruptions at work.*

It seems paradoxical that women should tend to be unacceptable in positions where commitments to the family might cause disruptions, when disruptions seem to be taken for granted in high-status occupations; more than that, status occupants often are congratulated for bringing honor to the organization by being wanted elsewhere.

Here the distinction mentioned earlier between status articulation and role articulation is especially relevant, although both role articulation and status articulation are likely to disrupt relationships in one role set; what organizations and professions try to avoid in high-status positions is status-articulation. Disruptions caused by women are not considered legitimate because they are seen as being due to a *failure* to meet occupational role expectations. In contrast, disruptions caused by men in high-status positions are legitimate because they are seen as being due to *fulfill-ment* of occupational role expectations.

Moreover, flexibility is built into the expectation of performance in high-status positions not only for role articulation but for occasional status articulation also. More generally, high-status occupants are not only more easily given what has been called "idiosyncrasy credit" (Hollander, 1958), being permitted some deviance by showing otherwise prized qualities (L. Coser, 1968), like the famous professors who can cancel classes more often than their less famous colleagues. It is not only that some measure of deviance is *tolerated* from high-status occupants; they often are being congratulated for showing that they take their status lightly by deviating from a strict adherence to its demands (cf. R. Coser, 1966; Goffman, 1961). This raises the more general problem of legitimate and nonlegiti-mate flexibility of role performance.

Concern with extra-professional issues testifies to the fact that the status occupant does not have "narrow" interests. If a man of high status takes time out to show concern for his family, he gives evidence of being a "good family man," a trait highly prized for a responsible position. As long as his attitudinal conformity cannot be questioned—and the likeli-hood of not having it questioned is directly associated with the prestige his status commands—occasional status articulation is permitted and may even call forth approving smiles from role partners, e.g., when the male executive announces in his office that he must take time off to buy his wife a valentine. For professional women, however, it is risky openly to artic-ulate their family status. The following conversations, which actually took place between two faculty members, illustrate this point:

> *Professor X to Professor Y:*
> I think that Joan [who is now giving only an introductory course] should be given a position in the department. She is a good teacher and does good work.
> *Professor Y:*
> I don't think so. The other day after classes I said to her: "We should have a conference about our next year's program. Can we talk about it now?" And she said, "No, it's too late, I have to go home because the children are home from school." She is just not committed as a profes-sional.
> *Two days later, Professor X to Professor Y:*
> We should have a meeting because the deadline for next year's curriculum is drawing close. How about meeting this afternoon since there are no classes?
> *Professor Y:*
> I can't today, I have to go home to babysit.
> *Professor X:*
> That's good of you. Perhaps we can meet tomorrow.

Although both Joan and Professor Y have in turn disrupted the relationship with a role partner by giving priority to parental obligations, only Joan is accused of lack of commitment to her work. In contrast, Professor Y—a male—was congratulated for taking time out for his family.

Women's occupational status is never quite legitimate. It is understood that if they have a family, this should command their major commitment, and this would cause a detriment to their occupation. Yet, if they are single, they are "deviant" and are looked down upon for not having been able to attract a husband. They are damned if they do and damned if they don't. If they are single and still young enough, they might yet succeed in finding a husband, in which case it is predicted that their career will be jeopardized. A faculty member from a high-prestige university, who prides himself on his liberal views, had this to say: "The chairman of my department refuses to give fellowships to women. He has a point. It's a bad investment. When they marry or have children, they drop out."

This is the process of the "self-fulfilling prophecy" (Merton, 1968: 475–490), by which opportunities are so structured that women will be less likely to be trained, and if trained, less likely to be employed in high-status positions, than men with equal potentialities for achievement. This process also accounts for the fact that many women drop out before getting their degrees. In most cases, however, women are likely to anticipate much earlier in life that marriage and children will make it difficult to use the qualifications they could acquire, and are, therefore, likely to refrain from seeking the training that would be commensurate with their abilities.

Summary and Conclusions

Societies always have social definitions of desirable life goals. In modern American society, men are to get occupational status and women are to get men who will get such status. Achieved status is the salient one in American society in that it tends to determine position in the stratification system. Hence, while men are in charge of placing their families in that system, women's statuses remain vicarious. Women tend to be deprived of the opportunity of obtaining achieved statuses for themselves. Another way of saying this is that men raise the family's status by raising their own, while women share in the family's status by denying their own. (By this is not meant that women who contribute to the family income do not help to raise its living standards; only that they have no claim to status recognition for doing so.)

Equal education for women helps them compete with one another to attract the most "valued men" and makes women capable of helping their husbands in their careers. Yet, modern American society also values equality of opportunity for its members. Hence equal education also holds out for women the opportunity for careers for themselves. Up to and including college, middle-class women are usually as well prepared as men to enter the occupational system and derive prestige from their participation in it (although we also know that their jobs command lower salaries and less prestige than those of men).

However, as long as the premise of women's cultural mandate is accepted, women will be considered a potential source of disruption in high-status positions as a result of their expected status articulation, which is seen as a potential threat of disturbance. The mechanisms of status articulation that operate in modern society to help routinize multiple status obligations and hence integrate the activity systems of family and occupations are not available to women to the extent that they are for men.

In an industrial society whose operation depends on the distribution of status positions according to achievement, attempts to shut the gates of opportunity, or even to leave them merely ajar, for one-half of the educated population on the basis of ascribed status cannot be maintained without considerable strain and conflict. If there is to be a change to reduce or eliminate contradictory expectations for women, it will have to be in the definitions of desirable life goals in American society. Many of our young men and women, who at the present time object to the frantic pursuit of money and status on the part of men, are ready for a scrutiny of alternative life-styles.[9]

Yet a change in the family structure need not threaten the solidarity of the family but may actually increase its cohesion. Solidarity in the family implies sharing commitments, both in caring for family members and in providing the financial means for its comfortable existence. If either spouse would spend a little more time in one of these activities than he or she does now, and a little less time in the other, children might grow up with the sense that both parents are committed to their vocation at work and to their calling at home as well; and that both these commitments can be deeply satisfying for adults of both sexes. This may help induce young men and women to want to grow up to become productive and committed adults. Nothing could foster solidarity and growth more than for parents to share the responsibility of providing for their children, of caring for them and for each other, at the same time as they are committed to their respective vocations outside the home.

If husbands were routinely expected to be as fully responsible for the management of disruptions in the family system as wives are now, it would become much more difficult to maintain the idea that higher-status professions have to be wary of women as potential disrupters of the routines of occupational life.

Notes

1. The rule of nepotism, which states that two members of the same family will not be permitted to work for the same employer, has its source in the functional requirement for modern organizations that they remain protected from familial concerns and allegiances during working hours. This is not only to avoid distraction; it is a response to the fact that different norms regulate behavior in the different activity systems. If it is objected that the rule of nepotism is obsolete because of the complexity of modern organizations, where the internal separation of offices and lines of command can insulate individual members of the same family, this confirms the point that is emphasized here. Separation between different areas of activities assures insulation from observability as well as involvement in a different authority structure, and this at least reduces, if it does not eliminate, the potential conflict.

2. In regard to "ego manipulation of . . . role structues," see Goode (1960).

3. On the dysfunctional aspects of the "husband-provider role," see Grønseth (1970).

4. The nature of the pressures deterring women from planning careers still awaits systematic investigation.

5. Typically, the woman takes her husband's surname. The negative connotation attached to the term *spinster,* in contrast to the lack of such connotation to the term *bachelor,* is due to the fact that the unmarried woman tends to be wanting in social standing.

6. For this observation, I am indebted to Steven Coser, who, when still in grammar school, remarked sarcastically: "How do you like the way this high school is integrated? The boys are on the football team and the girls are the cheerleaders!"

7. A mother reported proudly about her daughter: "She has her hands full. In addition to taking care of the house and the children, she writes book reviews for her husband." Asked who signs these reviews, she says: "He signs them, of course. *She is really very clever about that.*"

8. This is, of course, only a restatement of the familiar fact that women have lower status than men in the culture at large, and that this is carried over to female occupations in the public image. As a consequence, professions try to protect themselves lest too many women in their ranks depreciate their prestige with the public. The reluctance of medical schools to admit women students was similar to their reluctance in an earlier day to admit Jews. At that time, for a profession to be typed "Jewish" was as derogatory as it still is today to be typed "a woman's occupation."

9. As Gagnon (1969) has pointed out, equality of women would mean a truly revolutionary change because unlike other grants of equality to minorities, women's equality would affect the structure of the American family.

Sex Discrimination and Employment Practices: An Experiment with Unconventional Job Inquiries

RICHARD M. LEVINSON
Emory University

3. Consequences. Levinson and his students conducted a simple experiment, making inquiries about jobs for which they were inappropriate candidates—according to sex-role stereotypes. The students found some of the discouraging responses a "deviant" receives. Both women and men received responses that negatively sanctioned them for not adhering to "appropriate" stereotypes. In contradiction to the earlier findings of Gross from census data (1968), their survey found more discrimination against men who resist stereotypes than against women who do so. Can this be explained as a consequence of using different research methods? Do you think Levinson's descriptions of discrimination in job advertisements and responses to job applicants would still occur? Can you replicate this study in your community?

Although women have become increasingly involved in the labor force, their collective failure to achieve the occupational success of men is well documented (e.g., Epstein, 1970b: 6–11; Rossi, 1965; U.S. Department of Labor, 1969). Particularly accountable for this discrepancy is a pattern of job segregation—remarkably stable since 1900 (Gross, 1968; Oppenheimer, 1970; Wilensky, 1968)—by which women are disproportionately employed in low-status, low-income occupations (Gross, 1968; Knudsen, 1969; Kreps, 1971; Martin and Poston, 1972; Oppenheimer, 1970) or in lower, subordinate positions within occupational categories (Epstein, 1970a; Grimm and Stern, 1974; Gross, 1968; Kosa and Coker, 1965; Lopate, 1968; Martin and Poston, 1972). Additional explanations have been offered for the differential occupational distribution of women. Among them are sex role socialization (Davis, 1965: 46–48; Maccoby, 1963; Pavalko, 1971: 58–61; Simpson and Simpson, 1969: 202–205) conflicting demands of marital and parental roles (Garland, 1972; Kreps,

1971: 18–32; Rossi, 1965); extensions of cultural norms asserting that women are best suited for socioemotional or subordinate roles (Coser and Rokoff, this volume; Parsons, 1942; Prather, 1971a; Simpson and Simpson, 1969); psychological states of self-prejudice or lowered self-esteem (Goldberg, 1968; Horner, 1970); the sex typing of occupations themselves, which reinforces these processes by linking occupational roles and sex roles (Epstein, 1970a); and, of course, acts of discrimination (e.g., Bass et al., 1971; Bullough and Bullough, 1975; Levitin et al., 1971).

Sex segregation in occupations remains despite legislation such as Title VII of the 1964 Civil Rights Act forbidding discrimination by sex and the efforts of agencies such as the Equal Employment Opportunities Commission to enforce it. In 1968 the Commission ruled to forbid sex discrimination in help-wanted advertisements and outlawed sex-segregated classified advertisements. Nevertheless the advertisements themselves often make it clear what sex is desired. Consider some examples from the two major Atlanta, Georgia, newspapers in Spring, 1974:

> SUPER JOB FOR SUPER GAL—Need ambitious person for Gen. ofc, duties and tel. sales.
>
> SALESMAN—2 clean cut men to train as salesmen for Ga.'s oldest . . .
>
> PEST CONTROL—servicemen, driver's license necessary, unusually good opportunity for right men, will train.

This paper deals with the extent of sex discrimination during job inquiries. It examines discriminatory acts at recruitment which, by restricting access to certain positions, contributes to job segregation by sex.

Methodological Procedures

Working in teams of one male and one female, undergraduate sociology students selected several classified advertisements from two major Atlanta newspapers during Spring, 1974. Jobs were defined as "male" or "female" on the basis of their present sex composition (Kreps, 1971: 34–35; Oppenheimer, 1970: 66–67).[1]

In each team, one partner made an inquiry to a "sex-inappropriate" (SI) job followed approximately one-half hour later by a call from the other partner to the same number, a "sex-appropriate" situation (SA). For example, the female would first call to inquire about an auto sales position (SI). This would be followed by a call from the male (SA). The procedure would be reversed in the case of a "female" job. Students were instructed to be polite, use nearly identical words and mannerisms in their inquiries, and record in as much detail as possible the responses received from the employer to each call. In most situations, the following dialogue was used:

"I would like to inquire about your advertisement in the newspaper for a _____ " or "I am interested in applying for a job as _____."
"How/where can I apply?"

Again, each partner was careful to match the other in further inquiries and responses to the employer's questions. In conclusion, students thanked the employers and said they would "think it over." Thus, each call was a controlled experiment providing the employer with nearly identical inquiries from persons matched on qualifications and differing only in sex.[2] Variations in responses to different sex callers could be attributed to the voice-indicated sex of each person making the inquiry. Should one sex be treated distinctively more favorably than the other, one might reasonably assert this to be an incident of sex discrimination.

These procedures investigate only a small element of sex discrimination in employment. Employers may appear quite negative over the phone yet behave very differently when confronted in person by a sex-inappropriate applicant (e.g., see Deutscher, 1973; LaPiere, 1934). Conversely, employers who are particularly sensitive to charges of sex discrimination might resist openly refusing a caller simply on the basis of sex but discriminate in a more subtle fashion later on in the hiring process.

After all calls were completed, information contained on standardized forms used by students (job, caller's sex, and caller-employer dialog) was coded. "Clear-cut" discrimination was recorded in cases where employers clearly restricted or eliminated chances for employment due to sex. Cases where employers said one sex was unsuited for the job, when employers told an SI caller the job was filled but the SA caller it was still open, or when the SI caller was deemed unqualified but the SA person with identical characteristics found qualified were coded as "clear-cut" instances. Cases were coded as "ambiguous" when males and females were accorded different responses but given no impression that one would be excluded because of sex. Expressions of surprise or dismay, questions about why a person of that sex would seek such a job, differences in the amount and nature of information offered, encouragement or discouragement differentially offered were coded in the "ambiguous" category. With similar responses to each caller, the classification of "none" was used. Finally, when information did not permit a coding decision to be made, it was classified as "not discernible."[3]

Findings

Table 1 reveals that a substantial amount of sex discrimination was detected in job inquiries. Some 35 percent of the calls produced instances of clear-cut discrimination. Fewer (27 percent) showed "ambiguous" responses, while less than one-third (31 percent) treated both callers simi-

Table 1
Sex Discrimination in Job Inquiries

	Discrimination			
	Clear-Cut	Ambiguous	None	Not Discern.
(N)	(90)	(70)	(80)	(16)
%	35.2	27.3	31.2	6.3

larly. It appears that a large number of employers in the sample area practice discrimination by sex.

Clear-Cut Discrimination
Clear-cut discrimination took place in a variety of ways. In a few cases, the SI caller was told that the person responsible for hiring was not present or out of town, while the SA caller was told by the individual answering the phone to come in for an interview or to make an application. A variation on this strategy found employers telling SI callers that they were "too busy" to deal with them at the time and asking them to call back on "a better day" (with a very receptive response to SA callers). Another method of handling SI callers was to discuss their qualifications and declare them unqualified for the job while accepting the SA caller with identical qualifications. A female caller for a restaurant management training program was told that two years of college with no other management position was insufficient. A male who gave identical information was scheduled for an interview with the firm. A male caller for a secretarial position answered inquiries with an impressive list of skills, including a college degree, shorthand and typing skills, and previous experience, but was turned down since the employers declared they were looking for someone more "career oriented." The female was invited to fill out an application without hesitation or further inquiry. A male caller for a receptionist job was told that prior experience in credit checking was required for the job, while the female (who also said she had no experience in credit checking) was told to come in anyway for an interview.

In some cases, employers assumed the SI person to be unqualified simply because of sex and expressed this in the conversation before hanging up. A male inquiring about a "teacher-nurse-worker" position in a day-care operation was told, "Well this is with one-year-old children, and I doubt that you would want to work with them." A woman calling for a "mechanic's" job was told, "I really don't think a woman can handle this sort of thing." A female inquiring about a shipping-receiving job met the response, "Honey, I'm sorry, but we need a man to do that. All our employees are men, and you'd need to unload heavy equipment. . . . I'd like to help you, but we really need someone pretty strong." In each case, SA callers were encouraged to apply. One final example involves a female calling about a management trainee position for a tire corporation. She was told, "It's not for women. It requires lifting of 100-pound tires. I'm sorry—with the new laws, I couldn't put that in [the advertisement]." The male was given a job description that involved no lifting and told explicitly that it involved "no heavy work."

A blunt response that sex disqualified the caller (without any explanation) was another common occurrence. For example, women calling about jobs as liquor store manager, maintenance man, and fuel attendant were told, "The job's for a man," "We are only interested in men," and "Honey, we don't use girls as fuel attendants," respectively. Males calling for "female" jobs met similar responses. For a dental assistant inquiry, one was told, "We are just looking for a girl," and for a nurse's aid position, "Uh . . . we do not hire males . . . only females." In response to an inquiry about a medical secretary-receptionist, a male caller learned, "I'm sure the doctors would rather have a woman. . . . I'm afraid you're wasting your time because the doctors were quite specific about getting a woman," and a call about a receptionist-typist job was answered, "Well, sir, I'm not sure how to put this, but we're really looking for a nice young lady to fill the position, and you don't really meet this criterion."

Another group of employers told SI callers they were not suitable for the position but suggested an alternative job. The male caller for a clerk-typist opening was told he should instead apply for the (more prestigious and lucrative) job as claims adjuster, "a position for men." Similarly, a male caller for a "shampoo help" advertisement was told he could be a hairstylist, but "we don't hire men as shampoo help." A female inquiring about a janitorial position was told that it was filled (it was not, according to a later SA inquiry), but she could have a job as a maid (for a lower wage). The female who asked about a job servicing vending machines was informed that the company needed a "hostess" (at a lower salary). A final example involves a woman calling for a restaurant manager position. After indicating that she had a variety of work experiences and would be a business school graduate, the caller was told she would be better suited now for positions as "hostess, cashier, or waitress." The male caller was encouraged to interview for the manager position.

The most devious instances of clear-cut discrimination occurred when the SI caller was told the job was filled while the following SA caller was led to believe it was still open. This happened for such jobs as medical receptionist, waitress, typist, nurse's aide, auto sales, store manager, and truck driver.

Ambiguous Discrimination

Another set of responses was labeled "ambiguous" cases of discrimination. Some of these involved responses stemming from the surprise of finding a person of that sex interested in the advertised job, but in no instance did the employer eliminate the SI caller from consideration. For example, females heard the following comments not made to males applying for the same jobs:

> (pest control serviceman)
> "Do you want the job as secretary?" ("No, the pest control serviceman job.") "Well, er . . . oh maybe . . . I guess you can come in and apply."

> (production manager—carpets)
> "You *are* a female? And you're interested in this job?" ("Yes") . . . "You can come down, and we'll see if this job is suitable for you. If not, we can put you in the direction of where your interests lie."

Males were met with similar kinds of responses to SI calls not found in the female SA follow-up call:

> (secretary)
> "Are you inquiring for yourself?" ("Yes") "Well . . . I'm very surprised you're interested in this job . . . and you type pretty good, do you? Well . . . if you really are interested, I guess you can come on down for an interview. . . ."

> (drapery seamstress)
> "It's hard to believe a guy is really qualified for this work."

A large number of callers found employers trying to discourage them from pursuing SI jobs. But males and females found a different set of tactics applied in these "ambiguous" cases. Typically, males were told that jobs were either too simple, dull, or low-paying. On the other hand, women were told that jobs were too difficult, had "long or night hours," or required too much physical strength. While males were greeted with an encouraging reply for the following jobs, females heard the following:

> (laborer—lawn sprinkler installation)
> "Is this for *you?*" . . . Well, it's mighty hard work, out in the sun digging very deep ditches and the sprinkler systems are very complex . . . it's mighty hard . . . and long, long hours too."

> (gas station attendant)
> "It's pretty dirty work. Are you sure you wouldn't want to work somewhere else? The pay is minimum wage, and you might have to work late shifts."

Similarly, male callers were discouraged as illustrated by the following:

Table 2
Proportion of Inquiries into "Male" and "Female" Jobs with
Discriminatory Responses: Comparison of Totals

	Discrimination				
	Clear-Cut	Ambiguous	None	Not Discern.	Total
Female inquiries for "male" jobs	28%	31.5%	37%	3.5%	100% (N = 146)
Male inquiries for "female" jobs	44%	22%	24%	10%	100% (N = 110)

These data were dichotomized into a 2 × 2 table contrasting clear-cut by other categories. $X^2 = 7.45$, significant, $P < .01$.

(clerk-typist)
"I'm surprised you're interested in this. You realize it's general office work and typing—nothing very exciting."

(typist)
"It's only a part-time job without much security to it. We send typists to other offices with no guarantee of work all the time."

Comparison of Discrimination toward Males and Females

Responses to inquiries were compared for overall "male" and "female" jobs in Table 2. In this study, clear-cut discrimination against males was much more common than that against females. Forty-four percent of the males as compared with only 28 percent of the females faced job discrimination.

Discussion

Long ago, Hughes (1945) called attention to a process whereby certain combinations of status-determining characteristics (such as sex) came to be associated with a particular position. This results in the expectation that all incumbents of that position possess such auxiliary characteristics. Bird (1971: 69) has noted how capriciously such labels become applied by commenting that women are felt to be good for factory work on electronic circuits for the same reason men are said to be well suited for neurosurgery—finger dexterity and a steady hand. In this study, sex-typed jobs were approached by persons without those auxiliary characteristics. Their violation of social norms was sometimes negatively sanctioned by comments expressing surprise or derogation and/or discriminatory acts of exclusion.

But this does not explain the greater discrimination against male than female SI callers. Perhaps sex is a more *salient* characteristic of "female" than "male" positions, i.e., more essential for the performance of functions required by "female" than "male" jobs included in this study. Although Epstein (1969, 1970a) documents how gender sometimes interferes with female performance in professions of the male establishment, sex may be even more important for jobs associated with women, e.g., receptionist, secretary, fashion sales—at least for the men doing the hiring. A secretary may be expected not only to type but "decorate the office." As one male applicant for a receptionist's position was told by the (male) employer:

> "Well, you see, in our office there are many important customers coming into the office, and it just doesn't look right having a man behind the reception desk . . . it seems out of place . . . and it's liable to hurt the business. It shouldn't be that way, but you know how it is. . . . And also, speaking for the guys around here, I think the day would be a lot more pleasant with a pretty face around."

Similarly, it might be felt that a woman in sales who displays her products well (cosmetics, fashions) will be a more effective employee than a male. Thus, one explanation for the differential discrimination may be the feeling of (male) employers that being a female is more central to filling the needs of female sex-typed jobs than being male is for male sex-typed positions.

Another possible explanation for the differential discrimination might be related to aspects of personal character attributed to the caller by the employer. The male SI caller may be seen as more deviant or abnormal than a female SI caller. Observers of sex-role socialization (e.g., Lynn, 1961; Mussen, 1969) have noted that boys experience greater stigma and/or anxiety for acting like a girl ("sissy") than girls experience for acting like boys ("tomboys"). This may be the result of an identification process (Lynn, 1961) or the fact that male roles and traits are more culturally valued (Broverman et al., 1970; Mussen, 1969). As with stereotypic male characteristics, for women to seek more highly desired and prestigious male jobs may be perceived as rational, understandable, and sometimes admirable. However, the male seeking a less valued "female" position is likely, except perhaps in times of limited employment opportunities (Grimm and Stern, 1974: 693), to be seen as peculiar and, hence, an undesirable employee. Interestingly, several male SI callers were questioned about their "masculinity" (e.g., "Are you a queer?"), while no female SI callers reported such comments.

Finally, many employers were probably made sensitive to the legal consequences of discrimination against women through publicity of recent lawsuits, the activism of women's rights organizations, and government warnings. To date, men have rarely made use of the law to gain access to female sex-typed positions. Of twelve SI callers reporting an employer actually mentioning that he could not legally discriminate simply because of sex, ten (83 percent) were females inquiring about "male" jobs:

> (auto sales)
> "Well, I can't turn you down because you're a girl. But really, I think you're barking up the wrong tree."

> (manager)
> "Don't tell me *you* want this job?" ("Are only men eligible for the job?")
> "No, it would be discriminatory if we did that."

While there is evidence for the operation of each of these processes, the degree to which each accounts for our findings cannot be determined by these data.

Although the findings reported here indicate that women may find it easier gaining access to traditionally male fields than vice versa, others have argued just the opposite. Gross (1968) and Wilensky (1968) have speculated that traditionally female occupations have been more open to men than male occupations to women, and Gross (1968) has offered data to substantiate that most male fields have remained more segregated than most female fields. Apparently, the increased demand for labor in traditional female areas has not only absorbed growing numbers of women but attracted some men as well, mostly at higher supervisory positions (Grimm and Stern, 1974).

Several considerations may resolve the seemingly contradictory findings. First, our sample of occupations culled from classified advertisements are primarily nonprofessional, low-prestige positions. Occupations investigated by Grimm and Stern (1974) were semiprofessions (social work, teaching, librarianship, nursing) with some prestige, job security, a modest but adequate income, and opportunity for advancement. It is easy to understand why males might be attracted to such occupations, especially when they serve at the highest levels. By contrast, female occupations in this study are primarily dead-end positions without opportunity for mobility. (Eighty-three percent were classified as either secretary, receptionist, waitress, or maid.) While higher-status female semiprofessions may even actively recruit males to "upgrade the profession" (Gross, 1968: 51; Wilensky, 1964), there is no such self-conscious professionalization among female occupations in this study.

Our findings, in contrast to others, may also be a function of time. Several employers seemed very aware of the legal problems involved with discrimination against women. This study may have tapped a change taking place in which, as a result of increased feminist activism, employers are today much more hesitant to discriminate against women than men. Of course, employers might just be more cautious about giving overt refusals over the phone. Discrimination may occur later, in a more subtle fashion, yielding much less job access for females than is indicated by this study.

It is therefore unclear from the accumulating data how job opportunities for men and women will change in the future. If aggressive action on behalf of women is maintained, there may be some influx of women into jobs at all prestige levels formerly held by men. When there is a tighter job market, men might increasingly seek employment in formerly women's fields at all levels of prestige and begin to use the statutes to their own advantage if access is denied. If previous patterns continue (Grimm and Stern, 1974), those integrated occupations may become internally segregated and stratified by sex, with males continuing their domination.

Notes

Some fifty Emory University undergraduates were involved in the experimental procedures and collectively share the paper's authorship.

1. Although either sex could have performed tasks required by the 256 listed jobs, Merton notes that "occupations" can be described as 'sex typed' when a very large majority of those in them are of one sex and when there is an associated normative expectation that this is as it should be" (Epstein, 1970a).

    Very few advertisements included specific requests for a male or female (such as those already noted in the text), although some may imply sex by job title, e.g., waitress, office girl, or salesman, waiter.

    The following types of jobs were used: "*Male*" *jobs*—security guards, officers (17); garage workers and attendants, auto mechanics (18); automobile sales (13); other sales—sporting goods, large appliances, etc. (10); truck, bus drivers (13); manager, manager trainee in small business (restaurant, food, liquor, gas station, etc.) (12); skilled workers, servicemen (19); janitors, yardmen, maintenance, warehouse workers (29). "*Female*" *jobs*—receptionist (15); waitress, hostess (12); maid, housekeeper (11); secretary, office worker, etc. (53); cosmetic, fashion sales (8); other (Tupperware sales, dental assistants, day-care workers, nurse's aides, etc.) (11). Due to the nature of the jobs available through newspaper classified advertisements, few inquiries were made for jobs requiring advanced degrees, professional training, and accorded the highest prestige and income in this society.

2. In some cases, more than one set of calls was made to the same employer. They were counted only once in data analysis. Remarkably, in each case of overlapping calls the same employer response was independently found, a strong indication of reliability.

3. The information forms were independently coded by the author and an assistant using the four discrimination categories. Over 90 percent agreement was reached. Those for which there was no agreement were placed in the "Not Discernible" category.

    One issue in coding employer reactions involved the classification of responses to persons applying for positions in which sex might have some relevance for performance. For example, a male could adequately perform the tasks of a cocktail waitress, but the management might prefer an attractive female to lure a businessman clientele. Is refusal to hire males for such jobs discriminatory? The 1965 EEOC guidelines for employers took a narrow view of "bona fide sex qualifications." Preference for sex could not be given simply to please customers, co-workers, or clients or on the basis of generalizations about the ability of women or men in general (Bird, 1971: 13). Using EEOC guidelines, all such refusals by sex were classified as "discriminatory." It should be noted that such jobs comprised a small part of the total sample.

Finally, because our sample was restricted to the Atlanta, Georgia, metropolitan area, generalizability of the findings is limited. However, as a cosmopolitan and rapidly growing city in the otherwise traditional Southeast, Atlanta may be quite similar to other regional urban settings on dimensions likely to influence these findings.

Male and Female: Job Versus Gender Models in the Sociology of Work

ROSYLN L. FELDBERG
EVELYN NAKANO GLENN
Boston University

4. Implications. Feldberg and Glenn focus on what have been very limiting assumptions in previous research on men's and women's paid employment. They argue that previous research has mainly used a "job model" to explain male participation in the labor force and a "gender model" to explain that of women. The job model concentrates on working conditions, opportunities, and problems as the main source of explanations for what people do at and want from work. The gender model generally ignores type of job and working conditions to focus on personal characteristics, family circumstances, and an assumed "family first" commitment in explaining how women feel about their paid jobs and what they do at them.

Such sex-segregated theoretical models encourage picking and choosing in explanations of findings. Thus, as in the two studies in the sociology of work reviewed by Feldberg and Glenn, researchers consistently ignore family-related issues in explaining men's attitudes at work and job-related attitudes in explaining women's work attitudes and aspirations. What are the main recommendations Feldberg and Glenn make for overcoming the limiting assumptions common in the sort of "sociology of work" studies they discuss? If some of them seem more logical to you than others, on what grounds do you make your own evaluations of their work here?

Work has long been viewed as a central aspect of people's lives. It determines their daily activities, the rhythm of their days, the people they meet, and the relationships they form. In addition, work largely defines a person's class and status in the social structure. While issues of work are framed as universal ones, the actual study of work has proceeded along sex-differentiated lines.

These sex-differentiated lines lead to three problems which characterize the sociological literature on work. First, women are rarely included in research. Studies of work concentrate on white males, particularly those in managerial, blue-collar, and professional occupations (Hesselbart, 1978). Second, when women are studied, the analysis is shaped by sex-biased interpretations. Third, the entire analysis of work is distorted because certain factors are defined as appropriate either in the study of women's work, or in the study of men's work, but not in both.

Recently, the sociology of work has been criticized for its treatment of employed women. The critics argue that women have been excluded from the study of work and that, when they are studied, the analyses have been distorted by sexist assumptions (Acker, 1977; Acker and VanHouten, 1974; Brown, 1976; Kanter, 1975b; Oakley, 1974). While these writers have documented many specific instances of sexist interpretations, they have not identified the underlying paradigm that gives rise to sex-differentiated approaches to men's and women's employment.

Sex-Segregated Models

Separate models for men's and women's relationship to employment are a logical outcome of the sexual division of labor characteristic of the middle period of industrial capitalism. Although the separation of male and female spheres had long been part of the prescriptive literature in the United States and Britain, as well as elsewhere, the expansion of industry in the late nineteenth and early twentieth centuries made the realization of the ideal possible for middle- and upper-class women. During this period, the division of labor became more rigid as women were pressured to withdraw from production and to devote their attention to domestic concerns (Chafe, 1976). Women who remained in the labor force were primarily young and unmarried. Employment of married women (primarily black and some immigrant women) was viewed as the outcome of personal misfortune (Smuts, 1971). The dichotomy became men = breadwinners and workers, women = wives. It is assumed that all male-female differences flowed from that dichotomy. Rather than trying to determine how well this dichotomy applied to particular groups of men and women in specific historical periods, sociologists tended to incorporate it into their basic assumptions and concepts. Thus, even when women were employed, their employment was seen as atypical or as secondary to their "real" roles. The result is the creation of two sociologies of work: the job model for men and the gender model for women.[1]

Job Model
The *job model* treats the work people do as the primary independent variable. Researchers have used it to explain workers' behavior on and off the job.

Many aspects of the immediate job situation have been found to have an impact on workers' subjective reactions to their jobs (Kohn, 1976). Blauner's (1964) study of male industrial workers found that highly mechanized, routine, repetitive work was associated with higher levels of alienation, which he defined as powerlessness, meaninglessness, social isolation, and self-estrangement. Variations on this pattern have been confirmed for factory (Cotgrove, 1972), office and computer (Shepard, J., 1971, 1973), and professional workers (Pearlin, 1962).

In addition, quality of life "off the job" has been seen as affected by conditions and experiences in the work place, at least for men (Aronowitz, 1973; Israel, 1971; Kornblum, 1974; Mortimer, 1976; Ollman, 1971; Seeman, 1967, 1975). Kornhauser (1965) argued, on the basis of his findings, that job conditions in the automobile industry were the source of workers' mental health problems (cf. Gross, 1970). Finally, Meissner (1971) found that skills and the degree of judgment used on the job carry over to shape the off-the-job activities of male industrial workers (cf. Kohn and Schooler, 1978).

As important as the relationships the studies cover are the ones they ignore. First, they pay little attention to the effects of historical or geographical variations in the labor market (Kessler-Harris, 1973). Second, they overlook aspects of the life situation outside of work, such as ethnic culture and life-styles or family ties and resources.

Gender Model

While analyses of men's relationship to employment concentrate on job-related features, most analyses of women's relationship to employment (which are rare by comparison) virtually ignore type of job and working conditions. When it is studied at all, women's relationship to employment is treated as derivative of personal characteristics and relationships to family situations (Laws, 1976b; Oakley, 1974). This type of analysis is referred to here as the *gender model*.

Until the mid-1970s, researchers paid little attention to how the occupations or industries of employed women affected their responses to work. Instead, they used personal characteristics and family circumstances to explain the attitudes and behavior of employed women. For example, women's labor force participation rates were attributed to characteristics such as educational level, marital status, the number and ages of children, husband's income, and husband's attitude toward wife's employment (Mahoney, 1961; Mincer, 1962; Myers, 1964; Parnes et al., 1975; Sweet, 1973). Laws (1976b) points out that in this literature the decision to seek employment (or remain employed) and the choice of occupation are seen as products of unique "female" motivations, rather than of the structure of the local labor market and related factors (e.g., Eyde, 1962, 1968; Psathas, 1968; Rosenfeld and Perrella, 1965; Sobol, 1963; Williamson and Karras, 1970).

Consistent with the emphasis on the female role, many studies have tried to establish the effects on family life of married women "being employed" (Hoffman and Nye, 1974; Howell, 1973a; Nye and Hoffman, 1963; Safilios-Rothschild, 1970). Other studies have examined the impact of women's employment on division of household labor (e.g., Berk et al., 1976; Howell, 1973a; Szalai, 1972) and on power distribution in the family (e.g., Bahr, 1974; Blood and Wolfe, 1960; Heer, 1963; Scanzoni, 1970). In all of these "family consequence" studies, the supposed effects of women's employment are studied without reference to the actual activities of women on the job. Thus, they provide little information on how consequences vary for families of women doing different jobs under different working conditions.

Some recent research has been aimed at correcting distortions created by applying the gender model to women. In most cases, the approach taken is to apply the job model to women. Particular attention has been paid: to the impacts of institutional opportunity structures on women's evaluations of work and their aspirations for mobility (Kanter, 1977b; Wallace, 1976); to the effects of differential treatment of men and women, including different methods of worker control on women's work behavior (Acker and Van Houten, 1974;[2] Langer, 1972; Coser and Rokoff, this volume; Epstein, 1970b); and to the influence of conditions of housework on women's assessments of paid employment (Lamphere, 1973; Oakley, 1974; Walshok and Walshok, 1978). While these researchers realize the inadequacies of the gender model, they tend to overlook the shortcomings of the job model. Perhaps they are assuming that whatever model has been used to study men must be valid for all workers.[3] This is a reflection of the tendency to use men as the standard to define normal human behavior. However, we argue that the job model is, by itself, inadequate and that exclusive reliance on it leads to distorted conclusions about the meaning of work for both men and women. What is needed instead is an integrated model which takes into account the *interaction* between job and gender factors. The development of such an integrated model must begin with a careful analysis of the assumptions underlying each model and a systematic examination of their implications.

Assumptions of the Models

The sociology of work is essentially the study of how work connects individuals to the social structure. The models used in this field are, therefore, concerned with the nature of these links and their consequences. The most common topic for investigation is workers' response to work. However,

Table 1
Varying Assumptions in the Job Model and the Gender Model

Assumptions	Job Model	Gender Model
1. Basic social relation-ships determined by:	Work	Family
2. Family structure is:	Male-headed, nuclear	Male-headed, nuclear
3. Connection to family is:	As economic provider/worker	As wife/mother
4. Social position deter-mined by:	Work	Family
5. Sociopolitical behav-ior and attitudes de-rived from:	Occupational socialization, class/status of occupation, social relations of work	Gender role socialization, family roles, activities and relationships of household work
6. Central life interest[4] is in:	Employment + earnings	Family

the assumptions underlying the explanations encompass not only the work setting but also the basic connections of individuals to the larger social structure. These assumptions are different for men and women.

For men, it is assumed that economic activities provide the basis for social relationships within the family and in the society generally. For women, it is assumed that family caretaking activities determine social relationships. These different spheres of activity are, in turn, assumed to be combined in a nuclear family through sexual division of labor—that is, man as economic provider and woman as wife and mother. Furthermore, male-female differences in relation to the family are expected to lead to differences in the nature of men's and women's connection to other parts of the social structure. For example, social class is assumed to be determined by economic position (i.e., relation to means of production, occupation) for the male, and by position in the family (i.e., wife, daughter) for the female. Similarly, work attitudes and behavior of men are seen as consequences of occupational experiences (e.g., conditions of employment or occupational socialization), while responses of women are viewed as outcomes of family experiences (e.g., household burden, feminine socialization). The major assumptions are diagrammed in Table 1.

Two further points require emphasis. First, these differences in assumptions are themselves connected. They are complementary aspects of a single conception of social structure: what is held to be true for males is, by definition, held not to be true for females, and vice versa. Second, each model assumes homogeneity among members of each sex. Variations in the situations of members of each sex are ignored, and no allowance is made for class and ethnic differences or for changes over time.

Two Studies in the Sociology of Work

In this section, we will analyze distortions arising from the use of the job/gender models in two major studies. These studies share the rare characteristics of studying men and women in similar job settings, thus making possible a comparison of the conceptual frameworks developed to explain men's versus women's work attitudes and behavior. The authors of the two studies show differing degrees of awareness that they are using job and gender models.

The first study, by Blauner (*Alienation and Freedom,* 1964), compares men and women in somewhat different jobs within the textile industry. It illustrates the explicit use of a job model for men and a gender model for women. The job model is used to explain variations between groups of men; the gender model, applied only to the women, is used to explain differences between men and women. Beynon and Blackburn's study of English factory workers (*Perceptions of Work,* 1972) incorporates both job and gender variables. They recognize that differences in domestic situations *and* job conditions affect the work concerns of both men and women. Nevertheless, they tend to emphasize job factors for men and gender factors for women. Where women's behavior departs from sex stereotypes, they either deemphasize the behavior or discount its significance.

Blauner's Alienation and Freedom

Blauner's classic study of the relationship between the type of technology which characterized an industry and the degree of worker alienation rests on the job model. Generally, he finds that in mechanized industries, where jobs are less skilled and more subdivided, workers experience more alienation. When automated technology is used to create more integrated jobs, worker alienation is reduced, although it remains higher than in craft industry.

Blauner uses that model for industries which employ almost exclusively male workers. In studying the textile industry, the only one with large numbers of women, Blauner switches to the gender model to analyze the women's responses to employment. By doing so, he obscures the relationship between the conditions of employment and the degree of alienation.

Initially, Blauner emphasizes the traditions of the southern textile town, which stress community ties. Next, he examines the conditions of work in men's and women's jobs in the industry. Women are observed to be "especially unfree," performing "most of the unrewarding jobs" and working under the most objectively alienating conditions. Then, he compares men's and women's perceptions of their work. More women than men complain about their job conditions: 42 percent of women (versus 24 percent of men) say they have to work too fast; 49 percent of women (versus 29 percent of men) say they are "too tired" at the end of the day; and 49 percent of women (versus 27 percent of men) complain of "too much pressure" at work (pp. 71–72).

To be consistent with his overall emphasis on job conditions, Blauner should attribute the differences between women's and men's perceptions to differences in their working conditions. Instead, he shifts to a gender model to interpret the women's responses. He notes, "Since women have, on average, less physical stamina than men, and working women often double as housewives and mothers, it is to be expected that they would be more fatigued by their work" (p. 71).

This interpretation has two problems. First, by attributing complaints about work to female biology and family responsibilities, he obscures the previously argued link between working conditions and workers' responses. Second, he ignores data which show that women's work conditions are more demanding because they do more machine-paced work, which requires constant movement and is more closely supervised.

Blauner is either unaware of his shift to a gender model or takes it for granted as appropriate for employed women. He provides no evidence in support of the model. Thus, we do not know what proportion of the women are mothers and housewives, what family responsibilities the wives and mothers have, or whether the most tired women are, in fact, wives and mothers. At the same time, again without apparent awareness of his inconsistency, Blauner maintains the job model for analyzing men. He does not mention differences in tiredness among men or raise the possibility that any such differences could arise from variations in the levels of family responsibility.

If job conditions are poor, what are the workers' subjective responses to them? Blauner's analysis finds relatively little dissatisfaction and low levels of aspiration. This departure from the findings for other industries is attributed to low levels of education and the lack of alternative jobs, that is, to features of the southern textile town. But again, Blauner offers a separate gender-based analysis of women, who have even worse jobs, yet express no greater dissatisfaction than men. He says, "Work does not have the central importance and meaning in their lives that it does for men, since their most important roles are those of wives and mothers" (p. 87). Blauner also fails to consider that women's poorer prospects for advancement may depress their aspirations below those of the men. Here again, assumptions about the meaning of women's roles substitute for evidence.

Blauner next turns to a discussion of the impact of working conditions on the sense of self. He finds that 59 percent of men versus 41 percent of women would choose a different occupation if they were starting over. To Blauner, this suggests that men feel degraded by this work, while women do not. His interpretation is worth quoting at length:

> The submissiveness required of male textile workers must be damaging to the maintenance of a sure sense of masculinity; the low wages and status *undoubtedly* threaten the sense of worth and success in life. Despite the greater physical discomforts of her job, textile employment for the female worker is not as damaging to her sense of identity, since *successful work is not part of the traditional female role.* (P. 87; emphasis added)

The last two examples are interesting for several reasons. First, they show the author's tendency to use men's responses as normal, while women's responses are seen as variants. Second, they show that Blauner treats the unpaid work of women as nonwork, implicitly defining women as nonworkers. As a result, he is led to conclude that women are little affected by the *paid* work they do. Third, the examples show how reliance on separate job and gender models guides the analysis into stereotypical molds. In the second example, it is assumed that men's masculinity is measured by the paycheck. In the rural South, where low wages are endemic, they may not impugn masculinity. Men may establish their masculinity by other criteria—for example, having many children or being good woodsmen, hunters, farmers, or musicians. Similarly, southern women's greater submissiveness to male authority on the job may have nothing to do with the degree of centrality of work roles. It may be due to their socialization in patriarchal families; thus their submissiveness may be part of an established tradition.

Beynon and Blackburn's Perceptions of Work

Beynon and Blackburn's book represents a conscious attempt to overcome the false separation between the conditions of work and nonwork life. They criticize analyses that focus exclusively on either the technology and organization of work or the "orientations" which workers bring to work from their position in the social structure. They argue that the combination of these factors is necessary to explain workers' responses. By implication, one cannot focus only on family situations for women or only on work conditions for men.

The research setting offered an unusual opportunity for comparisons between men and women. Four groups of workers were studied: day men, who operated the basic production machinery or assisted the assembly-line workers; full-time women, who worked primarily on an assembly line wrapping and packaging the product; part-time women, who did similar jobs in separate units, but also moved around to fill in for full-time women where extra help was needed; and night men, who did both the production and packaging, including jobs considered "women's work" on the day shift. Each of the four groups represented a particular gender and marital status combination. The day men were mostly single, as were the full-time women. The part-time women and the night men were mostly married with children. With these four groups, the authors had an opportunity to examine the interrelated influence of conditions of work and family situations.

For the most part, Beynon and Blackburn succeed in avoiding many of the problems found in other studies. Unfortunately, the assumptions underlying the job and gender models are pervasive, and Beynon and Blackburn do not completely escape them.

First, they focus on behavior and attitudes which fit gender stereotypes and deemphasize those that do not. For example, they do not attach much significance to the fact that the full-time women are the most critical of the company and are most likely to press their grievances. Instead, they focus most of their attention on the part-time women, who are the least critical of the company, and who, therefore, fit the stereotype of the uninvolved worker.

Second, they overlook job factors that could explain women's responses, preferring to fall back on explanations based on "women's characteristics." In one chapter, they point out that the company accords special treatment—including leniency about work hours, leaves of absence, and the like—to the part-time women so that they can carry out their domestic responsibilities. Yet, they fail to suggest that it is the company's paternalistic policies toward them, rather than the women's commitment to family responsibilities per se, that explains these women's lack of criticalness toward the firm. With regard to the women's attitudes toward the union, Beynon and Blackburn overlook the influence of union policies and structure, which they earlier admitted ignore women and their concerns. Instead, they view women's critical stance toward the union as a reflection of a "different style of trade unionism."

Finally, Beynon and Blackburn, at times, explain similar behavior of men and women differently. In separate parts of the book, they point out that the day men and both groups of women express a concern with social aspects of the job. The men's focus on sociability is explained by the alienating job conditions and lack of opportunities for mobility, which turn the men's interests away from intrinsic job concerns (Chapter 3). The women's interest in social aspects is interpreted as a product of low commitment to work resulting from their primary commitment to family roles. This interpretation ignores the fact that job conditions and mobility are even worse for the women and that, therefore, their orientation can be explained in the same terms as the men's.

Moving from details of analysis, we find a more general pattern emerging: the authors devote substantial attention to describing and analyzing differences between the men and women but pass lightly over differences within sex—that is, between the day and night men and between the part-time and full-time women. As a corollary, little attention is paid to the similarities between the full-time women and the day or night men.

Throughout the various areas of response, the data presented indicate that the part-time women differ most from the other three groups. The full-time women's responses differ from those of the part-time women at least as much as they do from the responses of the two groups of men. In many areas—such as the meaning of work or sources of satisfaction—the full-time women's responses fall between those of the day men and the night men: sometimes more similar to the day men, sometimes more similar to the night men. Thus, the question should not be why women differ from men but why part-time women differ from the other three groups. Moreover, the answer should be sought not only in these women's family commitments but also in possible differences in their experiences in the workplace. Thus, we might ask, is the experience of doing part-time work, irrespective of family situation, sufficiently distinct that it leads to a divergent pattern of responses? Since there are no part-time men, this possibility cannot be tested. However, Beynon and Blackburn do not even mention it. Presumably, they are comfortable using gender assumptions to account for the results.

While assumptions from the job and gender models pop up throughout the book, it is in the conclusions that they emerge as the dominant framework. The contrast between specific analyses in the text and the summary statements in the concluding chapter illustrates this shift in framework. In Chapter 4, the women's specific dissatisfactions with their work are described graphically. One woman said that it is "terrible just thinking about coming to work in the mornings. It's not hard work, but it seems to wear you out" (p. 75). Another said, "You can't imagine how boring it is. It can really get you down. The girls are O.K.—they're great. It's just the job. The job is terrible." Yet, in the concluding chapter, the conditions that are complained about are minimized as a cause of major dissatisfaction. "Many of them found the work boring and tedious. However, they did not have high expectations of the intrinsic job, so that was not a major cause of dissatisfaction. Where they did expect some satisfaction was in social relationships, and it was here that they were critical of the firm" (p. 149).

This interpretation seems strangely distant from the data. Knowing that they have little hope of finding more interesting jobs, the full-time women concentrate on deriving satisfaction from their social relationships. One suspects that were men to respond similarly, their dissatisfaction would be fully acknowledged. Their emphasis on social rewards would be recognized as a tactic for coping with powerlessness. Further, their social ties might be seen as potentially useful in establishing solidarity and group control in the work situation.

At various points, the authors recognize and give lip service to the variety of oppressive conditions the women face in employment: limited job opportunities, paternalistic policies of the firm and the labor union, assignment to the poorest-paying and most boring jobs and, for some, heavy family responsibilities. Yet, the overall picture of women they construct is one of women as victims rather than as serious workers. The authors fail to appreciate that the women's responses may be strategies for wresting some satisfaction and autonomy from basically unsatisfying circumstances. Thus, the reader is left to fall back on "uniquely female characteristics" to account for the findings.

Discussion and Conclusions

The review of the two studies demonstrates the different ways job and gender models inform analyses of men's and women's responses to work. In some cases (e.g., Blauner), the models are explicitly incorporated into the analysis; in others (e.g., Beynon and Blackburn), the models are never explicitly elaborated, but some of the assumptions of the models slip in as taken for granted. Some analyses rely exclusively on job or gender variables to explain the behavior of one or the other sex, as does Blauner's treatment of women textile workers. Other analyses include a variety of other factors, such as labor market structure, as does Beynon and Blackburn's examination of women factory operatives.

Despite these differences in the mode of incorporation, the studies demonstrate similar distortions. First, data which do not fit the models are overlooked and ignored. Second, the significance of data which violate the model's assumptions is discounted or deemphasized in the interpretation. Third, when several alternative explanations could plausibly be invoked, the one that is most consistent with job or gender models is favored without adequate discussion. Finally, the search for alternative interpretations is short-circuited. The models offer a ready-made explanation, and the researchers follow the path of least resistance.

These distortions are serious enough. An even more serious consequence of the models is that they bias the entire direction of research. As with basic paradigms in science, the job-gender paradigm determines *what* is studied. The models direct attention to particular issues by defining them as problematic. The job-gender paradigm defines job conditions as problematic for men and family responsibilities as problematic for women, thereby directing research into these areas. The complementary issues, the impact of specific work conditions on women's responses to work, and the relationship of men's family roles to their work attitudes and behavior are viewed as nonproblematic and, therefore, have not been studied systematically in the mainstream literature.[5]

It is true, of course, that phenomena can be studied even in the absence of a supportive paradigm. When phenomena become sufficiently visible or widespread, they command public attention. Thus, in response to rising labor force participation among married women, increased research has been conducted on women in specific occupations (Epstein, 1970b; Walshok and Walshok, 1978), and on work-family linkages (Hunt and Hunt, 1977; Lein et al., 1974; Mortimer, 1976; Rapaport and Rapaport, 1971a). However, the research continues to focus on issues that are defined as problematic under the old paradigm. Both types of studies emphasize the strains for women and their families resulting from women having two jobs, while giving little consideration to the impact of conditions of women's employment in specific jobs.

What this suggests is that a new paradigm is needed. The concept of work needs to be made more inclusive, to cover unpaid as well as paid work. Moreover, it needs to be formulated so that the work people do can be located within the context of their whole lives. The development of separate job and gender models rests on a concept of work which arbitrarily separates paid employment from other work, identifying it as the only form of real work. As a result, other work tends to be treated as nonwork and women workers as nonworkers. This narrow conception leads us to ignore much of the work that is actually done. We lose sight of the distinct features of different forms of work, overlook the connections between types of paid work, as well as between paid and unpaid work, and fail to understand the impact of these connections on workers' experiences and responses. These connections are ignored not only at the individual level but also at the level of the political economy.

A more inclusive concept of work would render the distinct features of various kinds of work more visible. A beginning point is found in recent analyses of housework in which some of the categories ordinarily used to examine paid work are applied to the study of housework. Categories such as degree of control over the work process, types of work standards, extent of rationalization, and hours and pace of work have been found to be useful in examining women's behavior in attitudes toward housework (Dalla Costa, 1972; Glazer, 1976; Oakley, 1974). This kind of analysis needs to be extended in several directions. First, there are other types of unpaid work, such as community activities and dealing with social agencies and child care, that are not encompassed by the term "housework." These types of unpaid work are also part of the context within which paid work takes place. Thus, their contextual meanings should be included in the analysis of paid work. Second, the forms and conditions of these types of unpaid work need to be investigated, so that the kinds of work involved and the impact of doing that work become visible, no longer masked under the emotionally charged labels of "family responsibility" or "civic duty." Third, it is evident that men, as well as women, engage in unpaid work. The kinds of unpaid work commonly performed by men and the conditions of that work need to be studied, both independently of and in comparison to women's unpaid work. Finally, when considering paid work, closer attention must be paid to the actual conditions of work commonly assigned to women. Understanding women's responses to paid work requires a clearer, more precise picture of their work: again, hours and pace of work, extent of rationalization, kinds of skills, and types of work standards. In the absence of such information, attempts to analyze women's responses to employment must continue to rely on stereotypes, not only of female character but also of women's work.

A reformulated concept of work would also facilitate analysis of the connections between various forms of work and make clearer the distinction between work and nonwork. Again, there are beginnings in existing research. Studies of women clerical workers suggest that women's evaluations of the conditions of their jobs are based on comparison with the conditions of housework, as well as of previous jobs (cf. Lamphere, 1973; Walshok and Walshok, 1978). At the macro level, historical research has indicated some important connections between the conditions of paid and unpaid work for women: women's low wages and limited job opportunities in the labor force reinforce and are reinforced by women's disproportionate involvement in domestic labor (Caplow, 1954; Hartmann, 1976; Kessler-Harris, 1973). This research should be expanded to include the connection between paid and unpaid work for men. The relationship between variations in the extent and type of men's unpaid work and their responses to employment needs to be looked at more closely. For example, responses of men whose paid work is similar, but whose unpaid work differs, could be compared. Parallel historical research needs to be conducted on changes in the types and conditions of men's unpaid work and on shifts in the relationship between their paid and unpaid work.

A second area for major theoretical reformulation is the systematic incorporation of gender stratification into the analysis of work. Because male domination and female subordination have been taken for granted, gender stratification has remained largely invisible and unproblematic in the sociology of work. Changes in the economy and in social life have been accompanied by changes in men's and women's structural and interpersonal situations. As feminist analysts have pointed out, these changes reveal the extent to which gender stratification is socially created rather than natural. These analysts have begun detailed examination of the processes by which gender stratification is created and maintained in the family and other sociopolitical institutions. Similar examination must be made of work and the organization of work.

A beginning is found in recent studies which look at the consequences of differential assignment of men and women to positions in work organizations (see especially Kanter, 1977a,b). This research attempts to show that differences in men's and women's responses to employment are the outcome of their locations in hierarchies, their numerical proportions, and other structural features of organizations. The analysis stops short, however. It ignores the ways in which gender stratification, aside from its expression in organizational patterns, is structured into interpersonal relations. Acker and Van Houten's (1974) reexamination of the Hawthorne studies points out the different forms of social control imposed on men and women, independent of their organizational positions. For example, the controls imposed on female assembly workers were closer and more paternalistic than those imposed on male assemblers. Some observers have remarked on the parallels between paternalistic treatment of women in the workplace and their treatment in the family and other institutions (e.g., Glenn and Feldberg, 1977; Langer, 1972).

A fuller theoretical and empirical treatment of gender stratification would involve detailed consideration of both formal structures and informal processes. Examination of hierarchies and policies in specific types of organizations would help identify the conditions which create and maintain gender differences in work behavior and attitudes. Special attention needs to be paid to entry points for different hierarchies, the number of levels within them, access to experience or training needed for mobility, and the points of linkage between various hierarchies. This kind of detailed analysis is crucial to uncovering the less visible forms of stratification that do not appear as formal organizational categories. Analysis of informal processes is needed to identify norms governing interpersonal relationships between men and women in work organizations. An examination of interpersonal behavior among peers and between superordinate/subordinate pairs would enable us to sort out the impacts of formal organizational hierarchies and informal gender hierarchies, and the interaction between the two.

In what ways would these reformulations enhance the analysis of work? As an illustration, let us look at how the two studies we examined might be changed by the reformulations. Had Blauner seen the unpaid work women do as real work, he could not have dismissed them as nonworkers who are unaffected by the conditions of employment. Thus, for example, he would have had to think more carefully about the meaning of the extreme submissiveness required of the women who worked in the southern textile mills. The impacts of such conditions might have been analyzed in relation to the cultural prescriptions for women and their limited opportunities for other paid work. Overall, in analyzing the women's responses to this work, a more inclusive concept of work would have led Blauner to examine the actual conditions of employment, rather than relying on general beliefs about the priority of women's family (unpaid work) responsibilities.

Similar analysis could have been done of the impacts of required submissiveness on the male workers. Using this more inclusive concept of work, the analysis of men's responses would take into account men's family roles and the conditions of employment and labor market opportunities. Thus, the analysis of paid work for men and for women would take account of the context of their total life situations and would reflect the variations of life cycle, gender, and regional economy that characterize workers' lives.

Next, let us consider Beynon and Blackburn's analysis of men's and women's work attitudes in their treatment of differences in aspirations for mobility. They show clearly that full-time women, for the most part, do not want to become supervisors, while the men desire such promotions. The difference is reported without apparent awareness that it requires explanation. By failing to analyze the sources of women's reluctance, Beynon and Blackburn leave the impression that their response stems from feminine character or socialization. An analysis incorporating gender stratification of organizations would examine the position of female supervisors in the hierarchical structure, the links (or lack thereof) between these positions and higher positions, the degree of authority these positions command, the responsibilities they entail, and the entry points and career paths of those who reach these positions (e.g., whether or not they usually come up through the ranks). Comparison of female and male supervisory positions on these dimensions would yield a more comprehensive, and probably more valid, explanation of men's and women's different aspirations for promotion. Similar detailed analysis of gender hierarchies and norms within the company (and the union) would reveal the sources of patterns of differences and similarities among the four groups of men and women workers in such areas as attitude toward unions, dissatisfaction with work conditions, and orientation toward work.

In addition to enhancing the validity of specific studies, the suggested reformulations would enrich the sociology of work by directing inquiry into new areas. Research and thinking would be directed to aspects of work previously taken for granted or ignored. The analysis of women's work would include systematic study of both paid and unpaid work throughout the class structure, with careful attention to actual conditions of work and actual behavior of the workers. The analysis of men's work would involve learning about the kinds of unpaid work men do and the impacts of various off-the-job concerns (such as family responsibilities or ethnic and cultural values) on their responses to paid work.

These reconceptualizations should also provide points of entry into an understanding of work-family linkages for both men and women. In the introduction, we claimed that, since both men and women work and participate in families, a valid framework for the analysis of work must encompass these linkages on micro and macro levels. By reconceptualizing work and incorporating gender stratification, the study of work can be expanded to take into account the complex relationships between the organization of the economy, the labor market, the conditions of paid and unpaid work, and the conditions and structures of family life.

Notes

1. The basic assumptions of the sex-segregated models have never been wholly appropriate to men's or women's employment. As more women have become employees for longer periods of their lives, and as more questions are being raised concerning the division of labor by sex (in both paid and unpaid work), these models have become more of a barrier to understanding both men's and women's relationship to work.

2. This article is one exception to exclusive reliance on a job model and is, therefore, not subject to this criticism.

3. This tendency to rely exclusively on the job model in analyzing workers' responses to employment is not new. It is seen as early as the Hawthorne studies (Acker and Van Houten, 1974), as well as in Crozier (1964).

4. This assumption exemplifies the tenacity of beliefs which are congruent with the prevailing ideology of gender differences (cf. Laws, 1978). Dubin (1956) and Orzack (1959) showed that the degree of "central life interest" in work varied by occupation for men and women. Dubin and his associates (1976) have continued research in this area for over twenty years, yet the assumption persists that gender role, rather than occupation, is the primary variable which determines the degree of "central life interest" in work.

5. Interestingly, the relationship between men's employment and their family roles has been studied primarily for unemployed or underemployed men. Apparently, the problematic aspects of this relationship become more visible when the expected pattern does not hold.

II

Home Work and Market Work: Systematic Segregation

Today when meeting a man, many people still ask him what he does for a living, as one inoffensive way of learning something about a stranger and starting a conversation. But when meeting a woman, they ask what her husband does, unwittingly assuming not only that women are married but also that they do not have activities of their own worthy of conversation. Such different behavior denies variations in interests and life-styles, especially among women. It is an implicit devaluation of women's activities, and of women as well.

A major reason why such differing expectations exist is that in a capitalist system people who earn wages are valued as producers and those who work primarily at home are less valued, as dependents who consume what others have earned. While both activities are usually acknowledged as essential components of a functioning economy, they are often separated in explanations, with distinct spheres assigned to gender. Thus men who work where wages are earned and profits made are the producers, while women who work at home, where products are used, are consumers. The former activity is seen as of public or social value, the latter as of personal or private value.

A somewhat similar distinction, less tied to stereotypes of gender and work, is that between exchange value and use value. Any product which is consumed has a use value, i.e., is usable by someone. For example, both a toy made out of household items and a toy purchased in a store have use value. But only products which are bought or sold, such as the toy in a *store,* have exchange value. Thus we have two types of production—production of use value and production of exchange value. Capitalist society is the first society in history in which most production is of exchange value. We no longer produce most of the products we use; now we purchase most products in the

81

market. Money to make such purchases comes from the wages and profits of those involved, e.g., in industry, where production for exchange occurs. To the degree that men provide their families with money for exchange, women's dependency is objectively visible.

Neither pair of distinctions, however, permits adequate examination of the family as a complex economic unit. Where both men and women, husbands and wives, are involved in productivity and consumption, the unit is the family—not the individual. For example, if we think of money available for consumption as resulting from productivity, then a person providing necessary family services is contributing to family income. When a thrifty housewife shops carefully for inexpensive, attractive clothing or nutritious meals, she is saving income for additional purchasing power. Conversely, important consumption decisions about major family expenditures are rarely left solely to the wife. She may scout possible houses to rent or buy, research childcare options, and even talk to travel agents about vacation plans, but this leg work is conducted within family priorities. The decisions about these priorities are made jointly—or by the husband (Moore and Sawhill, 1978). In working-class families, when money is tight, it is women who manage it. They have to stave off creditors and make manageable budgets; when there is more money, husbands increase their participation or assume control over discretionary income (Rubin, 1976: 106–112).

The latter view of the joint efforts involved in production and consumption is not the usual one, however. Prevailing ideology describes work and family life as essentially different. Work occurs in the public arena, where exchange value is created; consumption takes place in the private family. Such a distinction between work and home life did not exist in the past, nor is it accurate today. Nevertheless, today the family is not seen so much as a part of the world as it is a refuge from that world. In the "real world" one works, contributes to the society, meets the required demands. In the family, one's personal needs are met and leisure activities take place (Lasch, 1977).

Economists have begun to realize that the distinction between work and leisure is more adequate for the analysis of how most men organize their time and effort than for that of women. It is both inaccurate and a sign of the devaluation of women's contribution to put their home time in the leisure category, for it supports a neglect or devaluation of the work at home. This misunderstanding creates special problems for women when they spend part of their work time in the paid labor force. Because women in the home are not viewed as workers, they are not perceived to have the skills and attitudes needed by workers in firms and industry. Some of the characteristics of a "womanly" woman, supposedly required to meet her responsibilities to husband and children, are considered antithetical to the demands of paid work: women should be warm, nurturant, supportive, and altruistic. But employers emphasize the value of workers who are impersonal, ambitious, and neutral but competent in their tasks. Therefore, when women work outside the home, they are often caught in a conflict between consideration by employers and co-workers as feminine women *or* as serious workers.

In the first reading in this section, Epstein gives a historical presentation of the development of this conflict by showing the social construction of the modern concept of femininity. We tend to assume that women today have more equality with men than they did in the past. But a comparison of our times with colonial and earlier industrial periods reveals that in many ways women once had more respect and recognition than they do now. That respect was based on their clearly understood economic contribution, as in work on the farm or in craft production. As this type of contribution became less available to women, popular opinion reflected that of some social thinkers of the day in explaining this change as "progress." They considered women better off when they were freed from work on farms or in factories. An upper- or middle-class woman could concentrate on being feminine within the home. By not being dirtied through the economic demands of the real world, women remained unsullied and thus purer than men. Epstein argues that this distinction between women and men was one adaptation to rising industrialization that especially benefited men. We can see how men gained a greater monopoly of social power through their control of money and goods for exchange. Married women were forced to become totally dependent on their wage-earner husbands.

We can see some support for this argument if we consider a current application of the view of "feminine" as separate from the world. Many who oppose the passage of the Equal Rights Amendment say that women will no longer be protected by the right to support from their husbands, even though such opposition ignores the many men who neglect this responsibility today. Currently 74 percent of all husbands default in the first year of court-ordered child support (*FEW*, 1980). ERA opponents also argue that its passage will expose women to forced participation in the military, not recognizing that Congress now has that conscription power if they choose to use it. Despite inaccuracies or selective attention only to those women who *have* some advantages, this "stay feminine" perspective still emphasizes that many benefits accrue to women who are not forced to participate in the real world.

Yet some men and women recognize the unfortunate consequences of this protectiveness toward women, consequences that are
common as long as contributions to the home and family are seen as
less significant than those made in the outside world. One such consequence is that women are seen as incapable and childlike rather
than healthy and adult. To be unsullied by learning to adapt to the
formal, impersonal, even dirty or inhumane demands involved in
earning a living means that one is not yet adapted to the adult
world—one has not matured. Such a view influences theories of mental health used by specialists in such work. Broverman et al. (1970)
found in a study of clinicians that their picture of a healthy man
matched that of a healthy adult, while their image of a healthy woman
matched that of a neurotic adult. These findings suggest that people
may give lip service to the belief that feminine characteristics are
prized but nonetheless devalue them in other, more direct ways.

Once we have this image of women as different, once the essence
of woman is associated with home and family, it becomes clear why,
as Feldberg and Glenn pointed out in the previous reading, even sociologists can uncritically assume that men's experience in paid work
is necessarily different from that of women. Note the circularity of
such reasoning: if occupational work is no different for women than
it is for men, then the women are not feminine. It is this restricting
definition of femininity and its converse, the restricting definition of
masculinity, which is the focus of much feminist criticism.

The pervasiveness of this ideology is most clearly illustrated by a
study of fifty-three dual-career couples conducted by Poloma and
Garland (1971: 741–761). They thought that the couples most likely to
reallocate family and occupational responsibilities anywhere would
be those who both had the opportunity to make a major contribution
to family income, to have flexibility in their work schedules, and to
receive respect for their work in the broader society. These families
would have the best opportunity for giving equal weight to the complexity of commitments facing both husbands and wives. Yet Poloma
and Garland found that only one couple in their study met this definition of equality. In all the remaining couples, the women adjusted
their own occupational commitments to demands of their husband's
career and their own household and child-care responsibilities. The
men supported their wives' work as long as it required no adjustment
in their own careers. The women's career commitments were devalued
by both wives and husbands.

These couples provide an example of what Pleck (in this section)
means by the asymmetrically permeable boundaries between paid
work and family tasks for each sex. Women's familial responsibili-

ties—their production in the home—intrude upon their occupational responsibilities (Silverstone and Ward, 1980, provide detailed examples from England). But intrusion can work in the opposite direction for men. Their occupational responsibilities spill over into family time. In the middle class, the work men bring home from the office takes priority over domestic responsibilities (Miller, 1971). In the working class, men refuse housework and child care because of physically and emotionally exhausting routine work as well as employer demands for overtime and for swing-shift work (Piotrokowski, 1980). Pleck analyzes the effect on the home of this distinction between boundaries of the tasks deemed appropriate to the masculine role and those appropriate to the feminine role. He argues that when women enter the labor force in greater numbers than they do now, the home tasks should be reallocated (Pleck and Pleck, 1980). The likelihood of this reallocation happening in the near future is questioned by a study of male college students. Komarovsky (1973) found that while these students believed that women should be able to work outside the home if they wished, they did not want their own wives to do so. And time budget studies of women who work 30 hours or more per week for wages found that they average 33 hours per week on housework, compared to 57 hours by women who work full-time in the house (Walker, 1970a). A national study in 1977 found that U.S. husbands of employed women do devote more time to housework than husbands of women who are full-time homemakers—about 1.8 more hours in household care and 2.7 more hours in child care per week (Pleck, 1979).

Bourne and Wikler look at a related conflict created for women from the vantage point of an upper-middle-class profession, medicine, in which men are dominant. These authors find that women are allowed this professional work as long as the male-centered demands of medical organizations need not be adapted to familial demands. Women doctors appear to have two choices. They may relinquish personal familial life and be perceived as foreswearing their femininity (as a "hen medic"); or they may choose among a limited number of less prestigious specialties which do not place extraordinary demands on family time. In showing how women are sanctioned if they request adjustments in the training process to accommodate family responsibilities, Bourne and Wikler demonstrate how women and their ability to contribute in the occupational world are devalued. Their needs are not significant enough to require an adjustment in the "male clockwork" of professional careers. This situation of negative sanctions and inflexible expectations results in what Bourne and Wikler call a "discriminatory environment." They are speaking of an environment in which there is no grossly unequal treatment, but in which women are continually told—in small but significant ways—that they do not belong. This communication is the same whether women are or are not married, and whether or not they are the sole support of their family. The ideological basis for the communication is found in pervading assumptions about femininity.

The inflexibility of occupations based on the male clockwork model as the only possible pattern is a sign that women in paid labor are still seen as atypical—as not feminine. Because, in this model, these women are atypical workers, there is no need to adapt ideal images of commitment or careers to the demands of their life cycle. As a result, the problems these women face are seen as personal ones requiring individual solutions, not social ones requiring group or institutional solutions. C. W. Mills (1959:9) remarked that an individual divorce is a personal problem, but when 25 percent of marriages end in divorce, it becomes an issue, a social problem. Perhaps we should also recognize the need to find a social solution to the conflicting demands placed on women in their home lives and in the work force. There have always been women in the labor force; immigrant women, poor women, and single women have always provided a major labor supply for American industry. Today it is common for women to work outside the home. As of 1974, 46 percent of all women of working age were in the labor force (Blau, 1978: 36). These women reflect the entire female population. They range from young to old; are members of all social classes; are white and nonwhite; mothers and nonmothers—married, single, divorced, and widowed. Yet we still expect these women to make individual adaptations to the demands of work both in the marketplace and in the home.

Some people have felt that modernization itself would lead to an egalitarian integration of women in the labor force. Osako's reading in this section describes another culture in which modernization has had no such consequence. Her study suggests that technological changes alone will not ensure improved opportunities for women in the paid labor force. In analyzing career opportunities in Japan, she points out that with modernization it is now harder, not easier, for women to enter the professional labor force. The Japanese occupational system is as firmly grounded in a male clockwork as any Western system. And in the newly prevalent nuclear family, demands are placed on the mother which cannot be shared as easily as in the more traditional Japanese family. In addition, the women in modern Japanese families are given status rewards for remaining in the home that they did not even receive in the traditional family. One aspect of modernization—the spread of the nuclear family pattern—is antagonistic to the other—the development of a supposedly rational economic system. Osako finds, as do Bourne and Wikler, that women who are able to maintain careers make idiosyncratic adjustments rather than challenge either the definition of commitment to work or the definition of the feminine role. Such adjustments tend to reinforce the definition of the problem as an individual one. We see the underlying social basis for inequality only when we recognize the devaluation of women implied in the inflexibility of structural arrangements and ideological patterns.

Industrialization and Femininity: A Case Study of Nineteenth-Century New England

BARBARA EPSTEIN *
University of California, Santa Cruz

5. Origins. Much sociology has assumed the naturalness of the current sex role division of labor. Parsons (1955), for example, has argued that men perform the instrumental and women the emotional roles in society; men produce goods and earn money, and women nurture children and maintain pleasant homes. Epstein shows us that the rigid separation of these responsibilities is fairly new. With the separation of home and work, men left the family and went from a family work site to an industrial one. Women could have done so also, Epstein argues. They didn't because an ideology had developed that women's primary responsibility was to rear children; motherhood had become a full-time job. The development and acceptance of the ideology of femininity have had drastic consequences for women in a society in which authority and prestige are gained from earned income, not from nurturance of the family. How might everyday life be organized today if women had not been restrained by the ideology of motherhood as a full-time job? How would your forecast affect each social class? Do you think we would be better or worse off today, as a nation? As individuals?

From the earliest days of American history, men's and women's roles in work, family, and society have been ordered according to ideas of what is appropriate for each sex. In the seventeenth century, white settlers brought ideas about masculinity and femininity with them from Europe and structured their families and communities in accordance with these ideas. During that century, and for most of the eighteenth century as well, most people took these sex roles largely for granted. It was not until the beginning of the nineteenth century, especially in New England, that the role of women became the subject of widespread concern and discussion. Out of that concern a changed concept of femininity emerged. In this paper, I will describe the concept of femininity, show how it was related to the emergence of an industrial economy, and suggest that the ideas about women that were established during that period were influenced by the develop-ment of capitalism and to some degree shaped its further development.

The change in women's roles from the seventeenth and eighteenth cen-turies to the nineteenth was dramatic. In the seventeenth and eighteenth centuries, the vast majority of New Englanders lived on family farms that were part of farming villages. Each family owned a plot of land that was large enough to produce a large variety of crops and to support some livestock or poultry; families used the common grazing and wood-gathering lands. There was a rough division between men's and women's work. The men were responsible for most of the work in the fields; the women, for looking after the infants, who arrived in rapid succession, and for work that could be done in and around the home. Boys learned to plant, cultivate, and harvest crops; girls learned the skills involved in turn-ing raw agricultural materials into usable goods. Women spun, wove, fin-ished cloth, and made it into clothes; they knitted and made candles, soaps, and brooms; they made liquors, cheese, and preserves; they made medicine and tended the sick. They also cooked, cleaned their houses, and took care of babies and small children. The division of labor between the house and the fields was practical rather than rigid. There was no taboo against women raising crops as long as they were close enough to the house to hear a baby's cry, and women often tended vegetable gardens and cared for poultry. Similarly, men worked in the house during the win-ter when there was little work in the fields, doing the work that was con-sidered too heavy for women, such as tanning leather or making furniture.

A farm could not operate without at least a husband and wife, and it helped to have a large number of sons and daughters. Sometimes, if a couple did not have enough children of one sex or the other, children from other families were brought in as servants and treated very much like the couple's children. The role of women on the New England farm was ex-tremely important. They bore, and largely raised, the children who pro-vided labor for the farm. Their work of turning raw materials into goods was essential to the family economy and to survival, no less so than the work of the men (Demos, 1970: Chapter 5; Morgan, 1944: Chapter 2; Ryan, 1975: Chapter 1).

In a limited way, Puritan law reflected the importance of women's role in the New England settlements. A Massachusetts law, taken over from English common law, required that a man leave a third of his estate to his wife as long as she had done a normal amount of work. The courts recti-fied wills that did not meet this standard. While Puritan law was biased against women as, for example, in the denial of property rights in a woman's first marriage, it was nevertheless more favorable to women than it would be in the nineteenth century, in New England or anywhere else in the United States. Puritan women had some limited property rights. Any property held by a woman became her husband's when she married, but if her husband died (or if the couple divorced, a rare event) and she remarried, she could retain ownership of any property she held (Flexner, 1968: 63 ff.; Morgan, 1944: Chapter 2). Beyond the relatively favorable position of women in Puritan law, the Puritan view that anything that transpired within Puritan society was the concern of that society often worked to women's benefit. If a husband's mistreatment of his wife came to the attention of the court, the court was obliged to interfere regardless of whether the wife complained about her husband's behavior. The husband's crime was against Puritan society and God himself, not only against his wife (Morgan, 1944: 39ff.).

It is true that very little of the land held by the Puritans was owned by women. But in a society in which land was relatively easy to acquire but could not be utilized without family labor, men and women were in important ways economically dependent upon one another, giving women a certain leverage within the family. Just as the economic position of Puritan women seems to have been stronger than was indicated by their property holding, the status of women in Puritan society seems to have been higher than would be indicated by the official, or biblical, view of women. Every Puritan child knew that "in Adam's fall, we sinned all," and that it was Eve and the snake who were responsible for that fall. Puritan ministers, on the relatively rare occasions when they preached or wrote about family relations, reminded their audiences that men held authority over women. As one minister wrote, "The Husband is called the Head of the Woman [1 Corinthians 11:3]. It belongs to the Head to rule and govern" (Wadsworth, 1712: 34).

Although, on the one hand, Puritan ministers quoted the Bible as the authority for this harsh view of women, on the other hand, they tended to moderate these pronouncements in their own discussions of women and family relations. One minister wrote in a tract on family relations, "Though the Wife is the Weaker Vessel, yet honour is to be put on her in her inferior Station. . . . Though the husband governs her, he must not treat her as a Servant, but as his *own Flesh;* he must love her as himself [Eph. 5:33]. He should make his Government of her, as easie and gentle as possible; and strive more to be loved than fear'd; though neither is to be excluded" (Wadsworth, 1712: 34–35; see also Mather, 1692).

There seems to have been more equality between husbands and wives than the biblical model of the family suggested. In the cooperative farm household, men's and women's roles often overlapped. In Puritan tracts on family life, men and women were as likely to be referred to as "heads of the household" or "parents" as they were to be spoken of as "husbands and wives" or "mothers and fathers." In these tracts, there was little discussion of "motherhood" or, for that matter, "fatherhood." Even in tracts that were specifically directed toward women, such as Benjamin Colman's *The Honour and Happiness of the Vertuous Woman* (1716), the woman's relations with her children were generally discussed under the heading of "parenthood," and the mother herself was as likely to be referred to as a parent as she was to be described as a mother. Except for childbirth, the nursing of babies, and a special responsibility to be models to their daughters (as were fathers to be models to their sons), Puritan ministers did not speak of responsibilities of mothers that were peculiar to them as women. This lack of attention to motherhood as a special category probably reflected the fact that on these family farms, child care was not solely a maternal responsibility. Boys often began to do some work with their fathers by the time they were six or seven, and in the winter months, when everyone in the family worked or played in the big room in the house, the father's authority over the children was as immediate as was the mother's.

Another indication that men and women had more actual equality in Puritan New England than ministers' pronouncements about male authority and female subjection would lead us to believe is the frequency with which women were brought to court for abusing their husbands or other men verbally or physically. John Demos (1970: 95) has found that in Plymouth Colony, women were as likely to be charged with "abusive carryage" toward their husbands or other men as were men to be charged with such behavior toward women. New England women seem to have been self-respecting and assertive. It seems likely that it was the role of women on the family farm and their security in the knowledge of their central role in family survival that made this possible.

Femininity as we understand it played little part in the Puritan understanding of women's role in the family or in society. Puritan women were told to obey their husbands, but the social graces, childlike innocence, and role of moral authority that later came to be associated with womanhood had little place on the New England farm. In Boston, however, and the other port towns, life was different, especially for the merchants, who began to form a community of their own in the seventeenth century. By the eighteenth century, the merchant class was a wealthy and powerful section of society, with strong ties to the English upper class and a life style that was increasingly influenced by English fashions. The men of this class were often able to support their wives through the profits they made in trade. These men could require less of their wives in the way of productive skills—clothes and other goods were imported from England and could be bought in the Boston stores—and more in the way of decorative qualities and social graces. Their homes were becoming centers of social life, and their wives were expected to develop those social graces which would allow them to be good hostesses (Ryan, 1975: 98 ff.). By the end of the eighteenth century, literature was being imported from England, and to

some extent published in the United States, that urged women of this class
to develop the graces of the lady. In these books, we can see the development of distinct models for masculine and feminine personalities. One author described the difference between the two:

> Women's brows were not intended to be ploughed with wrinkles, nor
> their innocent gaiety damped by abstraction. They were perpetually to
> please, and perpetually to enliven. If we were to plan the *edifice*, they
> were to furnish the *embellishments*. If we were to lay out and cultivate
> the garden, they were to beautifully *fringe* its borders with flowers. If we
> were to superintend the management of kingdoms, they were to be the
> fairest ornaments of those kingdoms, the embellishers of society, and the
> sweeteners of life. (Gisborne, 1797: 23)

This concept of womanhood retained, even accentuated, female inferi-
ority. Like farm women, these upper-class women were urged to develop
a range of abilities; motherhood had not yet become the primary focus of
women's lives. But the abilities that upper-class urban women were to cultivate were very different from those of rural women. One author wrote:

> To be obedient Daughters, faithful Wives, and prudent Mothers; to be
> useful in the affairs of a House; to be sensible Companions, and affec-
> tionate friends, are, without doubt, the principle objects of female duty.
> The accomplishments, therefore, which you should acquire, are those that
> will contribute to render you serviceable in domestic, and agreeable in
> social life (Bennett, 1795: 94).

This concept of womanhood was shaped by the experience of the English upper classes and formulated in such a way that it was attainable by
at least some women of the merchant class, especially its upper levels. Such
women could be supported by their husbands, had a fair amount of time
for social life, and could send their daughters to academies where their
education included decorative arts and their social graces could become
polished. While this style of femininity had no relevance for farm women,
it came to the United States at a time when, at least in New England, an
increasing number of families were congregating in town centers, where
the men earned a living by the crafts and trades, such as tanning, cabinet
making, forging iron, or milling flour—often the skills that had occupied
them part-time when they were farmers.

During the late eighteenth and early nineteenth centuries, a number of
inventions were brought to the United States that made it possible to produce cloth more cheaply in factories than at home. In 1813 the first New
England factory was established that produced cloth from start to finish;
from 1815 to 1830 the price of cotton declined from 42¢ a yard to 7½¢
a yard (Tryon, 1917: 276). For women who lived in or near towns, where
they could buy cloth from the factories or from stores, there remained

little incentive to work all day at the loom to weave four or five yards of such cloth. Some of this freed female labor was absorbed by the factories, which employed women almost entirely, especially young, unmarried women. And some women did piecework at home for the factory owners or merchants. But the number of women who worked in or for the mills was small in relation to the female population of New England. In 1832 only 2.2% of Massachusetts women worked in the mills (Abbott, 1906: 482). Most town women (and increasingly, farm women as well) found that they were spending less time making things for their families and more time cooking, cleaning their houses, and tending to the needs of their children and husbands. Their men were increasingly likely to spend their days away from home, working in shops, stores, or mills. Responsibility for child care and care of the home had devolved more and more upon the women.

At the same time that these changes were taking place in the commercial and industrial world, books began to appear in the Northeast, especially in New England, that described to women their duties as mothers and wives and instructed them in how to fulfill them. The men and women who wrote these books were often teachers, doctors, or ministers. Some of them wrote that their books were intended for women of the "middling classes"; most of the authors themselves could have been included in the upper level of this class.

These books reflected a sharp shift in the socially sanctioned roles women were expected to play in their families. Where for the Puritans, and for the authors of late-eighteenth-century ladies' books, motherhood had been only one of a woman's tasks, these nineteenth-century writers saw child care as the most important of a woman's responsibilities. Women were also urged to subordinate their own needs and desires to those of their husbands; the muted inequality of Puritan women had been replaced by a demand for outright subservience. The wife was to provide her husband with a refuge from the harsh outside world; she was to avoid disagreements with him and make sure that family life went smoothly. "The balance of concession devolves upon the wife," proclaimed one domestic guidebook. "Whether the husband concede or not, she must . . ." The same author saw domesticity, a willingness to stay at home, as central to a woman's subjugation of herself to her children and husband. Some women, he wrote, resented confinement in the home; but in this her desires were at odds with the happiness and well-being of her family and must be restrained. "She cannot discharge the duties of a wife, much less those of a mother, unless she prefers home to all other places and is only led abroad from a sense of duty, and not from choice" (Alcott, 1837: 83).

This increased emphasis on motherhood, and on the subservience of the wife to her husband, reflected the economic realities of the age and the concomitant loss of women's productive functions. These women were spending more time with their children because they had fewer other things to do and because, with their husbands working outside the home, they had more responsibility for child care than had their mothers and grandmothers. The loss of productive work also brought with it a greatly increased dependence upon men, and a corollary was heightened male dominance reinforced by the law.

Puritan law had been biased against women but had still allowed them some rights. They could appear in court in their own defense; in some cases, the courts intervened unasked on their behalf. With the weakening of the Puritan church, Puritan law concerning the family had gradually been replaced by English common law. According to this tradition, once women were married, they were represented legally by their husbands; they were "dead in the law." A married woman could not sue or be sued; she could not sign contracts; and any money that she inherited, earned, or brought to the marriage through a dowry was the property of her husband. Such laws had been gradually incorporated into state legal codes through the eighteenth century, but they affected fewer women in the Colonial economy, since few people earned money and the market was rudimentary. By the nineteenth century, with the development of towns and a growing market economy, laws excluding women from the courts and forbidding them to hold property put them at a serious disadvantage to men.

Furthermore, the supervision of family life that Puritan courts had engaged in was no longer possible. The individualist philosophy that was coming to pervade the towns and cities of nineteenth-century New England allowed for no such intrusions into the family, now seen as the private domain of the husband and father. One minister wrote, in a nineteenth-century guidebook to family life:

> Every family is a little state, an empire within itself, bound together by the most endearing emotions, and governed by its patriarchal head, with whose prerogative no power on earth has a right to interfere. Every father is the constituted head of his household. God has made him the supreme earthly legislator over his children, accountable, of course, to Himself, for the manner in which he executes his trust; but amenable to no other power, except in the most extreme cases of neglect, or abuse. (Humphrey, 1840: 16)

The loss of economic functions eroded the basis of women's power in the family; the loss of legal rights deprived them of weapons that they might have used to fight male domination. Industrialization made this weakening of women's position possible, but it did not make it necessary. As women's productive work was moved from the home to the factory, married as well as single women could have gone to work in the factories. Women could have gone to work in the town as storekeepers, artisans, and professionals. Children could have been cared for in nurseries and kindergartens, by grandparents, or by their fathers. It was not industrialization that kept women in their homes in the early nineteenth century, but the deeply engrained tradition of women's primary responsibility for home and child care. Once machines took production from the home, the political and economic power of men, together with the absence of much demand for female labor outside the home, combined to keep women in their domestic role.

It was women's dependence that laid the basis for the nineteenth-century ideology of female submission. If women were to accept that subservience, it was necessary that they internalize male dominance, rather than simply obeying men out of fear of the law or of withdrawal of economic support. The tasks that women retained when they ceased to produce goods were primarily emotional and psychological: raising children, helping them to develop personalities that would allow them to fit into the increasingly difficult roles of town life, and giving their husbands the emotional support that made it easier for them to function in society. Mere brandishment of male power was not enough to make women accept this limited role. They also needed to be convinced of its importance.

Making domesticity and subservience to men acceptable to women was the task of the guidebooks to wifehood and motherhood and, more generally, of the ideology of femininity. The elements of this ideology that were central to this task were, first, that children required full-time, undivided adult attention; second, that women were specially endowed to provide this care (and to create the homes that their husbands needed as well); and finally, that domesticity would shield women from the evil of the outside world and bring them status and power mediated through their families.

The Puritans had believed that children were born in sin, that it was the responsibility of parents to try to chastise them out of it, but that all, even adults who had evidence of salvation, were doomed to struggle against sinful impulses all their lives. Where Puritan parents were told that their children were fundamentally and irrepressibly sinful, nineteenth-century authors of women's books told mothers that their babies were innocent and pure and must be shielded from the corrupting influences of the outside world. One author wrote:

> The mind of a child is not like that of a grown person, too full and too busy to observe everything; it is a vessel empty and pure—always ready to receive, and always receiving. Every look, every movement, every expression, does something toward forming the character of the little heir to immortal life. . . . [If a child comes into contact with] evil passions

such as anger or other wrong feelings, evil enters into his soul, as the imperceptible atmosphere he breathes into his lungs: and the beautiful little image of God is removed farther and farther from his home in heaven. (Child, 1831: 9)

While children had to be protected from the corrupting influence of society, at the same time, at least if they were male, they had to be equipped to take part in that society. Thus child raising was a difficult and important task; the child's plasticity meant that every aspect of it required careful thought. Mothers were given detailed instructions. A typical book contained chapters on how to inculcate religion in children, how to train them to be obedient, and how a mother might achieve the firmness and self-control necessary to develop her children's characters (Abbott, 1833).

Raising children, then, was difficult, but fortunately, women were assured, they had special abilities for it, largely due to their innate warmth and morality. "The female breast is the natural soil of Christianity," wrote one author (Anon., *The American Lady's Preceptor*, 1813: 71). It was through their role as mothers that women could attain power, most importantly over their sons:

> The earliest days of our statesmen, of poets, of our men of profound thought and original mind, are passed in the nursery, under the constant care and superintendance of females. . . . How many a fair child has been nipped in the bud by improper treatment in early days; and how many have been brought to full perfection and beauty by the judicious care and attention of a mother. . . . (Anon., *The Lady's Companion*, 1856: 10)

Through their sons, women could exert a powerful influence over society without leaving their homes. Abbott (1833: 159) reminded them:

> Thus far the history of the world has been composed of the narrations of oppression and blood. . . . Where shall we look for the influence which shall change this scene, and fill the earth with the fruits of peace and benevolence? It is to the power of divine truth, to Christianity as taught from a mother's lips. . . . She who was first in transgression, must be yet the principal earthly agent in the restoration.

In arguing that children's innocence placed them in need of undivided attention, that women's nature equipped them for this role, and that through this role women could reform society, the authors of women's books assumed a view of human nature that differed fundamentally from the Puritan conception. These changed ideas about human nature were in part a product of the erosion of Calvinism in New England and the increasing dominance of New England's religious and intellectual life by liberal forms of Protestantism, especially Universalism and Unitarianism. Calvinism had preached the doctrine of original sin, the utter depravity of human beings, and their total reliance upon God for salvation. The liberals who began to challenge Calvinism in the second half of the eighteenth century rejected the idea of human depravity and replaced it with that of human ability, human potential for good and for an active role in salvation. Such ideas gained ground among the churches of early nineteenth-century New England and in the academies and colleges; most of the authors of women's guidebooks espoused this new liberalism.

In the conflict of these ideologies and the victory of liberalism, one can see the decline of an agrarian society, in which people felt little control over their world, and emergence of a capitalist system in which, in its early stages, some people sensed that they could affect their conditions and destiny and felt a new optimism and self-confidence. But the new concept of human nature also derived from changes in role requirements within the family, especially in the role of women; the idea that children were innocent and malleable helped to explain and justify women's confinement in the home. Probably child rearing had in fact become somewhat more difficult; fathers were not around much to help, and the life of an industrializing town, for which these children were being prepared, was more difficult and complex than life in a farming village had been. But child care could have been arranged in other ways. The main beneficiaries of women's domesticity were not the children but the men. It was they who were freed to participate full time in the industrializing market economy, to accrue the money and power that participation in that society could bring, and to gain the authority in their families that came with this division of labor.

This male power was not openly questioned, or even discussed, by early-nineteenth-century New England women. Self-conscious feminism did not appear until the mid-nineteenth century, and then it was strongest among women of professional families, often relatively well educated. But there is evidence that the town women of the "middling classes" felt and resented the increased power of their husbands and fathers. In a larger study (Epstein, 1975), I have shown that there was a striking change in the content of New England women's religious conversion experiences from the mid-eighteenth to the mid-nineteenth century. Eighteenth-century women's conversion experiences had, like men's, centered on remorse over a diffuse sense of sin, of distance from God and religion. In the nineteenth century, men tended to move away from orthodox religion, while women began to discover that their central sin was a desire to rebel: against God, the Bible, the minister. Women reported that they found themselves hating God's power and wanting to overthrow it. But they knew that such rebellion was both hopeless and damnable. They considered their conversions accomplished when they suppressed their fury, accepted God's omnipotence, and could regard him as a loving father rather than an enemy.

The center of conversion for these women was accommodation to the inevitable—male dominance. Rebellion itself was defined and defeated by the assumption that male power was unshakable. If to challenge God was hopeless and inevitable, acquiescence must follow. Some women, after conversion, carried rebellion into their families by going to religious meetings against the order of their husbands or fathers, or by denouncing their men for irreligion. Here again, male authority was challenged, but only in the name of obedience to higher male authority: that of God and Christ.

One reason that women tended to accept domesticity, with the male dominance that it involved, was that the other side of female subservience and economic dependence was male economic support. The grandmothers, and even the mothers, of these women had worked at demanding tasks for long hours. Most colonial farm women, especially in the early stages of settlement, worked from before dawn through the evening almost every day of the week at a series of complex tasks that left them with little freedom to enjoy a moment with their children or men.

Women were impelled to accept domesticity not only because of its material benefits but because it was surrounded by a seductive ideology. Women were told that in devoting themselves to their husbands and children, their position would be enhanced; that even though their work seemed trivial, in fact it held families together and was the basis of society itself. They were told that they were secluded from the outside society because they might otherwise be tainted by it, and that they were superior to it and to the men who inhabited it. And they were told that the seclusion that preserved their purity would also bring them power. The prospect of being relieved of productive work and of only having to mind the children, clean the house, and cook must have been very enticing. Unfortunately for these women, however, by the middle of the nineteenth century, the psychological strains brought on by powerlessness and dependency were already taking their toll; vague, often undiagnosable illnesses became widespread among women in the New England towns (Wood, 1973).

Finally, married women accepted domesticity because in early-nineteenth-century New England towns, most women did not have much choice. Some women could get jobs in the textile mills, but except in Rhode Island these mills employed only single women. Some women did continue to work instead of marrying, but this brought with it social isolation; there was no place for unmarried women in these towns. Thus they were pressed into domesticity by the constraints of the society in which they lived.

These women probably did acquire a certain dubious power through their acceptance of domesticity. To the extent that they did hold sway over family and personal life, men must have felt that women had the power to exclude them from or allow them into the realm of emotional ties and warmth. But the price of this nebulous influence was submission to male authority and adhesion to a rigid and antisexual moral code. Women were told to hold their own sexuality suspect:

> There is a species of love, if it deserves the name, which declines soon after marriage, and it is no matter if it does. . . . There can be no objection to external love, where it is a mere accompaniment to that which is internal. What I object to, is making too much of it; or giving it a place in our hearts which is disproportioned to its real value. Our affections should rather be based chiefly on sweetness of temper, intelligence, and moral excellency. (Alcott, 1837: 85)

The idea that women must put aside sexuality in order to be moral was a product of the Victorian view that sexuality was evil, but it also probably rested on a sense that concern with one's own satisfaction was incompatible with the selflessness required of the mother and the submission required of the wife.

Probably the great majority of married women in early New England towns stayed home with their children and were supported by their husbands. At this time, only the beginnings of what would become a working class existed in New England. Most men were farmers; those who left the farms became craftsmen, tradesmen, or professionals. There was a large group of servants, but these were usually young people who could expect to move up in society. Most factory jobs, especially in textiles, were filled by young women from rural or middle-class town families who would leave the factories when they married. This was a temporary labor force, not a working class. If industry had developed earlier than it did, or on a larger scale, women might have been drawn into work outside the home as they lost their productive role within it. But as it was, women's agrarian productive functions were destroyed without being replaced by industrial ones. It was in this vacuum that women's domestic role took shape, and in this situation the new concept of femininity was formulated.

As long as there was no working class in New England and its population was almost entirely native-born, English-speaking, and Protestant, domesticity was accessible to most town women. But after 1840 a working class, composed in large part of immigrants, began to develop in these towns. As new immigrant groups and then blacks entered the working class, the longer-established immigrants could move up in the occupational structure. It became possible for many women to stay at home, supported by their husbands. But the poverty of working-class life still precluded any real attainment of the domestic ideal. A woman who lived in a tenement could not give undivided attention to developing her children's personalities.

Through the nineteenth century and into the twentieth, most white Protestant urban women continued to stay at home, supported by their husbands, often in surroundings that made it possible for them to come somewhere near the domestic ideal. This role was a luxury made possible by
immigrant labor. Without it, the process of industrialization would have
pulled native-born Americans, both men and women, into industrial work.
The ideal of domesticity, formed in an earlier period of capitalism, was
kept alive not only because domesticity continued to be possible for native-
born women but because many of the immigrant groups brought with
them ideas about women's place that meshed with the American ideal. As
in the preindustrial United States, in these peasant cultures women had
worked in the home and cared for children. Some immigrants tried to
maintain this tradition by working as family units in industry or continuing to work at home, but for pay.[1] They maintained the hope that as they
rose in society, their women would be able to withdraw from industry and
devote themselves full time to the family. For many, this became possible.

The great wealth of the United States made possible the massive immigration of the late-nineteenth and early-twentieth centuries, which in turn
made possible the maintenance of the domestic role for so many American
women. The domestic ideal, established before the development of large-
scale industry, limited the options open to American capitalism by making
it more difficult to draw women into industry, adding to the pressures to
look outside the Northern states, to Europe and the American South, for
new sources of labor. But the domestic ideal also divided and weakened
the working class by providing an index of upward mobility, by holding
forth the elusive goal of a private life protected from the pressures of the
industrial world, and by making the housewife the symbol of that goal.[2]

Notes

* The name of the author in the article as originally published was Barbara Easton.
1. Jews were the only major immigrant group who had a tradition of women working outside the home. It was partly for this reason that Jewish women entered industry and the
   labor movement in such large numbers in the early twentieth century. Other immigrant
   groups resisted the incorporation of women into industrial work and the consequent disruption of traditional family patterns. Italians, for instance, often sought situations in
   which they could work as family units. Where this was not possible, the men might forbid
   the women to work (McLaughlin, 1971).
2. Other references on this topic include Cott (1977, 1978); Norton (1980); and Sklar
   (1973).

The Work-Family Role System

JOSEPH H. PLECK
Wellesley College

6. Current Expectations. Pleck looks at the conflict between work and family. Like Coser and Rokoff, he is interested in what he calls "structural buffers" to insulate men—and the occupational world—from conflict with changes in the family system. As long as the occupational world is sex-segregated, men are not directly threatened by women who have paid employment. But when women perform two roles—both the familiar male-occupational and the familiar female-home role—they face considerable problems of strain and exhaustion, while men's family life is not altered. Who benefits from this system? What do you think of Pleck's argument? Is the currently expected male role advantageous to all who play it? Under what circumstances is the female role more attractive? Are there important class differences in roles, in "structural buffers," and in related disadvantages for women?

The study of work and the study of the family have traditionally constituted separate subdisciplines in sociology. Rapoport and Rapoport (1965) and Kanter (1976c), among others, have aptly stressed the need for greater examination of work and family roles in relation to each other. Such joint consideration is necessary to describe how individuals' functioning in either of these spheres is affected by their involvement in the other. Further, the current examination of sex roles brings added impetus to the analysis of work-family interrelationships. A major part of what is usually meant by change in "sex roles" is specifically change in the traditional allocation of work and family roles between men and women. Traditional sex-role norms prescribed the specialization of work and family responsibilities by sex, but a new option for each sex to integrate roles in both work and the family is now emerging.

In this paper I analyze some aspects of the "work-family role system" composed of the male work role, the female work role, the female family role, and the male family role.

Female Work and Family Roles

Research on the effects of married female employment on the family (see Hoffman and Nye, 1974; Howell, 1973a,b) contains much information relevant to this link. The three major topics in this research have been the effects of wives' employment on children's psychological well-being, marital satisfaction and happiness, and marital power. The consensus today appears to be that when other variables are controlled, wives' employment has no clear positive or negative effect on children's well-being and, when freely chosen, has no negative effect on marital happiness and satisfaction. Most reviews (cf. Bahr, 1974) conclude that wives' employment is associated with some increase in wives' marital power (primarily assessed by wives' reports of how the couple would make various hypothetical decisions). However, Safilios-Rothschild (1970) has questioned the support for this and other aspects of the "resource" theory of marital power.

The most important aspect of married females' employment is simply its effect on the level of wives' performance of family roles. Blood and Wolfe's (1960) examination of the relation between household division of labor and wives' employment indicated that when wives held paid jobs, they reported doing a smaller proportion of the work performed by the couple on eight household tasks (not including child care). Several analyses of time budget data (Meissner et al., 1975; Robinson, Juster, and Stafford, 1976; Walker, 1969) have likewise shown, predictably enough, that wives holding paid jobs outside the home spend less time performing family tasks than wives not so employed. In Walker's data, for example, wives' average time in family tasks was 8.1 hours per day when not employed and declined, through several intermediate categories of part-time employment, to 4.8 hours per day when the wife was employed 30 or more hours per week.

Female and Male Family Roles

The first and most obvious feature of the articulation between females' and males' family roles is that women and men generally perform different family tasks.[1] That is, there is a marital division of family labor. There is no single accepted way of quantifying how far family tasks are segregated by sex, and any quantitative index would be strongly dependent on which tasks were selected for study and how narrowly or broadly each was defined. Duncan et al. (1974), in a Detroit sample in 1971, concluded that the general principle that household tasks should be segregated by sex had been maintained, with only slight adjustments on particular tasks, since the earlier study.

Ideological support for the traditional division of family labor by sex remains quite strong. Robinson, Yerby, Feiweger, and Sommerick (1976) note that in their national sample of married women in 1965–66, only nineteen percent responded "yes" to the question, "Do you wish your husband would give you more help with the household chores?" Repeating the question in a 1973 national survey, the percentage of agreement rose only four points to twenty-three percent. The increase in the percentage of wives wanting more help from their husbands in household work was considerably greater in certain subgroups, however. There was, for example, an increase of twenty percent of women who graduated from college. The increase in these groups may presage a challenge to the traditional division of household labor which will become more widespread in the future.

A second important feature of the link between male and female family roles concerns simply the relation between the overall levels of each. Though no direct analyses of this relation have been located, it can be inferred from the relation between males' family role performance and wives' employment status, since the latter is associated with variations in females' family role performance. Walker's (1970b) time budget data indicate that, on average, there is *no* variation in husbands' mean time in family roles (about 1.6 hours per day) associated with their wives' employment status. That is, husbands contribute about the same time to family tasks whether or not their wives are employed (and doing an average of 4.8 hours of work per day). Other time budget studies (Meissner et al., 1975; Robinson, Juster, and Stafford, 1976) confirm Walker's general findings. In Walker's data, husbands' family time does increase slightly, to 2.1 hours per day, when their wives are employed if a child under two is present, but otherwise the independence of husbands' family time from wives' employment status holds true when age and number of children are controlled.

The time budget data indicating that husbands do not increase their family role performance when their wives are employed are cross-sectional rather than longitudinal. It is possible, then, that longitudinal analysis might find changes in husbands' level of family work as their wives enter the labor force, leave it during childbearing, and then reenter it, in the family life cycle pattern so frequent today. Further, although there is no average increase in husbands' family time when their wives have paid jobs, this average lack of response may conceal subgroups of husbands who do take on a significantly greater family role. If so, there must be subgroups of husbands who actually decrease their family role when their wives work. More needs to be known about the determinants of individual variation in husbands' family role performance and in their responsiveness to their wives' paid employment.

Male Family and Work Roles

The effect of the male work role on the family is receiving increasing attention. Scanzoni (1970) notes that functionalist theory emphasized how the family is linked to the larger society through the husband-father's occupational role, and how this extrafamilial link affects family relationships. A number of studies and reviews (Aberle and Naegele, 1952; Aldous, 1969; Dyer, 1956, 1965; Grønseth, 1971, 1972; Miller and Swanson, 1958; Pearlin, 1974; Scanzoni, 1965, 1970) have considered how characteristics of the male's occupational role (especially his occupational status) affect the family, particularly the socialization of children.

The most obvious and direct effect of the male occupational role on the family, however, has so far received little analytical attention: the restricting effect of the male occupational role on men's family role. Again using time budget and division of labor measures, data from Walker (1974) and Blood and Wolfe (1960) indicate that role performances in work and family are inversely related to each other for husbands, as they are for wives.

While the extent of the husband's family role co-varies with the extent of his work role, variation in the extent of the husband's family role occurs around a low baseline *not* accounted for by the demands of his work role. Rather, men's family role varies within the limits imposed by the traditional division of family labor by sex. Though both men's and women's family roles vary according to their employment status, fully employed men still do only a fraction of the family work that fully employed women do—about one-third, according to Walker's data. To put it another way, though employment status has a significant main effect on family work, sex has a stronger effect and accounts for much more of the variance in an individual's time in family work than does his or her employment status.

Thus, it would be misleading to state that men's work role is the primary determinant of the limited family role men typically hold at present. It would be more accurate to say that the objective demands of the male work role are now a latent and secondary constraint, but will emerge as the primary constraint on men's family role if and when ideological support for the traditional division of family labor by sex is weakened. Until then, reduction in the demands of the male work role (for example, shortening the work week) may not lead to much of an increase in males' family role, as compared to increases in overtime work, the holding of two jobs, and leisure.

Male and Female Work Roles

There are two distinct contexts in which male and female work roles articulate with each other: work environments themselves and marriage. In the workplace, the most significant feature of the articulation of male and female work roles is the high degree of occupational segregation by sex (Blaxall and Reagan, 1976; Waldman and McEaddy, 1974), with females concentrated in lower-paying, lower-status occupations. Within this over-all occupational segregation, two dominant patterns for the articulation of male and female work roles can be distinguished. In the older pattern, typical in much blue-collar employment, women and men work in entirely separate settings and do not generally interact with each other in their work roles. Females are completely excluded from male workplaces. Males are not completely excluded from female workplaces, since women work under the authority and control of male employers. However, this control is largely administered through a cadre of female supervisors, thus greatly minimizing male-female contact.

A major source of this pattern of occupational segregation historically has been men's desire to exclude women in order to keep their own wages up (Hartmann, 1976). This pattern may derive from noneconomic sources as well. Caplow (1954) proposed that a fundamental norm that women and men should not interact with each other except in romantic and kinship relationships underlies this sex segregation of the workplace. Caplow speculatively argued that a major psychological source of this norm is that aggression toward females is severely punished in male childhood socialization and is therefore highly anxiety-provoking to males. Since interaction with work partners inevitably entails some degree of competition and aggression, Caplow argues, interacting with women in the workplace makes men anxious. We can also note similarities between these traditional norms prescribing complete segregation for male and female work roles and what anthropologists term "pollution ideology" (Douglas, 1970). According to pollution ideology, if certain categories of social objects (e.g., menstrual blood) are not segregated or handled in special ways, the order of the world is disturbed and catastrophe will result. In similar fashion, many miners and seamen in the past have resisted the introduction of women as co-workers because they superstitiously believed that women would be a "jinx" or "bad luck," bringing on mining disasters and shipwrecks.

The more recent pattern for the articulation of male and female work roles, whose ideal type is the modern office, is the integration of women into mixed-sex workplaces, but in roles that are segregated from and clearly subordinate to men's. Thus, women and men do not compete for the same jobs and do not have to interact with each other as peers. In this pattern, the potential for interacting with members of the other sex, particularly if unmarried, has almost attained the status of a fringe benefit. The shift from the first pattern of work organization to the second has not received sufficient attention. Several studies have examined how certain previously male occupations became female ones (Davies, 1974; Prather, 1971b), but that these occupational shifts transformed previously all-male work environments into mixed-sex ones has not been adequately analyzed as yet.

The second context for the articulation of male and female work roles is marriage. The critical factor affecting this link is primarily psychological, based on men's investment in their performance of the paid breadwinner role as uniquely validating their masculinity. Yankelovich (1974: 44–45) has suggested that for the large majority of men whose jobs are not inherently psychologically satisfying, daily work is made worthwhile by pride in hard work. The sacrifices made to provide for their families' needs validate them as men. Wives' work thus takes away a major source of these men's identity and is psychologically threatening.

Two dominant patterns for the articulation between male and female roles in marriage are apparent, corresponding to the two patterns noted in the workplace. In the more traditional pattern, husbands cannot tolerate their wives taking or holding any paid employment. Supporting this pattern, in many work places married women were ineligible for employment, and single women were dismissed if they married. In the more recent pattern, husbands can accept their wives' employment as long as it does not come too close to or, worse, surpass their own in prestige, earnings, or psychological commitment. The segregation of women in lower-paying, lower-status occupations helps insure that this limit is not breached. Further, husbands' acceptance of their wives' work in this pattern is conditional on their wives' continuing to meet their traditional family responsibilities.

Taking an overview of the workplace and marriage, the second pattern for the articulation of male and female work roles in each is not necessarily more equitable or less restrictive to women than the first. The emergence of the second pattern was, however, inevitable as the married female labor force has expanded over the course of this century. The question now is whether a third pattern can emerge on a widespread scale in which wives can have work roles of equal or greater status than their husbands' (Rapoport and Rapoport, 1971b), and in which female workers can interact with male workers as equals in the workplace.

Structural "Buffers" in the Work-Family System

What are the more general characteristics of the link in the work-family role system? How do these links affect whether change in one role does or does not lead to accommodating change in the other roles to which it is linked? We consider here two structural "buffers" in the links among these roles, limiting how much a change in one role affects the others.

The first kind of buffer is *sex-segregated market mechanisms* for both paid work and family work. A sex-segregated, dual market for paid work means that women and men do not compete for the same jobs. As a result, changes in the level of female employment occur neither at the expense nor to the benefit of male employment. Further, since women are segregated into not only different but also inferior jobs, women will rarely have jobs of equal or greater status than men's, psychologically threatening their husbands or co-workers. In these ways, the dual market for paid work insulates the male work role from the changes in the female work role that have occurred so far in our society.

Household work and child care can likewise be conceptualized as allocated by a sex-segregated, dual market mechanism. This market mechanism is supported by ideology concerning the appropriate household activities of the two sexes as well as by differential training in family tasks. The result is that the husband's family role is generally unresponsive to changes in the wife's family role. If a wife's employment requires her to reduce the level of her family role performance, the husband is unlikely to increase his. He may perceive that family work needs doing, but he will not perceive the kind of work that needs to be done as appropriate or suitable to him. The dual market for household work and child care thus has insulated men's family role from the changes in the female family role resulting so far from paid employment.

The second kind of structural buffer in the work-family role system is *asymmetrically permeable boundaries between work and family roles* for both men and women. For women, the demands of the family role are permitted to intrude into the work role more than vice versa. Though working mothers try to devise schedules to accommodate the demands of both roles, if an emergency or irregularity arises requiring a choice between the two, the family work often takes priority. For example, when there is a crisis for a child in school, it is the child's working mother rather than working father who will be called to take responsibility. This vulnerability of the female work role to family demands is an important part of negative stereotypes about women workers. It is also a major source of stress for women on the job, since the sex-role norm that women take responsibility for the family conflicts with the norms of the job role.

For husbands, the work-family role boundary is likewise asymmetrically permeable, but in the other direction. Many husbands literally "take work home" with them or need to use family time simply to recuperate from the stresses they face in their work role. Husbands are expected to manage their families so that their family responsibilities do not interfere with their work efficiency, and so that families will make any adjustments necessary to accommodate the demands of husbands' work roles.

Changes in the Work-Family Role System

As is well known, over the course of this century there has been a major increase in married women's rate of labor force participation (Oppenheimer, 1970). Married women's increased employment has induced a partially accommodating reduction in women's family role, but as yet almost no increase in husbands' family role, as indicated by the time budget data considered earlier. In consequence, employed wives face considerable problems of strain and exhaustion in both their work and family roles. As Rapoport and Rapoport (1972) have formulated it, there is a psychosocial lag between the changes occurring for women in the macrosocial world of work and changes in the microsocial world of the family. In their analysis, the psychosocial lag generates transitional problems of adjustment, but these will be resolved as the family "catches up" to changes in the workplace. Young and Willmott (1973) have likewise argued that the family is becoming more "symmetrical," that is, evolving toward a pattern in which each marital partner has a significant role in both paid work and the family. The analysis of the work-family role system developed here makes possible a more specific consideration of the issues these social changes will involve.

First, it is clear that one of the most pressing changes needed in the work-family role system is an end to the traditional norms prescribing the sex-segregated and unequal division of household work and child care. As noted earlier, however, if and when these norms break down, the demands of the male work role will emerge as the crucial constraint on how much men can increase their family role. Expansion of the scope of the male family role without accommodating changes in the male work role will lead to role strain in men similar to the strains now faced by working wives. While this distribution of strain throughout the role system will be more equitable than the current one, it will continue to be a source of instability. Husbands who are committed to equal sharing of household work and child care will find that the demands of their jobs make this quite difficult, and that a diversion of their energy from work to the family will penalize them in the competition for job advancement. The idea of paternity leave—admittedly only beginning to be raised in labor negotiations, and not widely taken advantage of in the few places where it has been implemented—is perhaps the first indication of the kind of workplace practices needed to legitimate a shift of husbands' energies from work to the family.

A second potential future change in the work-family role system is the breakdown of occupational sex segregation. Recent progress toward reducing occupational segregation, when it has been evident at all, has been dishearteningly slow (Blaxall and Reagan, 1976; Waldman and McEaddy,

1974). If occupational segregation is significantly reduced, major adjustments will be required in men's self-conceptions as primary family breadwinners and in the norms governing male-female interaction on the job. In addition, women holding higher-status jobs may give added impetus to the desegregation of family work and the enlargement of the male family role. First, women holding higher-status jobs may require that women's boundary between their work and family roles become more like men's; that is, their work role will more often need to take priority over their family role, and they will be able to do less family work. Second, women holding jobs more equal in status to their husbands' will give greater legitimation to the demand for a more equal sharing of family work. Contrary to these two effects, however, the increased income provided by women's holding higher-status jobs may make it more possible for families to purchase goods and services to compensate for the reduction in women's family role than is possible now when women are in relatively low-paying jobs. If these goods and services are available, purchasing them may be less stressful than trying to increase men's family role.

Third, if the sex segregation of both family work and paid work is significantly reduced, a fundamental change in the nature of the work role may be necessary, not just for men but for both sexes. As the paid work role has evolved in modern society, it has come to call for full-time, continuous work from the end of one's education to retirement, desire to actualize one's potential to the fullest, and subordination of other roles to work. This conception of the work role has been, in effect, the male model of the work role. Women, because of the family responsibilities traditionally assigned to them, have had considerable difficulty fitting themselves to this male model of work. To a large extent, it has been possible for men in modern society to work according to this model precisely because women have subordinated their own potential work role and accepted such an extensive role in the family. In doing so, wives take on the family responsibilities that husbands might otherwise have to fill, and in addition emotionally, and often practically, support their husbands in their work role.[2]

In the past, it has been possible for families to function, though not without strain, with one marital partner, the husband, performing according to this male work mode. Families have also been able to function, though with even more strain, with one partner conforming to the male work model and the other partner in a less demanding job role. Though it is stressful, especially for the wife, this kind of two-job family is on the verge of being the statistically dominant pattern (Hayghe, 1976). However, it does not seem possible for large numbers of families to function with *both* partners following the traditional male work model. Such a pattern could become widespread only if fertility dropped significantly further or if household work and child-care services became inexpensive, widely available, and socially accepted on a scale hitherto unknown.[3] In the absence of such developments, greater equality in the sharing of work and family roles by women and men will ultimately require the development of a new model of the work role and a new model for the boundary between work and the family which gives higher priority to family needs.

Notes

1. Glazer (1976) provides a useful analysis of current theoretical approaches to household work.
2. Mortimer et al. (1976) have drawn attention to the extent to which wives can directly contribute to their husbands' work as an alternative to holding paid work of their own, a further indication of the demanding nature of the male work role.
3. Safilios-Rothschild (1976) has analyzed in a somewhat different way the structural changes that may occur to accommodate families in which both parents have high-status jobs.

Commitment and the Cultural Mandate: Women in Medicine

PATRICIA GERALD BOURNE
NORMA JULIET WIKLER
University of California, Santa Cruz

7. Consequences. Bourne and Wikler illustrate and explain some of the problems women face when trying to combine professional and family life in our society. To do so, they introduce the concept of the "discriminatory environment." This idea indicates how current understandings about the meaning of commitment and sex restrict women from demonstrating their value and ability in nonfamilial employment. As long as sex and commitment are defined using familiar stereotypes of masculinity and of men's familial roles, women are precluded from being both feminine and competent in a profession. One way to manage the contradiction is to specialize in areas where there is less conflict. These authors note that women believe they have made their own decisions when choosing specialties or styles of medical practice, but in fact their decisions tend to decrease the conflict between familial and professional roles. Can professions ever integrate women throughout their ranks under these circumstances? What social policies could speed this effort? How could women and men work separately to establish such changes? How could they work together?

Since 1970, unprecedented numbers of women have entered traditionally male professions. Medicine is no exception. The proportion of women enrolled in medical schools in the United States rose from 9.6 percent in 1970–71 to 18 percent in 1974–75. By 1976, women comprised 40 percent or more of entering classes at many medical schools (URSA: 1976). A key question is: what are the implications of this recent influx of women for the organization of work and for the status of women in medicine? To a large extent, the answer depends upon the distribution of women among the kinds of work in the medical profession and the reasons for it.

Practical as well as theoretical concerns warrant the investigation of the factors and processes which affect the distribution of men and women among the medical specialties (cf. Davidson, 1979; Quadagno, 1976). Does the current distribution reflect choices made by women on the basis of their tastes, proclivities, feminine skills, and abilities, or is it due to overt and covert discrimination operating during medical school training? Though the study reported here [1] found little "actionable" discrimination in medical school admissions and training policies and practices (such as unfair grading, failure to refer or recommend women for further training or jobs) that would directly block women from entering various specialties, its findings reveal that the choices women make for further training and specialization are shaped and circumscribed by features of what we shall call a "discriminatory environment."

The discriminatory environment is a notion which has two components. The first—what we will term here "subtle" or "nonactionable" discrimination—has been widely recognized and documented. Rowe (1977) has described the *events* of subtle discrimination as forming a set of "Saturn rings" around a goal—specks of dust, each one in and of itself inconsequential but, in the aggregate, a concentric series of insurpassable barriers. Campbell (1973) has documented the many forms of this type of sexism encountered by women in medicine: acts of *commission* such as jokes demeaning to women, insults, and communications (verbal and nonverbal) indicating disrespect and disinterest; and acts of *omission* such as exclusion from conversation and from informal learning experiences. [2]

The second component of the notion of a discriminatory environment concerns the "maleness" of the medical profession and its institutions and is even more subtle (cf. Davidson, 1978). Though manifest and expressed in behavior, its source lies in the social structure itself.

There are two aspects to this component. First, medical schools are "male" in the sense that the personal characteristics expected and valued in physicians are those stereotypically deemed male. In his discussion of "status contradictions," Hughes (1945) argues that a status such as physician comes to be defined by the secondary characteristics of those who occupy the role (that is, men). In American society, the definition of what good doctors are like, how they look and behave, is overlaid and integrated with the characteristics and qualities ascribed to upper-middle-class white males. Male behavior and male ways of being (as social stereotypes) are expected of would-be physicians. They constitute the criteria by which medical faculty and, later, professional colleagues identify promising physicians and judge them worthy of special attention, encouragement, and professional opportunity. [3]

Women who enter the domain of medicine, which has been male-defined, are likely to find that their presence is jarring and upsetting to others. First, women are unexpected and therefore feared as unpredictable. Second, their personal "female" characteristics and qualities (which may be stereotypically imputed or actually theirs) are *incongruent* with those expected and valued for a physician.

Women arrive in medical school with the characteristics of the "ideal typical" American female ascribed to them. Thus, female recruits are assumed to have valued traits representing the warmth and expressiveness cluster such as gentleness, sensitivity, and tactfulness. They are also expected to have such generally *devalued* traits as passivity, indecisiveness, and dependence (Broverman et al., 1970). These latter characteristics are the opposite of those rewarded in medicine, for the "good" physician must demonstrate the stereotypically "male" competency cluster traits of assertiveness, egoism, and independence. With effort, the female medical student or physician can demonstrate to men and to other women that she is not a "typical" woman. She then faces their disapproval of her failure to meet role expectations of her as a woman. This "double bind," common to women who enter any traditionally male profession, is costly and difficult to resolve (Broverman et al., 1970; Davidson, 1975; Horner, 1972; Kamarovsky, 1946; Mead, 1949; Nadelson and Notman, 1974; Wikler, 1976).

The second aspect of the "maleness" of the medical profession is that the organization of work in medicine, the sequence of a medical career, and key professional norms are predicated on the conventional male role in the family and on the male biological "clock." Hochschild (1975) has demonstrated that the normative view of professional careers is based on male social roles in both professional and family life. Her analysis focuses on the career "clockwork" in the university setting, but the key features in medicine are not so different from academia. In both, the time of most intense career-building effort is simultaneous with the time of "building a family." The overlap of intense career building and the favored childbearing years creates particular pressures for women. Though male medical students may be deprived of time with their spouse and children because of the pressures of work, they will not have the anxieties women experience, related to the urgency of having children before growing too old. And because two important time- and energy-consuming endeavors overlap, male careers and institutions are thus predicated on the fact that every active professional needs a wife (Hunt and Hunt, 1977 and within this volume).

In this paper, we explore the role conflicts resulting from this structure which affect women's work choices: (1) the conflict between normative expectations about the qualities and characteristics of women and those about professionals; (2) the conflict between the allocation of time and energy to two social roles, doctor and wife-mother. Both conflicts crystallize for women in certain features of their professional training. By examining a particularly central and salient feature of medical work—professional commitment—we gain insight into the discriminatory environment and the conflict it generates for women.[4] Commitment to professional work is one of the most important values of behavior for an aspiring physician. Indeed, one of the most important criteria in choosing recruits to the medical profession and passing them on to prestigious and lucrative positions is a recruit's commitment.[5] Professional commitment is one example of a personal characteristic taken for granted in men but questioned in women. It is an aspect of behavior congruent with male sex-role expectations and incongruent with expectations about women.

We shall use data from interviews with medical school administrators, faculty, and students (both men and women in all cases) to illustrate how social assumptions about maleness, femaleness, and professional behavior and demeanor interact to the disadvantage of women.

Women and Commitment: Stereotypes and Expectations

Male faculty persistently expressed stereotypes in the interviews concerning the professional commitment of women medical students. Sometimes male suspicion of female students' commitment was expressed directly. More often it was implicit in views on the role of women in medicine today, their special qualities, the kinds of medical problems they are suited for, and the work settings which best accommodate their needs, interests, and skills.

Until recently, so few women sought medical training that their professional commitment was not of major concern; it was clear that their sole interest and obligation was their medical work. A stereotype of the woman doctor as "hen medic" developed. Hen medics were not necessarily mannish, but they were clearly unfeminine—that is, unattractive and unmarried. These women doctors were seen as dependable because they were free from competing priorities.

The recent dramatic rise in women applying and admitted to medical school has thrown the stereotype and its attendant behavioral expectations into confusion. Clearly, all cannot be defined as unattractive and unmarriageable. But if not, their commitment may be viewed as problematic. One faculty member articulated this view in describing a colleague's behavior:

> I don't ask them [applicants] questions about marriage and family. It is none of my business. I know one of my colleagues asks this question, but of good-looking women only, not of average-looking women—or of men. (Male faculty, Mansfield Med)[6]

Though male physicians virtually never articulated reservations about the capabilities of women in medicine, they frequently expressed reservations about the "payoff" in training women as physicians. These reservations were generally expressed in a low key, as by a male faculty member at Middleton: "I just have a feeling that we get considerably less working years out of women; it's variable and intermittent." At the heart of this reservation is the assumption that a woman will not practice, or will practice much less, if she is married. Being married is viewed as a handicap for a woman. As this faculty member put it:

> I don't recall any bias [against women] myself. I don't happen to have run across it. When women are married, a woman must often sacrifice her own career goals. Medicine is very demanding. If you have any handicaps, it makes it very difficult. (Male faculty, Middleton Med)

Because a medical career and marriage are often viewed as mutually exclusive, it is expected that a woman will renounce the former in favor of the latter. Women frequently report that this expectation is conveyed to them explicitly when they express their intention to go to medical school. As one woman put it:

> When I would tell people that I wanted to be a doctor, they would say to me, "Sure you'll be a doctor. In college you'll get married, you'll have babies, and that will be the end of that." (Female student, Madison Med)

The implicit belief is that women may intend to have a career but will be overwhelmed by a stronger desire to get married and have children. Once they become married and mothers, they will lose interest in a career. If women are considered attractive, it is assumed that marriage will win over career. A story related by a woman at Marshall Med is illustrative:

> One of my favorite high school science teachers, one who'd been really helpful and encouraging to me, wrote in my high school yearbook, "You'll never make it as a doctor because you're much too cute." It made me furious. He gave me encouragement with the one hand then said, "*But* you'll get married and have kids." (Female student, Marshall Med)

Dual Commitments and Time Binds

Assumptions about women's lack of commitment to professional work are based not only on stereotypes about what women value but also on realities about what is normally required of women as wives and mothers, and what is therefore unavailable to them in professional roles. Men know that they could not do what they do professionally if they had to do what their wives do for them in addition to their work. And men know that they could not do their work as they currently do it if they lacked a wife to keep their private lives in order. Thus, not only do they realize the difficulty of doing two jobs, they recognize the difficulty of doing just one without the home support system.

In a study of the psychological strains of everyday medical school life, Coombs (1971: 39) documents the expectation and importance of this support system. An unmarried male medical student told Coombs he envied married male peers because they have "someone who has dinner ready for you, rubs your back, provides a shoulder to cry on at any hour, and builds you up when you're down."

The knowledge that they will have to play the roles of doctor, wife and mother, and social worker, while their male counterparts have only the role of doctor, was very much on the minds of women medical students in the interviews. Those who are already married find that the double demands on their time create friction with their mates. Those who contemplate marriage and children know that it will be a difficult logistical task; they fear that professional involvement means that they will not be able to provide a professional husband with the support system that he will need to do his work well. Consequently, these women fear that a professional career will diminish their value as a potential wife and render relationships more than usually problematic. Should they hope to have children, simply running their lives seems to demand superhuman energy.

Typically, the women interviewed in this study wanted to do well in medical school but also held high standards for their current or potential role as mate and mother. Their anxiety was increased by surrounding evidence that medical school and problems with relationships go together. Whether or not the incidence is really any higher in their environment than in others, they attribute to it the difficulties inherent in life as a physician or medical student. A female student at Marshall Med summed up an often voiced perception: "It just seems like medicine and divorce go hand in hand." A classmate concurred: "I don't know very many people who've formed relationships, but I know a lot who've busted."

In the course of medical school, women students think often about how to manage their dual roles. They generally put the burden on themselves. "Somehow" it will all work out because of extra energy and planning on their part:

> When I was thinking of going into medicine, I told myself, "Well, you're not going to have any children because you're not going to have any time. If you want to be a good mother, you're going to have to have all your time for the formative years." But now I feel differently. However, that hasn't changed my feelings about children, but I do feel it can be done. I think it requires more energy and a lot of planning and a lot of help from the outside. (Female student, Middleton Med)

Usually these concerns form a steady undercurrent of feeling. On occasion, they come to a head in genuine desperation:

> I am at a point where I dread the next step. I know I will be tired, unhappy, out of control of the situation, feeling inadequate, that I don't know anything, that I don't know how to handle anything, and there will always be that lack of time in managing my home.

> I'm much more supportive of his career than he is of mine. I don't know what's going to happen when I start clinical. This morning I was thinking of quitting. I just want to be happy. Why do I have to achieve something? Why do I have to *be a thing?* A name, a doctor? Other people live without it, there are other things in life. But I like it a lot and I'm beginning to see myself *do* it, even though I dread it. (Female student, Mayberry Med)

What is perhaps most remarkable is how much they define the problem as a personal rather than a structural one, and the solution as solely their responsibility. Revealing, in part for its uniqueness, is this account of a woman faculty member who described how she had managed her first child at the expense of her career. Now well established in her field with three children none the worse for wear, she spoke of how she managed her fourth child by having the confidence to ask others—the child, her husband, the job—to bend a little, rather than doing all the bending herself:

> I found out I was pregnant about midway through my senior year and had to drop out of the internship matching program—or at least at that time I thought I did. I recently had another baby, and I didn't drop out of anything.
>   When I was a resident I went so far overboard, I had to be the perfect resident. With this last child, I had the confidence to ask the system to bend for me. I would bring the babysitter to work sometimes, and sometimes my husband came over. Women deprive themselves of a lot. I find it's so important not to drop out altogether. (Female faculty, Marshall Med)

This way of managing is unusual. It is difficult for women physicians to make such demands of others for it seems to prove the stereotype that they will not, in fact, be able to manage. The pressure not to appear weak, to ask special favors, or to make demands of others, and even to define the problem as a structural rather than a personal one, is what sometimes forces women to choose between family roles and professional commitments, as predicted by those who establish the criteria of commitment.

Dual Commitments, Cultural Mandate, and the Double Bind

Women in medical school are up against something more complex than the stereotypic expectations which male faculty, administrators, and students have of their commitment priorities and the competing demands for time and energy from their family roles. Coser and Rokoff (1971) have proposed a theoretical framework for considering how expectations of commitment influence the effectiveness of women professionals. They argue that the conflict experienced by professional women between family and work stems in only a relatively minor way from their participation in two roles with competing claims on their time. More important, they argue, is that the social *values* which underlie these dual time demands are contradictory in a deep, normative sense. Thus, as professionals, women are expected to be committed to their work, as men are. But as women, they are normatively required to give priority to their families. The demonstration of commitment to work by a woman may be negatively sanctioned and disapproved (Coser and Rokoff, 1971 and in this volume).

The interview data substantiate Coser and Rokoff's argument. While men are angry if women are prevented from doing their work by other obligations, they simultaneously disapprove if a woman seems to be allowing work commitments to interfere with family obligations:

> At Mayberry Med [during an admissions interview] I was asked by a professor of gynecology, "Won't this interfere with your husband's career? You should be home with your child." He went on to suggest that I was simply the type of person who likes to set difficult goals for herself and that I would eventually be dissatisfied with medicine. (Female student, Middleton Med)

But it is clear that when women try to establish a new pattern of training to manage this pressure from home, they engender anger and objection. When a woman medical student asked to rearrange the order of her clerkships, she was perceived as asking for special favors as a woman and thus injuring her medical future:

> I'd taken all of my third year clerkships up until the last two and I was really tired, really exhausted. I went to the Dean and I said, "Look I don't want to take ob/gyn this month. I'm planning on going into that field and I'm too tired to do it justice. I'd just as soon take radiology." I've never been so hassled in my entire medical career. He threatened me with the fact that I would be ruining my career, that they would think I was too weak. I went and talked to the head of the ob/gyn department and he told me this was injuring me, that this would be a very important consideration in my evaluation because I was not strong enough to take it. (Female student, Mayberry Med)

A woman at Middleton Med described the process by which she resolved her dilemma:

> When I entered, I thought it seemed easy to do everything. Now I realize that wasn't realistic. It's not just medicine, it's a profession. So, now I plan to pick out an area of medicine I want and do that area to the extent I feel comfortable. I'm interested in cardiology; you can do that now forty hours a week. You give up something with that, a certain relationship with your patients. The one-hundred-hour-week routine is stupid to do to anyone. If women stand up, maybe men will be able to too. (Female student, Middleton Med)

The problem with this resolution is, of course, that one does not attain authority, leadership, or high income by limiting one's commitment to work. This holds for men as well as for women. Top jobs do not come to those who have not persuaded others of their full and intense commitment. But what is important here is that this phenomenon operates differentially on men and women and thus has a discriminatory effect on women.

The interaction of the structures of family and professional careers means that women are much less free to choose an intense commitment to work (it is our guess that many more would, if the price were not so high) because of the threat to chances of a satisfactory personal life. For women, the choice of a high level of commitment risks not only a sacrifice in quality of family experience but of not having the experience at all. Whenever professional work is predicated on a base of a home support system and lack of responsibility for one's personal life, that will discriminate against women. They just cannot find "wives" to do it for them.

Perhaps the clearest indication of the damage done to women physicians by this feature of their environment—the requirement for a high degree of professional commitment, judged appropriate to and possible only in males—is the definition of women-appropriate work which now seems to be operating in medicine.

Women's Commitment and Women's Work

Male expectations and prescriptions that women will, and should, give priority to marriage and family over medicine have led to the definition of certain types of medical work and certain categories of patients as appropriate for women. In the interviews with male faculty and administrators, almost universal approval of women's presence in medicine was expressed. But these statements of approval were nearly always couched in the context of observations that the structure of work in medicine has changed to allow some people to participate on a limited basis.

The shift toward group practice and the demand for physicians in institutional settings has created roles for which less than full professional commitment is seen as nondisruptive, and where the presence of women is viewed as appropriate. The dean at Mansfield Med summed up the trends and the way a changed structure allows for women:

> I think the situation has changed a great deal in terms of the development of specialists and away from the old-time situation where to be a doctor meant willingness to be a one-man fire department, on call seven days a week, all night, every night, every weekend. That was a form of living that was reasonably incompatible with the male physician having a decent home life, but very incompatible with the female physician looking forward to what is usually referred to as the hen medic, and it was a mas-

culinizing situation. Now, it's entirely different. Let me give you an example—physicians in student health services in colleges and universities. It's an ideal situation for women physicians. (Male dean, Mansfield Med)

The shift from entrepreneurial to bureaucratic medicine also facilitates the participation of women in the profession. Health Maintenance Organizations are designated "women suitable":

Medicine is a taxing field, around the clock. It's harder to accept the kinds of responsibilities that are necessary, if she has in mind having a family, *if* we were operating on the entrepreneurial model. Now there's a change toward shared responsibility. It's easier for women to fit in. At Kaiser, for instance, I know of two women who are splitting a position. (Male faculty, Middleton Med)

It appears that women are perfectly acceptable to most male members of the profession *if* they agree to work in areas where their divided commitment will not disrupt the work and will not disrupt the expectations of proper behavior for a married woman. One of the women students provided a particularly well-articulated description of what male definitions of "women's commitment" and "women's work" look like:

I've learned that you're supposed to say that you want to have children because that's normal. And you're supposed to have plans set up and assume that you'll work in group practice. And you're supposed to say that you'll wait until you're out [to have children] and you'll go into a field like pathology where you'll have good hours. (Female student, Mansfield Med)

Such a scenario is "what you are supposed to say" because it does not threaten expectations of women as good wives and mothers, but allows them a role in limited areas of work in the profession where their divided loyalties will not disrupt professional work.

Constructing positions in which women may limit their hours without disruption is only one of the components of the emerging definition of what is appropriate work for women in medicine. They are also thought to be better suited to working with certain kinds of patient groups. Women's gynecological medical problems are often cited as appropriate work for women:

I think women students contribute something to the atmosphere—an appreciation of certain patient problems. I can't document that very well, but I *feel* it. For instance, the hysterectomy. It's being brought to our attention that that's an operation that is perhaps being done much too often. I hadn't ever really thought about that, where I certainly would have if the operation in question had been removal of the testicles. (Male faculty, Middleton Med)

The dean of Mansfield Med summed it up: women are capable of an appreciation and understanding of *certain* patient problems:

> A number of women are attracted to pediatrics, and I think they do very well there. You know, it's very interesting that the veterinarians find that women are excellent; they excel in a subtle thing. You can't quantify it, but they seem to have a way with animals that men don't quite have, and I think there may be a form of that in pediatrics, too. (Male dean, Mansfield Med)

Conclusion

These definitions of women's work and women's commitment are part of the environment in which women are professionally socialized. Whether these expectations and male assumptions about women's place in medicine are ever communicated directly, their existence constricts the range of women's options. Single women who are convincingly uninterested in family life or unmarriageable may be presumed by male faculty to have sufficient professional commitment. Yet, they will still have difficulty overcoming the sex stereotypes of "appropriate" medical specializations and "suitable" contexts for medical work. Since married women are neither expected to give nor rewarded for giving full commitment to professional life, their struggle to achieve full professional status is laden with additional difficulties.

Few of the women interviewed would use the term "channeled" to describe the process by which they chose medical specialties or selected contexts for professional work. The term implies that forces other than free choice determine their decisions, and they believe that they have freely chosen. But it can be argued that channeling is precisely what occurs. In some measure, women collude with the stereotypes held by men, and their careers are invisibly shaped by their own expectations of women's roles. Women's choice of specialty and work setting cannot be called "free" when those choices are made in a discriminatory environment such as we have described. Not surprisingly, women will "choose" to go where they feel comfortable, welcomed, and competent. These "comfort zones" will be chosen to reduce the stress accompanying the violation of deeply held norms of women's role and place. To accommodate by "choosing" to abandon marriage or children to carry out the role is no less costly.

This analysis suggests that affirmative action policies to increase the number of women in medical training institutions are indispensable for ultimate change but are impotent *at present* to correct the effects of a discriminatory environment. Numbers alone will not undo the norms and values we have observed. These will remain until we change the relation of male roles to the family and crucial features of the structure and organization of professional work.

Notes

The authors of this study are listed in alphabetical order. Their contributions are equal.

1. Our analysis is based on, and uses data from, a recent exploratory national study of sex discrimination in health professions schools (URSA, 1976). The study was conducted by Urban and Rural Systems Associates (URSA), a San Francisco firm, under contract to the Women's Action Program, Office of Special Concerns, HEW contract #HEW-OS-74-291. The URSA study team visited twenty-seven health professions schools across the country where extensive semistructured interviews were conducted and taped with administrators, faculty members, and students. The professions included were: medicine, osteopathy, dentistry, veterinary medicine, optometry, podiatry, pharmacy, and public health. We confine ourselves to materials from the nine medical schools included in the sample.

2. Covert messages may be transmitted by touch and gesture (Henley, 1977), by language (Thorne and Henley, 1975), and by conversational and nonverbal interactional strategies (West, 1977a).

3. The role of expectations in engendering self-fulfilling behavior and the implications in general of Rosenthal and Jacobson's (1968) work here are apparent but so far unexplored in this context. Cynthia Epstein's (1970a) discussion of the creation of confidence under these conditions is also illuminating.

4. Central to the status of a profession is a field's ability to induce members to do their job no matter how long it takes and no matter what other demands are made on their lives. These requirements are stringent in medicine, where lives may be at stake in the physician's decision about how high a priority should be given to finishing a job.

5. Medical schools place enormous emphasis on the personal qualities of potential recruits. Schools will often interview 700 or 800 qualified (as judged by grades, test scores, and letters of recommendation) applicants in order to choose a class of 100 students. Much more faculty and administrative time is lavished on this effort than in other professional and graduate schools.

6. All quotations are from tape-recorded field interviews, unless otherwise noted. Names of people and medical schools are fictional. The latter were chosen at random from the "M" town listings in an atlas of the United States.

Dilemmas of
Japanese Professional Women

MASAKO MURAKAMI OSAKO
University of Illinois, Chicago Circle

8. Implications. One conventional argument is that industrialization or modernization leads to growing equality for women. Looking at the Japanese experience, Osako finds no such correlation; she shows how women are virtually excluded from managerial or professional positions. In Japan "moving up" is highly valued, but in corporations this is often a matter of (1) male sponsorship, (2) moving up as a *group*, (3) spending long hours with your group— both in overtime work and in social activities, and (4) gaining seniority. All these customs tend to keep women out of such work and, if they enter it, from advancing. Osako shows how the nuclear family, which has emerged as a viable unit through industrialization, increases women's conflict between responsibilities at home and expectations involved in paid work. What are the similarities between the picture painted by Osako and that by Bourne and Wikler? What are the differences (in opportunities and handicaps) when Japanese and American women are compared? What differences in organization, strategy, and tactics would you expect in the women's movements in the two societies?

A visitor to a Japanese corporation invariably notices that virtually all the women employees in the office look very young, except perhaps the sweepers, who are mostly middle-aged. Women employees in nonmanual occupations commonly work only until they marry or have their first child. In most corporations, they are placed on a career track separate from men and receive differential treatment in task assignment, wages, promotion, and retirement. Even though Japan has undergone remarkable economic development during the last few decades, this condition has not changed.

The economic development, in conjunction with the Allied Occupation, produced a number of significant social changes in Japan, such as complete legal equality between the sexes, improved living standards, and extensive urbanization. Since 1955, the number of women entering college has increased by 300 percent and the female work force in nonagricultural sectors has doubled (Ministry of Education, 1972). At the same time, the proportion of professional and managerial workers in the entire female labor force increased from 3.5 percent in 1955 to 8.6 percent in 1977, while the comparable figures for males changed from 8.5 percent to 12.3 percent. The sex ratio in these occupations also increased from 30.4 percent to 42.0 percent within this period (Japan Census Bureau, 1977).

The present study focuses on the dynamic interaction between sexual inequality [1] and institutional and cultural changes within Japanese society. The major portion of this paper considers how the sexual inequality experienced by Japanese professional women [2] persists, *despite* recent changes or *because* of them. Urbanization, the nuclearization of family, and extensive educational opportunities are some salient features of modern Japan (Reischauer, 1974, 1977; Vogel, 1963).[3] If recent normative and institutional developments are forcing a change in women's professional work experience and status, then we would expect a new direction in the future, unless other counteracting forces arise. But if their experience of inequality and segregation is rooted in the very nature of Japan's modernization, then it is reasonable to expect that the situation will remain stable.

The term "professionals" is used here to include "managers and officials" in addition to "professionals and technicians." Japanese themselves do not distinguish between managers and professionals in their everyday activities, for in the normal career progression, most professionals are eventually promoted to administrative or managerial positions. Therefore, to be precise, the present analysis is about employed professional and managerial women in Japan.

Japanese professional women, as noted, have kept employment patterns largely intact since World War II. College-educated women still continue to retire for marriage and childbirth without later reentering the professional labor force. The labor shortage in the early 1970s encouraged married women to return to work, but usually they were hired as temporary help in production and service sectors (Office of Prime Minister, 1974:180). Consequently, professional women have made little progress; most major companies have continued to exclude women from managerial positions. A government survey reports that 50.1 percent of the firms do not have women at *any* level of supervisory and administrative positions and that only 12.1 percent had at least *one* woman in the section head position or above (Office of Prime Minister, 1974:182). The pattern of sexual segregation as measured by the sex ratios in traditionally female-dominant occupations (for example, nurses, elementary school teachers, dieticians) and male-dominant occupations (for example, physicians, attorneys, architects) has remained virtually *constant* since the 1950s (Japan Census Bureau, 1951–1976).

Why have professional women in Japan failed to achieve greater equality with men despite economic development and sharply expanded participation? The lack of strong career orientation (Benedict, 1946; Norbeck, 1965; Vogel, 1971; Wagatsuma, 1977), inadequate child-care facilities, and protective legislation (Fundanren, 1975; Lebra et al., 1976; Ministry of Labor, 1972) may stand as immediate causes. The present analysis will focus on the conditions in the family and office which not only underlie these immediate causes but also directly affect the working woman's thought and behavior (cf. Boulding, 1976a) Epstein, 1970b).

Method

The data analyzed in this paper are obtained partially from the author's observation and partially from Japanese publications (for example, The Federation of Japanese Teachers Unions, 1975; Kato, 1971; Ministry of Labor, 1972; Office of Prime Minister, 1974; Watanabe, 1973). The author's observation includes: (1) semistructured interviews with thirty-three Japanese women professionals in 1975, (2) research at a large Japanese auto factory (cf. Osako, 1977), and (3) close acquaintance with Japanese businessmen and their families as fellow PTA members at a Japanese language school in Chicago, Illinois. This last group provided the views of professional women held by male colleagues and housewives. Each of the thirty-three interviews, lasting one to three hours, covered aspects of work activities and family relations.[4] The sample was selected to represent a wide variety of occupational and familial backgrounds from the alumni directories of a national university and a public high school the author attended.

The sample consists of nine college professors, eight journalist/editors, six government bureaucrats, three primary school teachers, three physicians, two lawyers, and two others. Their ages range from twenty-six to fifty-five, with a modal age of thirty-six. Among these thirty-three, twenty-six were married (twenty-one with children), five were single, and two were divorced.

Women's Role in the Japanese Family

The traditional extended Japanese family observed patrilineal succession. Since the continuation of the lineage was the family's foremost concern, the bride's most important duty was to provide the family with a male heir (Hsu, 1974). Women in the traditional household actively participated in various phases of production. And the family often regarded the bride more as an additional helper than as the son's companion. She served the family under the guidance of her mother-in-law. A well-known Confucian saying states, "A woman is to obey her father as daughter, her husband as wife, and her son as aged mother."[5]

Urbanization and modernization during the past several decades have brought structural changes to the Japanese family and increased the housewife's authority in domestic decision making. Now a majority of Japanese families (77.3 percent) are nuclear (Fundanren, 1975: 15), and 75.8 percent of the male workers are employed outside the family (Japan Census Bureau, 1975). A large majority of families are no longer economically producing units, and their major functions are reduced to procreation, socialization of children, consumption, and tension management (cf. Parsons, 1949). The differentiation between family and workplace has resulted in increased sexual division of labor: workplace as man's sphere, and home as woman's domain. The typical Japanese salaried man spends long hours away from home in work, socializing with colleagues, and commuting (Vogel, 1963; Wagatsuma, 1977). This custom places an increasingly large domestic responsibility upon the wife's shoulders, since the parents are generally not living with her and, in addition, their influence is rapidly declining. The average Japanese housewife not only has considerable autonomy but also is sure of her importance at home. This discourages her from pursuing a career if it hinders her from being a good mother and wife.

Contrary to the common myth of subservient Japanese women, the middle-class wife in Japan regards her husband as if he were the oldest son, who must be respected but who is not fit to handle delicate matters such as dishes and babies. Especially in the sphere of consumption and child rearing, the wife is entrusted to gather information through media and friends and to make proper decisions, since the husband has little time for them (Vogel, 1963). Thus, a Japanese wife who uncomplainingly serves her husband may appear subservient to Westerners but may feel she is running the home (Reischauer, 1977).

Her sense of well-being and accomplishment is augmented by three additional factors. First, Japanese culture emphasizes the importance of motherhood as a sacred mission. This notion is still widely accepted by today's women. It may be more honored where choices are few, but none of the married professional women interviewed wished not to have children (see also Paulson, 1976). Second, Japanese society values the contribution to collective goal achievement more highly than individualistic achievement (cf. Bellah, 1957). It also credits indirect contributions as much as direct ones. Therefore, a woman is considered more virtuous if she devotes herself to the advancement of other family members (notably sons and husbands) rather than pursuing her own career. Third, Japanese middle-class women can expect to be secure in their familial roles, for the divorce rate has been consistently low since the 1930s (102 divorces per 1,000 marriages in Japan, in contrast to 470 per 1,000 in the United

States; Goode, 1971). In addition, the middle-class husband's stable employment, guaranteed by the practice of job tenure, increases the economic security of the family. For these reasons, many married women do not feel the need to pursue careers to prove their worth or to obtain an independent basis of security.[6]

A competitive entrance examination system places further constraints on married women to remain full-time homemakers (Vogel, 1963, 1977). In Japanese society, a degree from a prestigious university is a license for employment in stable, large, and reputable business establishments. Entrance to a university is based on the applicant's performance on the competitive entrance examination. Children often begin preparing for the examination as early as age five, for the admission to a reputable primary school means a solid education and is likely to lead to select high schools and eventually to good universities. The mother is expected to assume a central role in the child's education, supervising and assisting in homework. A hired hand or a grandparent cannot perform the strenuous task of helping with the children's homework, which may last into the early morning hours. Some professional mothers who are successful survivors of the Japanese examination system decide to leave employment for the sake of their children's future. In contrast to American mothers, who frequently reenter the labor force as the last child starts primary school, Japan's professional mothers have to face another obstacle to their own employment when the first child is about to prepare for the junior high school entrance examination.

How Working Mothers Cope at Home

Despite the conditions inhibiting professional women from employment, a small minority do continue their careers throughout marriage and child rearing. One source estimates their number as 4 percent or less (Women's Bureau, City of Tokyo, 1974). Do these women pursue careers at the cost of foregoing or underemphasizing familial role expectation? The experience of the thirty-three women interviewed sheds some light on the issue since twenty-six were married (twenty-one with children). These women are neither immune to familial problems nor uncommitted to the importance of familial roles. The married respondents widely share the problems of child-care arrangement (78 percent) and older children's homework (30 percent) and face the criticism of in-laws or neighbors (56 percent). Furthermore, all the working mothers mention greater concern with the children's health and school work than do the sample of PTA members not employed. These women said they tried hard to provide adequate care for the children, taking time from their busy schedules to cook hot breakfasts and never missing a school open house.

If they are committed to the cultural emphasis on familial roles, how do they manage dual roles at home and work? The endeavor demands much energy and organization, especially when children are young. An examination of family situations suggests a few consistent patterns. Seventeen of the twenty-one married women with children lived with or near their own parents or in-laws. In a typical arrangement, the grandparents watched the children after the day-care center closed (or the hired nurse left) and shared whatever housework was to be done. No respondent enjoyed the service of live-in help because it was too expensive and her house was too small. When the professional woman's mother was widowed, she was likely to live with the daughter. Some of the older women were hesitant about soliciting parents' or in-laws' help, for however devoted they might be, they were either getting too old for the rigorous job of child care or incapable of supervising a high schooler's homework. However, the majority of the respondents were satisfied with their arrangements and felt that without parental support there was no way to combine dual careers.

A supportive husband appears to be another necessity for the wife's continued pursuit for her profession. Our married sample's spouses were atypical in that they wanted their wives to be professionally active and willingly accommodated themselves to the wife's demanding schedule. Most families practiced a flexible division of labor at home. Chauffeuring the children to the day-care center in the morning and bathing them in the evening were commonly chores of the father.

There is a limit to what respondents could expect from spouses in the way of substantive (in contrast to psychological) support. About two-thirds of the couples were in the same profession. Therefore, except for those in teaching positions, husbands were also in rigid and demanding work schedules. A municipal government employee with two small children confided that when she had to stay up in the office all night, her husband did not mind taking over cooking and child care for two successive nights. Beyond that, he became irritable and the children would have to be taken to the grandparents' home.

In contrast to this group of liberated husbands, our respondents themselves were unexpectedly traditional in certain aspects. They made the point very clearly that the husband's job is *extremely* important. They said they took pains not to disrupt his work performance, even at their own inconvenience. For instance, an editor in a unionized publishing firm where her husband also worked reported that when the child got sick, she stayed home until she used up all her sick leave, and then her husband took over. Women were not embarrassed to report that their husbands took the first bath and received the first serving of rice. The working mothers in our sample, instead of asserting equality with the spouse, were generally grateful to spouses generous enough to let them work. Thus, it is not the women's demands for domestic equality or the rejection of traditional emphasis on motherhood that enabled the couple to continue dual careers.

Women's Role in the Office

The Japanese company is commonly characterized as a community, also as like a kinship group or fraternity, where the members share a strong sense of group identification and diverse extrawork activities (Abegglen, 1958, 1973; Cole, 1971; Dore, 1973). Several features of this kinshiplike organization generally handicap women in their endeavor, particularly in private industries (Abegglen, 1958; Dore, 1973; Nakane, 1970; Osako, 1977).

The Japanese white-collar worker normally starts employment immediately after his graduation from college and stays at the same company until retirement. In this permanent employment system, the employee enjoys economic and psychological security as an integrated member of the factory community. Promotion and wage increase in the Japanese company are primarily based on length of service and only secondarily on merit, especially in the lower and middle strata. Thus, the longer the person works for the company, the higher the status and salary. If he leaves the place of employment, not only are the chances for respectable reemployment small, but he has to start at the bottom of the status-salary ladder.

This condition seriously handicaps women's occupational advancement in two ways. First, they cannot reenter employment with full status once they leave for childbearing. Second, when the husband is transferred, his working wife has virtually no chance to obtain a position equivalent to the one held at her old firm.

The emphasis on group loyalty is another notable feature of the Japanese factory. Loyalty to one's work group, superiors, and the company as a whole are stressed equally. The employee's loyalty to the group is expressed by long working hours and intensive social involvement with colleagues. The employee not only actively participates in a wide array of company-sponsored cultural and recreational activities but also shares many informal social hours with colleagues. Seriously career-minded women are clearly aware of the strategic importance of these hours in exchanging information and cementing social networks. The women surveyed echoed the typical male view that unless a woman plays mahjong and visits bars with male colleagues, she cannot really be a part of the group.

Informal clique networks are another intricate aspect of occupational life that women face. A clique is vertically organized, and with a core unit consisting of a pair of sponsors and their protégé (Halloran, 1972). As a new college graduate enters the office, he is assigned to a section. As he moves through a few positions in the first several years, he cultivates a tie with a potential sponsor who is several years older than himself, a graduate of the same university, and personally compatible. The pair may share the same academic major and hobbies such as mahjong and golf. When promotion time comes for the junior executive, the senior executive informally negotiates for him with the senior's own superiors and colleagues, and he sponsors the junior's promotion to the position within the executive's own division that eventually leads to the junior man's post. The sponsor guides the protégé in work and personal matters, while in return the latter assists in clique politics, work, and private matters. Even wives may form a vertical friendship tie. For instance, the senior executive's wife may recommend a reputable private school (which the former's children attend) to the junior's wife and may serve as an intermediary between the school's admission officer and the junior's family. If everything goes well, the sponsorship, once formed, is nearly permanent.

Unlike the American manager, whose business skill involves a deft shifting of alliance from a declining clique to a rising faction, the Japanese white-collar businessman is expected to stay with the original clique (just as the *samurai* did in feudal society). This pattern encourages a sense of solidarity because members of the clique share a common fate in its rise and fall. When a man does not have a sponsor, his chance for respectable promotion is slim, though he will still enjoy the basic security of a permanent employment system.

It is rare for a woman to find patrons within the upper-echelon staff, who are invariably older males.[7] The patronage tie exists within a group (clique) context, and the patron's concern is to select a protégé who enhances his influence and the clique's solidarity. The risks of picking a protegée (the suspicion of colleagues, weakened solidarity in the clique, uncertainty about her future performance) clearly outweigh the potential benefits. In addition, most office staffs are unsympathetic toward working women, and the pressures from affirmative action programs are nonexistent.

From the woman's perspective, finding a mentor may not be worth the effort, especially if a woman wishes to have children. Since under Japanese law every company has a formal provision for extended maternity and child-care leave, it is technically possible to take leave for a few years, but, as noted, it would be professional suicide. Such an act is interpreted as a lack of commitment to the career and the company. In any case, a leave would sever the sponsor-protegée tie should one exist. Moreover, a leave would bring disgrace to the sponsor, who could be criticized as misjudging his protegée's commitment.

How Women Cope in the Office

This typical Japanese factory structure seems a formidable obstacle to women professionals planning careers. But some determined women do enter certain professions, notably teaching, research, government, and media, and many even continue employment through marriage and childbirth. The interviews with thirty-three professional women and analysis of the literature (Duke, 1973; Ichibangasa et al., 1973; Kato, 1971; Lebra et al., 1976; Thurston, 1973; Watanabe, 1973) indicate that the workers in these fields do not encounter the discrimination common in manufacturing, finance, and trading. Women in teaching, research, government, and media are given job assignments comparable to men's even though, for example, a woman reporter may cover home-related rather than political issues. The base wage for male and female workers with comparable job responsibilities tends to be equivalent, even though the male may receive a somewhat larger salary because of his head-of-household status and specially favorable evaluation (Mouer, 1976). The availability of promotion opportunities varies from one occupation to another. More equality is found in government offices, where the *nenko joretsu* (promotion by the length of service) is strictly observed; opportunity is less equal in the media (Paulson, 1976). In education, very few principals are women, although female teachers' lack of interest in the position is often used to explain the difference rather than discriminatory practice (Mouer, 1976).[8]

Why do these areas provide better opportunity for women than other areas? Despite their seemingly diverse job requirements and organizational structure, they exhibit certain characteristics. These occupations generally require clearly defined skill and allow considerable autonomy in work performance. Skills that permit objective evaluation are found in lower-level teaching and municipal government offices, where standardized examinations are the major basis for promotion to administrative positions.

Further, work organization is only moderately hierarchical, except in the universities and government offices. Typically, the basic unit (school or department) consists of one head (principal, editor-in-chief, or equivalent), one assistant head, and ten to forty regular staff members. Often little status difference exists among nonsupervisory staff, except for length of service. In journalism, for instance, supervisory or administrative positions are not necessarily desired by such staff as television producers and editors.[9] Frequently they do not wish administrative responsibility or hope to become free-lancers. A moderately hierarchical organizational structure, especially in combination with strict observance of *nenko joretsu* and considerable intrinsic job satisfaction, tends to reduce the necessity for collegial competition. Our data suggest that this may be the case for some jobs in teaching, research, government administration, and journalism. This arrangement is favorable for women if one can assume that intense competition for higher status and wages tends to escalate the level of discrimination (cf. Wagley and Harris, 1964).

Conclusion

We began our analysis by asking, has the inequality of Japanese professional women continued *because* of or *despite* recent social changes? We have found that the current status of Japan's professional women is highly consistent with the state of the family and the factory. The Japanese housewife's domestic authority has increased as the family has become more nuclear and the sexual division of labor more explicit (that is, man's sphere at work and woman's place at home). But this trend has not been paralleled by a comparable gain in the occupational sphere. To the contrary, increases in domestic authority have encouraged mothers to stay home. The domestic trend is supported by women's understanding that in the paternalistic company, professional and managerial women's chances for uninterrupted careers and orderly promotion are slim and costly. The firm continues to demand intense loyalty to the group as well as continued service. Partly because of this dismaying situation at the office, only a small minority of women seriously pursue careers in the mainstream of the economy. Persistent sexual inequality (measured by the attainment of organizational status) and sexual segregation are rooted in the very nature of the current Japanese social system.

Despite various obstacles, a small proportion of married Japanese women do pursue careers in the professions and attain relatively orderly advancement. They do so with the help of supportive relatives and by selecting occupations with accommodating working conditions and organizational structures. Will this group of women increase in the future? One way to explore this question is to examine family and industry in a larger social and historical context. The crux of the matter is that Japanese women do not see themselves as victims of sexual inequality. Some middle-class housewives may be discontented with their lives, but they do not regard an occupational career as a viable means to improve their lot. The large majority wish to remain in their place at home. Thus far, women's liberation has never been established as a serious political movement. As a result, there is no effective political group to press the implementation of the equal rights guaranteed in the Japanese Constitution. The traditional management policy of sexual discrimination persists. Pessimism about changes in this trend is warranted. The home-oriented majority are likely to raise their daughters in conformity with conventional sex-role definitions.

Improved child-care facilities may encourage women's work participation. But given the demands of the Japanese office, the regular nine-to-five day-care center cannot adequately meet professional women's needs. Competent live-in help could ease the burden. However, ordinary professionals cannot afford this help because of crowded housing conditions and the wage system. Since Japanese wages are based on length of service more than on technical qualifications, when the woman is young enough to have small children, her and her husband's wages are low.

Problems for working women are exacerbated since Japan, unlike other Asian nations such as the Philippines and India, suffers from a short supply of domestics. The advanced Japanese economy has plenty of openings for women in factories and stores, and the school system provides every child with a full nine years of compulsory education (that is, the attainment of a sufficient aptitude to develop skills required for nondomestic jobs).

What is the theoretical implication of our research, which finds that rapid economic development in the last few decades has not encouraged professional women's active participation in the mainstream of the Japanese economy? Convergence-divergence controversy over the social outcomes of industrialization is a major perspective in sociology (Form, 1969; Moore and Feldman, 1960; Moore, 1964). Those supporting the convergence theory argue that industrialization results in basically homogeneous modern cultures and institutions despite wide variations in indigenous traditions. In contrast, divergence theorists argue that traditional culture significantly affects the processes and consequences of industrial development. Paralleling this disagreement, in the study of women's work activity and economic development, Wilensky (1968) stresses the correlation between the level of development and the pattern of female labor force participation while Langlois and Collver (1962), Youssef (1974), and Clignet (1977) focus on the wide variation in the mode of female work participation among nations with similar degrees of industrialization. The latter group explains the diversity in terms of the nature of family and of industry, which either hinders or encourages women's occupational participation.

Our findings appear to support the divergence theory to the extent that a few decades of economic development have left the traditional patterns of sexual segregation in work intact. Furthermore, the conjecture that economic difficulties such as an energy shortage and recession may force Japanese industry to adapt more rational practices emphasizing technical skills rather than sex or length of service is unlikely to be true. Past economic adversity, such as widespread bankruptcy and unemployment, has increased the exclusion of women from professional and managerial positions because men have the cultural prerogative to support a family.

The application of the convergence-divergence perspective suggests that, however consistent our results seem to be with the divergence theory, there is a possibility that the Japanese situation today is a result of cultural lag, which will be adjusted in the future. The contribution of this research is not so much to add a new piece of evidence to the dispute as to demonstrate that common sociological indices, such as the rate of women's labor force participation and occupational distribution, do not by themselves constitute self-sufficient indices of social behavior. Such indices must be interpreted in their full empirical context, as has been attempted here in the case of Japanese professional women.[10]

Notes

1. Sexual inequality refers to how much men and women differ in prestige, power, and wealth. Sex-based segregation in work and discrepancy in organizational status attainment between male and female are two major indices of sexual inequality in occupation.

2. Occupational categories in the United States and Japanese censuses are highly comparable.

3. In 1975, 75 percent of the Japanese population lived in urban areas; 78 percent of the families were nuclear; and over 90 percent of the teenagers completed at least twelve years of education. The comparable figures for 1955 were 52 percent, 60 percent, and 45 percent, respectively (Japan Census Bureau, 1951–1976).

4. The aspects of work explored include: the job content, salary, fringe benefits, promotion opportunity, office politics, social relations, and the union. In addition, the respondent discussed her relationship with the spouse (affective aspect, division of labor at home, authority dimension), children (social and academic adjustments), relatives (support patterns and emotional relationship), and neighbors.

5. Despite this Confucian teaching, examination of historical evidence suggests that in certain contexts Japanese women enjoyed considerable responsibility and authority in managing family businesses and farms (Goode, 1970).

6. Even though the present paper does not focus on the strains and problems experienced by Japanese housewives, serious problems do exist. For instance, the suicide rate for Japanese women is among the highest in the world (see Cecchini, 1976).

7. Henning et al. suggest that sexual attraction and exploitation are a significant element that the American managerial woman has to deal with in the work organization. However, sexual themes are notably absent in our interviews, as well as in the literature on Japan's professional and managerial women despite the fact that sex is freely discussed in contemporary Japan. Japanese men may have less need and fewer opportunities to treat their female colleagues as sexual objects. Unlike the United States, where men *achieve* masculinity by purposeful action, it is an ascriptive characteristic in Japan (cf. Fiedler, 1968). Thus, Japanese men are not under pressure to prove their masculinity by sexually attracting women. In addition, if a Japanese man wishes to have an extramarital relationship, he can have one with a *geisha* or a bar hostess without incurring serious societal objections. Third, since much of collegial social interaction occurs within a group, an employee has little chance for an individual liaison. The society frowns upon an illicit relationship with an "amateur" woman; if discovered, a sexual relationship with a colleague can damage the careers of those involved. In short, seriously career-minded men can see that the costs of sexual involvement with a female colleague exceed the benefits.

8. We did not have sufficient data to ascertain if lack of interest is the primary reason for the small number of female principals. The principalship is not a popular position in Japan. It involves mostly administrative tasks; it rarely leads to a higher position; the work schedule is very demanding; and the salary is not high enough to compensate for its heavy responsibility.

9. The media involve a wide range of occupational settings. Newspaper, TV, and radio enterprises appear to be more discriminatory against women than companies engaged in journal and book publication.

10. Other references on this topic include Osako (1981) and Plath (1980).

III

Invisible Work:
Unacknowledged Contributions

Generally in our society the capitalist view predominates. "Real work" produces income, and that, characteristically, is what men do. Men dominate the public world, where they produce goods and services with exchange value; women's production of goods and services is for use within the family world. Such home work and the work many women do in and for their communities is unpaid labor. Because it is unpaid, it is devalued; much of it is so taken for granted that it is often not even seen as work.

It is thus not surprising that the actual importance of much of the work women do not only in maintaining a family and a home but also in establishing community life, facilitating interaction within and between families and throughout communities, has still not even been systematically studied. In our society, for example, the work of volunteers is given lip service as honorific, but little attention is really paid to how the society would function in its absence. Women assume most of the responsibility for providing linkages between home and school in organizations like the PTA. Women raise money for the church, welfare, the elderly, and for children's activities, and provide staffing. But the value of that work in our cash-nexus economy and the worth of those who do it are left ambiguous. Like other currently conventional forms of women's work, such as writing family letters, it may be praised but it seldom has exchange value in market terms. It is not figured into such estimations of economic productivity as the Gross National Product. Again, much of community work *is* skilled and requires training. But when fund raising, public relations, and political organizing are done by women in volunteer work, the efforts involved tend to be ignored—considered work that anyone can do in spare time.

137

Elise Boulding (1976c) has called the hidden work that women do the "underside of history." In paying attention to this work here, we have the opportunity to rethink the contribution of women through recorded time. As she notes, in addition to their own special work, more women do work like that of men than is often realized. Women, as we noted earlier, have always been involved in the manufacture and trade of goods, but they have also often participated in political and cultural life. When societies are in upheaval, women, like men, fight, in battles, join migrations, and participate in social movements. Much of this activity was once performed within the household unit, and the family's efforts were attributed to the legally dominant males of the household—even when they were dead or absent. Women managed homes and estates during the Crusades, for example, as agents of their husbands. Because women's work has been understood as part of the contribution to family, church, and society that males plan and direct, it has been relatively easy to overlook or ignore entirely what is seen as only the acceptance of assigned tasks.

If the directly economic work of women can be ignored when they participate with men, it is even more easily ignored when women are independent or isolated. They may be totally self-sufficient (as in some nunneries) or formally sequestered (as in societies that practice purdah); more often, they are informally hidden behind the scenes through custom and tradition. But important work performed exclusively by women, as in medieval convents, has almost been lost to recorded history.

The low esteem in which much of women's work is held often carries over to *any* work they do. When women do work that is similar to that of men, it is so often overlooked and forgotten that women come to expect that their activities will not be acknowledged as work. The stigmatizing consequences of attaching a woman's name to work was recognized by women novelists in the early nineteenth century, for example. They sometimes chose male pen names to avoid the negative appraisals women writers would automatically receive. These women resisted societal expectations about what work was proper for women; yet their use of pseudonyms showed their appreciation of the strength of those expectations. Women artists suffered the same consequences in the patriarchal family system (Greer, 1979: 28–35). Often brothers and fathers would sign the works done by wives and daughters.

In our own times, another arena in which this "stay backstage" pattern appears is politics, where women work behind the scenes to make the visible (male) candidates look good. Women spend hours organizing meetings at which men spend a short time managing the business or speaking to audiences. Margolis (1979) asked why women who were active in local political organizations did not move into public office. She found that male officials did not regard the organizational work of politics that women do as important enough to earn women much of a share of the political rewards or appointments. Women's work behind the scenes may have made the public success of others possible; yet it was a backstage performance and thus easily taken for granted or forgotten by political decision makers.

The value of much of the work that women do has been seen as subordinate for so long that even feminist social scientists, such as Ernestine Friedl (1975), point up the higher status of the work that men more often do. She emphasizes that producing for exchange outside the home is the work which automatically brings higher status in societies throughout the world, because it can mean more control over any surplus above subsistence requirements. The question of why or how this greater degree of discretion is so often acquired by and associated with men has not yet been sufficiently examined.

One general problem in assessing the worth of women's work is that no serious attention has been paid to how their efforts make the accomplishments of men possible. We really do not even have well-established terms to discuss the work not only of reproducing but of maintaining new members of the society, and that of providing the support for those who do paid work at various class levels—although some critical scholars are attempting such analyses (Bourdieu and Passeron, 1977; Eisenstein, 1978; Papanek, 1979). Nor do we have a clear terminology for the work of maintaining society by facilitating and managing the flow of communication. Yet these are activities in which women do most of the work. They are also kinds of work men tend to overlook or undervalue. Because of gender inequality, men are in situations similar to those of the upper class in a class-stratified society. Like the members of the upper class with their servants, men generally do not notice the skill or effort required to maintain their comforts.

Generally men see the value of their own work more readily than that of women. As Boulding argues, when men write the histories of civilizations, they focus on what they see as important, what is easiest for them to remember: the "important" events of the government, economy, and military dominated by men. Social histories have only recently become popular that describe everyday life for the common man and woman (Cott, 1977; Tilly and Scott, 1978). These histories provide the data to refute the notion that women have made no significant contribution to society. But in the recent past, many men and women have shared the view that women's work is not significant—as evidenced in the tone of apology used by women who identify themselves as "just a housewife." This view ignores all the interactional work of maintaining relationships as well as women's important contributions in childbearing, child care, and homemaking.

As we have seen in earlier sections, such distorted perceptions derive partly from the historical movement of production of goods away from the home. Women lost the ability to produce family income or many of the goods once made for family use—with the development of factories, the centralization of labor in cities, and both the opportunity and the need to purchase mass-produced household items. Women continued to labor, but the meaning of *work* in the developing economic system became associated with the opportunity to produce for exchange (see Kessler-Harris, 1981). Such a definition ignores the work which facilitates home life and involves rearing the children and supervising their life in the community.

Chodorow, for example, analyzes the unrecognized work involved in developing gender identity. Building on Freud's theory of the Oedipal complex, Chodorow argues that the whole "sex-gender system" we take for granted is dependent on mothers as the primary nurturers. If this dependency were to change, she suggests, the basic emotional styles of men and women would change. Today men tend to be emotionally dependent on women, while women have learned not to rely on men for emotional closeness. This pattern develops when boys inhibit the expressions of emotion to the first important person in their lives—their mothers—in order to form a male gender identification. Such inhibition is then reinforced because it is required and rewarded in the occupational world where men move as adults. Conversely, because growth for the young girl does not have the same emotional requirements, women can grow up still being participants in the emotional areas of adult life. Thus the first form of hidden work that women do is their work as primary nurturers, with a major influence on the formation of adult personality. The irony is that their work preserves a gender identification system that, as we see in Sattel's and Fishman's articles in this section, inhibits egalitarian relations.

The overly narrow contemporary definition of work also obscures such societal work as the reproduction and training of the sort of labor force that industry and bureaucracy prefer. Kohn (1977) argues that mothers train their children to meet the occupational demands they will face as adults. Middle-class mothers are concerned with the development of self-direction and self-control; working-class mothers expect obedience to externally defined standards. Thus middle-class children learn to work independently, and working-class children are prepared for the close supervision they will find in blue-collar work.

While women's work is often overlooked by the general public, governmental population policies indicate that those in authority at the national level have often recognized women's work in providing "manpower." As the Ryder reading in this section shows, women become politically relevant as reproducers even when individually or collectively lacking legitimate power. When governments see a greater need for armies, for example, abortion becomes difficult to obtain or financial incentives are given to encourage childbearing; but opposite policies are established when there is a surplus of workers. On the issue of child rearing, we should recall Huber's point (in the "Division of Labor" section): biology may dictate that only women give birth, but it is social policy (as enacted in legislation) and cultural mandates (as expressed in the pressures from employers, husbands, and relatives) that assign women the major responsibility for parenting. In fact, women have little option; there are no social supports for alternatives. It is the forces constituting what even social scientists often uncritically call "society" (in a sense implying "we all agree") that require women to be the direct caretakers for children and that designate men as the breadwinners outside the home. Coser's functional analysis shows how the stratification system of our society depends on this use of women's labor for parenting. Educating children to assume their parents' class position involves developing cultural and political attitudes as well as attitudes about work; and much of such education depends upon the mother organizing her children's use of space and time. She supervises their activity and its placement in suitable environments populated with appropriate peers. Middle-class children, for example, are transported to special lessons so that they will develop appropriate cultural interests. At the same time, their mothers try to control peer associations possible in public schools which might encourage values and interests parents do not want their children to have. Thus, Coser argues that what appears as service to the family is also service in the maintenance of the stratification patterns of society.

Coser's functional approach focuses attention on the interdependence of various parts of society—in this case, the way the responsibilities of motherhood reinforce the stratification system. An interactional approach focuses attention on how people understand their part in this system and how they maintain it through appropriate behavior. The articles by Sattel and Fishman provide two ways of examining those interactional processes. They show how daily verbal and nonverbal behavioral exchanges between men and women selectively emphasize patterns of dominance for men and submission for women, and so reinforce a sex stratification system which helps maintain the current invisibility of much work women do.

Sattel challenges the view of theorists like Chodorow, who say that men are incapable of emotional expressiveness. He argues that men can selectively use both expressiveness and inexpressiveness to maintain their power—in work situations and in sexual relations. Women teach men how to be more expressive, but men also learn to use their inexpressiveness to shield their intentions, cover their weaknesses, and gain time for reflection and decision making. Both expressiveness and inexpressiveness can thus become assets in gaining or asserting power over others. The dominant man can force the other to accept his terms or to take responsibility for the breakdown of the interaction. As the invisibility of much of their work suggests, women are likely to acquiesce in this arrangement, partly because of their training, which stresses that they should be supportive and obliging, and partly from fear of abandonment in a society where it is difficult for women to survive on their own. Acquiescence is also encouraged by the higher evaluation of women who are linked to men.

In the communication patterns that Fishman studied, we watch women work hard to maintain conversation. Men often ignore (and so redirect) women's efforts in this social interaction; women continue to search for topics that men will accept. Conversely, women respond to almost any topics raised by men, even when those topics require an abrupt change in direction. Thus, men define where interactional work shall be focused, but women put forth the effort to assure that it occurs and continues.

Ryder's analysis of how societies depend upon women to bear and rear children, Coser's study of women's work in status placement and maintenance, and the interactional work studied by Sattel and Fishman all bring out evidence of women's invisible work. This work has been relatively easy to ignore from the male perspective; it is not men's work, nor will it directly produce income. The larger significance of women's work often becomes visible only when there is a breakdown in the status-role system that allocates different functions to men and women. Earlier, in the reading by Coser and Rokoff, we saw how conflicts arise when mechanisms of status articulation break down. When gender stereotypes about the division of labor are maintained, the system works smoothly for those with the most power in the larger society; women's work in maintaining the larger society remains invisible. For example, women's work makes it possible for men to devote their time to paid work, while women provide the household services on which workers (and their employers) depend.

But when women enter the larger economy and so cannot provide the expected (though hidden) maintenance services to the society through their work in the family, the system breaks down and the formerly invisible work is revealed.

The societal acceptance of what Hanna Papanek (1973) has called the "two-person career" becomes clear when a husband and wife strive to maintain a dual-career family. As Hunt and Hunt point out in the final reading in this section, the trials and conflicts such a couple must face raise many of the issues posed earlier in this section by Ryder. When both members of a couple want paid careers outside the home, no one remains behind to provide comforting and supporting services required by the demands of professional work. This situation can put both persons at a competitive disadvantage. For example, shared parenting handicaps both men and women in their career. They cannot devote the expected time or emotion to their work—the time and emotion that men who do *not* share parenting can give. Egalitarian expectations for dual careers (Berger et al., 1978) may also founder because of the difficulties of finding two good positions when one partner must move for career reasons. Today many young women expect that equality of opportunity in the labor market will make it possible for them to combine home and family, not just with "paid jobs" but with professional careers. Hunt and Hunt find that the experience of those who have tried this alternative shows how difficult it is for a dual-career *family* to meet the demands made on individuals by the male clockwork of professional careers.

These problems are compounded by familiar, if currently challenged, social expectations that the man's job is more important for the family welfare and for his ego. Even those who begin with egalitarian aims may consequently be pressed into the model in which the husband's work comes first and the wife works around her household responsibilities. Very similar problems are part of everyday life in working-class families, where women may have similar aspirations but much less cultural support for them and much less social support for child and home care, except when relatives are available (Ota, 1980).

The Future of American Fertility

NORMAN B. RYDER
Princeton University

9. Origins. Ryder, showing that there is a continuing decline in fertility, explains why this should be the case and worries about the social consequences if the trend continues. He reasons that "our past success at population replacement . . . has been conditional on the discriminatory treatment of women." He suggests that many women, finally given the choice to earn the prestige and authority derived from paid work, will find child care comparatively unrewarding. Invisible work in the family can be less appealing than visible work in the marketplace, with its rewards in social status and income. While no society can continue without replenishing the population, Ryder believes that individual choices are preferable to governmental policies, although he suggests that our society may have to consider paying women to stay home and rear children. Can you think of alternative social policies to solve the interrelated problems Ryder notes in his identification of historical patterns and predictions of future trends? Both Huber and Ryder argue that demographic (and historic) variables have influenced women's press for equality. Because of these changes, they argue that the women's movement cannot be reversed. What do you think? Why?

In every society, the family is the institution charged with responsibility for replacement of the population. In premodern times, high mortality made that a very large responsibility indeed, but our survival as a species shows that the traditional family proved adequate to its assignment. It is beginning to look as if the modern family is not.

I want now to suggest some characteristics of change in the family during the course of modernization which may be the source of the problem. In premodern times, the family was the basic unit in the economy. The head of the family was by virtue of that fact the owner and the employer. To the individual member, the family represented the source of technical education, the avenue of employment, the channel of credit and social security, and the source of protection and defense. The gravity of the responsibilities of the traditional family were manifest in its authoritarian structure, specifically, the power of parent over child and male over female. In the community at large, the most important piece of information about a person was his or her family name. The family indeed has been the foundation of all systems of ascribing status on the basis of characteristics fixed at birth, and thus of stratification systems, whether they are oriented to caste or race.

How different it is with the modern family. One by one, its functions have been shifted to the specialized institutions characteristic of the developed society. The father is no longer the source of land or other capital, or the person under whom one could serve an appropriate apprenticeship. The head of the family can no longer act as if he owned his wife and children. The intrusion into the family structure of an ideology emphasizing the individual has diluted respect and gratitude alike. The parents can no longer control the marriage of their child, nor indeed is it important to them that they do so. The new calculus of production emphasizes not who a person is but what he or she can do, and that in turn depends more on one's individual accreditation in educational institutions, controlled not by the family but by society.

Fertility was once high for a simple reason: the productivity of the child accrued to the benefit of the parent. But then the fundamental direction of obligation in the intergenerational contract shifted from what the child owed the parent to what the parent owed the child. As the benefits of children to parents approached the zero point, the costs of children to parents rose, without an apparent ceiling to date. Is it any wonder that fertility fell? Indeed, a more interesting question is what might stop it from falling.

Those who view the modern family with alarm are apt to emphasize its conjugal aspects. For example, there is great concern about the prevalence of divorce, and indeed, this has grown to disconcerting proportions. Yet it seems to me that frequent divorce is the understandable consequence of making the satisfaction of the individual the test of a good marriage. The burden of proof has shifted from what the individual can do for the family to what the family can do for the individual. Yet I doubt that the frequency of divorce is a distinctive signal of the disintegration of the marital institution. As the family was stripped of its economic and political responsibilities, it too became a specialized institution, specialized in the development and maintenance of the individual self. In a modern society, the individual has greater need for emotional support, and the conjugal family is more exclusively the source of that support. The family provides an emotional haven to comfort individuals on their return from exposure to the frequently damaging consequences of participation in the impersonal, competitive modern economy. One testament to the continuing importance of marriage as an institution is the alacrity with which most divorced persons choose to remarry, as a vote of confidence in the institution which has failed them only in particular.

A second example of concern with conjugal aspects of the family is the growing practice of young people living together without taking vows, a practice my generation views with antipathy or at least unease, as well as a covert admixture of envy. I think the young are making a mistake if they consider sex to be an appetite which can be adequately satisfied without a sense of commitment—they are denying themselves the fullness of the experience—but I seriously doubt that their experimentation is a threat to the idea of marriage. As a companionate institution, marriage will survive, if only because the individual has such a need for it. The risks and loneliness of an uncommitted life are too evident and too large.

What concerns me most about the modern family are not these conjugal aspects—for such problems, no matter how perplexing, are essentially irrelevant to the reproductive issue—but its generational aspects, the other dimension of the family. To be explicit, I think the child has come to mean rather little to the parent today, and the parent rather little to the child. The generations were once bound together by concern of the parent for the child and respect of the child for the parent, a concern and respect that were solidly embedded in the importance of each for the future of the other. But now almost the only bond is love, and that tends to be fragile and brittle.

There was a time when parents assumed total responsibility for the socialization of the child, but now the traditional functions of the family are passing out of the home and into the hands of professional providers. Perhaps the most important institutional encroachment was the compulsory public school, but parents have also been displaced by doctors and nurses, community workers, playground leaders, probation officers, and psychiatrists. As responsibility for the child is shifted from the parents to the agencies, the ties between parent and child are weakened. It is almost as if the child is too important to the society to be left to the parents. Society has a large stake in a healthy, educated, and socially conforming child, and inept parents cannot be allowed to stand in the way.

Perhaps the principal reason for the recent decline in fertility is the possibility now gradually opening for women to derive legitimate rewards in the pursuit of activities other than motherhood. At considerable risk of oversimplification, I would assert that our past success at population replacement, throughout all of human history, has been conditional on the discriminatory treatment of women. If we are now prepared to consider this as fundamentally inequitable, and are ready to respect the woman who chooses a nonmaternal way of life, we may be pulling out the prop that has all along made possible our survival as a species. Although I am apprehensive about the consequences, I believe we must accept them, because it is meet and right and proper for women as well as men to be self-determining persons.

Despite the evidently inferior positions to which we still assign women in the occupational sphere, the labor force now has only one-third fewer women than men. Although some may be propelled into a job by family financial problems, others are unwilling to remain trapped at home with the children and the housework. The word is out that the satisfactions of raising children require more personal sacrifices by women than by men. Women are now entering the marketplace with greater confidence, expanding their social circles beyond that of their husbands' friends, and experiencing more independence. Those who remain housewives now feel obliged to apologize. Being a wife and a mother is no longer an occupation sufficient unto itself. And the plain fact is that working and mothering are competing activities. As women gain access to the full range of educational and professional opportunities—and they still have far to go—the alternative opportunity cost of reproduction will rise and press fertility further downward. This is the final frontier of modernization—the elimination of discrimination by gender.

In summary of this account of the present family, I believe that there is less satisfaction from parenthood today, and there are alternative modes of living which appear preferable to a significant proportion of young women. This is not to predict that many will decide against parenthood, but rather that enough will exercise a legitimate option to keep fertility low. Simply speaking, we should be prepared for population size to decline.

Imperceptibly but inexorably, the population of the future will come to differ in many important respects from anything we have known (Ryder, 1975). Before touting what I think some of those differences will be, two points need to be made clear. First, the propositions to be advanced do not depend on complete acceptance of what I have so far been saying; they hold within a rather broad range of fertility forecasts. Second, the problems to be advertised are not new; they are all with us now. The point of the exercise is not that new problems will be created by prospective demographic change, but that old problems will be exacerbated by it.

The first fact about the new world ahead is that our population will be much older than it is now. In particular, the proportion of people who are above age 65 will approximately double. This prospect has already aroused considerable concern about the financing of social security, for example. When the problem of supporting a dependent population is raised, it is not always recognized that while elder dependents will increase, younger dependents will decrease. The total quantitative burden (to use the ugly jargon word) on those of working age will not change. Still, the transformation of the family institution has long since produced a more evident and perplexing quandary: what is the most fitting and humane social setting for old people? I wish I could provide an answer.

An associated fact about the world to come is that the working population itself will be older. What does that signify? The typical commentary asserts, with little solid evidence, that an older work force will be a less productive one. Younger workers are considered superior in strength, speed, and energy, whereas older workers are given the edge in skill, dependability, and wisdom. Such tradeoffs seem more reasonable, of course, to each cohort as it gets older. More worrisome than such cross-sectional considerations, in my view, is the fact that age signifies time of birth, and thus the historical location of one's training. Perhaps the most sensible way to solve that problem would be for us to shake off the shibboleth that all education must precede all labor force participation. Why should we not contemplate opening the doors between the world of work and the world of education throughout the entire life span?

The problems of the productivity of an older workforce have their parallel in the question of the willingness of older entrepreneurs to take risks. Just as older workers tend to be less flexible and less mobile, because they have more to lose from change—they have paid off more of their mortgage—so older entrepreneurs may tend to err on the safe side, to the detriment of initiative and innovation. Maybe that is a valid generalization about the attributes of age, but maybe it just reflects the sociological truism that older persons, like everyone else in an ascribed system, tend to behave in the ways they are expected to behave. Until more and better research is done on the subject, we should withhold judgment. Moreover, organizations need not be intimidated by the seniority principle. Surely, we can find ways of transferring leadership and power from the older to the younger members of organizations without sacrificing altogether the assets those older members represent, perhaps by putting a strict time limit on tenure in high office. The one proposed answer to the problem of the older work force with which I am least in sympathy is the Procrustean solution of lowering the retirement age. In my opinion, retirement is a major cause of death.

Furthermore, there is reason to doubt that the principal issue for the future is whether we will be sufficiently productive. Indeed, in a sense, we are already overproductive. We no longer need the work of youth, any more than we need the work of the old, or of women, or of the depressed minorities. Yet to say that our society can afford the luxury of idleness does not mean that the individuals themselves can. In a society in which work gives meaning to life, obligatory idleness is less a privilege than a curse. The challenge of our future is much less to increase productivity than to find meaningful roles for all of our citizens.

It seems to me that the most important socioeconomic implications for the future lie in what may be called the processual rather than the structural characteristics of the population. There are only two ways in which a population can be transformed—by some process in which its constituent members assume different characteristics, and by the replacement of individuals of one kind by individuals of another kind. The latter mode of transformation I have termed "demographic metabolism" (Ryder, 1975). The evidence is strong that the technological evolution of developed societies has been accomplished mainly by the recruitment of members of new cohorts, i.e., by metabolism, rather than by the retraining of the members of old cohorts. Of course, personnel turnover in itself is not important. What matters is the opportunity that turnover provides for modification of the system of role allocation and the socialization of entrants. Just like any other population, the working population has a kind of birth rate, i.e., rate of entry into it. With the shift from a growing to a declining population, the birthrate of the labor force will decline by some 40 percent. The problem, in principle, applies to all organizations—political, cultural, social, and educational. One of the ways we try to keep our research institutions alive is by linking them with graduate education, in the belief that the continual infusion of fresh young minds will invigorate the enterprise. If comparable possibilities become substantially more scarce, it is incumbent upon us to devote much more attention than now to recruitment, selection, and training so that we may maximize the efficacy of demographic metabolism, as well as enlarge the opportunities for those already within the system to improve their credentials and refresh their education, to help compensate for more sluggish turnover.

The final point concerning the implications of low fertility is the most obvious one: the population will be smaller than it would otherwise have been. There has been a large amount of literature, some of it credible, concerning the relationship between population size, on the one hand, and resources and the environment, on the other (Ryder, 1973). I would be more cheered by the prospect were I not convinced that the problems of most concern are rooted elsewhere than in the sheer numbers of people. But rather than alienate the considerable numbers of zealots on such questions, let me concede that the task of solution by whatever means will be easier if there is less population growth.

I have been presenting an assessment that population decline is a likely prospect, and that it will highlight institutional flaws for which we must find institutional rather than demographic remedies. Is there an acceptable demographic solution to the problems posed by population decline? One logical option would be to restrict access to the means of fertility regulation, for example, by passing legislation against sterilization and abortion and banning the production of the oral contraceptive. In my view, such actions, even if they could be enforced, would be politically and morally regressive. The issue is not survival willy-nilly, but survival of what we believe in. Would it not be tragic if, in an attempt to preserve our population size, we so departed from our ideals that what persisted was not worthy of preservation? Similarly, if my diagnosis is correct that the crucial source of low fertility is the newfound women's freedom, then, in theory, men could save the day demographically by ordering women back to the kitchen. Would we really prefer to live in such a world? Measures which improve the quality of life of individuals—such as freedom of fertility regulation and freedom from discrimination on the basis of gender— should surely be pursued even if they exacerbate prevailing population trends.

Because the society has such a large stake in the production of sufficient numbers of new members, it would seem appropriate that the society assume a larger share in the cost of bearing and rearing children. Efforts in this direction have been tried, and they have been to little avail so far as the birthrate is concerned. I see no evidence from the research to date that suggests that if people only had higher incomes they would surely have more children. In brief, I don't think we can buy babies. One encourages fertility with family benefits, geared to birth orders above two, and help to mothers in combining a job with family responsibilities. One cannot easily combine working and mothering under the rules of full days and full weeks of work; perhaps we need new ways of working. The price for sustaining a replacement level would undoubtedly be high, and the magnitude of the income transfer sufficient to inspire a taxpayers' revolt. The problem is that one occupation, that of housewife and mother, is now very low paid, and the nonmaterial rewards are apparently insufficient to compensate for the low pay. Is the government prepared to guarantee an annual wage to the housewife/mother?

The public authorities may not be able to exert an appreciable influence on the level of fertility. Although economic hardship may balk a few people in their desire for more children, others have different reasons they consider overriding and decisive. If a program of income transfer would suffice to raise fertility, it would seem to follow that a general rise in income would have the same effect. But there is no historical evidence that this is true except in the short run.

It is possible to counteract population decline by immigration, but nearly all countries cherish the idea of a one-culture nation-state. Although this was the way America was populated, we have not yet learned, nor have most comparable countries, how to manage decently a multicultural society. With large income differences between wealthy and poor nations, there will be a strong migratory pull on the developing countries, so that we could set high qualifications on entry. But that would make high the cost to the sending country. The populations of labor-exporting countries are disadvantaged if they are deprived of their more vigorous and qualified elements. Immigration can offset main structural rigidities of the labor force in the short term, at the lower levels of the economic hierarchy deserted by the domestic work force, but it entails serious social tensions. I have a long-run vision of a world in which national boundaries become progressively permeable, to the point of erosion of the very concept of a nation-state, so that some day every child born into the world is looked on as our child—but I recognize that to be a utopian contribution to a realistic policy discussion.

It does seem unlikely that any nation would long tolerate a negative rate of natural increase. I read recently in the *New York Times* a warning by the President of France to his countrymen that no nation with a middle-sized population could realistically aspire to grandeur. The article continued with what I take to be their operational definition of grandeur. It was observed that, in the Napoleonic era, France had three times as many people as Britain. Population stimulants are associated with raising armies and the Nazi era. Thus, although France may dare to call for subsidization of larger families by appeal to French nationalism and the nation's military credibility, there is squeamishness about such exhortations in West Germany. The apprehensions go beyond national boundaries. Similar thinking produces the warning that the West may soon be hopelessly outnumbered by the Third World, and such a disparity in size will create a dangerous political imbalance. This is a primitive logic, but it is a prevalent political reality, which probably plays an implicit part in the demographic philosophy of many national leaders.

Past population policy pressed the cause of what were perceived to be collective interests over what individuals were clearly signaling was in their interest. In my view, the burden of proof is squarely on the government to make an unequivocal case for such collective interests relative to individual well-being. Governments are ambivalent about population size and the rate of growth. They know the case that can be made for reduction of growth as an aid in solving the problems of resource depletion and environmental pollution. For all the apprehension about the negative consequences of a stationary or declining population, there are positive consequences as well, and I have been arguing at many points here that the negative ones are more likely to respond to institutional than to demographic remedies.

The past history of governmental action in the field of fertility has been pronatalist—especially through inhibiting individual access to satisfactory fertility regulation—but individuals and families proceeded in an antinatalist direction nevertheless. What is happening to our fertility now is mostly based on the choices people are making about how they can best achieve an optimum quality of life in the prevailing circumstances. I propose that governments treat such choices with the respect they deserve.

In conclusion, then, I think we are in for a considerable demographic transformation, but not one to be feared. I doubt that governments are able to modify the trend of fertility more than marginally, provided they can be restrained from regressive measures. And I doubt that they should even if they could—because the people know what they are doing.

Stay Home, Little Sheba: On Placement, Displacement, and Social Change

ROSE LAUB COSER

State University of New York at Stony Brook

10. Current Expectations. Coser reiterates a theme suggested in the readings by Huber and Ryder—that the most radical and far-reaching demand of the Women's Movement is availability of full-time child care. It would free women for demanding work commitments by no longer requiring them to be at home. Such day care is expensive and may be possible only if national economic priorities are altered—as part of a radical reorganization of society. Could such a restructuring of our society arise in part *because* in the present system it *is* women who still have most of the everyday responsibility for transmitting social class expectations to children? What will happen to the family if women do have the same freedom of movement as men? How could the allocation of parental roles be revised to make this freedom possible? Is it possible to make major alterations in parental roles without making parallel changes in the economic and political system?

The possibility for radical change in America was considerably delayed when Richard Nixon killed two measures in December, 1971, and June, 1972, respectively: the busing of school children and federal support for child-care centers. Different as they are, both programs could have been important instruments for radical change in American society by altering the social placement function of the American family.

The first program, busing, could undermine the stratification system by disturbing an important mechanism for keeping children within the strata in which they are born. This mechanism maintains the insulation between social classes provided by residential segregation. The second program, child care outside the home, would weaken the intensity of social control by giving mothers the chance to pursue other activities and encourage their occupational commitment. That is, these programs would have permitted the relocation of people in social space so that their role relations would become crucially restructured. Busing would permit children to move to schools away from the neighborhoods where they live; child-care centers

153

would give mothers the option of movement to activities not available at home base.

The use of physical space is typically linked to the regulation of social relations. In the specific cases I have mentioned, if two measures, busing and child-care centers, were to become an important part of the American way of life, much of the social placement function would be taken out of the family's hands.

Up to now, the family's most important function in society has been the placement of its members. The husband-father determines the social status of the family members through his occupational status, and the wife-mother executes the social placement function through her control over scheduled activities at home and away from home. The family chooses, and mother supervises, the processes of gatekeeping and traffic direction for the children. These processes begin at an early age to ensure that the children will move on controlled tracks.

A key to this gatekeeping function is the assurance of predictability about the whereabouts of the family members. This is not peculiar to modern society. Every society controls the spatial movements of its members. Questions such as "Where have you been?" "When will you be home?" and "How long will it take you?" belong to the daily language of family life. As long as children go straight to school from home, or straight home from school; as long as the husband comes straight home from work; as long as the wife comes straight home to fix the family meal, all is well. If there is a time lag between the place of work and the home, people must account for themselves: the executive was at a meeting, the child had a piano lesson or went to see a friend, the husband had to see a customer, the wife was detained in church or other community activities. (For her to be detained at work, by the way, would usually not be quite legitimate, for her work is not supposed to interfere with her family obligations.) We must account for our travels; they are not a matter of exclusive personal concern.

The spatial movements of children, their maternal control, and the control of the controllers are what is at stake in busing and in child-care centers. Removing children from home territory arouses social anxiety because adults feel they may lose control over their children.

This is how we must understand Nixon's statement, when he vetoed the child-care bill on December 9, 1971, that child-care provisions would "commit the vast moral authority of the national government to the side of communal approaches to child rearing against the family-centered approach. Good public policy," he continued, "requires that we enhance rather than diminish both parental authority and parental involvement with children." Senator Strom Thurmond (R., S.C.) said that the bill would allow the federal government to "mold the characters of our nation's young" (Facts-On-File, 1971).[1]

To be sure, Nixon did not literally mean parental involvement; he meant, of course, *maternal* involvement. There is little objection to men having occupations that demand travel and becoming truck or taxi drivers, pilots, or traveling salesmen. Only a few female occupations that take women far from home are regarded as proper, and these are typically short-term jobs. The youthful appearance of stewardesses, while meant to emphasize their appeal as sex symbols, is even more important as a symbol of the transitory status of the young woman, one that is acceptable before but not during motherhood. A mother belongs at home, not on the road or in the air.

The mother at home and the father on the move—this arrangement maintains the stratification system. It is through the mother, who gives primacy to the place of residence, that the kinship system is integrated with the stratification system, much as the local public school (or the private school) helps maintain the social placement function of the family. This arrangement would be seriously hampered by both busing and child-care centers. Giving children a residentially segregated education and keeping the mother at home fulfill the same function and reinforce each other. With the mother in control of the family and the local school limiting the geographical radius of the children's movements, the social network of the children can be controlled as well, so that their values, their tastes, and their internal dispositions will be prepared for later adult roles that will not depart too much from those of their parents.

Stability of place is an important condition for role enactment, while displacement in space carries with it the strong possibility of status change. Geographical displacements had better not go uncontrolled, for they imply status uncertainty. Therefore all traveling, whether it be short- or long-distance, has to be patterned in such a way that it will not interfere with the existing pattern of role relationships; and if it is to help change role relationships, the change has to take place in an orderly way. If not, displacement is tantamount to invasion and conquest of alien territory, and to liberation for those who are so engaged.

This is what busing, and the freeing of women to go where they please, is all about. The type of new associates busing provides is unpredictable and is therefore feared to be undesirable for the children as well as for the parents. This travel is seen as a revolutionary activity; it arouses social and political disapproval.

The opportunity to travel, like all opportunities, is not randomly distributed. First, there is, of course, the simple problem of resources. Access to means of transportation, as to other resources, is differentially distributed. Plane travel enables the well-to-do to travel far afield in the search for jobs, while those who do not even have access to a car may be literally mobility blocked or without a job. Elliot Liebow shows this in *Tally's Corner* when he tells us:

Many of the nonunion jobs are in suburban Maryland or Virginia. The
newspaper ads say, "Report ready to work to the trailer at the intersection of Rts. 11 and Old Bridge Rd., Buston, Virginia (or Maryland)," but
this location may be ten, fifteen or even twenty-five miles from the Car-
ryout. Public transportation would require two or more hours to get
there, if it services the area at all. Without access to a car or to a car-pool
arrangement, it is not worthwhile reading the ad. So the men do not.
(Liebow, 1967: 44)

The transportation system could fruitfully be studied from the point of
view of its class-maintaining arrangements, as did Linda Hunkins in New-
ark, New Jersey (1973). But here I shall limit myself to opportunities for
travel that do not directly derive from material resources. Some occupations have built into them the opportunity for extending the role set,[2] and
such extension in itself is likely to encourage growth. It is well known that
organisms that reach outward have more survival value than organisms
dependent only on the immediate environment. Whether we compare
shellfish with mammals, or the newborn with a baby that can walk, or the
self-sufficient small farm with the large farming enterprise, always it is the
case that interdependence with other organisms creates increased opportunities for survival and growth. The extension of the role set for an individual, that is, the addition of new role partners,[3] assures an expansion of
activities and is the source of subtle or not so subtle rewards. A trip to a
conference, or to a lecture, makes the academic person known and therefore leads to invitations to more conferences, more lectures, and even job
offers that can either be accepted or used to bargain for better rewards on
the present job. The opportunity to travel within one's occupation enhances the person's value on the occupational market (cf. Sieber, 1974).

Opportunities to travel are not distributed randomly. In addition to
mere access to means of transportation, opportunities to travel are often
built into the high rungs of the occupational ladder in business or in the
professions. Industrial workers, or others in low ranks, secretaries, nurses,
carpenters, or shoemakers, do not have these opportunities. The Matthew
effect,[4] which refers to the biblical wisdom that to those who have shall
be given, means that inequality is cumulative in the sense that opportunities themselves generate new opportunities. The opportunity that comes
with traveling in relation to one's occupation is only one example among
many of the cumulative impact of inequality.

Inequality is not simply a condition similar to that of a race, in which
some people start the race later than others. It is similar to a race in which
some people have a handicap that puts them farther behind with every
move. Not only are the possibilities for the extension of one's role set, and
hence for the multiplication of occupational opportunities, reserved to elite
occupations; ipso facto, they are reserved to men. Women are largely de-

prived of this type of traveling opportunity because they rarely participate in the elite professions. They maintain, at home, the family as a permanent institution by remaining available to its members, including the traveling husband-father when he returns. By remaining home, women give stability to lives that are much disrupted by frequent travels and the formation of ephemeral—though useful—relationships.[5] Women provide the stable pole in the flux of events. If women were to join men in the elite professions, they would be as free as men to move about, to seize opportunities to address meaningful audiences, to establish potentially profitable relationships. But their restriction of horizontal movement means restriction of upward mobility; it means restriction of opportunities. To remove this restriction from women would mean to weaken their guardianship of the home. If women really had full equality of opportunity with men, the family as an institution, while probably not disappearing, would cease to be what it has been so far.

Such a radical change in the structure of the family would help bring about a radical change in the structure of society because the displacement of women from the home would seriously jeopardize the social placement of the family's members. Nixon may well be right that child-care centers would give women the opportunity to move about freely, and would create a more communal way of life than individualistic Americans have so far envisaged.

The opportunity to travel with the purpose of expanding the role set is also afforded through the institution of busing school children, but in this case, the nature of new associations is unpredictable, and if predictable, undesirable. The manifest purpose of busing is to bring about racial integration, in order to counteract residential segregation with its concomitant racial segregation. But it is precisely residential segregation that helps maintain the class system, for it is through such segregation that the interactional network is controlled, especially for the children. In American society, propinquity provides a claim to interaction at the same time as it provides an obligation to interact. Children provide much of the opportunity for this interaction. PTA, Cub Scouts, and Brownies are some of the institutions that pull the parents, especially the mothers, out of their homes, at the same time restricting them to the community. If neighbors within a certain radius in a middle-class community did not interact with one another on behalf of their children, years could go by in many of our urban or suburban areas without next-door neighbors even seeing each other for more than an occasional hello. Hence, by busing children out of a middle-class community, much opportunity for community interaction is lost. Also, the new contacts the other school provides are not of one's choosing, and they are unpredictable or undesirable. As to the children who are bused into the middle-class community, if they should become integrated—which is, after all, the purpose of the whole procedure—they would interact with the middle-class children, whose parents would then have to relate to these new friends of their own children. But these new friends come from a social class that the middle-class parents have not chosen as a preferred social context for their own children's socialization. While busing provides the opportunity for the underprivileged to extend their role set through integration, it creates status anxiety on such a large scale that it becomes a political issue.

The Supreme Court affirmed the importance of residential segregation on July 24, 1974, when it ruled that the busing of school children be limited within school districts. About four months earlier, on March 31, there was another ruling in which the Court upheld the constitutionality of a Long Island village ordinance prohibiting more than two people unrelated by blood, marriage, or adoption from occupying a one-family house, thus preventing students from obtaining rental in an area that is zoned for one-family living. These two rulings, taken in conjunction, exemplify a policy for the prevention of territorial invasion. Spatial movement is controlled to provide reasonable assurance that territoriality will remain integrated with the stratification system.

Like other opportunities for spatial movement, the opportunity to travel is socially patterned not to interfere with the class structure. In Parsons' terms, it contributes to pattern maintenance. Where traveling away from home threatens the class structure, it creates social disruption. The community rallies to put people back in their place by stating that children belong to their parents' residential radius—conveniently forgetting that the children of the rich have always been "bused" away to private schools for the sake of social-class exclusiveness. But busing the children of the poor becomes a threat to those who extoll the American way of life, and who are also likely to maintain that women belong in the home. Hence child-care centers, which would permit women to move out of the home for more than three or four hours a day, also become a threat to those who extoll the American way of life. Better stay home, little Sheba.

I have chosen the issues of child-care centers and busing to demonstrate that seemingly small changes in the pattern of daily life may well help produce radical social change. Sociologists know that the strength of a social value is measured by the reaction of others when it is in danger of violation. The strong negative reaction of the public and of the Nixon administration to such measures as child-care centers or the response of the Reagan administration to busing children testifies to the radical implication of these seemingly minor issues.

Notes

1. Almost three years later, on September 6, 1974, President Ford "told the heads of 16 of the nation's best-known women's organizations that he had 'serious reservations about the desirability of creating a program of government-financed child-care centers' " in spite of the fact that he "reiterated his support for the Equal Rights Amendment" and "his commitment to search actively for women to fill appointive positions" (*New York Times,* Sept. 7, 1974).

2. These variables—observability, control, and involvement—are the ones, it will be recognized, that Merton uses in formulating the mechanisms through which "roles in the role-set become articulated so that conflict among them becomes less than it would otherwise be" (Merton, 1968: 425–430).

3. Cf. "Libidinal diffusion is the social cement which binds living entities together. The more objects an individual can cathect at once, the larger the number of individuals who can cooperate in a joint endeavor. Furthermore, as libido becomes further diffused, and gratification becomes less complete, the individual experiences a constant tension and restless energy which can be harnessed to serve socially useful ends" (Slater, 1974b: 111).

4. For an application of this principle to the world of science, see Merton, 1973: 439–59.

5. The Israeli sociologist Rivka Bar-Joseph (1974) reports that during the 1973 Yom Kippur War, Israeli soldiers at the front were heard to say that they like the idea of having a woman at home who maintains the home for their return.

The Inexpressive Male: Tragedy or Sexual Politics?

JACK W. SATTEL
Normandale Community College

11. Consequences. Sattel sees male inexpressiveness as a statement about who holds power in the relationship between men and women. He points out that men are inexpressive only when they want to be. They *can* learn expressiveness and use it to attract their wives or other women. Where social interaction is valued, this inexpressiveness is a strategy that forces women to do the work of understanding men. Women draw men out, helping them express emotions; or women must do the work of expressing men's feelings for them. In Sattel's view, men may even use their alleged inability to be expressive as a strategy for requiring women to take on the responsibility of teaching men how to be expressive—or communicative—about their emotions. He argues that this strategy may become yet another kind of work that is women's responsibility. Do you have any experience of your own to support or contradict Sattel's contentions? What are the conditions under which men are most and least likely to use women to express emotions?

In this brief essay, I am concerned with the phenomenon of "male inexpressiveness" as it has been conceptualized by Balswick and Peek (1971). In their conceptualization, male inexpressiveness is seen as a culturally produced temperament trait which is learned by boys as the major characteristic of their forthcoming adult masculinity. Such inexpressiveness is evidenced in two ways. First, adult male behavior which does not indicate affection, tenderness, or emotion is inexpressive behavior. Second, and somewhat differently, behavior which is not supportive of the affective expectations of one's wife is inexpressive behavior. It is the latter variety of inexpressiveness which occupies the major concern of Balswick and Peek. They suggest that the inability of the American male to unlearn inexpressiveness in order to relate effectively to a woman is highly dysfunctional to the emerging standards of the companionate, intimate American marriage. Ironically, Balswick and Peek see inexpressiveness in contexts outside the marriage relationship as functional insofar as in nonmarital

160

situations the inexpressiveness of the male to females other than one's spouse works to prevent threats to the primacy of the marital bond, that is, it presumably functions to ward off infidelity. The authors further suggest two styles of adult inexpressiveness: the "cowboy—John Wayne" style of almost total inarticulateness and the more cool, detached style of the "playboy," who communicates only to exploit women sexually.

The article has proved to be an important one in forcing sociologists to rethink old conceptual stereotypes of masculinity and femininity. In part, it has helped to contribute to efforts to rescue for both sexes qualities and potentials that previously were thought to belong to only one sex. On the other hand, it would be unfortunate if Balswick and Peek's conceptualization would enter the sociological literature as the last word on the dilemma of male inexpressiveness—unfortunate because, despite their real insight, I think they fundamentally misconstrue both the origin and the playing out of male inexpressiveness in our society.

In the note which follows, I would like to reconsider the phenomenon of male inexpressiveness, drawing upon my own and other men's experiences in consciousness-raising groups (especially as recounted in *Unbecoming Men: A Men's Consciousness-Raising Group Writes on Oppression and Themselves* (Bradley et al., 1971), as well as some of the literature which has appeared since Balswick and Peek first published their article.

Becoming Inexpressive: Socialization

The process of becoming inexpressive is cast by Balswick and Peek in the traditional vocabulary of the literature of socialization:

> Children, from the time they are born both explicitly and implicitly are taught how to be a man or how to be a woman. While the girl is taught to act "feminine," . . . the boy is taught to be a man. In learning to be a man, the boy in American society comes to value expressions of masculinity . . . [such as] physical courage, toughness, competitiveness, and aggressiveness. (1971: 363–364)

Balswick and Peek's discussion of this socialization process is marred in two ways. Theoretically, their discussion ignores the critique of the socialization literature initially suggested by Wrong (1961) in his analysis of sociology's "over-socialized concept of man [sic]." Wrong, using a largely Freudian vocabulary, argued that it is incorrect to see the individual as something "hollowed out" into which norms are simply poured. Rather, "conformity" and "internalization" should always be conceptualized as problematic. For example, if we consider inexpressiveness to be a character trait, as do Balswick and Peek, we should also be aware that the normative control of that trait is never complete—being threatened constantly by both the presumably more expressive demands of the id and the excessive ("perfectionist") demands of the "internalized norms" of the superego. Wrong's point is well taken. While the norms of our society may well call for all little boys to grow up to be inexpressive, the inexpressiveness of the adult male should never be regarded as complete or total, as Balswick and Peek would have it.

For them to have ignored this point is particularly crucial given their concern to rescue some capacity of authentic expressiveness for the male. Their suggestion that men simply "unlearn" their inexpressiveness through contact with a woman (spouse) is unsatisfactory for two reasons. First, it forfeits the possibility that men can rescue themselves through enhanced self-knowledge or contact with other men. Second, *it would seem to make the task of rescuing men just one more task of women.* That is, the wife is expected to restore to her husband that which was initially taken from him in socialization.

A second problem with Balswick and Peek's discussion of socialization and inexpressiveness is that they ignore the peculiarly asymmetrical patterns of socialization in our society which make it much more dangerous for a boy to be incompletely socialized than a girl. For example, much of the literature suggests that parents and other adults exert greater social control to insure that boys "grow up male" than that girls "grow up female" (Parsons, 1951)—as can be seen in the fact that greater stigma is attached to the boy who is labeled a sissy than to the girl who is known as a tomboy. Failure to even consider this asymmetry reveals, I think, the major weakness of Balswick and Peek's conceptualization of male inexpressiveness. They have no explanation of *why* male inexpressiveness exists or *how* it came into being and is maintained other than to say that "our culture demands it." Thus, while we can agree that male inexpressiveness is a tragedy, their analysis does not help us to change the social conditions which produce that tragedy.

Inexpressiveness and Power

To break this chain of reasoning, I would like to postulate that, in itself, male inexpressiveness is of no particular value in our culture. Rather, it is an instrumental requisite for assuming adult male roles of power.

Consider the following. To effectively wield power, one must be able both to convince others of the rightness of the decisions one makes and to guard against one's own emotional involvement in the consequences of that decision; that is, one has to show that decisions are reached rationally and efficiently. One must also be able to close one's eyes to the potential pain one's decisions have for others and for oneself. The general who sends troops into battle must show that his decision is calculated and certain; to effectively implement that decision—hence, to maintain his position of power to make future decisions—the general must put on a face of impassive conviction.

I would argue, in a similar vein, that a little boy must become inexpressive not simply because our culture expects boys to be inexpressive *but because our culture expects little boys to grow up to become decision makers and wielders of power.*

From this example, I am suggesting that inexpressiveness is not just learned as an end in itself. Rather, it is learned as a means to be implemented later in men assuming and maintaining positions of power. More generally:

> (A) INEXPRESSIVENESS in a role is determined by the corresponding *power* (actual or potential) of that role.

In light of this generalization, we might consider why so many sociologists tend to merge the universalistic-particularistic (rational) and the affective neutrality-affectivity (expressive) distinction in any discussion of real social behavior. In the case of the general, it would seem that the ability to give an inexpressive—that is, an affectively neutral—coloring to his decisions or positions contributes to the apparent rationality of those decisions or positions. Inexpressiveness validates the rightness of one's position. In fact, the social positions of highest power—not incidentally always occupied by men—demand veneers of both universalism and inexpressiveness of their incumbents, suggesting that at these levels *both* characteristics merge into a style of control. (Consider both Kennedy in the missile crisis and Nixon at Watergate. While otherwise quite dissimilar, in a crisis and challenge to their position, both men felt that "stonewalling" was the solution to the situation.)

From the above, it also follows logically that inexpressiveness might be more a characteristic of upper-class, powerful males than of men in the working classes. Many people—sociologists included—would probably object to such a deduction, saying the evidence is in the other direction, pointing at the Stanley Kowalski or Marty of literary fiction. I am not so sure. To continue with examples from fiction for a moment, the early autobiographical novels of, say, James Baldwin and Paul Goodman, dealing with lower- and working-class youth, consistently depicted "making it" as a not unusual tradeoff for one's sensitivity and expressiveness. More empirically, the recent work of Sennett and Cobb in their study of working-class life, *The Hidden Injuries of Class* (1972), suggests that upward mobility by working-class men was seen by them as entailing a certain phoniness or inauthentic relationship with one's *male* peers as well as a sacrifice of a meaningful expressive relationship with children and wife. The result of this for the men interviewed by Sennett and Cobb was often a choice to

forego upward mobility and power because it involved becoming something one was not. It involved learning to dissemble inauthentic displays
of expressiveness toward higher-ups as well as involving the sacrifice of
already close relationships with one's friends and family.

Inexpressiveness and Power as Situational Variables

In their article, Balswick and Peek include a notion of inexpressiveness not
just as a socially acquired temperament trait but also as a situational variable. Thus, while they argue that all males are socialized into inexpressiveness, they also argue that "for many males . . . through progressively
more serious involvements with women (such as going steady, being
pinned, engagement, and the honeymoon period of marriage), [these
males] begin to make some exceptions. That is, they may learn to be *situationally rather than totally inexpressive*" (1971: 365–366). As noted
above, this is seen by Balswick and Peek as functional for men and for the
marriage relation in two ways. It meets the wife's expectations of affective
support for herself while usually being accompanied by continued
inexpression toward women who are not one's spouse. Thus, in this sense,
the situational unlearning of inexpressiveness enhances the marital relationship while guarding against extramarital relationships which would
threaten the basic pairing of husband-wife.

There is, on the surface, a certain descriptive validity to Balswick and
Peek's depiction, although, interestingly, they do not consider a latent
function of such unlearning. To the extent that an ability to be expressive
in situ with a woman leads to satisfactory and gratifying consequences in
one case, it probably doesn't take long for the male to learn to be expressive with *any* woman—not just his spouse—as a mode of approaching that
woman. Some men, for example, admit to this in my consciousness-raising
group. This, in fact, is a way of "coming on" with a woman—a relaxation
of the usual standards of inexpressiveness as a calculated move to establish
a sexual relationship. Skill at dissembling in this situation may have less to
do with handing a woman a "line" than with showing one's weaknesses
and frailties as clues intended to be read by her as signs of authentic male
interest. In many Latin cultures, which might be considered to epitomize
traditional male supremist modes, the style of *machismo*, in fact, calls for
the male to be dependent, nominally open, and very expressive to which-
ever woman he is currently trying to "make." The point of both these
examples is to suggest that the *situational unlearning* of inexpressiveness
need not lead to strengthening the marriage bond and, in fact, may be
detrimental to it, since what works in one situation will probably be tried
in others.

Following the argument developed in the previous section concerning the interplay between power and inexpressiveness, I would suggest a different conceptualization of the situational relevance of inexpressiveness:

(B) EXPRESSIVENESS in a sexist culture empirically emerges as an effort on the part of the male to *control* a situation (once again, on his terms) and to maintain his position.

What I am suggesting is that in a society such as ours, which so permeates all social relationships with notions of power and exchange, even what may appear on the surface to be authentic can be an extension rather than a negation of (sexual) politics.

This is even more true of male inexpressive behavior in intimate male-female relationships. The following dialogue is drawn from Erica Jong's novel of upper-middle-class sexual etiquette, *Fear of Flying*. Consider the political use of male inexpressiveness:

SHE: "Why do you always have to do this to me? You make me feel so lonely."
HE: "That comes from you."
"What do you mean it comes from me? Tonight I wanted to be happy. It's Christmas Eve. Why do you turn on me? What did I do?"
Silence
"What did I do?"
He looks at her as if her not knowing were another injury. "Look, let's just go to sleep now. Let's just forget it."
"Forget what?"
He says nothing.
"Forget the fact that you turned on me? Forget the fact that you're punishing me for nothing? Forget the fact that I'm lonely and cold, that it's Christmas Eve and again you've ruined it for me? Is that what you want me to forget?"
"I won't discuss it."
"Discuss what?" "What won't you discuss?"
"Shut up! I won't have you screaming in the hotel."
"I don't give a fuck what you won't have me do. I'd like to be treated civilly. I'd like you to at least do me the courtesy of telling me why you're in such a funk. And don't look at me that way . . ."
"What way?"
"As if my not being able to read your mind were my greatest sin. I *can't* read your mind. I *don't* know why you're so mad. I can't intuit your wish. If that's what you want in a wife you don't have it in me."
"I certainly don't."
"Then what is it? Please tell me."
"I shouldn't have to."
"Good God! Do you mean to tell me I'm expected to be a mind reader? Is that the kind of mothering you want?"
"If you had any empathy for me . . ."

"But I *do*. My God, you just don't give me a chance."

"You tune out. You don't listen."

"It was something in the movie wasn't it?"

"What in the movie?"

"The quiz again. Do you have to quiz me like some kind of criminal. Do you have to cross-examine me? . . . It was the funeral scene . . . The little boy looking at his dead mother. Something got you there. That was when you got depressed."

Silence

"Oh, come on, Bennett, you're making me *furious*. Please tell me. Please." (He gives the words singly like little gifts. Like hard little turds.) "What was it about the scene that got me?"

"Don't quiz me. Tell me!" (She puts her arms around him. He pulls away. She falls to the floor holding onto his pajama leg. It looks less like an embrace than a rescue scene, she sinking, he reluctantly allowing her to cling to his leg for support.)

"Get up!"

(Crying) "Only if you tell me."

(He jerks his leg away.) "I'm going to bed." (Jong, 1973: 108–109)

One wonders if this is what Balswick and Peek mean by a man "un-learning" his inexpressiveness. Less facetiously, this is clearly an example which indicates that inexpression on the part of the male is not just a matter of inarticulateness or even a deeply socialized inability to respond to the needs of others. The male here is *using* inexpression to guard his own position. To *not* say anything in this situation is to say something very important indeed: that the battle we are engaged in is to be fought by my rules and when I choose to fight. In general:

> (C) Male INEXPRESSIVENESS empirically emerges as an inten-tional manipulation of a situation when threats to the male position occur.

Inexpressiveness and Male Culture

Balswick and Peek see inexpressiveness as a major quality of male-female interaction. I have tried to indicate about where they might be right in making such an attribution as well as some of the inadequacies of their conceptualization of the origins of that inexpressiveness. A clear gap in their conceptualization, however, is their lack of any consideration of the inexpressive male in interaction with other men. In fact, their conceptual-ization leads to two contradictory deductions. First, given the depth and thoroughness of socialization, we might deduce that the male is inexpres-sive with other men, as well as with women. Second, the male, who is only situationally inexpressive, can interact and express himself truly in situations with other men. This latter position finds support in the notions of male bonding developed by Lionel Tiger (1969). The former position is validated by some of the contributors to Pleck and Sawyer's recent reader on *Men and Masculinity* (1974; esp. Candell, Jounard, and Fasteau). In this section, I would like to raise some of the questions that bear on the problem of male-to-male inexpressiveness. (1) Is there a male subculture? Subcultural differences are usually identified as having ethnic, religious, occupational, etc., boundaries; gender is not usually considered to define subcultural differences. This is so even though gender repeatedly proves to be among the most statistically significant variables in most empirical research. Yet, if we think of a subculture as consisting of unique patterns of belief, value, technique, and language use, there would be a *prima facie* case for considering "male" and "female" definitive of true subcultures in almost all societies. (2) What is the origin of male and female subcultures? This question is probably the most inclusive of all the questions one can ask about gender and sex-role differences. It thrusts us into the very murky swamp of the origin of the family, patriarchy, sexism, etc. Sidestepping questions of the ultimate origin of male and female cultural differences, I would only suggest that a good case might be made for considering the persistence— if not the origin— of male and female subcultural differences as due to male efforts to maintain privilege and position *vis-à-vis* women. This is the point anthropologists have been quick to make about primitive societies. The ritual and magic of the males is a secret to be guarded against the women's eyes. Such magic is privy only to the men, and access to it in rites of passage finally determines who is man and who is only *other*. Similar processes are at work in our own society. Chodorow's distinction between "being" and "doing" (1971) is a way of talking about male and female subcultural differences that makes it clear that what men "do" defines not only their own activity but the activity ("being") of women as well. Benston's (1969) distinction between male production of exchange-value in the public sphere and female creation of use-value in the private sphere captures the same fundamental differential of power underlying what appears to be merely cultural. (3) Is male culture necessarily inexpressive? Many observers would say it is flatly wrong to assert that men are inexpressive when interacting with other men. Tiger (1969), for example, talks of the games (sport) men share as moments of intense and authentic communication and expression. In fact, for Tiger, sport derives from the even more intense solidarity of the prehistoric hunt—a solidarity that seems, in his scheme, to be almost genetic in origin. I think Tiger, and others who would call our attention to this capacity for male expressiveness, are saying something important but partial. Perhaps the following example drawn from adult reminiscences of one's fourteenth year can make this clearer:

> I take off at full speed not knowing whether I would reach it but knowing
> very clearly that this is *my* chance. My cap flies off my head . . . and a
> second later I one-hand it as cool as can be. . . . I hear the applause.
> . . . I hear voices congratulating my mother for having such a good ath-
> lete for a son. . . . Everybody on the team pounds my back as they come
> in from the field, letting me know that I've *made it.* (Candell in Pleck and
> Sawyer, 1974: 16)

This is a good picture of boys being drawn together in sport, of sharing
almost total experience.

But is it? The same person continues in the next paragraph:

> But I know enough not to blow my cool so all I do is mumble thanks
> under a slightly trembling upper lip which is fighting the rest of my face,
> the rest of being, from exploding with laughter and tears of joy. (Candell
> in Pleck and Sawyer, 1974: 19)

Why this silence? Again, I don't think it is just because our culture demands inexpression. I think here, as above, silence and inexpression are
the ways men learn to *consolidate* power, to make the effort appear as
effortless, to guard against showing the real limits of one's potential and
power by making it *all* appear easy. Even among males alone, one maintains control over a situation by revealing only strategic proportions of
oneself.

Further, in Marc Fasteau's very perceptive article "Why Men Aren't
Talking" (Pleck and Sawyer, 1974), the observation is made that when
men do talk, they talk of "large" problems—war, politics, art—but never
of anything really personal. Even when men have equal credentials in
achieved success, they tend not to make themselves vulnerable to each
other, for to do so may be interpreted as a sign of weakness and an opportunity for the other to secure advantage. As Fasteau puts it, men talk,
but they always do so for a *reason*—getting together for its own sake
would be too frightening—and that reason often amounts to just another
effort at establishing who *really* is best, stronger, smarter, or ultimately,
more powerful.

Inexpressiveness and the Sociology of Sex Roles

In the preceding sections, I have tried to change the grounds of an explanation of male inexpressiveness from one which holds that it is simply a
cultural variable to one which sees it as a consequence of the political
(power) position of the sexes in our society. I have not tried to deny that
male inexpressiveness exists but only that it does so in different forms and
for different reasons than Balswick and Peek suggest. I am making no
claims for the analytic completeness of the ideas presented here.

A direct result of the feminist movement has been the effort on the part of sociologists concerned with family and sex-role-related behavior to discard or recast old concepts in the face of the feminist critique. One tendency of this "new sociology" has been an attempt to rescue attributes of positive human potential from the exclusive domain of one sex and, thus, to validate those potentials for all people. Although they do not say this explicitly, some such concern certainly underlies Balswick and Peek's effort. I think that this is social science at its best.

On the other hand, I am not convinced, as Balswick and Peek seem to be, that significant change in the male sex role will be made if we conceptualize the problem as one that involves individual males gradually unlearning their inexpressiveness with individual females. Balswick (1974) wrote an article based on the analysis developed with Peek entitled "Why Husbands Can't Say 'I Love You' " and printed it in a mass distribution women's magazine. Predictably, the article suggests to the wife some techniques she might develop for drawing her husband out of his inexpressive shell. I think that kind of article—at this point in the struggle of women to define themselves—is facile and wrongheaded. Such advice burdens the wife with additional "emotional work" while simultaneously creating a new arena in which she can—and most likely will—fail.

Similarly, articles that speak to men about their need to become more expressive also miss the point if we are concerned about fundamental social change. Such arguments come fairly cheap. Witness the essentially honest but fatally narrow and class-bound analyses of Korda (1973) and Farrell (1974). Their arguments develop little more than strategies capable of salvaging a limited number of upper-class male heterosexual egos. The need I see and feel at this point is for arguments and strategies capable of moving the majority of men who are not privileged in that fashion. What such arguments would say—much less to whom they would be addressed—is a question I cannot now answer. But I know where my work lies. For if my argument is correct—and I believe it is—that male inexpressiveness is instrumental in maintaining positions of power and privilege for men, then male sociologists might well begin to search through their own experiences and the accumulated knowledge of the sociological literature for sensitizing models which might indicate how, and if, it would be possible to relinquish the power which has historically been ours.

Interaction: The Work Women Do

PAMELA M. FISHMAN
Brooklyn, New York

12. Consequences. As Aristotle said, "Man [sic] is a social animal."
This statement has been accepted for more than 2,000 years. Now
we are asking: who makes it possible for social life to occur? Fishman shows that conversation is part of the effort involved in producing social life. To produce social relationships requires attention, skill, and responsiveness to others. In her analysis of
conversations between couples in their own homes, Fishman dis-
covers that the work of establishing and maintaining conversations
is women's work. Men may choose the topics—by ignoring those
that women introduce—yet it is up to the women to keep interaction going by being responsive. Can you devise an experiment, or
make a series of observations, to see if Fishman's findings can be
replicated in other settings? Under what circumstances might these
findings *not* hold true? Do you agree with her conclusions about
men's power, e.g., to "define reality" through silence and other
means of controlling conversations?

The oppression of women in society is an issue of growing concern, both
in academic fields and in everyday life. Despite research on the historical
and economic bases of women's position, we know little about how the
hierarchy is routinely established and maintained. In this paper, I attempt
to direct attention to the reality of power in daily experience by analyzing
conversations between men and women in their homes. The paper focuses
on how verbal interaction helps to construct and maintain the hierarchical
relations between women and men.

Weber (1969: 152) provided the classic conception of power as the
chances of one actor in a social relationship to impose his or her will on
another. Berger and Luckmann (1967: 109) have discussed power as a
question of potentially conflicting definitions of reality; that of the most
powerful will be "made to stick." That particular people have the power
to construct and enforce their definition of reality is due to socially prevalent economic and political definitions of reality.

Imposing one's will can be much more than forcing someone else to do
something. Power is the ability to impose one's definition of what is pos-

170

sible, what is right, what is rational, what is real. Power is a product of human activities, just as the activities are themselves products of the power relations in the socioeconomic world.

Power usually is analyzed macrosociologically. It cannot be solely a result of what people do within the immediate situation in which it occurs. What people do in specific interactions expresses and reflects historical and social structural forces beyond the boundaries of their encounters. Power relations between men and women are the outcome of the social organization of their activities in the home and in the economy. Power can, however, be analyzed microsociologically, as in this paper. Power and hierarchical relations are not abstract forces operating on people. Power must be a human accomplishment, situated in everyday interaction. Both structural forces and interactional activities are vital to the maintenance and construction of social reality.

Recent work on gender and the English language shows that the male-female hierarchy is inherent in the words we use to perceive and name our world. The use of generic "man" to refer to the human species (Miller and Swift, 1976); the addition of suffixes ("authoress," "actress," "stewardess") when referring to female practitioners (Miller and Swift, 1976); the asymmetrical use of first and last names—women are more often called by their first, men by their last, even when they are of equal rank (Thorne and Henley, 1975); women's greater vocabulary for sewing and cooking, men's for mechanics and sports (Conklin, 1974). These studies of grammatical forms and vocabulary document the male-dominated reality expressed through our language.

Much less attention has been directed toward how male-female power relations are expressed in conversation.[1] By turning to conversation, we move to an analysis of the interactional production of a particular reality through people's talk.

This activity is significant for intimates. Berger and Kellner (1970: 64) have argued that at present, with the increasing separation of public and private spheres of life, intimate relationships are among the most important reality-maintaining settings. They apply this argument specifically to marriage. The process of daily interaction in the marital relationship is ideally "one in which reality is crystallized, narrowed, and stabilized. Ambivalences are converted into certainties. Typifications of self and other become settled. Most generally, possibilities become facticities."

In these relationships, in these trivial, mundane interactions, much of the essential work of sustaining the reality of the world goes on. Intimates often reconstruct their separate experiences, past and present, with one another. Specifically, the couple sustain and produce the reality of their own relationship, and more generally, of the world. I shall focus upon the interactional activities which constitute the everyday work done by intimates. It is through this work that people produce their relationship to one another, their relationship to the world, and those patterns normally referred to as social structure.

Work in Interaction[2]

Sometimes we think of interaction as work. At a party or meeting where silence lies heavy, we recognize the burden of interaction and respond to it as work. The many books written on the "art of conversation" call attention to the tasks involved in interaction. It is not simply an analogy to think of interaction as work. Rather, it is an intuitive recognition of what must be accomplished for interaction to occur.

Interaction requires at least two people. Conversation is produced not simply by their presence but also by the display of their continuing agreement to pay attention to one another. That is, all interactions are potentially problematic and occur through the continual, turn-by-turn efforts of the participants.

The work of Sacks and his followers (Sacks et al., 1974; Schegloff, 1972; Schegloff and Sacks, 1974) attempts to specify how conversationalists work to accomplish such things as beginnings and endings. They have ignored, however, the interaction between intimates. Schegloff and Sacks (1974: 262) characterize intimates in home situations as "in continuing states of incipient talk." Thus they contend that their analysis of the activities involved in opening and closing conversations, as well as those involved in keeping conversation going, does not apply to intimate conversations. But this perspective disregards the many conversations which do not begin with greetings or end with good-byes. If one sees a movie with friends, conversation afterward does not begin again with greetings. In social gatherings, lulls occur and conversations must begin anew. In any setting in which conversation is possible, attempts at beginning, sustaining, and stopping talk still must be made. And these attempts must be recognized by both parties for them to move between states of "incipient" and "actual" conversation.

In a sense, every remark or turn at speaking should be seen as an *attempt* to interact. It may be an attempt to open or close a conversation. It may be a bid to continue interaction: to respond to what went before and elicit a further remark from one's partner. For an attempt to succeed, the other party must be willing to do further interactional work. That other person has the power to turn an attempt into a conversation or to stop it dead.

Method

The data for this study consist of fifty-two hours of tape-recorded conversation between intimates in their homes. Three couples agreed to place tape recorders in their apartments. They had the right to censor the taped material before I heard it. The apartments were small, so that the recorders picked up all conversation from the kitchen and living room as well as the louder portions of talk from the bedroom and bath. The tapes could run for a four-hour period without interruption. Though I had timers to switch the tapes on and off automatically, all three couples insisted on doing the switching manually. The segments of interrupted recording vary from one to four hours.

The three couples had been together three months, six months, and two years, respectively. All were white and professionally oriented, between the ages of twenty-five and thirty-five. One woman was a social worker, and the other five people were in graduate school. Two of the women were avowed feminists, and all three men as well as the other woman described themselves as sympathetic to the woman's movement.

The tape recorders were present in the apartments from four to fourteen days. I am satisfied that the material represents natural conversation and that there was no undue awareness of the recorder. The tapes sounded natural to me, like conversations between my husband and myself. Others who have read the transcripts have agreed. All six people reported that they soon began to ignore the tape recorder. Further, they were apologetic about the material, calling it trivial and uninteresting, just the ordinary affairs of everyday life. Finally, one couple said that they forgot the recorder sufficiently to begin making love in the living room while the recorder was on. That segment and two others were the only ones the participants deleted.

I listened to all of the tapes at least once, many two or more times. During this period, I observed general trends of the interactions as a whole. Three transcripts were chosen from five hours of transcribed conversations for closer, turn-by-turn analysis of the progress of concrete interactional activities. I chose these three because they were good examples of conversation that appeared to be problematic for the man, for the woman, and for neither.

Preliminary Evidence

Some evidence of the power relations between couples appeared while I was still collecting the tapes. During casual conversations with the participants after the taping, I learned that in all three couples the men usually set up the tape recorders and turned them on and off. More significantly, some of the times that the men turned the recorders on, they did so without the women's knowledge. The reverse never occurred.

To control conversation is not merely to choose the topic. It is a matter of having control over the definition of the situation in general, which includes not only what will be talked about but whether there will be a conversation at all and under what terms it will occur. In various scenes, control over aspects of the situation can be important. The addition of a tape recorder in the home is an example of a new aspect of the routine situation. The men clearly had and actively maintained unilateral control over the new feature in the situation.

This research also involves the issue of a typically private interaction becoming available to a third party. Usually the men played the tapes to censor them and made the only two attempts to exert control over the presentation of the data to me. One case involved the "clicks" that are normally recorded when the recorder is turned off. Since more than one time segment was often on the same side of a tape, I relied on the clicks, as well as my sense of the conversations, to know when a new time segment began. One man carefully erased nearly all the clicks on the tapes, making it difficult to separate out recordings at different time periods.

The second instance was a more explicit illustration of male censorship. Early on, I made the error of asking a couple to help transcribe a segment of their tape. The error was doubly instructive. First, I saw that the participants could rarely hear or understand the problem areas any better than I, even though they had been "on the spot" and were hearing their own voices. Second, the man kept wanting to know why I was interested in the segment, repeatedly guessing what I was looking for. At the time, I only knew that it was an example of decision making and did not know specifically what I wanted. He never accepted this explanation. He became irritated at my continued attempt at literal transcription and kept insisting that he could give me the sense of what occurred and that the exact words were unimportant. He continued the attempt to determine the meaning of the interaction retrospectively, with constant references to his motives for saying this or that. It took hours to withdraw from the situation, as he insisted on giving me the help that I had requested.

Findings: Interactional Strategies

Textual analysis revealed how interactants do the work of conversation. There are a variety of strategies to insure, encourage, and subvert conversation.

Asking Questions

There is an overwhelming difference between female and male use of questions as a resource in interaction. At times, I felt that all women did was ask questions. In seven hours of tapes the three men asked 59 questions, the women 150, nearly three times as many.

Other research (Lakoff, 1975) notes that women ask more questions than men. Lakoff has interpreted this question asking as an indication of women's insecurity, a linguistic signal of an internal psychological state resulting from the oppression of women. But a psychological explanation is unnecessary to reveal why women ask more questions than men. Since questions are produced in conversations, we should look first to how questions function there.

Questions are interactionally powerful utterances. They are among a class of utterances, like greetings, treated as standing in a paired relation; that is, they evoke further utterances. Questions are paired with answers (Sacks, 1972). People respond to questions as "deserving" answers. The absence of an answer is noticeable and may be complained about. A question does work in conversation by opening a two-part sequence. It is a way to insure a minimal interaction—at least one utterance by each of two participants.

Once I noted the phenomenon of questions on the tapes, I attended to my own speech and discovered the same pattern. I tried, and still do try, to break myself of the habit, and found it very difficult. When I succeeded in making a remark as a statement, I usually did not get a response. It became clear that I asked questions not merely out of habit or from insecurity but because it was likely that my attempt at interaction would fail if I did not.

Asking "D'ya Know"
In line with the assumption that children have a restricted right to speak in the presence of adults, Harvey Sacks (1972) describes a type of question used extensively by children as a conversational opening: "D'ya know what?" As with other questions, it provides for a next utterance. The next utterance it engenders is itself a question, which provides for yet another utterance. The archetype is, "D'ya know what?" "What?" "Blahblah (answer)." Sometimes, of course, the adult answers with an expectant look or a statement like "Tell me what." Whatever the exact form of that first response, the idea is that the first question sets off a three-part sequence, Q–Q–A, rather than a simple Q–A sequence.

Sacks points out that children's use of this device is a clever solution to their problem of insuring the right to speak (at the same time, their use of this strategy acknowledges that restricted right). In response to the "What?" children may say what they wanted to say in the first place. Finding such three-part "D'ya know" sequences in interaction informs us both about the work of guaranteeing interaction and about the differential rights of the participants. In the five hours of transcribed material, the women used this device twice as often as the men.

Attention Beginnings
The phrase "This is interesting," or a variation thereof, occurs throughout the tapes. When conversation is not problematic, the work of establishing

that a remark is interesting ideally is done by both interactants, not one. The first person makes a remark; the second person responds to the remark, thus establishing its status as something worthy of joint interest or importance. All this occurs without the question of its interest ever becoming explicit.[3] The use of "This is really interesting" as an introduction shows that the user cannot assume that the remark itself will be seen as worthy of attention. At the same time, the user tries singlehandedly to establish the remark. The user is saying, "Pay attention to what I have to say; I can't assume that you will." In the five hours of transcribed material, the women used this device ten times, the men seven.[4]

There are also many instances of "y'know" interspersed throughout the transcripts. While this phrase does not compel the attention of one's partner as forcefully as "This is interesting" does, it is an attempt to command the other person's attention. The phrase was used thirty-four times by the women and three times by the men in the transcribed conversations.

Minimal Response
Another interaction strategy is the use of the minimal response, when the speaker takes a turn by saying "yeah," "umm," "huh," and only that. Men and women both do this, but they tend to use the minimal response in quite different ways. The male usages of the minimal response displayed lack of interest. The monosyllabic response merely filled a turn at a point when it needed to be filled. For example, a woman would make a lengthy remark, after which the man responded with "yeah," doing nothing to encourage her or to elaborate. Such minimal responses are attempts to discourage interaction.

The women also made this type of minimal response at times, but their most frequent use of the minimal response was as "support work." When the men are talking, the women are particularly skilled at inserting "mms," "yeahs," "oh's," and other such comments throughout streams of talk rather than at the end. These are signs from the inserter that she is constantly attending to what is said, that she is demonstrating her participation, her interest in the interaction and the speaker. How well the women do this is also striking; seldom do they mistime their insertions and cause even slight overlaps. These minimal responses occur between the breaths of a speaker, and there is nothing in tone or structure to suggest that they are attempting to take over the talk.

Making Statements
Finally, I would like to consider statements, which do nothing to insure their own success or the success of the interaction. Of course, a statement does some interactional work; it fills a space and may also provide for a response. However, such statements display an assumption on the part of

the speaker that the attempt will be successful as is. It will be understood, the statement is of interest, there will be a response. It is as if speakers can assume that everything is working well; success is naturally theirs.

In the transcribed material, the men produced over twice as many statements as the women, and they almost always got a response, which was not true for the women. For example, many times one or both people were reading, then read a passage aloud or commented on it. The man's comments often engendered a lengthy exchange; the woman's comments seldom did. In a discussion of their respective vitas, the man literally ignored both long and short comments from the woman on her vita, returning the conversation after each remark of hers back to his own. Each time, she turned her attention back to his vita "as directed." Listening to these conversations, one cannot conclude from the substance of the remarks that the men talk about more interesting things than the women. They take on that character by virtue of generating interaction.

Interactional Progress

The simple narration of the use of strategies obscures one important quality of interaction: its progression. The finding and frequency of strategies are of interest, but seeing the use of strategies in the developing character of interaction reveals more about the differential work done by the sexes.

One short segment of conversation is discussed. It is from the transcript originally chosen for analysis because the conversation appeared problematic for the woman. This segment is the beginning of an interaction during which the woman is reading a book in her academic specialty and the man is making a salad. The woman's opening remarks set up two "d'ya know" sequences, demonstrating her lack of certainty, before anything has been said, that the man will pay attention—a safe assumption, since the conversation never gets off the ground. The "d'ya know" only solves the minimal problem of getting a response. She cannot get a continuing conversation going.

Her second attempt at a conversation uses both the "d'ya know" strategy and an attention beginning of "That's very interesting." This double attempt to gain his participation manages to evoke one statement of continuation from him, but her follow-up calls forth only silence.

Her third attempt uses the attention beginning which had some small success the last time. She adds a few "y'knows" throughout her utterance, asking for attention. She finally achieves a minimal response when she repeats something. Though she makes further attempts in the remainder of the interaction (not reported here), a conversation on the topic never does develop. After three or four more minutes, she finally gives up.

One might argue that because the man is making a salad he cannot pay attention to the conversation. However, while still at work on the salad, the man introduces his own topic for conversation, remarking that then-President Nixon was a former lawyer for Pepsi-Cola. This topic introduction engenders a conversation when the woman responds to his remark. They go through a series of exchanges which end when he decides not to continue. This conversational exchange demonstrates that the man was willing to engage in discussion, but only on his own terms.

The transcript demonstrates how some strategies are used in actual conversation. It also documents the woman working at interaction and the man exercising his power by refusing to become a full-fledged participant. As the interaction develops and she becomes more sure of her difficulties, she brings more pressure to bear by an increased use of strategies. Even so, she is able to insure only immediate, localized responses, not a full conversational exchange.

Conclusions

There is an unequal distribution of work in conversation. We can see from the differential use of strategies that the women are more actively engaged in insuring interaction than the men. Women ask more questions and use attention beginnings. They do support work while the men are talking and generally do active maintenance and continuation work in conversations. The men, on the other hand, do much less active work when they begin or participate in interactions. They rely on statements, which they assume will get responses, when they want interaction. Men much more often discourage interactions initiated by women than vice versa.

The women seemed to try more often and succeeded less often than the men. The men tried less often and seldom failed in their attempts. Both men and women regarded topics introduced by women as tentative; many of these were quickly dropped. In contrast, topics introduced by the men were treated as topics to be pursued; they were seldom rejected. The women worked harder than the men in interaction because they had less certainty of success. They did much of the necessary work of interaction, starting conversations and then working to maintain them.

The failure of the women's attempts at interaction is not due to anything inherent in their talk, but to the failure of the men to respond, to do interactional work. The success of the men's remarks is due to the women doing interactional work in response to attempts by the men. Thus, the definition of what is appropriate or inappropriate conversation becomes the man's choice. What part of the world the interactants orient to, construct, and maintain the reality of, is his choice, not hers. Yet the women labor hardest in making interactions go.

It seems that, as with work in its usual sense, there is a division of labor in conversation. The people who do the routine maintenance work, the women, are not the same people who either control or benefit from the process. Women are the "shit workers" of routine interaction, and the "goods" being made are not only interactions but, through them, realities.

Through this analysis of the detailed activity in everyday conversation, other dimensions of power and work in interaction are suggested. Two interrelated aspects concern women's availability and the maintenance of gender. Besides the problems women have generating interactions, they are almost always available to do the conversational work required by men and necessary for interactions. Appearances may differ by case. Sometimes women are required to sit and "be a good listener" because they are not otherwise needed. At other times, women are required to fill silences and keep conversation moving, to talk a lot. Sometimes they are expected to develop others' topics, and at other times they are required to present and develop topics of their own.

Women are required to do their work in a very strong sense. Sometimes they are required in ways that can be seen in interaction, as when men use interactional strategies such as attention beginnings and questions, to which the women fully respond. There are also times when there is no direct situational evidence of "requirement" from the man, and the woman does so "naturally." "Naturally" means that it is a morally required and highly sanctionable matter not to do so. If one does not act naturally, then one can be seen as crazy and deprived of adult status. We can speculate on the quality of doing it naturally by considering what happens to women who are unwilling to be available for the various jobs that the situation requires. Women who successfully control interactions are derided, and doubt is cast on their status of female. They are often considered abnormal; terms like "castrating bitch," "domineering," "aggressive," and "witch" may be used to identify them. When they attempt to control situations temporarily, women often "start" arguments. Etiquette books are filled with instructions to women on how to be available. Women who do not behave are punished by deprivation of full female status. One's identity as either male or female is the most crucial identity one has. It is the most "natural" differentiating characteristic there is.

Whereas sociologists generally treat sex as an ascribed rather than as an achieved characteristic, Garfinkel's (1967, chap. 5) study of a transsexual describes one's gender as a continual, routine accomplishment. He discusses what the transsexual Agnes had shown him: that one must continually give the appearance of being male or female in order for one's gender to be unproblematic in a given interaction. Agnes had to learn these appearances, and her awareness of them was explicit. For normally sexed people, it is routine.

The active maintenance of a female gender requires women to be available to do what needs to be done in interaction, to do the shit work and not complain. Since interactional work is related to what constitutes being a woman, with what a woman *is,* the idea that it *is* work is obscured. The work is not seen as what women do, but as part of what they are. Because this work is obscured, because it is too often seen as an aspect of gender identity rather than of gender activity, the maintenance and expression of male-female power relations in our everyday conversations are hidden as well. When we orient instead to the activities involved in maintaining gender, we are able to discern the reality of hierarchy in our daily lives.

The purpose of this study has been to begin an exploration of the details of concrete conversational activity of couples in their homes from the perspective of the socially structured power relationship between males and females. From such detailed analysis, we see that women do the work necessary for interaction to occur smoothly. But men control what will be produced as reality by the interaction. They already have, and they continually establish and enforce, their rights to define what the interaction, and reality, will be about.

Notes

A fuller report on this research, including examples from the transcripts, can be found in the original article.

1. A notable exception is the work on interruptions in conversation by West (1977b), West and Zimmerman (1977), and Zimmerman and West (1975). Hirschman (1973, 1974) has also examined the interactive production of language in male-female settings.

2. Throughout this paper, I use the terms "interaction" and "conversation" interchangeably, although it is not meant to suggest that conversation covers all the essential components of interaction.

3. The notion that joint expression of interest is a necessary feature of conversation is discussed by Garfinkel (1967: 39–42).

4. Unlike the use of questions and "D'ya know," which were randomly scattered throughout the transcripts, six of the seven male usages occurred during one lengthy interaction. The conversation had been chosen because it was one of the very few cases in which the man was having trouble maintaining interaction. In contrast, four of the female usages were from one transcript, and the other six were scattered. My impression from listening to all the tapes was that a complete count would show a much larger proportion of female-to-male usage than the ten-to-seven figure indicates.

Dilemmas and Contradictions of Status: The Case of the Dual-Career Family

JANET G. HUNT
LARRY L. HUNT
University of Maryland

13. Implications. Surveys show that the ideal life-styles many young women expect today will include marriage, children, and work outside the home (Cummings, 1977), but other surveys show that many young men do not want their wives to have careers (Komarovsky, 1973). In this article, Hunt and Hunt argue that women who hold these ideals will not be able to manage the combination easily, even if they find men willing to marry them. Hunt and Hunt believe that in the current economic system the dual-career family, in which both partners work for income and also share the housework and child-care responsibilities, is not a viable alternative because today it is a two-person job to develop and maintain one professional career. Hunt and Hunt see the problem not only as logistical but also as one of limited resources. Who will supply the supportive emotional environment of the home when both partners are exhausted by the efforts of working? They argue that the occupational world cannot accept this added labor force without becoming more competitive. More able candidates will appear for each job. All who do not have the resources of a nonworking partner will be at a disadvantage. Judith Syfers (1972) wrote an article entitled "I Want a Wife;" Hunt and Hunt argue that in a dual-career family, both partners will feel that way. What structural supports would be required to minimize this feeling? What strategies are currently available for the dual-career family? What efforts are those in the Women's Movement making to change the way in which occupational expectations now produce problems for couples interested in dual careers? Consider some of the problems facing women who try to coordinate work at home and work in the labor market. In what ways is the effort both easier and more difficult for middle- and upper-class women? In what ways is it easier and harder for blue collar working-class women? Can you think of ways in which the problems are the same?

In the dual-career family, both spouses have careers simultaneously.[1] Until recently, this arrangement has implied little or no modification of other traditional aspects of familial division of labor (Garland, 1972; Miller, 1972; Poloma, 1972). Increasingly, however, both the members and analysis of dual-career families appear to see it as a life-style[2] which not only tolerates career pursuit on the part of wives but facilitates the wife's career by altering the allocation of responsibilities within the family. Husbands assume some of the domestic and child-care responsibilities which customarily fall exclusively on wives (Bird, 1979; Hall and Hall, 1979; Holmstrom, 1972; Nadelson and Nadelson, 1980; Rapoport and Rapoport, 1969, 1971b, 1976). This modification of family sex roles, together with the extension of support services, is seen as altering a major structural barrier to women's achievement and making easier the changing status of women in contemporary society.

The problem with this view is that it attends to selected aspects of the connections between the family and personal achievement but ignores other key features of this complex relationship. The contemporary nuclear family emerged with the process of industrialization and represents a series of adaptations to the industrial productive system. With the new degree of separation of productive work from the household, strategic changes in the nature of the family occurred. Husband and wife are no longer a productive team but have a division of labor which casts him in a predominantly public and productive (instrumental) role and her in a private and domestic (expressive) role.[3] Further, the nuclear family is no longer as clearly connected to larger networks of extended kin or community (urban and suburban housing developments, while euphemistically called "neighborhoods," are not the locus of modern life). Instead, it is a highly private social island sharply demarked from public life. We argue in this essay that the private nuclear family form, with its instrumental/expressive division of labor, provides a very important support system for the individual worker or achiever in the present structure of industrial society, and that the dual-career family is thus a questionable vehicle for women's status enhancement. The reasons are that it (1) may not be able to provide careerists with the supportive services necessary to make them competitive in the career market, (2) may compound this problem by introducing into the market a previously excluded element—qualified women—which has kept competition artificially low, (3) may exaggerate rather than ameliorate the dysfunctional tradeoffs attendant on the supportive (functional) role of the modern nuclear family, and (4) may accentuate the status problems generated by the modern nuclear family for social categories other than wives.

The "Two-Career Family" Versus the "Two-Person Career"

Successful careerists tend to possess status characteristics, such as those pertaining to race, ethnicity, and sex, in addition to the formal status requisites (Hughes, 1945). They also tend to have supportive services pro-

vided by wives which, though not formally required or recognized as productive, are important if not essential for optimal performance. In fact,
with her concept of the "two-person career," Papanek (1973, 1979) suggests that the auxiliary role of wives in the career development and success
of their husbands is sufficiently extensive to warrant analytic treatment of
a career as a two-person phenomenon. Yet there has been little attention
given to the dilemmas this poses for dual-career spouses.

The role of the wife in the two-person career has many aspects, both
practical and symbolic. The division of labor in the contemporary nuclear
family responds to the industrialized productive system by providing the
worker with a nonworking (nonproductive) partner (Brown, 1970; Dahlstrom and Liljestrom, 1967). To this domestically based partner falls the
responsibility for housework, child care, consumption, integrative and supportive functions, and maintenance of social networks (family ties to kin,
friends, business associates). In all these aspects of family life, specific major decisions may be deferred to the household's "head," but this should
not obscure the fact that the wife invests the larger share of time and
assumes the day-to-day responsibility.

The services of the wife free the worker to assume a public, productive
role without forfeiting family-based roles and identities. Further, her availability is an important mark of status-group membership. Just as America
as a nation has taken the low level of participation of its women in the
labor force as an index of its high standard of living, so the "idle wife" of
each American male who can "afford" one is an addition to race, ethnicity, and sex as an informal indication of formal status attainment.

The point of these observations is that the division of labor in the contemporary nuclear family is an important component in individual career
success, and that the dual-career family, by altering this division, undercuts
the career potential of each spouse in a way not adequately anticipated in
the literature on this family form. While the supportive rather than per-
sonal-achievement role of traditional wives is widely recognized, it is
viewed primarily as an obstacle to women's career success rather than as
having strategic significance for the male careerist. The liability carried by
dual careerists competing without auxiliary partners is therefore given too
little attention.

The tendency to underestimate the importance of the wife's auxiliary
role is evidenced by the fact that where the problem of spouses pursuing
careers without "wives" has been considered, it has been related primarily
to the issue of the dual-career couple's capacity to manage family responsibilities—not to the question of their capacity to be successful in their
careers. Thus, the difficulties associated with child care and housekeeping
in the dual-career situation are discussed primarily from the standpoint of
"work overload" (Rapoport and Rapoport, 1969, 1971b, 1976), an

overly simplistic treatment of the problem. By considering only the tangible aspects of the wife's traditional obligations, and then treating these as tasks that can be arbitrarily apportioned between spouses and/or delegated to extrafamilial agents, this approach ignores the extent to which these functions combine in a single coherent role symbolizing both support and the success of the careerist. The problem of how to survive without a wife, in other words, is not simply a logistical one of covering the workload, but also a social-psychological one of sustaining the careerist's personal and social identity.

In pursuing careers without traditional auxiliary partners, both spouses in the dual-career family share some of the problems of the single male (who may be handicapped by the absence of a wife as a symbolic and social asset) *plus* the problem of child care and domestic-work overload, which the single male without children does not incur. This can place the dual careerists in double jeopardy relative to their traditional counterparts—married males with conventional wives. And from this perspective, their rate of success should be expected to be comparatively lower.[4]

The Limited Career Market

Advocacy of the dual-career family was forged in a period of optimism concerning the possibility of change in the structure of American life. During the 1960s, many concerned with social change and alternative lifestyles sensed an increased openness in society. Mobility into professional roles was sought by increasing numbers of persons, and oppressed minorities moved to secure rights and rewards previously denied them. In this atmosphere, women's concerns for a new level and quality of participation in public life were articulated, and many believed that increased sexual as well as racial equality was around the corner—a possibility which would become a reality in the 1970s. However, a politics of scarcity has since come to dominate national life, blunting those trends and the visions which guided them. This development highlighted the failure of reformists to consider not only the liberalizing climate of attitudes but the actual capacity of the career market to absorb substantially larger numbers of persons without major institutional modification.

The sexual division of labor created by the intersection of the nuclear family and the industrialized economy has historically rendered American women a largely nonproductive, dependent element in the social order. Without radical restructuring of work and redefinition of jobs and careers, the progressive participation of women (and minorities) can mean a larger throng pursuing a stable or declining number of jobs under increasingly competitive conditions. Such heightened competitiveness can accentuate the disadvantage of the dual careerists and generate pressures to alleviate strain by getting women to withdraw once again from the job market.

Increasing job scarcity may adversely affect the survival chances of dual careerists in at least two ways. First, it may make them individually less competitive in the job market. The professional glut of the 1970s already means elevated standards applied at training, hiring, and promotional states of career development. This makes it increasingly difficult for any aspirant who assumes a significant portion of family responsibilities to compete successfully with persons without children and/or spouses working full time.

Second, job scarcity greatly accentuates the problem of coordinating the career paths of spouses. Even in the best of times, coordinating two careers—each involving training, the pursuit of jobs, and periodic job moves—constitutes a monumental task for the dual careerist. But as the opportunity structure tightens, coordinating two careers may no longer be just difficult; it may be a luxury that is entirely beyond the grasp of many independently well-qualified aspirants. This difficulty arises partly because, with fewer opportunities open to each spouse, the possibilities for finding workable combinations are mathematically reduced. However, it is also because a major survival strategy adopted by dual careerists in the past— that of one spouse, usually the wife, pacing herself more slowly to cover family responsibilities and/or avoiding reaching critical career junctures at the same time (Bird, 1979; Holmstrom, 1972; Poloma, 1972; Rapoport and Rapoport, 1969, 1971b, 1976)—is far less feasible in today's job market. This market increasingly demands a full effort on the part of all who would remain competitive.[5]

Resolutions to these problems of the dual careerists in an ever more competitive job market are potentially twofold. One spouse can withdraw to facilitate the success of the other and/or preserve the family unit, or the couple can separate to pursue careers without the constraint of coordination. Either way, the dual-career family dissolves, and such dissolution may well become the norm, not the exception, among those who pursue the dual-career life-style.

The Impact of Dual Careers on the Nuclear Family

The dual-career family is not only problematic from the standpoint of the career market but is also questionable from that of the family style itself. One source of strain is that the progressive extrication of the modern family from the networks of extended kin, larger households, and communities has resulted in the breakdown of historical mechanisms of social control. When public and private lives were less segregated, much of family life was accessible to the view and supervision of nonfamily members.

Now, civility and restraint from abuse rest primarily on the fragile basis of the mutual feelings of two adults. And in light of such indices as the incidence of child abuse and domestic violence, this may be only marginally sufficient (Laslett, 1973; Skolnick, 1978).

The dual-career family may have, at best, mixed implications for this problem. Insofar as this family form involves women and children outside the private context of the household and/or introduces hired help into the household, it reduces the family's isolation and may tend to ameliorate the social-control problem. On the other hand, demands on the couple's time and the absence of a traditional wife to perform socio-emotional functions create increased tension. Further, the dual-career family's "deviance" constitutes a barrier to its ready assimilation and acceptance within traditional social circles, which may work to make this family even more isolated than its more conventional counterpart. The Rapoports (1969) acknowledge the "network dilemmas" created by dual careers but do not address their social-control implications.

A second source of strain associated with the nuclear family results from changing values. The contemporary family finds its members caught between the conflicting cultural ethics of work and duty, on the one hand, and fun and personal freedom, on the other. The family is romanticized as offering a synthesis of these virtues through the coupling of the marriage contract and parental obligation with free choice of marital partners and voluntary control over family planning, but its members often find it in tension with impulses for new experience, spontaneity, personal growth and development, and the like (Putney, 1972; Skolnick, 1978).

The implications of this problem for the dual-career family are only superficially positive. It can be argued that the greater opportunities for personal fulfillment offered women by this family form reduce their value tension by giving them the terms men have had for realizing both ethics in different phases of their lives. However, careerism does not really offer women the life-style men have enjoyed, because women cannot fully delegate their family responsibilities. Women have always experienced problems of role conflict in their attempts to combine family and career (see, e.g., Coser and Rokoff, in this volume). This role conflict is a female variant of the value tension the nuclear-family system creates. Inasmuch as dual careerism increases the domestic responsibilities of men, it reduces their insulation from the acute role conflict women experience when pursuing careers and may simply make such conflict a problem for both spouses.

A final factor affecting the nuclear-family system is contraction of the motherhood role. The extension of life expectancy and the spread of contraception have had the effect of drastically reducing the proportion of women's lives that is consumed by childbearing and child rearing. This makes increasingly obsolete a definition of women's roles in home-bound terms and calls for cultural redefinitions of sex roles acknowledging women's availability and need for greater participation in extrafamilial spheres of life. And the dual-career family is hailed by many as the obvious response to the shrinking place of mothering in a woman's life (Bird, 1979; Dahlstrom and Liljestrom, 1967; Friedan, 1963; Holmstrom, 1972; Rossi, 1964).

But this view takes the logic of what is happening to the meaning of being a mother and parent only halfway. Contraception has eliminated the inevitability of parenthood. Industrialization has eliminated the economic advantage of having children and transformed it into something of a liability. And the participation of women in careers may work to reduce, for these women and their spouses, any remaining incentives for having children. As some women have had children primarily to fill a void created by the absence of alternative opportunities, careers may remove this incentive by filling the void. Moreover, if child rearing becomes more personally demanding for men, who have previously enjoyed a kind of "absentee parenthood," men's desire to have children may be reduced. Thus, while some may see the dual-career family as a realistic development in light of women's need for greater domestic equity and social participation, the dual-career life-style is probably more likely to evolve into an adult-centered rather than a family-centered one.

These considerations suggest the strong possibility that the dual-career family form will not strengthen the nuclear family by offsetting its major weaknesses, but may instead further reduce its viability. If so, the combination of dual careers and nuclear families cannot be forecast as a social pattern that will spread widely throughout American society.

Further Status Implications of the Nuclear-Family System

Dual careerism responds to the problems of women by seeking to equate the terms on which spouses assume family responsibilities and pursue extrafamilial goals. In doing so, it would exaggerate the status dilemmas of two other social categories directly affected by the contemporary nuclear-family system: (1) the service workers needed to maintain the private nuclear household, and (2) the children, who, even more than wives, are captives of this structure.

While proponents of the dual-career family emphasize its implications for a redefinition of sex roles and greater sharing of child care and housework responsibilities by spouses, a major theme running through discussions of this family form is the need for more adequate support systems in the form of extrafamilial child-care facilities and paid domestic help within the household (Feinstein, 1979; Holmstrom, 1972, Miller, 1972; Rapoport and Rapoport, 1971b; Rossi, 1964). Particularly where the emphasis is on hired help within the home, this stress on support systems would seem to betray some rather elitist assumptions. Hired help on a single-family basis involves a category of workers that must be paid out of the take-home earnings of the nuclear unit. Consequently, the dual-career family is premised upon the increased use of a class of workers locked into a standard of living considerably lower than that of their employers.

To the extent that the dual-career family would require support systems involving a category of relatively low-paid workers, it would provide for the liberation of one class of women by the continued subjugation of another. It would base sexual equality on the perpetuation of class differences. This may not only pose an ideological dilemma for some who might choose the dual-career life-style but also presents practical problems with respect to the continued availability of support-system personnel. As the ideology of equality is assimilated not only by educated white women but by the less privileged classes and minority peoples who have traditionally provided cheap services for the more affluent, the potential pool of support-system workers may diminish.[6]

The other social category which may emerge as a powerful interest group to be reckoned with is children. The support system espoused by dual-career family advocates would further professionalize and institutionalize the child-rearing process. Many hail this as providing a more stimulating, healthful, and egalitarian developmental and socialization experience for children (Figes, 1970; Firestone, 1970; Holmstrom, 1972; Rossi, 1964; Safilios-Rothschild, 1974). But others suggest that it is extending the trend toward schooling, which oppresses children by robbing them of individuality, overly formalizing the learning process, and arbitrarily limiting their participation in, impact upon, and independence within society (Goodman, 1964; Gordon, 1971; Illich, 1971; Plumb, 1974). School, in other words, does to children many of the things that domestic confinement does to women, and any policy to emancipate women by further confining and excluding children may place the interests of these two groups at odds. As children (and their advocates) continue to articulate their right to "deschooling," to work, and to self-determination, women (and dual-career husbands) who have founded their careers on professional child care may be vulnerable, both practically and ideologically, to an erosion of their career commitment and involvement.

Conclusions: Beyond the Dual-Career Family

Proponents of the dual-career family see its major strength as permitting real sex-role change without abandoning existing economic and familial institutions. We submit that the failure of the dual-career family to move beyond these institutional constraints constitutes its major weakness. The dual-career family seeks to combine the luxury of two full-time, continuous careers and a private nuclear-family household. Yet as Slater (1974a) observes, probably no social order can provide for the realization of all values simultaneously. If sexual equality is finally to become a central social value, it cannot realistically be expected to coexist with social institutions which are the outgrowths of the excesses of a patriarchal society.

Careers are based on a subordinate female class which frees the male, supports him in his career pursuits, and manages the consumption of the goods and services he produces. Each private nuclear-family household requires a full-time child-rearing and home-management specialist who must either be a captive wife or a low-paid servant. To alter these patterns, we cannot simply expect women to take up careers next to their husbands, turn domestic work over to a servant class, and confine children to the supervision of hired help and child-care institutions. A significant number of people may find the dual-career family to be the most desirable and realistic method for personal survival within the existing social order, but it can probably never provide a generalized solution to the problem of sexual inequality. Such a solution should meet several conditions that the dual-career family does not:

1. Provision for the radical redistribution and restructuring of work and compensation, so that an expanded group, including more women, minorities, and children could share participation in a nonexpanding economy (e.g., through compensation for housework and the development of noncontinuous, part-time, and/or shared work roles, combined with larger households supported by multiple wage earners).

2. Reduction of the amount of domestic service persons would need or expect from others, so that no class of persons would have to work simply to provide a more privileged life-style for others (e.g., through more limited involvement in public work roles, expanded households, and/or simplification of life-style).

3. Establishment of informal, extranuclear, and intergenerational social networks within which children would have to be neither overschooled nor smothered by full-time mothering. Instead, under the diffused nurturing and "benign neglect" of a social unit larger than the family but smaller than the school, they could be raised as children have historically been— as participating members of human communities (e.g., through larger households, communes, apartment coalitions or cooperatives, and the like).

While it is difficult to see any movement toward these social developments, social policy concerned with effecting changes in patterns of sexual inequality must look beyond fitting two careers into nuclear families.

Without fundamental reordering of work and life-style, the current wedding of the occupational world and the nuclear family—as surely as the more obvious social and political realities of traditional status-group relations—will continue to result in a marked status advantage for now-ascendant social categories. And the idea that this status advantage can be removed without major modification of these institutions simply diverts attention from this fact and may well prove conservative in its implications.

Notes

1. The Rapoports (1971b) distinguish the dual-career family from the dual-worker family in which both spouses have jobs. Dual-worker families (and, we might add, families in which one spouse has a career and the other works at a job) are far more numerous but lack some of the key elements of the dual-career pattern. The distinction hinges upon the difference between career and work at a job in terms of the degree of personal commitment (jobs are taken for more purely economic reasons) and continuity of employment (jobs are more subject to interruption and lack clear developmental stages and accumulation of expertise).

2. While dual-career families are but one of myriad alternative life-styles on the upswing, they are perceived as having perhaps the most direct implications for the status of women. Patterns, such as gay, swinging, and heterosexual communal living, seem to be responses to personal fulfillment needs that are largely unrelated to achievement or career development, particularly for women. Other alternatives, such as single and lesbian life-styles, while they may be more closely associated with women's status concerns, have less chance of becoming general, insofar as they are more radical departures than the dual-career family from the standard nuclear form still considered basic for the socialization of children. This latter assumption is one that is questioned in this essay, but nonetheless probably accounts for the emphasis on the part of advocates of sexual equality in the dual-career family.

3. The wife's role is nonproductive in that it is not paid public production (Benston, 1969) and insofar as a major function of her work is to provide expressive symbolism (e.g., food preparation could be accomplished by the man himself after work or professionally, but when the task is performed by a wife, it takes on a supportive dimension). Nonetheless, it should be acknowledged that the instrumental and expressive functions of work cannot be sharply separated. Women's work does indeed have a productive component, whether this is recognized and compensated for or not. (See, e.g., Benston, 1969; Pyun, 1969.)

4. Some of the literature hints that there may be significant compensations in the dual-career pattern which offset its liabilities. Dual-career spouses must be able to offer each other unique kinds of mutual support by virtue of their overlapping or common life experiences (especially when they are pursuing careers in the same profession). And dual-career families might be relieved of some of the make-work and status-displaying responsibilities generated by the traditional division of labor. (See, e.g., Bird, 1979; Butler and Paisley, 1980; Epstein, 1970b; Rapoport and Rapoport, 1971b, 1976.)

5. The phasing out of the option of a slower-paced and perhaps even interrupted career path for the female careerist during the early stages of family development and at critical phases of the husband's career development has occurred in the name of "universalism" and illustrates the naïveté and implicit individualism of such a principle (Slater, 1974a). The principle would treat each individual equally, as if all persons were similarly free to pursue

success goals. But as they are not, the application of universalistic criteria—blind to all auxiliary dimensions of status and selected and enforced by those who possess the favored auxiliary characteristics—is inherently and systematically discriminatory. While particularism restricted women's training and employment opportunities, excluded them from top positions, and contained them at low salary levels, it granted them a unique career path which was compatible with their family roles. Universalism has reduced some of the old injustices but ignores the constraints placed on women (and, increasingly, on dual-career husbands) by the nuclear-family system, making them probable casualties of equal treatment.

6. It might be objected that there are many women whose only employment prospect is domestic service work, particularly in the face of contracting opportunities for alternative forms of employment. These women would certainly not benefit from reduced demand for their services. To such an objection, we would submit that in the short run the demand for these services will probably not be reduced but will expand, as higher-status women increasingly seek liberation from the household. In the long run, should the radical transformation of the economy and social order envisioned in the concluding section of this paper occur, the domestic-labor class we now have would no longer exist. The services they now render would be to some degree eliminated (e.g., with the development of a variety of professional household-maintenance specialists paid by multiple wage earners), and to some degree diffused and performed informally (e.g., housework would become a shared responsibility of all household members). As for those people, largely women, who have performed these services, radical reorganization of the economy would give them new forms of work and/or compensation so that they would no longer be available on exploitative terms.

IV

Women and the Dual Economy: Continuing Discrimination

Single, divorced, widowed, and poor women have always worked outside as well as in the home; now more and more married women with working husbands are joining them. Today, nearly 58 percent of the U.S. female labor force is composed of married women; in 1940, only 15 percent of such women were employed outside the home (Odendahl, 1978; Smith, 1979). Despite widespread support for the belief that women should stay home to care for "their" children (Fraiberg, 1977), the major increase in women joining the paid labor force is among married women with children below the age of six. Between 1960 and 1967, that set of mothers doubled in the paid labor force— from 15 to 33 percent for mothers of children under three and from 25 to 42 percent for mothers with children from three to five. This increase was larger than among women with older children (Almquist, 1977).

The growing number of women seeking paid work do so for many reasons. Women tend to live longer than men, and so there are many widows in the labor force. Increasing divorce rates require more women to go outside the home to work. These trends swell the ranks of women from all social classes and races who are heads of households; 36 percent of all black families, 21 percent of all Hispanic families, and 11 percent of all white families are headed by women (FEW, 1980). Among married women, many seek paid work primarily to keep family income above the poverty line.

In addition to those who work outside the home because they must, a growing number of women prefer to do so. Some women find full-time housework an unsatisfactory occupation (Berk and Berk, 1979). Still others, especially those with college education, want an opportunity to use their knowledge and skills to achieve the degree of independence and respect that one's own earnings can provide (Friedan, 1963). These women add to the numbers of women returning to work or preparing for that return by enrolling in professional schools. Seminaries, graduate programs, and law schools all show a dramatic rise in enrollment by women in the last decade (Association of American Colleges, 1980).

So many women have so many reasons for entering the labor force that we might wonder why even more women are not doing so. We have already discussed the cultural mandate for women to put family first (Coser and Rokoff, this volume). This mandate conceals the interests of those men who benefit both from women's support services and from their relegation to a secondary position in the labor market. We have also noted that the extra demands placed on women who do not have a supporting network at home and instead must provide that network for others limit the time available for a commitment to paid work (as the Hunt-Hunt and Pleck readings pointed out earlier).

All these obstacles are exacerbated by the experiences women face in the paid labor force. Clearly, they are at a disadvantage when evaluated on expectations of behavior based on the male clockwork (discussed in earlier introductions and in the reading by Bourne and Wikler). In addition, women are limited by the effects of pervasive sex segregation within the paid labor force itself. Such segregation seems so natural to many that they notice it only when the norm is challenged, as when a male voice answers as the telephone operator or a woman arrives to make telephone repairs. In this section we show why, because of this segregation, women's entrance into the labor force by itself cannot be considered a sign of growing equality.

If we consider how industrialization began, we see that it originally depended upon a segregated labor force, in rough imitation of the division of labor in the family work unit. Men worked at the more skilled jobs, while women and children were assistants, preparing working materials and cleaning up afterward. This imitation of the pattern in the craft worker's family productive unit was, for a while, supported by early industry owners, who gave men the wages earned by their wives and children (Tilly and Scott, 1978: 112). When industrialists hired individuals rather than families, the differential in jobs and wages between men and women continued. The low wages women received were rationalized on the basis that they were young and single, living in households with other people, or that they were wives supplementing a husband's income. There was no effort to accommodate women without family support or women who were heads of households. In fact, the system of differential jobs and pay for women forced many into marriage, where they hoped to benefit from a man's wage (Tilly and Scott, 1978: 128).

Sex segregation of the paid labor force, with the corresponding differential rates of pay between typical women's and men's jobs, continues today. One reason for women's continued disadvantage in the marketplace has been their lack of organization by unions. With union support, men in skilled jobs were able to fight for better wages and protected jobs; women, like other unskilled workers, had no such advantage. Though unions were growing in the late 1800s, their leadership resisted organizing women. Because of the pervasive stereotype of women as temporary workers who leave the labor force for marriage, it was assumed that the continual need to educate new women workers to appreciate the value of unionization would use too many scarce resources. And transitory workers would have no reason to strike for improvements of primary benefit to others (Kessler-Harris, 1981: 51). This image of women as unorganizable existed although they had organized and struck for better wages and conditions in the mills of Lowell, Massachusetts in the 1830s (see Dublin, 1975; Eisler, 1977, for some of that early history). While there were few married women gainfully employed during this period, those who were, along with widows, single, and deserted women, were almost 20 percent of the labor force (Hill, 1929).

The second reason for the lack of interest in organizing women is one which causes difficulties in the labor movement to this day. In the nineteenth century, employers trained women to do unskilled labor once performed by skilled male workers. The increased technology that made unskilled labor profitable also created opportunities for workers with little training who could work at machines. Women and children who had to work could then be used as strikebreakers when men refused to work for the low wages accompanying unskilled jobs. As a result of these tactics, women were seen as unfair competitors by many unionized workers. There were serious arguments in the early days of the American labor movement about how to overcome competition from women. Some argued that women should be organized along with men to prevent employers from using women as a cheap labor supply to undermine male demands for better wages. Others argued that women should be excluded entirely from the labor force and that men should receive a family wage sufficient to support wives and children. The ideology that women belong in the home was frequently invoked. Labor leaders also argued that all unskilled workers were easily replaceable and thus unorganizable. While skilled workers could bargain with employers who did not want to pay the cost of training replacements, employers faced little cost

in replacing unskilled workers. The latter consequently had little leverage for bargaining (Milkman, 1980). By using women and other
unskilled workers—mostly immigrants and their children and other
minorities—to threaten the pay of skilled workers, employers set
workers against one another and forestalled a unification of American
workers (Reich et al., 1973).

Instead of improving women's working conditions by extending the
benefits of union membership to them, unions turned their efforts
toward promoting legislation that would better these conditions. This
protective legislation did improve the life of those women in the most
oppressive work by setting minimal health and safety standards, but
at the same time it reduced the economic desirability of women
workers. While employers could still pay women less than men, it
was costly for them because employers were not required to meet
these health and safety standards if all the workers were adult men.
Protective legislation helped men in that women could no longer be
used as competitors to force wages down. But women were even
more rigidly excluded from the better-paying jobs (Kessler-Harris,
1981: 93).

Expanded commerce and trade, as well as the rise of large corporations, did lead to the possibility of white-collar jobs just at the time
many industry jobs were closed to women. But discrimination continued much as before. Employers preferred women for the newly developing jobs because they could be hired for half the pay of men.
Without other alternatives, women would not ask for the promotions
men expected in order to support their families (Kessler-Harris, 1981:
96). By 1900 the pattern was firmly set for most women to work in
poorly paid jobs open only to them. (See Tentler, 1979, for conditions
of work for women from 1900 to 1930. Broader views of the struggle
waged by women to better their conditions in the twentieth century
are provided by Baxandall et al., 1976; Foner, 1980; Wertheimer, 1977.)

While thousands of industrial workers—male and female—were organized with the rise of the industrial union in the 1930s, this commitment to organization of all industrial workers did not include a
commitment to equality of treatment. The women who were organized were largely those in blue-collar production jobs, where terms
of unequal pay were often written into the contract. No attempt was
made to develop principles of comparable pay for women's and
men's sections in the same industry (Milkman, 1980: 126). And no real
effort was made to organize office workers, the majority of whom
were women. After World War II, though unions would have preferred conditions of full employment, when such conditions did not
develop, they signed contracts giving preference for jobs to men over

women. Women had to return to lower-paying jobs as service workers, office workers, and domestics, even though 75 percent of those
interviewed during the war years and at demobilization said they
wanted to remain in their industrial jobs (Kessler-Harris, 1981: 143).

And so, as Gross argued (1968), the pervasive pattern of lower pay
for women's jobs combined with their segregation in the work force
to ensure continued inequality. He found that the increasing numbers of women entering the labor force by 1960 were still either in
these segregated women's jobs or in newly available jobs, such as
key punch operator, which immediately became female ghettos.
Where desegregation did occur, men were entering women's fields
but not the reverse. And the men who entered women's occupations,
such as nursing or elementary school teaching, were overrepresented
in the senior positions in those fields. A related study by Hedges
(1970: 19) found that in 1969 half of all employed women were in 21
of 250 occupations listed by the Census Bureau. One-quarter of all
women in the study were in five jobs: secretary-stenographer,
domestic, bookkeeper, elementary school teacher, and waitress. In
contrast, half of all male employees were spread among 65 occupational categories. In a follow-up of Gross' study, Williams (1975)
found that the historical tendencies noted by Gross as of 1960 were
continuing into the 1970s, though changes in methods of categorizing
jobs in different periods made precise comparison difficult.

What has happened is that although women are now entering the
labor market in growing numbers, they are largely restricted to jobs
in the *peripheral* or secondary sector of the economy, where productivity is lower and firms want a labor force willing to accept inferior
working conditions, lower pay, and precarious job stability. The jobs
available to women in these firms typically require few skills, have
low wages, offer few opportunities for advancement (and minimal on-
the-job training), and have high worker turnover. White men predominate in the *core* sector of the economy, typically in jobs with
high skill requirements, high wages, good advancement possibilities,
and low worker turnover (Beck et al., 1980). In these industries, sophisticated technology guarantees that worker productivity is high.

According to classical economic theory, employers suffer for their
discrimination by not getting the best workers and thus not being
able to compete in the market (Becker, 1957). What this viewpoint
ignores is the fact that owners and employers in industries with minimal technological development benefit by employing a poorly paid
worker who makes few demands for training, wages, or promotion.
In our dual economy, women neither compete with white men nor
benefit from the employment advantages gained by unionized work-

ers in high-productivity industries. In peripheral industries, low-skilled and poorly unionized women and other minorities are easily replaceable and have been unable to make demands and receive benefits, as have workers in the core sectors of the economy. But in a classic case of blaming the victim, women themselves are often deemed responsible for the characteristics of the jobs available to them. Employers point to such workers' lack of training and unstable work histories as a justification for low wages and lack of job-training opportunities, though the only work they offer characteristically has high worker turnover and provides no training (Beck et al., 1980). But it is discrimination which leads to low productivity of women workers. After controlling for education, experience, and all other factors which might cause differences in productivity—and thus increase the value of the employees to the employer—the proportion of sex differential in wages which is unaccounted for and thus attributable to pure discrimination is estimated at between 29 and 43 percent (Sawhill, 1973). This differential is not as great between black women and black men, but it does not disappear.

The readings in this section show how the process of sex segregation within the job market is maintained by interrelated social, economic, and technological constraints. Glenn and Feldberg describe the proletarianization process in clerical work: reduced skill and increased routine; closer control and more impersonal relations; lower prestige and lower pay. With increased automation, years of experience may mean increased wages for seniority but no increase in level of skill and few chances for promotion. A new employee can be trained in a few days to do the job of someone with years of seniority. In these circumstances, white-collar employees, like unskilled blue-collar workers in peripheral industries, are afraid to make demands for better wages or express complaints about working conditions. Women's acceptance of these conditions thus comes not only from socialization to be "nice" and cooperative but also from their realistic appraisal of lack of alternatives available in a segmented labor market.

Employers may explain their unwillingness to provide job training and opportunities for advancement to women workers as a response to their experience that women are not stable employees. But it has long been known that rates of job turnover are related more to type of job than to characteristics of the job holder. Turnover is greatest in the lowest level of poorly paid, dead-end jobs. Given that more women compared to men are in such low-reward jobs, the overall turnover rate makes women seem less stable (U.S. Civil Service Commission, 1963).

The reading by Kanter in this section, a forerunner of ideas and evidence in her *Men and Women of the Corporation* (1977b), emphasizes that many aspects of women's aspirations, attitudes, and behavior in paid work are related more to characteristics of hierarchical organizations than to those assumed to be based on gender or personality. Many supposed "traits" of women workers, such as a concern with friendships developed on the job, are a function of their positions in the hierarchy, e.g., whether they are in low-status, low-skill jobs or in jobs requiring extensive skill and formal education. It is not personality characteristics but the opportunity to gain mobility and power that affects the organizational behavior of women (and men). Kanter suggests that in business and industry, women (and men) may believe they are making individual decisions, yet their behavior may be seen more accurately as adaptations to existing hierarchies and distributions of opportunities. Her point is quite similar to that made by Bourne and Wikler in their reading (earlier) on the situation women face in medicine. When women say they are not as ambitious on the job (or in their careers) as many men are, they may often express not an early and conscious choice but a cumulative response to the limited opportunities actually available to them.

With an understanding of the historical development of a dual economy and also of the ways in which organizational structure itself can limit opportunity, it is no longer easy to explain patterns in women's market work as based on personality or sex differences. Both blue-collar and white-collar women have long been subject to the same sorts of occupational discrimination that ethnic and racial minorities have experienced, and economic, structural, and technological constraints are still used in various combinations to maintain such discrimination. But many of the restrictions of opportunity involved are also reinforced and maintained every time a decision is made by people (at all levels in the occupational world) who take such restrictions as given or necessary. Hillsman and Levenson help us understand the existence and persistence of the dual labor market from the interactional perspective. They show how vocational school counselors maintain job segregation between white and minority women graduates by making everyday decisions that guide the students into "appropriate" subfields, i.e., those the counselors have come to believe will make employees acceptable to employers. The counselors come to this understanding through a selective focusing of their everyday experience and through interpreting employment statistics, without realizing how both types of evidence are partly created and maintained by their own counseling practices.

Hillsman and Levenson's study of the discriminatory consequences of school and job counselors' expectations, like that of Kanter on how owners' and managers' expectations are expressed and experienced at various levels of the corporate structure, illustrates the power of what Merton (1968) might call "self-fulfilling prophecies" about the work that women can do. Stereotypes of all kinds, about the right kind of work for women, their capacities, priorities, commitments, and motivations, continually influence the kind of work they are ultimately able to get. As long as we do not examine, for example, how owners, employers, and lower-level officials make decisions that open or close opportunities for women, we tend to confuse behavior and motivation. What people actually do may not tell us as much about what they want to do as it does about what others they are dependent on will encourage or allow them to do.

Affirmative action policies have ostensibly been introduced to break the self-fulfilling processes maintaining the segmented labor market and the disadvantaged position of women and minorities within it. Some hoped that, with affirmative action legislation, women's positions in paid work would improve rapidly. But Hacker's detailed study of the American Telephone and Telegraph Company's response to legal requirements for affirmative action during a period of technological innovation suggests that fundamental changes will not occur as long as employers maintain stereotyped images of women. These images assume what women will respond to and accept in their participation in the paid work force. For example, AT&T did make categories of jobs in installation and repair available to women, but at a time when overall planning in the company assured that these categories were to be phased out. Some of the managers realized that the women were being moved into another dead-end job. Others assumed that women move in and out of the work force at a constant enough rate to provide a natural form of attrition, obviating the necessity for layoffs with the introduction of new technology. Whatever the motives of AT&T managers, these and other changes also deflected the anger of male workers away from the job reduction resulting from long-planned increases in automation and toward competition with women over affirmative action. As in so many other periods of economic hardship in this country, any potential unification of the labor force was averted.

The barriers to the liberal ideal of equal opportunity are far from disappearing; they are continuing in new socioeconomic and technological forms. It is growing recognition of their historical and continuing segregation in the labor force that has recently led women to raise the issue of comparable pay for work of equal worth (Celarier, 1981; Perlman and Ennis, 1980). This new policy will address the needs of women who are not fully recompensed for either their experience or their training. The struggle to give everyone in the society an equal opportunity to succeed in the marketplace is far from over. But as long as women (and minorities) are restricted to positions in which marketable experience and training are not available to them, even such a more sweeping challenge to the existing political and economic system as comparable pay for comparable worth will not fundamentally improve women's position.

Degraded and Deskilled:
The Proletarianization of Clerical Work

EVELYN NAKANO GLENN
ROSLYN L. FELDBERG
Boston University

14. Origins. In this section, Glenn and Feldberg's study of clerical work shows how women are used for low-paid and alienating labor. Using the concept of proletarianization, these authors argue that as clerical work became more routinized, wages were lowered and the field was opened to women. Women's lack of experience in organizing to fight for their rights and their willingness to be agreeable and helpful have been turned to employers' interests; more work can be expected from female workers without raising wages. Clerical work, like much service work, becomes a female ghetto as men find better positions. Do you think men might move back into secretarial work? Can you explain recent trends in another proletarianized occupation—telephone operator—which men now enter? (See the Hacker reading below as well.) What are the main social, economic, and technological influences on women's work as clerks that Glenn and Feldberg discuss?

As the American dream of upward mobility through hard work dissolves in the face of limited opportunity, analysts have turned their attention to the meaning of routine work. The pioneer studies of the 1950s and 1960s examined blue-collar work in large, highly mechanized factories (Blauner, 1964; Chinoy, 1955; Gouldner, 1964). Recently, it has become fashionable to say that white-collar work, particularly clerical work, is becoming factory-like. A federal task force reports:

> Secretaries, clerks and bureaucrats were once grateful for having been spared the dehumanization of the factory . . . they had higher status than blue collar [workers]. But today the clerk . . . is the typical American worker . . . and such positions offer little in the way of prestige . . . imparting to the clerical worker the same impersonality that blue-collar workers experience in the factory. (*Work in America*, 1973: 38)

The acknowledgment of change has not yet led to detailed study of the actual conditions of clerical work and the implications of these conditions for 11.7 million female clerical workers (Manpower Report of the President, 1975). The research reported in this paper is the first exploratory stage of such a study. The paper analyzes the changing conditions of clerical work, examining the extent to which they can be understood by the concept of proletarianization.

Proletarianization can be defined as a "shift in middle-class occupations toward wage workers, in terms of: income, property, skill, prestige or power, irrespective of whether or not the people involved are aware of these changes" (Mills, 1956: 295). Following Mills, we use the term "proletarianization" to refer to objective conditions rather than to the workers' subjective feelings and identities.

The features that distinguish clerical work, justifying its inclusion among "middle-class" occupations, are: clean physical surroundings, an emphasis on mental as opposed to manual activities, reliance on workers' judgment in executing tasks, and direct personal contact among workers and between workers and managers. *Proletarianization occurs as clerical work loses these special characteristics, i.e., as work is organized around manual rather than mental activities, as tasks become externally structured and controlled, and as relationships become depersonalized.* We therefore examine changes in condition in three areas: the organization of clerical activities, the control of the work process, and the social relationships in the office.

We will argue that increased size of organizations, the application of machine technology, and prevailing organizational goals have had a proletarianizing effect in all three areas. However, we will also argue that proletarianization has progressed at different rates for workers in different specialties and in different types of organizational settings.[1]

Organizational and Technological Changes in the Office

Clerical work is, above all, work in organizations. It does not and cannot exist as an independent occupation. In turn, the characteristics of the organization define the nature of clerical work within it. The easiest way to appreciate the way organizational structures shape clerical work is to compare the small office of the nineteenth century with the large contemporary office.[2]

The Nineteenth-Century Office
In the older offices, the clerical staffs were small. Clerks were "all-around" workers. They handled all phases of an assignment, both organizing and executing it, and they did a wide variety of tasks. In 1905 Dorothy Richardson was "entrusted with the revision of the least important manuscripts" in the office of a publishing company, where she also took dicta-

tion and typed (Richardson, 1972: 272). Clerks often had extended responsibilities that today would be classified as managerial or administrative (Lockwood, 1958). A bookkeeper, intimately familiar with all of the financial details of a firm, might be readily consulted on financial decisions. In the 1920s, for example, one secretary ran a business for most of the year while the head of the firm lived in the Southwest for his health (Bureau of Vocational Information, 1929). The organization of the work in the old office allowed the worker to develop skills and to identify as a skilled craftsman, a professional, or a part of management (Lockwood, 1958).

The Growth of Organizations
The rise of large national companies in the latter part of the nineteenth and early twentieth centuries profoundly changed the office (Stinchcombe, 1965). The demand for clerical services soared, not only absolutely, but also disproportionately to the growth of production (Melman, 1951; Rushing, 1967). National companies established central administrative offices with huge clerical staffs (Mills, 1956). Industries such as banking, insurance, and brokerage, whose primary workforce was clerical, accounted for an increasingly large share of the economy (Braverman, 1974).

The demand for clerical services was met by hiring more workers, by introducing machines, and by bringing "scientific management" into the office. The numerical growth of clerical workers between 1870 and 1970 is documented in Table 1. At first, simple machines such as typewriters were introduced; after World War I, multiple function machines, for example, bookkeeping machines which performed a sequence of tasks, were used to speed up operations (Baker, 1964). Scientific management was used to break jobs into a series of steps, which were then reordered to save time, and/or divided among different groups of workers. Physical rearrangements eliminated wasted motions.

These changes in office routine transformed the office hierarchy. A new male managerial stratum took over the quasi-managerial activities of the clerks, leaving the detail work to the now predominantly female office staffs (Crozier, 1964; Mills, 1956). Two distinct occupational hierarchies evolved: a male one, made up of many layers of managers, and a female one of file clerks, typists, stenographers, clerical supervisors and secretaries (Coyle, 1929; Davies, 1974; Mills, 1956; Rotella, 1974). Thus began an increasing distinction between those conceptualizing a task (mental work) and those doing it (manual work).[3]

The Modern Office
To appreciate and evaluate the effects of these as well as more recent organizational and technological changes, we now look at the large contem-

Table 1
Growth of the Clerical Force: 1870–1970[1]
(in thousands)

	1870	1880	1890	1900	1910	1920	1930	1940	1950	1960	1970
Total clerical workers	91	186	492	770	1,885	3,311	4,274	4,847	7,632	9,783	13,714
As % of employed persons	0.7%	1.1%	2.1%	2.6%	5.1%	8.0%	9.0%	9.1%	12.8%	14.7%	17.4%
Female clerical workers	2	8	83	204	677	1,601	2,223	2,549	4,597	6,629	10,233
As % of all clerical workers	2.4%	4.3%	16.9%	26.5%	35.9%	48.4%	52.0%	52.6%	60.2%	67.8%	74.6%

[1] Figures are not strictly comparable due to minor reclassifications of occupational categories.
Sources: 1870–1940 Total Clerical Workers, Female Clerical Workers, compiled from Janet M. Hooks, *Women's Occupations Through Seven Decades*, U.S. Department of Labor, Women's Bureau, Bulletin #218, Washington, D.C. 1947. Table 11A: Occupations of Women Workers, 1870–1940; Table 11B: Occupations of All Workers, 1870–1940.
1870–1940 Employed Persons from U.S. Bureau of the Census, *Historical Statistics, Abstracts of the U.S.*, Series D57-71.
1950–1970 U.S. Bureau of the Census, *Statistical Abstract of the U.S.*, 1972. Table 366: Employed Persons, by Major Occupation Group and Sex: 1950–1972.

porary office. In such offices, workers are organized into functional sub-units (e.g., sales, accounting, inventory control). Within units, clerks are further subdivided according to task. In fact, the most striking features of "paper work" in large organizations are the elaborate subdivision of tasks and the extreme specialization of workers.

Two current developments furthering these trends are the use of electronic data processing (EDP) and pooling arrangements, most fully developed in the IBM Word Processing System.

Computers routinely perform a wide range of clerical functions, from keeping inventories to maintaining insurance policy records and processing banking transactions. EDP is seen by experts as the latest stage in automation; the previous stages were "manual" processing (simple and multifunction machines) and "mechanized" processing (cardpunch systems) (Rico, 1967). The most significant features of the computer compared to earlier stages are its speed and capacity to store huge quantities of information. The effects of EDP on clerical work have been widely studied, leading to contradictory conclusions (e.g., International Labour Review, 1960; Rico, 1967; Shepard, J., 1971).

Computers are seen as labor-saving devices. Yet the computer's capacity to process vast amounts of information has increased the demand for data, on the assumption that more data results in more rational, better-informed decisions. Thus, the introduction of a computer rarely reduces the size of a clerical staff, since many clerks are needed to prepare the quantities of data involved.

Observers disagree about whether automation encourages further fragmentation of work. Shepard, J. (1971) and Rico (1967) argue that fragmentation is characteristic of mechanized rather than automated processing. They point out that more sophisticated systems allow reintegration of previously separate activities. For example, in later-model computers, information is entered directly in the department generating the information, eliminating a separate keypunching section.

However, we have found that clerical workers have not experienced increased autonomy or decreased fragmentation as a result of automation.[4] Regardless of technical differences among automated systems, all require that "information be handled in standardized and regularized form, which, in turn, implies that previous steps have been taken to put the information in such form" (Hall, 1975: 319). Moreover, when a system covers an entire firm, all activities must be translated into the same format (Rico, 1967: 31). As a result, work throughout the organization is structured by the requirements of the computer. Although the clerk may be less directly supervised, she does not gain autonomy; the requirements of the machine replace the directives of an immediate supervisor. Her mental choices are limited to predetermined categories. She has little discretion to do the work as she sees fit or to set her own pace, since her work has to feed into subsequent stages. As these changes occur, the worker is proletarianized according to our definition.

Although many routine clerical jobs, such as tabulating, are eliminated, other equally routine jobs are created—jobs such as transporting tape decks and keypunching. New skilled jobs, such as programming, are also created, but clerks are rarely upgraded to fill the new jobs (Hall, 1975; International Labour Review, 1960). Instead, professional and technical workers, recruited from outside the organization, form a new, higher-status group within the office hierarchy. The proportion of low-level clerical jobs remains the same.

The trend toward subdivision and specialization has also been furthered by clerical pooling arrangements. Pools have long been used for routine tasks such as typing and tabulating. The new pooling arrangements extend the use of pools to secretarial functions, with automatic machinery downgrading the skills required. These features are evident at Public Utility, where IBM's Word Processing/Administrative Support System has been introduced.

Previously, managers (called "clients" in the new system) were serviced by one-to-one secretaries, supplemented by a typing pool. Now secretarial work is divided among three pools. The first pool is the Word Processing Unit, made up of eight "general service clerks" who do all the typing, using "automated typing and dial dictation equipment" (Hilaael, 1975). Two "clerical assistants" also type and help to supervise the work. A supervisor receives assignments and instructions from clients and parcels out the work. In the second pool, the Administrative Support Center, ten to twelve women handle all nontyping clerical tasks. They answer telephones, schedule appointments, order supplies, and keep records and charts. This unit is similarly supervised by a head supervisor and two working assistants. This unit handles thirty-to-forty clients. The third pool, consisting of four or five men and women, does all reproduction work.

Dividing up secretarial work in this way makes it easier to identify the elements of each task and to set up standard procedures for carrying them out. For example, Public Utility has developed rules for transferring phone calls received by an administrative support clerk. Ostensibly, proper routing does not depend on the clerk's special knowledge of her clients' duties. This job no longer requires the general knowledge that characterized the all-around secretary.

Current Patterns and Trends

Clerical work is still undergoing change, and its conditions vary in different settings. Although we interviewed women from many companies and organizations, we studied five in greater detail. Of the five organizations,

Big City Insurance and Public Utility have subdivided clerical work the most, using extensive automation and pooling. Progressive Products, in contrast, retains all-around clerical and secretarial arrangements with finely graded steps for upward mobility. Rationalization has been resisted because the founder's belief in meaningful work still molds company policies. Proponents of rationalization argue that this company's creed can be adhered to only because the company is financially successful. Brand Name Foods, a medium-sized regional firm, and Personal Manufacturing, a national giant, fall somewhere between these extremes. They retain middle-level, all-around secretaries but also rely on a separate staff to perform highly routinized and mechanized clerical chores.

Many managers believe that Public Utility and Big City Insurance are establishing the pattern for the future. Although the exact details may change as systems are tested and "debugged," the general outline is clear. New office systems will use a technology based on subdivision and standardization. Choices among different work structures now available to workers will be considerably narrowed for those working in large organizations.

Impact of Changes on Clerical Activities

As a result of the changes described above, old skills have been made trivial and opportunities to develop skills have been reduced. Traditional specialties such as stenography and bookkeeping, which required extensive training, have been displaced or simplified beyond recognition. The skills now required are more *mechanical,* as in operating a Xerox machine, *lower level,* as in typing addresses on automatically typed correspondence, and/or *narrower,* as found in the administrative support center. Many clerical jobs can be taught with step-by-step manuals in a few days. A supervisor at Big City Insurance claimed that the work of "transferring policies" was so standardized that she could tell on the first morning of training whether a girl would do well.

In these low-skill jobs, women are unable to develop and maintain the skills they have. A thirty-seven-year-old clerk at Public Utility wanted to keep up her typing, but all of the typing was done in a separate pool. She did not want to type full-time; as a result, she never types at all.

The simplification of jobs and the absence of mental activity actually make many jobs more demanding. The worker experiences great pressure to work quickly and accurately, and to maintain the pace set by machines. The strain of routine jobs is demonstrated by workers' emphasis on temperamental qualities rather than skills. "Patience" was mentioned by fourteen of thirty workers. A twenty-one-year-old typist in Word Processing stated:

> You need a lot of patience. You need to be more or less good-natured, easy-going. Sometimes the tension gets really bad. Some people look on it as boring. If you go on saying, "Oh God, another day!" you wouldn't last too long.

Since the reorganization of clerical work began, managers have looked for "clerks who are satisfied to remain clerks" (Coyle, 1929: 185). Opportunities for upward mobility, never very extensive, have been further curtailed by the collapse of meaningful skill differentials. The more energetic and ambitious workers reach the top of their job ladders in a few years, then find themselves blocked.

Routine computer jobs such as keypunching are "universally regarded as dead-end occupation(s)" (Hoos, 1962: 75), but even the "better" computer jobs offer few opportunities for learning and experimentation. A young woman, promoted and trained in computer operation at Brand Name Foods, repeats the same operations day after day. "At first there was a lot to learn, but now that I've mastered it there's nothing new. I know the work backwards and forwards." The next step up for her was "nowhere"; the company would be reluctant to move her. She would have to be trained for a different position and someone else trained to replace her.

The main avenues of mobility for clerical workers are either horizontal or downward. A woman working for East City said:

> I thought about changing my job, but it took ten years of seniority to get a month's vacation. If I left and went to another job, I'd have to start up the levels again and I don't know how long it would take.

Clericals have become similar to blue-collar workers, and unlike professionals, in that experience on the job does not qualify them for better positions in new settings.

Control of the Work Process

Subdivision and standardization of the work process have been accompanied by changes toward more rational and impersonal methods of control. This close association has led some observers to argue that subdivision and specialization were not instituted primarily for the oft-stated reasons of efficiency (Gorz, 1973; Marglin, 1974). Rather, they were designed to increase the company's control over the work, as shown in recent studies of steel manufacturing (Stone, 1973) and computer programming (Kraft, 1975). However, it is important to note the managerial ideology that rationalization of work and formal control ensure profitability.[5] Managers consider the work process and the worker the means—and sometimes the obstacles—to realization of this goal. Both need to be controlled.

To appreciate the changes in control mechanisms, it is useful again to look at the early office. Workers were no less closely controlled than workers today, but the control was more personal and dependent on internal motivation. Clerks were few and worked in close physical proximity to, and under the visible eye of, the employer. Moreover, the work of the clerks and that of the employer were inseparable: the activities of the owner generated the work of the clerks, while the clerks' activities made it possible for the owner to carry on his business. Relationships were often paternalistic, reinforcing age and class divisions. The owner's authority was easily accepted. Relationships typically involved mutual loyalty and obligation. The clerk performed a variety of both official and personal functions. In return, he was afforded a measure of leniency and protection. In short, the organization of the office and the conditions of work created direct bonds between boss and clerk, encouraging the latter to identify with the former.[6]

Formal Controls

As businesses grew, sheer numbers of clerical workers made face-to-face controls impossible. More formal, administrative controls were introduced. An increasingly fine hierarchy, headed by an office manager and staffed by unit supervisors and assistants, supervised the clerks. In addition, subdivision and standardization made impersonal control easier and more necessary.

Personal forms of control imply a certain degree of flexibility in the pace and organization of work. However, subdivided work requires inflexible routines to insure that the subparts fit together. Subdivision prevents workers from gaining an overview of the total work process, thus necessitating external coordination, supplied by managers. They devise a work plan to be implemented by supervisors who divide the work load and see that production requirements are fulfilled. External coordination requires standardization, introducing new opportunities for control. As the work becomes standardized, the supervisor can regulate the worker simply by observing her movements. A supervisor at Big City Insurance reported that she can tell at a glance whether a worker is doing her assigned task.

These external controls over the work process increase the worker's vulnerability. The worker is open to constant inspection (similar to the "listening in" method of monitoring telephone operators; Langer, 1972). Her errors can't be hidden. The more clearly bounded her job is, the easier it is to assess her output—how many forms she checked or the number of pages she typed. It's a simple matter to rate her on numerical production, and it can be argued that as a job is reduced to quantifiable elements it loses status, thus contributing to its proletarianization.

The worker's hold over her position becomes precarious; her services are interchangeable and replaceable. Speed and dexterity, rather than finely honed skills, are required. The older and more experienced workers do the same work as younger, less experienced ones. A forty-nine-year-old clerk-typist for Municipal Offices says, "If I left tomorrow, they'd get someone else. Sometimes they'll give me [forms to type] and say I can do it better. I'm not flattered when I know someone else could do it as well." An experienced worker who complains or becomes expensive through raises can be easily replaced.

Processes that depend on particular individuals with specialized skills and knowledge can be disrupted by absences and turnover. Large organizations can avoid disruption and gain control through standardization. Public Utility requires each clerk to write a desk manual detailing duties and daily routine, including instructions on how to answer the telephone, how to deliver mail, etc. As one clerk said:

> If I'm out, my fill-in should be able to to what I do. It took two weeks to do it [the desk manual], one or two hours a day. . . . It's writing yourself out of a job. Everything is written in logs and on paper.

Once formal controls are instituted, they become increasingly necessary because they undermine workers' internal motivation. Personal control provides incentives to do a good job or to complete tasks before the end of the day; impersonal control leads them to work by "rule"—to put in the required number of hours and to do only their defined tasks, regardless of the organization's needs. A secretary transferred to supervising a pool says, "I used to work until 7 or 8 p.m. to get things done. Now, as soon as it's 4:30, I'm out the door." A vicious cycle arises. As Gorz (1973) describes the cycle: (1) the less management is willing to rely on workers' motivation, the more extraneous, regimented, and idiotic work has to become, and (2) the more extraneous, regimented and idiotic work becomes, the less management *can* rely upon the worker's motivation.

In this transitional period, some workers act as though the older conditions of work still existed. A nineteen-year-old typist says, "When I type, I don't like to make mistakes. When I finish it gives me a feeling of satisfaction." A thirty-two-year-old staff secretary says, "When I clear up everything on my desk, then it's been a good day. I don't like to leave stuff hanging over until the next day." Employers benefit even while the changes they have introduced are undermining the basis of these internal standards.

Sex as a Basis for Control

American managerial responses to issues of control have been shaped by the belief that workers are irrational, individualistic, and lacking in long-term perspectives (Kanter, 1975b). Thus, managers rely on external controls to ensure that workers do what they are supposed to do. In the case of clerical workers, managers are also influenced by prevailing stereotypes about women, viz. that they are oriented toward pleasing others, are more sensitive than men to the quality of their surroundings, and are more honest and less mercenary. Acker and Van Houten suggest that "unique mechanisms (may be) employed in organizations to control women" (1975: 153). Clerical workers are sometimes thought to be treated "better" than production workers. On closer inspection this "better" treatment may disguise closer, more restrictive controls. Langer (1972) shows how the New York Telephone Company "rewards" workers while maintaining both control and low wages. The women are "treated" to candy on holidays, jewelry on their anniversaries with the company, and appliances for recruiting new employees. "Niceness" is stressed throughout the company to create a pleasant atmosphere. The "niceness," which extends to sharing work loads, helps the women cope with the strains of constant supervision and rigid formats; it thus enables the company to continue imposing "unreasonable" demands. Similarly, in an ostensibly more enlightened setting, clerks in a college business office are allowed to cover for each other, thereby insuring that work gets done at no extra cost (Garson, 1973).

Orders to women are cloaked in the guise of personal requests, which they find difficult to refuse. A typist for Technical Research reports, "I don't have time to go to the bathroom" when typing a proposal to meet a deadline. The president of the company always sends her a memo of appreciation for extraordinary efforts when a proposal is completed. Sometimes changes in routine, designed to formalize control, are presented as moves to improve personal relationships, presumably because women would welcome such changes. A clerk at Public Utilty reports, "When they set up the administrative services center, they said it was more democratic. We wouldn't have "bosses" anymore, just clients. But they were just trying to save money. A clerk gets $150 a week while a secretary gets $185, for serving just one person." Even when management is aware that its employees see through its rationale, they rely on them to act like ladies and to continue to be loyal, dependable, and polite.

Extending Control: Why Secretaries Are "Out"

How far control over the worker has been extended can be appreciated by looking at the one group that has seemingly escaped control—the private secretaries. Within the office structure, the secretary is both a personal assistant and a company employee. However, the secretary's principal tie and loyalty is to her boss rather than to the company. The secretary to the president of Techtronics describes her duties in this way: "Basically, I try to help my boss succeed. If he succeeds, I succeed." The company rarely measures a private secretary's performance directly. Her status and pay reflect her boss' position—they rise as he moves up.

Researchers have long recognized that a secretary's status is tied to that of her boss (Benét, 1972; Mills, 1956; Moore, 1951), but they have rarely explored the implications of the tie on organizational control. The secretary is accountable to her boss; in return, the boss protects her from company scrutiny. A secretary at Progressive Products reported that her boss screened out unpleasant assignments and safeguarded her free time. The company has little control over the secretary's activities, and management complains about "underutilization" of the secretary's time (Hilaael, 1975). Replacing private secretaries with pools is, therefore, another way to extend company control over employees.

Relationships Among Workers

Changes in the work process and in the control structures have also transformed relationships in the office. We will look at two sets of relationships: those between supervisors and those they supervise, and those among lower-level workers.

Again, it is useful to compare these relationships with those in offices of an earlier period. Relationships there were face-to-face. The experienced specialists, such as bookkeepers and chief clerks, occupied positions analogous to that of "master craftsmen" in the trades. They took charge of the whole work process, aided by junior bookkeepers, copiers, and office boys. Like apprentices, these assistants learned first the rudiments and later the refinements of their specialties by working alongside the senior clerks (Braverman, 1974). Since each individual made a unique contribution, the interdependence among individual workers was immediately obvious. At the same time, the paternalistic structure of the office encouraged them to identify with those above them (Mills, 1956).

Supervisors, Secretaries, and Clerks

In the large, modern office with specialized clerical units, the relationships between higher and lower levels are impersonal. Contact with managers is limited and filtered through several layers of supervisors. Because of the separation between planning and doing in modern offices, the supervisor does not directly generate the work for those under her. Her authority stems more from her formal position than from her expertise as a skilled craftsperson. Like the factory foreman, she oversees routines and enforces rules set up by others. She stands in for management, sheltering it from direct confrontation with workers. An assistant supervisor at Big City Insurance complained that she had to do all the "dirty work." "If there's any disciplining, I have to do that," as well as "correcting our children's mistakes" (cf. Hughes, 1959).

Supervisors are defined as first-level management and are paid entry-level managerial salaries. However, since the position does not lead to higher grades, the supervisor occupies a no-man's land. By defining supervisors as "management," companies remove them from the worker category, creating barriers to personal relationships. They also enforce informal rules to forestall face-to-face relationships which might undermine impersonal control. A recently promoted supervisor at Public Utility reported: "They don't like management people socializing with nonmanagement. They think it hinders work. I don't think it does. I used to have lunch with one girl and I had to stop, and I couldn't even tell her [why]. My supervisor told me I couldn't have lunch with her any more."

It isn't surprising that many workers shy away from promotion to supervisory positions. They recognize the conflicts inherent in the position. A typical remark was made by a twenty-six-year-old clerk at Giant Investment who said, "I wouldn't want to be responsible for more people, but I would want to be responsible for more work." This remark illustrates an underlying problem: since workers don't aspire to the supervisor's position, there is little basis for identifying with her. This is quite unlike the close identification the assistant bookkeeper could form with the head bookkeeper, the person she could see herself becoming.

The other high-status clerical position, the secretary, is also isolated from the lower levels. Unlike the supervisor, the top-level secretary rarely begins in the clerical ranks and so lacks a common base of experience with other clerical workers. The top-level secretaries we studied entered at, or near, the top, like the nineteen-year-old secretary to the president of Technical Research. She came directly from a secretarial school which taught not only technical skills but also poise, grooming habits, and general polish. A secretary for a high-level executive has to protect her reflected authority by keeping her distance, by not mixing too much with others in the office. The secretary to the vice-president of Techtronics said she was well suited to her job because she was a "loner."

Relations Among Lower-Level Workers

If workers no longer identify with higher-level supervisors and secretaries, what happens to relationships among workers at lower levels? Within work groups, individuals are no longer interdependent, since everyone does the same job. The interdependence is between clerical units, a much more abstract concept. As a result, it is difficult for individual workers to know what others in different units do, and whether they share common conditions and occupy comparable positions in the hierarchy.

Divisions are reinforced by physical separation. In Public Utility and Big

City Insurance, different clerical units are located in separate parts of the building. An administrative assistant in Giant Investments, which employs hundreds of clerks, claimed that after five years she knew only the two other women working her own unit. Clerks rarely move around or observe workers in other parts of the building. Messengers deliver and pick up communications. At Big City Insurance, clerks must stay at their desks except during designated break periods. These arrangements are defended on the grounds of efficiency. However, they also limit workers' opportunities to form face-to-face relationships with other workers.

Within units, external supervision and standardization of activities create contradictory forces. On the one hand, workers are tempted to ease the strains through cooperation and solidarity. On the other hand, workers feel vulnerable, which decreases their desire for personal ties. Some women are fearful of being too open. A typist at Technical Research says, "They [the company] are aware of what's going on, sometimes too aware." When asked whether she had close friends at work, a clerk at Public Utility replied: "To me a close friend is someone you can divulge anything to. But here, you are reluctant to talk about personal things. . . . In a large company there is a lot of gossip and things spread."

Traditionally, lower-level clerical workers were said to lack worker identity because they identified with their superiors. With impersonal control, this tendency has been reduced. Now other structural factors make worker-worker identification problematic.

Conclusion

Proletarianization is an outcome of changes in the organization of work designed to increase managers' control of the work process. It affects workers psychologically, economically, and politically—both as individuals and as members of a class. In future papers we will explore the effects of proletarianization on worker consciousness. Here we turn our attention to three other interrelated outcomes: first, the downgrading of the work itself and consequent changes in the workers' relationship to it; second, the resulting inefficiencies in carrying out clerical work and coordinating throughout organizations; and third, the way workers as consumers bear the costs of both outcomes.

The transformation of clerical work itself has been analyzed in the body of the paper. The changes remove the very features that once made clerical work interesting, attractive, and of higher status. At a more abstract level, the changes alter the relationship of the workers to their work, to each other, and to management (Ollman, 1971). As managerial decisions are substituted for workers' decisions, the workforce becomes an inert collection of bodies mechanically related to a set of materials and sustained in motion by external force. Managers' greater control is control over a transformed work force: less knowledgeable, less involved, less committed, and therefore, less able and willing to respond to variation.

If the process is carried far enough, the very efficiency managers claim to seek is sacrificed (Marglin, 1974). Clerical work itself becomes less efficient, as illustrated in a recent evaluation of a Word Processing/ Administrative Support System (Hilaael, 1975). Managers found that their telephones were answered quickly under the new system and they were pleased with the "good coverage." However, once the phones were answered, problems arose. Some unimportant calls reached managers directly, while more important ones were transformed into messages. With subdivided tasks and standardized procedures, the workers who answered the telephones had neither the information nor the authority to handle routine matters or even to sort routine from important information.

When clerical work cannot be performed efficiently, the control structure it services is similarly hampered (Giddens, 1975). Clerical units have been described as the "arteries through which the life blood flows." Activities such as recordkeeping, scheduling, and copying link the various internal departments of an organization and connect it to "other businesses and to the rest of the people" (Mills, 1956: 190). These connections are essential for maintaining control of the various departments in an organization and for coordinating their activities. Changes which rigidify or interfere with these connections can result in a form of organizational paralysis. The paradox is that as managers gain greater control over clerical activities, they may become less able to manage their organizations.

This is one irony. The second is that workers who have suffered the direct effects of new control strategies, now, as consumers, pay the costs of the inefficiencies resulting from these transformations. As the Word Processing example shows, customers are unable to get satisfactory responses to their request for service. At the same time, they are paying higher prices for goods. The effects of proletarianized clerical work are less direct than in the case of production work, where slowdowns, sabotage, absenteeism—the well-known workers' responses to the worsening conditions of work—have direct, obvious effects on prices. Nevertheless, because clerical work mediates the delivery of consumer goods and services, its transformation similarly contributes to higher prices. Thus, the burdens of the changing structure of clerical work are borne by the workers directly as workers and indirectly as consumers.

Notes

We appreciate the cooperation of the clerical workers who told us what their work involved and how they felt about doing it.

1. The materials for this paper are drawn from several sources, the most important of which

are informal observations of clerical arrangements in five large organizations (which we have assigned pseudonyms such as Progressive Products, Brand Name Foods, Big City Insurance); discussions with managers about the organization and functions of clerical work; and intensive interviews with thirty clerical workers. These workers were classified as secretaries (ten), miscellaneous clerks (nine), typists (five), supervisors and assistant supervisors (three), and administrative assistants (three).

No attempt was made to draw a random sample. We did, however, obtain a range in terms of type of employer, age, education, and marital status. The employers included manufacturing (eleven), insurance (four) and utility companies (three); government (state and municipal) agencies (five); and universities, medical and other service institutions (seven). The age distribution was: ages 18–24 (eleven), 25–35 (twelve) and over 35 (seven). The educational distribution was: less than high school graduation (two), high school graduation (five), high school plus vocational courses (five), business or secretarial school (five), one to three years of college (six), and four or more years of college (six). Of the thirty women, seventeen were single, ten were married and living with husbands, and three were divorced or separated. Seven were mothers; four had three children, one had two children, and two had one child. Six had children under eighteen.

The interviews, based on open-ended questions, took from one-and-one-half to three hours and covered a wide range of issues concerning specific jobs and work in general. We collected detailed information on job histories, job activities, relationships with other workers, and related topics.

We assess changes in the conditions of work by identifying common patterns across interviews, interpreting these patterns in light of data from other studies and from our observations. Individual quotes are used in the text to illustrate and clarify our analysis, although the workers may not share the interpretations we offer. The quotes should not be taken to mean that workers necessarily *feel* "proletarianized"—some do, some do not.

2. The small offices of today are located somewhere between these two types. Although we interviewed women in small offices who were "all-around" workers, we do not analyze their situation in this paper.

3. As Stone (1973), Braverman (1974), and others point out, the distinction between those conceptualizing a task and those doing it was introduced to facilitate mass production in large organizations while insuring managerial control.

4. The examples of increased autonomy are drawn primarily from production workers. Automation may reduce the machinelike requirements of assembly-line jobs. However, for clerical workers comparable changes may limit rather than expand the worker's scope of activity. The long-term result may be to make semiskilled production jobs and lower-level clerical jobs comparable, through "improvements" in the former and "downgrading" of the latter.

5. Nonprofit and governmental organizations are not exceptions, since they are typically accountable to outsiders for maintaining the appearance of productivity. Standards can be nonmonetary (e.g., number of clients served) as well as monetary (e.g., the cost of servicing each client). Because of the lack of a profit measure, large nonprofit organizations often develop elaborate bureaucratic standards to assess efficiency.

6. It is important not to romanticize clerical jobs in the old office. Workers were frequently overworked and underpaid, and the personal controls could be oppressive and arbitrary. Some of these problems have been eliminated through standardization and formal controls. However, the workers we interviewed generally prefer personal control, even with its potential abuses.

Job Opportunities of Black and White Working-Class Women

SALLY T. HILLSMAN *
Vera Institute of Justice
BERNARD LEVENSON
Mount Sinai School of Medicine, CUNY

15. Current Expectations. Hillsman and Levenson began their work knowing that the black women graduates of a vocational high school did not have the same employment success as white women. Their study shows that black and white women do not have different motivations, but that both school and state employment counselors tracked women into different fields based on the counselors' own myths of racial interests and competencies. The authors show the advantages of being in a dominant racial group, and how outsiders (or people new to a situation—and therefore knowing less about the informal opportunities available) can limit their own opportunities. Black and Hispanic women, with fewer connections to more prestigious jobs, were more dependent upon resources of the school and state placement offices and did not demand equal opportunities with white women. Because such officials believed that only white women were hired for the better jobs, they usually did not even try to place the minority women in them. Are there situations of such discriminatory training and hiring patterns in your own community? Would you tend to benefit or to be disadvantaged by such discrimination if you were looking for such work? Are there ways in which all paid workers lose when such discrimination persists? Can you think of ways to break discriminatory patterns in school and in occupations?

This paper is concerned with working-class women's first attempt to secure employment. When seeking their first full-time jobs, the women discussed in this paper share the triple disadvantage of sex, age, and class; however, some are additionally burdened by race. Research on men has found early experiences in employment to be critical to successful integration into the labor force.[1] (See, for example, Blau and Duncan, 1967, and Freedman, 1969.) Yet little research on the employment problems of working-class women exists, though their careers are vitally important to the economic well-being of countless American families. Employment problems which disturb their careers, including sexism and racism, have serious consequences for many families near the bottom of the class system.

Our specific concern is with differences in the quality of entry-level employment secured by black, Puerto Rican, and white working-class women who have received vocational training and graduated from high school. We will examine the first employment of a group of women who entered an urban labor market during the same years after graduating from training programs in the same vocational high school. The dual purpose of our analysis is to evaluate the independent impact of race, preemployment training, referral, and recruitment on differential success in securing good entry-level employment and to identify the consequences of racial discrimination. Our data clearly show that from the start minority women do not share the occupational success of their white counterparts. The data indicate that discrimination is a two-part process at this crucial early stage of career development. It appears in the job referral and placement activities of the school and State Employment Service and in the recruitment of entry-level workers into various industries.

Research Setting

The vocational high school is a strategic site for examining the early phase of the occupational cycle. Generally, those who choose and successfully complete secondary vocational programs do not suffer lack of motivation (Purnell and Lesser, 1969). On the contrary, compared with many of their peers, they are sufficiently motivated to have completed high school. Moreover, they have undergone more extensive training for labor market competition than other young workers, and they enter that arena with salable skills. Good vocational schools are integrated into the industrial community by maintaining close relations with employers, unions, and State Employment Services. As a result, there are greater possibilities for their graduates to have access to regular and good employment than for graduates of other terminal programs (Eninger, 1967; Kaufman et al., 1967).

This description of good vocational education is generally less applicable to the training of young women. Much vocational education for women is in home economics and does not produce job skills. However, the specific school discussed in this paper trains young women in relevant industrial skills. The High School of Fashion Industries (HSFI) in New York City is a unit-trade school specializing in apparel production. By the classic criteria suggested above, it is a good school. It provides quality industrial training for jobs available to women;[2] it is selective in its admissions policies;

it maintains close ties with employers and labor unions; and job referral placement for graduates is one of its major concerns.

Our analysis of working-class women's transition from high school to work is based on data obtained from HSFI student records combined with Social Security work history records. Merging these two data bases is an extremely fruitful way of examining the *early* career stage.

The Structure of Employment Opportunity

Job opportunities available to these women are affected by the structure of general employment in their community. Obvious as this seems, the local labor market rarely is used as a context for evaluating the success of training efforts.

The general structure of employment in New York City is diverse. Therefore, the labor market within which these graduates search for jobs is both large and characterized by sizeable employment in almost all major divisions of the economy. This school's graduates are successful in securing entry-level employment in virtually all sectors of the local economy.[3] The great diversity of jobs obtained by the 1,402 graduates studied (three-quarters of whom are women) is demonstrated strikingly in Table 1. At least one graduate (often more) during the seven years studied was employed in fifty of the sixty-seven major industries in New York City as distinguished by the SIC.

These data suggest that available employment opportunities are far more diverse than generally expected for graduates with vocational diplomas and narrow manual training for jobs in a highly specialized industry. Obviously, these credentials do not bar them from employment in most industries. Nevertheless, upon closer examination, the last column of Table 1 indicates that students from the school are underrepresented in many local industries, that is, they do not obtain as *much* employment in some areas as is clearly possible. If the graduates' employment was determined solely by the opportunity structure (i.e., a matter of chance), the proportions in column A would be close to those in column B.

The second row of Table 1 demonstrates that HSFI graduates are expectedly overrepresented in Apparel Manufacturing firms (SIC #23): 565 graduates, over four times that expected by chance. Graduates are overrepresented in all but two of the seven local industries where apparel construction skills are in demand. (These industries are underscored in the table.)

While this analysis suggests that the school is successful placing its graduates in relevant, training-related jobs, it also calls attention to something neither expected nor obvious. Two of the three industries in which graduates are *most* overrepresented do *not* have much, if any, need for apparel manufacturing skills (Row 1, Apparel and Accessory Stores; Row 3, General Retailing Stores). In addition, graduates are not as highly overrepresented in the apparel construction industries as we anticipate from the combined effect of the school's specialized training, vigorous placement efforts, and the numerous jobs available in these industries. We would expect at least *four times* as many to have found jobs in Apparel Manufacturing *by chance alone* because there are considerably more jobs in this sector of the economy than in Apparel Retailing (9 percent versus 2 percent). But these data suggest that many students avoid employment in the apparel industry. Neither their explicit training nor the abundance of jobs draws then to this sector of the economy.

Closer inspection of local employment opportunities for the graduates of this school reveals important reasons why many resist referral to training-related employment. The quality of apparel jobs is lower than that of jobs elsewhere on most dimensions. Apparel jobs, particularly those held by women, are generally blue-collar, low-paying, low-skilled, sex-segregated, limited promotionally, and often in old, ugly factories (Helfgott, 1959a; Richards, 1951). Yet as we have seen, the city's labor market contains a wide variety of industries which offer higher-status, white-collar occupations to this school's graduates (especially industries in SIC Divisions E, G, and F, for example, Banking; and some industries in SIC Division H, for example, Educational and Legal Service industries). In addition, many nonapparel firms are large, with higher wages and job structures offering greater promotion potential than is possible in the similar apparel firms. Earnings in trade-*unrelated* employment exceed earnings in training-related employment. In each trade, white graduates earn more by "defecting" from the apparel industry; in all but two cases, the same is true for minority women.

The import of this analysis is paradoxical. Because the school has an active placement policy, some graduates are directed to training-related jobs rather than to *better* positions which are not related to their narrow manual training. Job referral and placement, therefore, restrict the career opportunities of some students. The school continues this restrictive pattern because it is never required to evaluate its graduates' career success *relative to available job opportunities.* Indeed, the reverse is the case. The school's *own* success as a training institution is officially and unofficially measured by the proportion of its graduates placed in training-related employment. Like most vocational programs, its continued public support is at least partially contingent upon its "success" as a source of young apparel workers. Unfortunately, this success criterion is typically used without qualification. While such a measure may benefit employers who receive trained entry-level workers without having contributed to their training cost, it does not necessarily foster the careers of individual graduates. In

Table 1
Placement of High School of Fashion Industries Graduates (1956–1963)
and Distribution of Workers in New York City (1959)* (N = 1,402)

SIC Code	Description of Major Industrial Group	No.	HSFI Graduates Proportion (A)	NYC Workers Proportion (B)	Col. A/ Col. B
1. 56	Apparel & accessory stores	176	.126	.0218	5.76
2. 23	Apparel & other textile products Mfg.	565	.403	.0940	4.29
3. 53	Retail gen'l merchandise	135	.096	.0227	4.24
4. 22	Textile mill products Mfg.	36	.026	.0107	2.40
5. 31	Leather & leather products Mfg.	29	.021	.0106	1.95
6. 25	Furniture & fixtures Mfg.	12	.009	.0066	1.31
7. 30	Rubber & plastic products Mfg.	5	.004	.0033	1.08
8. 39	Misc. manufacturing industries	31	.002	.0211	1.05
9. 727	Personal services—garment pressing, etc.	26	.018	.0209	.88
10. 76	Misc. repair services	4	.003	.0034	.83
11. 57	Furniture & home furnishings	7	.005	.0060	.83
12. 48	Communications	31	.022	.0267	.83
13. 26	Paper & allied products	10	.007	.0090	.79
14. 61	Credit agencies other than banks	4	.003	.0039	.73
15. 80	Medical & other health services	28	.020	.0305	.66
16. 73	Misc. business services	36	.026	.0407	.63
17. 82	Educational services	6	.004	.0084	.48
18. 503	Wholesale trade—apparel	76	.054	.1078	.50
19. 59	Misc. retail stores	10	.007	.0146	.49
20. 67	Holding & investment companies	2	.001	.0030	.48
21. 36	Electrical equipment & supplies	11	.008	.0167	.47
22. 60	Banking	16	.011	.0256	.44
23. 54	Food stores	14	.010	.0228	.44
24. 63	Insurance carriers	19	.014	.0311	.44
25. 15	Gen'l bldg. contractors	4	.003	.0072	.40
26. 49	Electric, gas & sanitary services	5	.004	.0097	.37
27. 24	Lumber & wood products	1	.001	.0020	.36
28. 47	Transportation services	3	.002	.0060	.36
29. 27	Printing & publishing	19	.014	.0409	.33
30. 64	Ins. agents, brokers & service	3	.002	.0088	.31
31. 78	Motion pictures	3	.002	.0069	.31
32. 81	Legal services	3	.002	.0070	.30
33. 52	Bldg. materials & farm equipment	1	.001	.0024	.29
34. 65	Real estate	15	.011	.0371	.29
35. 38	Instruments & related products	3	.002	.0076	.28

Table 1 (*continued*)

SIC Code	Description of Major Industrial Group	No.	HSFI Graduates Proportion (A)	NYC Workers Proportion (B)	Col. A/ Col. B
36. 79	Amusement & recreational services	3	.002	.0078	.28
37. 58	Eating & drinking places	15	.011	.0398	.27
38. 89	Misc. services	5	.004	.0136	.26
39. 32	Stone, clay & glass products	1	.001	.0027	.26
40. 34	Fabricated metal products	5	.004	.0141	.25
41. 17	Special trade contractors	7	.005	.0259	.19
42. 42	Trucking & warehousing	3	.002	.0127	.17
43. 28	Chemicals & allied products	2	.001	.0088	.16
44. 35	Machinery except electrical	2	.001	.0089	.16
45. 86	Nonprofit membership organizations	4	.003	.0224	.13
46. 55	Auto dealers & service stations	1	.001	.0068	.10
47. 45	Transportation by air	1	.001	.0094	.08
48. 20	Food & kindred products	2	.001	.0242	.06
49. 70	Hotels & other lodging places	1	.001	.0153	.05
50. 62	Security & commodity brokers	1	.001	.0158	.04
51. 44	Water transportation	0	—	.0107	.00
52. 29	Petroleum & coal products	0	—	.0007	.00
53. 19	Ordinance & accessories	0	—	.0005	.00
54. 33	Primary metal industries	0	—	.0031	.00
55. 37	Transportation equipment	0	—	.0034	.00
56. 16	Heavy construction contractors	0	—	.0038	.00
57. 75	Auto repair, services & garages	0	—	.0044	.00
58. 41	Local & interurban transit	0	—	.0097	.00
59. 66	Combined real estate ins., etc.	0	—	.0008	.00
60. 84	Museums, botanical gardens, zoos	0	—	.0008	.00
61. 07	Agricultural services & hunting	0	—	.0002	.00
62. 21	Tobacco manufacturers	0	—	.0002	.00
63. 10	Metal mining	0	—	.0001	.00
64. 13	Oil & gas extraction	0	—	.0001	.00
65. 09	Fisheries	0	—	.0000	.00
66. 14	Nonmetalic minerals except fuels	0	—	.0001	.00
67. 46	Pipeline transportation	0	—	.0001	.00

Industries which are underscored are considered to contain a high proportion of entry-level jobs for which HSFI graduates are directly trained.

* U.S. Bureau of the Census and U.S. Bureau of Old-Age and Survivors Insurance, cooperative report, *County Business Patterns, First Quarter 1959*. Part 3A Middle Atlantic States (New Jersey, New York), U.S. Government Printing Office, Washington, D.C., 1961.

the case of HSFI, this contrast is clear. However, the potential for a similar discrepancy between the evaluation of program success and the evaluation of career success is present whenever evaluation fails to include the comparative *quality* of jobs *relative* to what is available. This problem is particularly likely to hinder adequate evaluation of vocational training efforts for women since such programs typically prepare women for low-level, sex-typed occupations.[4] By traditional measures, the successful training programs are those which assure that their female graduates actually enter such occupations.

In conclusion, while this school's program is reasonably successful by traditional standards (45 percent of employed graduates placed in apparel jobs during these years), we may legitimately question its efforts from the perspective of its students' relative job success. Students themselves implicitly question the school's perspective by their defection from its training. For the most part, graduates placed in higher-status, more financially rewarding, and more stable employment are those located outside the industry of training. While the attractions of nonapparel jobs are obvious, they are not always sufficient to counter the school's vigorous placement efforts. The school is, after all, close at hand during these women's three years of high school—a formative period in the transformation of aspirations into concrete career decisions. It is a strategic source of job information and referral for those with little personal experience in the work world. However, the school's impact on career opportunities is not uniform among all groups of students.

Equality of Employment Opportunity: Job Referral and Placement

To investigate whether some women profit more from the broader opportunities in this labor market, we shall use several indices to examine the entry-level jobs of black, Puerto Rican, and white graduates of the school's core curriculum—the four Womenswear Production trades.[5] Black and Puerto Rican women profit the least. Regardless of the trade in which they were trained, minority women more frequently enter blue-collar (generally apparel) manufacturing jobs, in contrast to their white classmates, who are more likely to be placed in white-collar (nonapparel) jobs.

This pattern of job placement depends more upon these women's race than upon differences in their training. While all of them are trained for production jobs in womenswear, at entry in school they are assigned to different trade groups. This tracking supposedly reflects differences in ability and potential. An analysis of the tracking criteria used (Baker [Hillsman], 1975), however, suggests that this is not an entirely accurate picture of the trade assignment process. There is considerable evidence that race is used directly and indirectly as an independent indicator of potential "talent" or "ability" in assigning entering students to the elite curriculum. Black and Puerto Rican women, therefore, are assigned more frequently to lower-status, less-skilled trade groups (particularly Garment Operating and secondarily Dressmaking). White students are assigned most frequently to the "elite" trade, Fashion Design.

Across the entire employment spectrum, *job referral and placement depend more upon race than vocational training.* Race has substantial consequences for determining which of these women will secure white-collar jobs. This factor then influences the nonmonetary prerequisites associated with their employment, their entry-level earnings, and their advancement potential.

If preemployment skill and training differences are in *any* way important to the job placement of these young women, we would expect more graduates of the most skilled and prestigious curriculum (Fashion Design) to enter jobs requiring apparel skill. Empirically, however, there is an inverse relationship. As Table 2 indicates, 33 percent of the elite Fashion Design graduates enter apparel trade jobs after graduation, in contrast to 45 percent of the Dressmakers and 55 percent of the Garment Operators. Thus, we have another paradoxical result. Women given choice curriculum assignments are less likely to translate that training into relevant employment. While this may raise doubts about the training program, it augurs well for these women's personal success. The well-trained graduates are attracted to the generally higher-status and higher-paying white-collar jobs in the community rather than to apparel jobs.

Table 2 also demonstrates that race influences which graduates within each trade successfully resist referral to trade-related jobs. Whereas 25 percent of white Fashion Design graduates are placed in apparel employment, 40 percent of black and Puerto Ricans are; the same holds for Dressmaking graduates (47 percent compared to 76 percent) and Garment Operating graduates (40 percent compared to 73 percent). Again, placement in training-related work depends more upon the graduate's race than preemployment skill and training. Using data from Table 2, we compare Dressmakers and Garment Operators to measure the relative effects of training and race. How much difference does training make?

Finally, the impact of skill and training differences emerges when we confine our analysis to women actually placed in Apparel Manufacturing (SIC #23). Even here, considerations other than training are powerful determinants of placement. Comparing the first line of Table 3 with the other lines, we see that white graduates are more favorably placed within available Apparel Manufacturing jobs than blacks and Puerto Ricans. Outerwear firms are characterized by more expensive production items, greater responsiveness to style changes, and require greater adaptability by workers. In contrast to working on undergarments or nightwear, the work in

Table 2
Proportion of Womenswear Graduates "Defecting" from Needle Trades
Employment,* by Trade Group and by Race

Race	Fashion Design-Technical	Fashion Design	Dressmaking	Garment Operating
White	.81 (67)	.65 (43)	.76 (124)	.73 (73)
Black and Puerto Rican	.67 (42)	.56 (68)	.47 (314)	.40 (373)
Total:	.75 (109)	.59 (111)	.55 (438)	.45 (446)

* Needle Trade Employment: SIC #22 (Textile Mill Products Manufacturing), SIC #23 (Apparel Manufacturing), SIC #25 (Furniture Manufacturing), SIC #31 (Leather Products Manufacturing), SIC #503 (Apparel Wholesale), SIC #727 (Garment Pressing, Repairs, Alterations).

Outerwear production (men's and women's) is more interesting and the pay generally higher (Helfgott, 1959a). White women, regardless of training, are employed more frequently in outerwear firms than their minority classmates.

The career consequences of these patterns are serious. We have already seen that minority women's early careers are restricted in a variety of ways because the school's referral and placement activities "help" them to be more "successful" at translating their education and training into trade-related work. Referral activities, therefore, not only restrict minority women's access to white-collar jobs but also encourage their employment in an industry characterized by little advancement opportunity, poor working conditions, seasonal employment, and low earnings.

Equality of Employment Opportunity: Industry Recruitment

Thus far, we have examined inequality of opportunity as seen from the perspective of school referral and placement. Examining the transition from school to work also raises questions about the *complementary* perspective, namely, employers' recruitment practices. Our data suggest that discrimination is the result of a symbiotic but often unspoken relationship between placement personnel and employers. It is clear that placement personnel do not send students to various jobs randomly; nor, however, do they place students only according to their personal perceptions of the appropriate relationship between race and trade-related employment, with its resulting career consequences. Quite distinct racial patterns of industry recruitment can be described using data on these graduates' entry-level employment. While at this level of analysis we cannot completely separate the deeply interwoven effects of placement and recruitment, these data do

Table 3

SIC Classification of Womenswear Graduates Employed in Apparel
Manufacturing, by Curriculum and by Ethnicity
(Four to six months after high school graduation)

		Curriculum							
		Garment Operating		Dressmaking		Fashion Design		Fashion Design Technical	
SIC Code	Primary Activity of Firm	Black & PR	White	Black & PR	White	Black & PR	White	Black & PR	White
233	Women's outerwear	.18	.38	.27	.53	.58	.46	.30	.86
234	Women's undergarments	.44	.25	.11	.21	.12	.27	.10	—
236	Girls', children's outerwear	.10	.19	.20	.11	.12	.18	.10	.14
239	Misc. textile products	.15	—	.23	—	.08	—	.10	—
238	Misc. apparel	.08	.06	.06	—	.08	—	.30	—
235	Millinery	.02	.06	.05	—	—	—	.10	—
231	Men's outerwear	.01	.06	.06	.16	.04	—	—	—
232	Men's furnishings and work clothes	.02	—	.01	—	—	.09	—	—
237	Fur goods	.01	—	—	—	—	—	—	—
230	Apparel manufacturing, n.e.c.	—	—	.01	—	—	—	—	—
	Total:	1.01	1.00	1.00	1.01	1.02	1.00	1.00	1.00
	(Number)	(198)	(16)	(143)	(19)	(26)	(11)	(10)	(7)

reveal distinct patterns of industrial preferences for employees of different
races. That these patterns reflect *recruitment* preferences is documented in
the last section of this paper. It is also corroborated by an extensive independent study of employment discrimination by industry in New York
City (Hiestand, 1967).

We will restrict our discussion to the Dressmaking graduates because
this large group is the nearest to parity of the three racial groups and
because these graduates have been trained in a curriculum which is neither
at the bottom nor at the top of the school's skill and status hierarchy.

We carried out a chi-square test for the distribution of graduates by industrial division. The results lead us to conclude that these women's recruitment is dependent upon their race.

The consequences of discrimination in hiring are important for these women's work lives. While HSFI is a relatively well-integrated school (29 percent white, 24 percent Puerto Rican, and 47 percent black), its graduates appear to be recruited and placed in work situations characterized by greater racial homogeneity. It should not be thought that this ghettoization at work is unique to HSFI graduates, to the apparel industry, or to women workers. It is a national pattern. Siegel (1965), for example, employed an index of dissimilarity between the occupational distributions of white and minority *males* aged 25 to 64 for 1950 and 1960. His data suggest a small reduction in occupational segregation over the decade. What is most interesting and relevant here, however, is his finding that the highest indices of occupational dissimilarity for men of different races occur about the ages when youths graduate from high school or during the first year or two of college—the very levels which minorities are reaching in appreciable numbers for the first time. Siegel's data cover aggregate occupational data for the country. From our data, we get a glimpse of how this process of dispersion and segregation operates among working-class women who graduated from the same curriculum in the same high school, who were trained in the same skills, and who entered the same general labor market.

The pattern of progressive racial segregation as these young women prepare for and enter the work world is unmistakable. They enter a relatively integrated high school but are quickly tracked into more racially homogeneous trade groups. While 49 percent of the Fashion Design students are white and 25 percent black, 69 percent of the Garment Operating students are black and 12 percent white. After formal technical training and informal career socialization, they are referred to jobs based more upon their race than their skill and training and are recruited into work settings which tend to be not only sexual but racial ghettos.

The Hiestand study of employment opportunity and racial discrimination in New York City (1967) calls attention to an extremely important consequence of this progressive ghettoization. Hiestand emphasizes that, in spite of clear industry patterns of discrimination, there are actually many white-collar jobs potentially available to minority applicants. But they are widely dispersed. Even firms in industries characterized by relatively high proportions of minority workers show great variation in the number they typically hire (some hiring virtually none, others many). This means that to improve equality of opportunity for doubly disadvantaged minority women, access to the widest number and range of firms must be assured. Yet we have just demonstrated that the referral and placement activities of this school and State Employment Service *restrict* rather than expand the labor market search of minority graduates, who are also the most dependent upon them. To secure good jobs, minorities must rely more heavily than whites on sources of referral other than friends and family. Otherwise they are handicapped by previous patterns of job discrimination. Therefore, *any* restrictions created by school referral and placement services affect the job opportunities of minority women more than those of equally trained and educated whites. Minorities must rely more heavily on these formal services to help spread their job search net wide enough to locate firms willing to hire them for good entry-level positions.

Pressures to Discriminate in the Job Referral Process

While we dealt earlier in this paper with the reasons behind the school's restriction of students' access to nonapparel jobs, we have not directly confronted the issue of why they impose these restrictions more severely on minority women. The answer begins with our demonstration that employers' hiring patterns are racially restrictive. To understand how and why *marketplace* patterns influence the operation of the *school's* referral activities, we must closely analyze the direct and indirect ties between the school and the labor market.[6]

While both school and employment service personnel are committed to their students' welfare, they are obviously also committed to their own program and job security. The criterion by which their personal and program performance is judged—training-related employment of graduates—leads them not only to restrict some graduates' job search but also to discriminate racially. Pressures to discriminate are subtle but pervasive. They are built into the central role relationships that placement personnel must maintain to carry out their assigned tasks. To an important extent, their own job security depends upon the successful placement of graduates (see Blau, 1955), and this in turn rests on adherence to whatever hiring criteria are considered relevant by employers in (and out of) the apparel industry, including race, sex, personality, or class.

School and Employment Service personnel are fully aware of the racial, ethnic, and sexual stratification systems which characterize the city's apparel industry (see, for example, Helfgott, 1959b; Herberg, 1953; Hill, 1963). They report feeling that they must take into account images employers have concerning who are desirable, "suitable" workers at different job levels. If they do not, they report that employers sanction them and impede their placement success.

"One firm in the industry said to me that Negroes don't work out."

"Puerto Ricans have a much better image in the industry [than blacks]."

"Salesrooms . . . only want whites; their excuse always is that they have 'southern buyers' who would be offended [by minorities]."

"This summer I sent a couple of 'hippies' out for jobs. They were hired because they were white—in spite of their dress and the possibility they were on drugs. If I'd sent a *Negro* like that, I would have gotten a call saying how dare I send someone with that appearance and probably taking drugs too!"

Placement personnel perceive what our data substantiate—that employers' images of desirable, "appropriate" employees are not always related to students' skill or training; they are, however, affected by racial stereotypes: [7]

"[Blacks] haven't the thousand year tradition of craftsmanship that they have in the Orient, in Europe, and among the Jews. I'm not saying they can't, but let's see where they are a thousand years from now, or five hundred, or two hundred."

"[Blacks] don't have the ability—the creativity, initiative, or interest—the ability you are born with."

"You want to send to jobs the ones who are pleasant to have around. The motivated ones. It's things about the student and not her ability you look for. The attitude is really more important than the skill."

Placement personnel are pressed by the criteria used to judge their own performance to act upon these images. As a good vocational school, HSFI is expensive and held publicly accountable through an evaluation of the "trade-relatedness" of its graduates' employment. Likewise, the job security of State Employment Service personnel is linked to student placements in the apparel industry. Although supervisory personnel claim this is no longer the case, interviews with placement counselors and observations of their counselling and referral activities indicate that they experience daily pressures from the school, employers, and their own organization to produce apparel industry placements.

There is, however, another paradox here. We have just described the negative racial attitudes placement personnel report on the part of apparel employers. Yet, as we saw earlier, black and Puerto Rican women represent the majority of the referrals to that industry. In spite of their negative attitudes, employers accept these minority women because there is almost always a shortage of workers willing to take the low-level, low-paying, seasonal sewing jobs which lack promotional opportunity and which are traditionally sex-typed female. Blocked from job opportunities in other industries by discrimination in hiring and job referral, and socialized during high school to believe their white-collar aspirations are unrealistic,[8] these minority women are more willing than their white counterparts to accept poor employment, *even though they are high school graduates.*

The need of school and Employment Service personnel for trade-related placements is met, therefore, by placing minority women in low-level apparel jobs. The better apparel jobs occasionally available are reserved for the few white graduates who resist the temptations of white-collar employment because they are committed to fashion careers. These women are more acceptable to employers for the few female jobs having skill and pay potential. Observation and interviews in the school reveal that most white students are able to defect from the industry without serious opposition by teachers and Employment Service staff and often with the help of the latter, who receive some white-collar job listings. Their career advantage is allowed because the performance goals of trade-related placements have been sufficiently met by minority women to assure the program's continuation.

Conclusions

This paper is a small part of a growing body of empirical evidence that preemployment education and training *alone* cannot answer the problem of economic inequality. While we must continue to strive toward equality of education, the data presented in this paper suggest that career disparities among workers cannot be understood without more emphasis on the early stages of their career development, particularly job referral, recruitment, and search.

Equal credentials and educational performance do not assure equal careers. The work histories of these working-class women demonstrate that differences in race are far more influential than differences in training when translating their education into jobs. The discrimination occurring at this phase of the career cycle can be linked directly and indirectly to the *images* employers have about the suitability of job applicants. These images have little or nothing to do with the training or skill characteristics of applicants, but they are used in personnel evaluation nonetheless. Here again, more research is necessary on how employers actually evaluate employees at the entry level and for promotion.

From a policy perspective, these materials indicate the importance of reducing discrimination in job referral and hiring. At least as much emphasis is required on this phase of the career cycle as is now placed on improving skills and educational credentials prior to employment; if not, the latter will have little impact on reaching equality.

Clearly, the traditional concern with evaluating job training in terms of the training-relatedness of job placements also needs alteration. It is the absolute quality of the jobs and their quality relative to other jobs available that are crucial to career progress. This issue is rarely dealt with. The present pattern of evaluation also supports the continued separation of labor markets by race and sex by encouraging traditional patterns of job referral which narrow these workers' job opportunities. For equality of opportunity to be realized, job search networks must be broadened for all groups that suffer discrimination. Formal job referral and placement services must be specifically designed to locate and, where necessary, develop openings for such workers in high-quality and probably nontraditional settings. This is particularly important for those who are multiply disadvantaged, as are youthful female high school graduates, many of whom are our also black and Puerto Rican.

Notes

* The name of the senior author in the article as originally published was Sally Hillsman Baker.

1. Our own follow-up research on the women discussed here indicates that initial career differences do indeed affect later earnings (Baker [Hillsman] and Levenson, 1975). However, more detailed longitudinal research on the career patterns and cycles of both men and women is critically needed.

2. While there is no doubt that HSFI is an excellent school, it unfortunately also illustrates many of the problems faced by young women trying to prepare seriously for future employment. Vocational programs typically are sex segregated. The sex segregation reflects and reinforces the sex segregation of occupations and jobs found throughout the labor market. It is clear that in the United States (and elsewhere), men and women compete in totally different labor markets, and this operates to restrict women's access to better-quality, higher-paying employment (Kreps, 1971; Oppenheimer, 1970; Sullerot, 1971). The apparel industry in New York City is a heavily female industry, and training throughout the New York school system reflects this pattern. HSFI, for example, is 80 percent female. The apparel industry is also generally low-paying. While some jobs, especially for cutters and pressers, are relatively well-paying, they are almost exclusively reserved for men. At HSFI, only men are taught cutting and pressing skills.

3. Data on entry-level job placement were obtained from Social Security work history records. The records classify each graduate's employment during any quarter according to the Standard Industrial Classification code (SIC). This is a nested classification of firms based upon the type of product or service; a close version is also used by the Census Bureau (see U.S. Bureau of the Budget, 1957). In examining graduates' entry-level employment, we selected the second calendar quarter after graduation, that is, the months October through December. This quarter was chosen to assure that most graduates had been placed in jobs by avoiding the generally low-employment summer months.

4. In New York City, for example, over 90 percent of the female vocational school students are trained in cosmetology, office skills, low-level health occupations, distributive education, and apparel manufacturing; less than 4 percent of the male vocational students are trained in these same areas. In contrast, over 80 percent of the males are enrolled in training for technical, mechanical, or repair skills (e.g., computer technology, TV broadcasting technology, auto, aviation, business machine, radio-TV mechanics); skilled crafts (e.g., carpentry, plumbing, printing); and other skilled work (e.g., computer programming, drafting, sheet metal work). Less than 3 percent of the women are enrolled in these training programs. New York City is not alone in these training patterns (Sullerot, 1971).

5. The full curriculum is divided into ten apparel-related trades. Two-thirds (virtually all women) are graduated from the Womenswear Production Division, which consists of four

trade groups: Garment Operating, Dressmaking, and two Fashion Design sections (which are both the smallest and considered most desirable). Students in the "technical" section of Fashion Design take college-preparatory academic courses, but most graduate with the standard Vocational Diploma anyway.

6. The materials in this section were derived from an extensive field study conducted in the school by one of the authors (Baker [Hillsman], 1970).

7. There is woefully little research on exactly how employers evaluate existing or potential employees (notable exceptions are Freedman, 1969, and Berg, 1970). However, that they often make judgments unrelated to applicants' technical talent or trainability or the relationship of these to performance has been suggested by numerous researchers. Economist Lester Thurow (1972), for example, points out that since employers often prefer to train workers on the job, their unverified judgments concerning workers' trainability rather than their existing skill is critical to the hiring decision. Thurow suggests that employers have only minimal data on what it costs to train different types of workers and what personal characteristics are good predictors of workers' trainability. The job-testing and employee-selection literature supports Thurow on this point. Therefore, the desirability of a particular worker or group of workers is heavily influenced by employers' personal predispositions and the prevailing social perceptions about what individual characteristics (including age, sex, race, educational level, test scores, etc.) are associated with good, cheap, "suitable" employees. (See also Thurow and Lucas, 1972.)

8. While school and Employment Service personnel need not be personally prejudiced for such discrimination to take place, they often need to personally justify their behavior. This is accomplished by asserting that they send most students to jobs the students themselves prefer. When there is an overt discrepancy between the student's preferences in employment and where the teacher believes she ought to work, the teacher labels it an "unrealistic" aspiration and tries to dissuade (counsel) the student from her goal. When the teacher later refers the student to the job she considers appropriate, there is no question in her mind that it is in the student's best interests.

The Impact of Hierarchical Structures on the Work Behavior of Women and Men

ROSABETH MOSS KANTER
Yale University

16. Consequences. What are often interpreted as sex differences in work behavior (aspirations, concern with co-worker friendship, leadership styles) may be more accurately explained as organizational behavior. Studies show that those who are disadvantageously placed, whether men or women, limit their aspirations and are less likely to be perceived as promotable, thus completing a vicious cycle. Kanter shows us how career advancement for women is affected by a commonly held belief that men are better leaders than women. She argues that the way subordinates respond to superiors is partly based on how supervisors assess their own present (and future) power. Those who have power can help subordinates; those who do not, act in both controlling and negative ways toward subordinates. Thus those who have power are more apt to be liked, while those without power are more apt to be disliked. This article shows us that it is necessary to see how hierarchical structures affect workers' behavior rather than assuming that differences in worker behavior stem from gender or personality differences.

Find men and women in low-level, low-mobility jobs and interview them about their careers. How long have they been in their present job? How long do they expect to stay? Where do they get most of their personal satisfaction or sense of achievement: at home, at work, somewhere else? Collate and contrast their statements. If you have access to any high-status, high-aspiration workers, and if you can find both men and women in such positions, interview them about their experiences and perspectives on work and career; then identify and analyze the similarities and differences. Finally, contrast your findings about men and women in low- and high-status occupations. Pay particular attention in your analysis to the types of structural influences Kanter emphasizes.

Three structural variables—the opportunity structure, the power structure, and the sex ratio—shape the behavior of women in organizations, just as they shape the behavior of men. If women sometimes have lower aspirations, lesser involvement with work, and greater concern with peer group

234

relations, so do men in positions of limited or blocked mobility. If women are sometimes less preferred as leaders, generate lower morale among subordinates, and use directive-interfering leadership styles, so are men with relatively little organizational or systemwide power. If women in managerial or professional positions are sometimes isolated, stereotyped, overly visible, and cope by trying to limit their visibility, so are men who are "tokens" and therefore rare among a majority of another social type.

In other words, structural position can account for what at first glance appear to be sex differences and perhaps even explain more of the variance in the behavior of women and men. It becomes important to understand how women and men get distributed across structural positions and how this differential distribution affects behavior—not how women differ from men. In this analysis, sex is one criterion for social placement, one sorting mechanism among others, that accounts for which positions and roles are considered appropriate for people. Women may be more likely to face discrimination than men, and more women than men may be found at the bottom of opportunity and power hierarchies. If given the opportunity, women may more often find themselves alone among other-sex peers. But the behavior of women at the bottom (or alone) should be seen as a function of *being* at the bottom, and not primarily as a function of being a woman.

This paper considers two structural effects of hierarchical systems on behavior: the opportunity structure and the power structure. It deals primarily with the behavioral consequences of disadvantaged positions. To explain fully the behavior and problems of women in more advantaged positions requires the introduction of the third variable, the sex ratio, for women more highly placed in hierarchies are often "tokens" in groups numerically dominated by men. The effect of tokenism on women and men is discussed at length elsewhere (Kanter, 1975a, 1977b).

Work Orientations, Aspirations, and Location in an Opportunity Structure

It is tempting to conclude, on the basis of research evidence and common-sense observations, that women's work orientations, on the average, differ from those of men. Isn't this, after all, compatible with the "primary" socialization of women for family roles and men for work roles? Women, this thesis goes, tend to be less involved in their work and less committed to it than men, interrupting their careers whenever they can. They are more concerned about their relationships with other people than with the task or reward aspects of their jobs, and they have lower levels of aspiration. I review some of the evidence for these statements below. But I also argue, instead, that all of these findings can be explained by the nature of the *opportunity structure* in which people find themselves in an organization, whether they are men or women. People in low-mobility or blocked-mobility situations tend to limit their aspirations, seek satisfaction in activities outside of work, dream of escape, and create sociable peer groups in which interpersonal relationships take precedence over other aspects of work. When women occupy low-mobility positions, they tend to exhibit these characteristics. Since most of the women studied in organizations tend to be disadvantageously placed in the organization's opportunity structure, they confirm the generalizations made about "women's organizational behavior." Yet, when we observe *men* disadvantageously located in the opportunity structure, they tend to demonstrate the same characteristics. What one line of thought considers a "sex difference," I consider a structural phenomenon. (See Laws, 1976c, for a psychological version of a similar argument.) This is consistent with the prevalent finding in organizational behavior that people at upper levels of organizations tend routinely to be more motivated, involved, and interested in their jobs than those at lower levels (Tannenbaum et al., 1974: 1).

Opportunity and Limited Aspirations
The evidence for women's more limited aspirations and greater concern with peer relationships comes from a variety of sources. Several studies conclude that women more than men tend to be concerned with local and immediate relationships, remaining loyal to the local work group even as professionals, rather than identifying with the field as a whole and aspiring to promotions which might cause them to leave the local environment. Several studies of male professionals in organizations have found a correlation between professionalism and a "cosmopolitan" rather than a "local" orientation, using Merton's terms. The one exception was a study of nurses by Bennis and colleagues (1958b). In this *female* group, the more professionally oriented nurses "did not differ from others in their loyalty to the hospital, and they were *more* apt than others, not less, to express loyalty to the local work groups" (Blau and Scott, 1962: 69). While Blau and Scott conclude that this is due to the limited visibility of the nurses' professional competence, it is also compatible with the response of people to a professional opportunity structure characteristic of nursing, which does not offer much mobility out of the current organization and in which good peer relationships are likely to be an important component of competent work performance. Similarly, Costantini and Craik (1972) found that women politicians in California were oriented intraparty and locally more than men, while the men were much more often oriented toward higher office. The difference in the opportunity structures for women and

men in politics at the time this research was carried out is well known, making the women's preferences understandable on structural rather than characterological grounds.

In a dissertation research project on a major corporation, Homall (1974) surveyed 111 nonexempt (i.e., hourly) employees on their attitudes toward promotion. Using an expectancy-value theory, she found that men show greater motivation to be promoted than women and perceive the greater overall desirability and likelihood of the possible consequences following a promotion. The men also perceived themselves to be more competent in basic managerial skills than the women did and to receive more encouragement from superiors to improve and advance. But newer employees were also more likely than older ones to show high motivation for promotion, and the better educated more likely than the more poorly educated, indicating that not only sex but also other characteristics affecting the employee's real advancement opportunities played a part in the results.

Homall also found that *neither* men nor women *reported* perceiving many real advancement opportunities for themselves. Yet, in this company, like most, the differences in the *actual* opportunities for men and women, and the mobility hierarchies in which they are located, are quite striking and dramatic. About two-thirds of the women nonexempts in the company unit from which the sample was drawn were secretaries. The secretarial hierarchy is a short one, with increased rank reflecting the status of the boss rather than the secretary's work, and leading to executive secretary as the highest position. Until recently, practically no executive secretary was ever promoted into the exempt (salaried) ranks, and those promoted represent a minuscule proportion of either secretaries or exempt personnel. The other women in Homall's sample were predominantly clerks in dead-end jobs. It is not surprising that the aspirations of women in such an organizational situation should be limited, that they should turn to other sources of satisfaction. Indeed, in a study of the values of 120 occupational groups, secretaries (the only predominantly female category studied) were unique in placing their highest priorities on security, love, responsibility and happiness—not job advancement (Sikula, 1973). The men in Homall's sample, on the other hand, were a much smaller proportion of the nonexempt population. The majority worked as accounting clerks or in the international exports department in a customer relations function that led directly to the exempt ranks of the company. Their mobility prospects were strong.

There is evidence that, in general, the jobs held by most women workers tend to have shorter chains of opportunity associated with them, to contain fewer advancement opportunities. In a study of eleven industries employing about 17 percent of the U.S. work force (motor vehicles and parts, basic steel, communications, department and variety stores, commercial banking, insurance carriers, and hotels and motels), a consulting group found that as the amount of progression possible in nonsupervisory jobs increased—the number of steps of opportunity it contained—the proportion of women declined markedly (Grunker et al., 1970). Women represented 46% of all nonsupervisory workers, but they were a whopping 64% of workers in the "flattest" jobs (least advancement opportunities) and a minuscule 5% of workers in the highest opportunity jobs.

Thus, the Homall results and others showing women's "lower" work involvement and aspirations can be more profitably read as reflecting a response on the part of both employees and their managers to the worker's placement in an opportunity structure. Those who are disadvantageously placed limit their aspirations and are less likely to be perceived as promotable, thus completing a vicious cycle. Those who are more advantageously placed are likely to maintain higher aspirations and to be encouraged to keep them. The sex typing of jobs in this major corporation, as in others, means that a *social structural effect* might be misleadingly interpreted as a sex difference. My own interviews, in the same company Homall studied, with women who are advantageously placed in a high-mobility opportunity structure (as sales personnel in a hierarchy that regularly leads directly to management positions), indicated that they are highly motivated and aspire to top management positions.

But it is not only women who respond to blocked mobility by limiting their aspirations, lowering work commitment, and dreaming of escape. Men poorly placed in an opportunity structure tend to behave in similar ways. A number of classic studies of male blue-collar workers indicate that work commitment and aspirations are both low where advancement opportunities also are low. Dubin (1956) concluded that work is not a "central life interest" of industrial workers. Other research confirms this finding. Purcell (1960) studied male workers in three meat packing plants. Around half were negative about their chances for advancement, and many denied that they would ever *want* to be foremen. Bonjean and his associates (1967) also found that individuals with negative mobility perceptions tend to have low aspirations. Where work is boring or repetitive and chances for mobility are low, people tend to develop little attachment to work and seek their major satisfactions in the family realm. They also seek to leave the organization whenever possible. Mayer and Goldstein (1964) and others offer evidence that the "interrupted career" pattern is true for men as well as women. Blue-collar men leave organizations to start small businesses and then return when (as is statistically likely) the business fails.

Concern with Peer Group Relationships

Along with more limited aspirations, women are said to be more concerned than men with interpersonal relationships on the job, more involved with other people than with the intrinsic nature of the task. In attitudinal studies attempting to distinguish job aspects motivating increased performance ("motivating" factors) from those merely preventing dissatisfaction ("hygiene" factors), attitudes toward interpersonal relations with peers constituted the only variable differentiating men and women. (The women in two major studies include those in both relatively high-level and relatively low-level jobs.) For women, peer relationships were a motivational factor, spurring them on, whereas for men they were only a hygiene factor, which the men would miss if it were not there but which did not push them to perform (Davis, 1967: 35–36). One of the few significant sex differences found by University of Michigan researchers in their national survey of the attitudes of 1,472 working men and women lay also in this area. More women (68%) than men (61%) indicated that is was very important to them that their co-workers be friendly and helpful (Crowley et al., 1973; see also Johnston, 1975).

Some laboratory studies also suggest that the tendency of more women than men to be concerned with the quality of relationships affects those women's behavior and performance. Female game-playing strategy, in a series of experiments, tended on the average to be "accommodative," including rather than excluding, and oriented toward other people rather than toward winning, whereas the male strategy was more often "exploitative" and success-oriented (Uesugi and Vinacke, 1963; Vinacke, 1959). But even here, later investigators have challenged the sex-differences interpretation and offered an explanation based on situational characteristics. Lirtzman and Wahba (1972) have pointed out that the Vinacke experiments used minimally competitive social games with uncertainty and risk reduced once coalitions were formed, permitting any sort of partnership relationship. In their own experiments, using a highly competitive game with high uncertainty about the consequences of behavior, sex differences disappeared. Women as well as men behaved competitively, aggressively, and exploitatively, trying to maximize their chances of winning. In other words, the context shapes organizational behavior. A concern with relationships tends to arise for women in low-risk, low-uncertainty environments, where opportunities will not be lost if one accommodates to others.

The opportunity structure is an important part of the context that defines for organization members how important good, accommodative relationships with peers ought to be, and whether or not minimizing peer relations in favor of competition or distance has a payoff in mobility. High-mobility situations foster rivalry, instability in the composition of work groups, comparisons upward in the hierarchy, and concern with intrinsic aspects of the job. Low-mobility situations, however—those characteristic of most of the working women studied—foster camaraderie, stably composed groups, and more concern with extrinsic rewards, social and monetary. In a classic piece of sociological analysis, Merton (1968: 233) argued that amount of upward mobility as an institutionalized character-istic of a social system generates either vertical or horizontal orientations. When people face favorable advancement opportunities, they compare themselves upward in rank, with one foot already out of the current peer group in the process he called "anticipatory socialization." Unfavorable advancement opportunities, on the other hand, lend themselve to compar-ison with peers and concern with peer solidarity. Pennings' (1970) study of white-collar workers with high or low mobility opportunities (measured by promotion rates) offers confirmation. The importance attached to in-trinsic job characteristics, to the nature of the job itself as opposed to such external factors as relationships with co-workers, varied with promotion rates.

Work-value orientations and the importance of interpersonal relations, then, are a function of the structure of opportunity facing people in differ-ent parts of the organization by virtue of the category into which they fall. There is evidence that men as well as women turn to relationships with work peers as an alternative interest when mobility opportunities are lim-ited or blocked. Under such circumstances, men, like women, form strong peer groups that value solidarity and loyalty within the group and look with suspicion upon fellow workers who identify or interact with anyone outside the group. One example is the men in the bank wiring-room group in the Hawthorne studies (Roethlisberger and Dickson, 1939), who cre-ated a strong peer group which restricted work output. Burns' (1955) ob-servations of a factory in an uncertain, changing environment showed dra-matically the differences in interpersonal orientations of low- and high-mobility men. The older men, considered "over the hill" and in positions outside of the main career advancement ladders, formed "cliques" oriented toward protection and reassurance. These peer groups represented, to Burns, organized retreats from occupational status into the realm of inti-macy. The younger men, on the other hand, who still had opportunities, formed a very different kind of group, "cabals" which plotted an increase in their status. The younger men oriented themselves around power, while the older ones substituted intimacy and support. Tichy (1973) hypothe-sized that in no-mobility systems friendship needs are the primary pressure for group formation, and that lack of ability to envision other rewards in the future encourages people to seek more immediate socio-emotional re-wards in the present situation. (See also Cohen, 1958.) Initial placement in an opportunity structure, then, helps determine whether a person will de-velop the aspirations and orientations that make further mobility possible. Women in low-mobility organizational situations develop attitudes and orientations said to be characteristic of "women as a group" but which can more profitably be seen as human responses to blocked opportunities. (Some of these responses, of course, may have positive rather than negative social value.)

Leadership Attitudes, Behavior, and the Power Structure

There is no research evidence that yet proves a case for sex differences in either leadership aptitude or style. A wide variety of investigations, from field studies of organizations to paper-and-pencil tests, indicate that the styles of men and women vary over the same range, and there are no conclusive sex-related preferences (Bartol, 1974, 1975; Crozier, 1971; Day and Stogdill, 1972; Rousell, 1974). In an organizational simulation using college students, Bartol found that the sex of the leader did not by itself affect follower satisfaction, even when female leaders were characterized by high dominance, a trait most likely to offend male subordinates (Bartol, 1974, 1975).

Even attempts to prove that women leaders are perceived and evaluated differently from men—a not unlikely occurrence—have resulted in very few significant results. In a study of high school departments, Rousell (1974) found that teachers' ratings of their department heads' aggressiveness, suggestibility, and professional knowledge did not discriminate between the sexes. Bartol and Butterfield (1974) asked subjects to make judgments about male and female leaders exhibiting a variety of styles. The evaluations of men and women did not differ significantly on most variables, including such critical ones as "production emphasis," but there was a tendency to give higher ratings to men than to women when they "initiated structure" and higher to women than men when they showed "consideration," demonstrating some propensity for raters to "reward" people for sex-role-appropriate behavior. (See also Rosen and Jerdee, 1973.)

On the other hand, there is considerable evidence for a general cultural attitude that men make better leaders. A large number of studies have concluded that neither men nor women want to work for a woman (although women are somewhat more ready to do so than men, and people who have already worked under a woman are much likelier to be favorable toward doing so). In a 1965 *Harvard Business Review* survey of 1,000 male and 900 female executives, for example, an educated and experienced sample, over two-thirds of the men and nearly one-fifth of the women reported that they themselves would not feel comfortable working for a woman. Very few of either sex (9 percent of the men and 15 percent of the women) felt that *men* feel comfortable working for a woman, and a proportion of the male respondents said that women did not belong in executive positions. A total of 51 percent of the men responded that women were "temperamentally unfit" for management, writing comments such as "They scare male executives half to death. . . . As for an efficient woman manager, this is cultural blasphemy" (Bowman et al., 1965). At the same time, there is a prevalent stereotype of the "woman boss" as rigid, petty, controlling, and too prone to interfere in the personal affairs of subordinates. (See Laird and Laird, 1942. My own interviews confirm this stereotypic picture.)

It is too easy to explain these findings only by reference to abstract notions of sex discrimination. Here too, I want to invoke a structural explanation that can account for a preference for male leaders and for women's occasional use of authoritarian-controlling leadership styles. Both of these phenomena are understandable given the current distribution of men and women in the power structure of organizations. The nature of the power structure of the organization as a *total* system can account for (1) which leaders are preferred and considered effective by subordinates, and (2) which leaders are likely to use and be perceived as using overly directive, overly interfering styles.

Leadership Effectiveness and Power Position
What makes leaders effective with subordinates? Attempts to distinguish more effective and less effective styles have generally failed, in part because there are tradeoffs associated with emphasizing one or another form of supervision, as early studies of authoritarian, democratic, and laissez-faire leaders showed. While human relations skills are considered important if coupled with a production emphasis, the evidence is mixed enough to permit few conclusions about leader traits alone (Tannenbaum, 1966: 78–79). Marcus and House (1973), for example, tried to differentiate instrumental and expressive exchanges between superiors and subordinates as a way to predict interaction and group process. The distinction was ultimately not very useful. Subordinates reported getting about equally as much job-related information whether the leaders tended to be instrumental or expressive, and they found very little relationship between styles of leadership behavior and subordinate group process. This is one of a number of studies that fail to demonstrate that leader strategy alone makes much difference and, as I have already indicated, there is no firm evidence that men and women differ in characteristic choice of style anyway.

But what *does* seem to make a difference is the leader's own position in the power structure of the wider organizational system. Early theory in organizational behavior assumed a direct relation between leader behavior and group satisfaction and morale, as if each organizational subgroup existed in a vacuum. However, Pelz (1952) discovered in the early 1950s that perceived influence *outside* the work group and upward in the organization was a significant intervening variable. He compared high- and low-morale work groups to test the hypothesis that the supervisor in high-morale groups would be better at communicating, more supportive, and more likely to recommend promotion. Yet, when he analyzed the data, the association seemed to be nonexistent or even reversed. In some cases, supervisors who frequently recommended people for promotion and offered sincere praise for a job well done had *lower* morale scores. The differentiating variable that Pelz finally hit upon was whether or not the leaders had power outside and upward: influence on their own superiors and how decisions were made in the department as a whole. The combination of good human relations *and* power was associated with high morale. Human-relations skills and low power (a likely combination for women leaders) sometimes had negative effects on morale.

High external status, sometimes taken as a shorthand symbol for potential or actual power and influence, also contributes to leader effectiveness. It adds a power base outside of the legitimate authority vested in the current office. Subordinates are more likely to inhibit aggression and negativity toward a demanding person of higher than lower status (Thibaut and Riecken, 1955). People who come into a group with higher external status tend to be liked more, talk more often, and receive more communications (Hurwitz et al., 1968). Leaders with higher-status characteristics are generally assumed to be capable of greater influence in other parts of the organization. This gives people of higher credentials and higher status ascribed characteristics an obvious initial advantage over those with lesser assets, and, to belabor the obvious, gives men an edge over women on this variable.

An advantageous location in the power structure has real as well as symbolic payoffs. It gives leaders more rewards to dispense to subordinates, as they may have more claim over the resources of the organization. It means that the leader can more effectively back up both promises and threats and can, indeed, make changes in the situation of subordinates. Such organizational power comes from several factors that are themselves structural: (1) close contact and good relations with other powerholders in the system and (2) advantageous location in the opportunity structure and favorable mobility prospects. The first guarantees influence through present relations and present interactions; the second through bets about future increases in power, giving subordinates a chance to capitalize on the success of a "comer" in the organization (see Stein, 1976).

Women are currently likely to be disadvantaged on both grounds and thus less likely to act as though they have, and be perceived by subordinates as having, organizational power. In business organizations, those systems in which the most negative attitudes toward working for women are consistently expressed, women are both numerically rare and structurally isolated as managers or supervisors of any kind. Statistically, they represent about three percent of all managers and officials in the 1970 U.S. census, but even within this category they tend to be concentrated in staff rather than line positions, where they often lack supervisory responsibility (Kanter, 1975b). Accumulating evidence indicates that women leaders, under such circumstances, may be excluded from the informal network of organization managers (Cussler, 1958), just as they may be excluded from the influential networks of professional peers in male-dominated professions (Epstein, 1970b). Even if she occupies a leadership position, then, a women may have less influence in the wider organizational situation because of her rarity and isolation, and this may interfere with her effective exercise of leadership, with subordinate satisfaction, or with the likelihood of subordinates to prefer her to a man, *regardless* of her own style or competence. This proposition may account for evidence of the importance of a male sponsor in the success of women executives (Cussler, 1958; Hennig, 1970). A high-status man bringing a woman leader up behind him may provide the visible sign needed by subordinates that the woman does have influence outside and upward. While sponsors serve multiple functions (such as coaching and socialization in the informal routines), the reflected power they offer may be even more important for women than for men who are protégés. Indeed, the dozen women I interviewed who are the first to sell industrial chemicals (on a sales force of over 300) reported that their influence with customers is partly a function of how much their manager indicated he will back up and support their decision. They can be more effective at selling if they look as if they have organizational power.

Power, Powerlessness, and Leadership Style

Leaders with favorable mobility prospects are also likely to please their subordinates more than those who appear stuck. Here there is a complex interaction between leader power, leader behavior, and subordinate perception. People well placed in the opportunity structure are already likely to be paying more attention to those upward in the organization and to be less critical of them, and thus to be making the connections that give them organizational power. They are also likely to be less rigid, directive, and authoritarian than low-mobility leaders (Hetzler, 1955). And they offer more opportunity to subordinates to move up right along with them. Under such circumstances, we can guess that leader actions are likely to be seen as helping rather than hindering the groups's performance and that morale would be high.

The only significant sex-linked difference found in a study of high school department heads lay in just these group climate characteristics, and they can be traced directly to differences in the organizational power of the men and women leaders, even though the researcher does not herself make this interpretation. Rousell (1974) studied 205 teachers and 40 department heads, 25 male and 15 female, working with small departments of roughly equal sex distribution. Departments headed by men were perceived as higher in "esprit and intimacy"—a good indicator of morale—and those headed by women in "hindrance"—an indicator that the leader was seen as getting in the way rather than promoting subordinates' interests. But mobility prospects and the likelihood that leaders would be moving up in the organization also appear to have been very different for the men and the women. For one thing, there were no women *above* the level of department head in the whole county. Secondly, the women seemed to have risen to their last position. They had moved to this position more slowly than the men (they were older, more experienced, and had spent a longer time in their previous positions), and they had more limited aspirations (one-seventh of the women, as compared with half of the men, expressed a desire for further promotion).

Levenson (1961) has also suggested that the fact of promotability itself influences style of supervision and subordinate attitudes, evoking good leadership practices. *Promotable* supervisors are more likely to adopt a participatory style in which they share information, delegate, train, and allow latitude and autonomy—in order to show that they are not indispensable in their current jobs and to fill the vacancy created by their promotion with someone they have trained. *Unpromotable* supervisors, on the other hand, may try to retain control and restrict the opportunities for their subordinates' learning and autonomy, as they themselves are not moving up, and a capable subordinate represents a serious replacement threat.

Thus, when people in middle-management positions have lower advancement potential and a less favorable position in the power structure (because of their age, ascribed characteristics, or present achievements), they tend to "take it out" on their subordinates in the form of greater directiveness and increased control. So do people who feel relatively powerless or relatively insecure in their jobs. In other words, under these circumstances more likely to be encountered by women then by men, *men as well as women* begin to act in those ways said to characterize the negatively stereotyped "woman boss."

Hetzler (1955) conducted an attitude survey of male Air Force officers. He found that leaders of lower status and advancement potential favored more directive, rigid, and authoritarian techniques of leadership, seeking control over subordinates. Subordinates were their primary frame of reference for their own status assessment and enhancement, and so they found it important to "lord it over" group members, just as some women have complained women supervisors do to them. They also did not help talented members of the group get ahead (perhaps finding them too threatening), selecting immediate assistants of mediocre rather than outstanding talent. A series of laboratory experiments confirm these field observations. People who find themselves relatively powerless, because they lack confidence in their own abilities or because they encounter resistance from their targets of influence, tend to use more coercive rather than persuasive power (Goodstadt and Kipnis, 1970). Furthermore, the "psychologically powerless"—as people who know they are going no further in an organization are likely to be—are more likely to use coercive power to elevate their own sense of worth and dignity, especially when their control over subordinates is threatened by someone's "poor attitude" (Goodstadt and Hjelle, 1973).

Finally, people who feel vulnerable and insecure are most likely to be authoritarian-controlling leaders. The behavior attributed to women supervisors is likely to be characteristic of new and insecure supervisors generally. Gardner (1945) noted this during World War II, when the demands of war production brought women into formerly all-male positions. Even women, he observed, complained that women supervisors were unfriendly, too critical, too concerned with petty details, and too strict in disciplining them. But Gardner concluded that newly promoted men given supervisory jobs without sufficient training also showed these tendencies:

> Any new supervisor who feels unsure of himself, who feels that his boss is watching him critically, is likely to demand perfect behavior and performance from his people, to be critical of minor mistakes, and to try too hard to please his boss. A woman supervisor, responding to the insecurity and uncertainty of her position as a woman, knowing that she is being watched both critically and doubtfully, feels obliged to try even harder. And for doing this she is said to be "acting just like a woman." (1945: 270–271)

We again come full circle. Those favorably placed in the power structure are more likely to be effective as leaders and thus likely to gain even more power. The attitudes toward women leaders in organizations where they are most likely to have an unfavorable position in the power structure, despite the authority of their office, become understandable not just as an example of sex discrimination but as an example of a general organizational process that can also affect men. If some women respond, as some men do, by turning to control over subordinates as their internal measure of success, this reaction is also understandable as a response to structural circumstances.

Conclusion

It is time to move beyond "sex differences" and "sex roles" in our understanding of the observed behavior of women in organizations, and to return to classic and emerging social psychological and structural theories that explain behavior as a function of position in a network of hierarchical relations. By looking at the larger organizational context in which relationships and interactions occur, we can account for the behavior of both men and women who'find themselves in similar positions in an opportunity or power structure or in a similar sex ratio. Tannenbaum and colleagues reach this conclusion in another context in their study of fifty plants in five nations: that social structure rather than interpersonal relations is the more substantial basis for understanding outcomes such as the distribution of reactions and adjustments within a system (1974: 205).

We thus avoid the "blame the victim" approach that locates explanations for work behavior in dispositions in the individual (whether planted there by temperament or socialization). The real villain of the piece in a structuralist model turns out to be the very nature of hierarchy. Complex organizations whose opportunity and power structures routinely disadvantage some kinds of people (whether women or men) are likely to generate the behavioral consequences of such disadvantaging. On the other hand, the creation of a class of advantaged persons who are offered the prospects for increasing their opportunities and power does not itself always lead to desirable consequences, for those people may become more involved with the politics of climbing than with the human side of the organization or the personal side of life.

The structuralist perspective that I have outlined here suggests a different kind of social policy and intervention strategy for the elimination of sex discrimination than the "sex difference" or "sex roles" schools of thought (Kanter, 1976). Instead of retraining women (or men) as individuals to acquire work-appropriate behavior, attitudes, and motivation, or providing different models of socialization, change strategies would focus on the structure of the organization as a total system. It is much easier, of course, to approach the individual, the family, or the school with change policies and research programs, as these are relatively small and powerless elements of the society compared to work organizations. But I argue that it is those complex organizations that more critically shape the prospects for the work life of adults, and it is thus those systems we must investigate and understand. It is the nature, form, and degree of hierarchy that should bear the burden of change.[1]

Note

1. Other references on this topic include: Bennis (1958a), Cattell and Lawson (1962), Dittes and Kelley (1956), Kanter (1977c), Langer (1972), Mensel (1957), Millman and Kanter (1975), Waters and Waters (1969), and Wild (1969).

Sex Stratification, Technology and Organization Change: A Longitudinal Case Study of AT&T

SALLY L. HACKER
Oregon State University

17. Implications. Hacker studied AT&T when it was under a court order to meet affirmative action guidelines. This was also a period of technological change in which some low-level technical and supervisory positions were scheduled for elimination. Hacker shows that technological change may have different consequences for men, for women, for whites, and for persons of color. In this case, white women were displaced while women of color advanced. Men gained more traditionally women's positions than the reverse. Are such effects typical? How does Hacker explain such differences in consequences? Is the dual economy involved? Is AT&T unique? How will legislation affect different groups? How can affirmative action legislation be phrased to minimize the risk that potential gains for employees historically discriminated against might be eliminated by planned technological change? What does Hacker mean by "backlash myths"? By "automation clauses"? Do you agree with the conclusion in her final sentence? Principles of seniority are strongly upheld by labor unions. What do you think about the arguments for and against seniority? How do these principles affect the chances for advancement of working women? Under what circumstances do you think these principles should be modified to encourage affirmative action?

Mainstream sociological research on stratification has generally ignored women (Acker, 1973), but research on women—especially as related to employment—is deeply concerned with sex as a variable of stratification. Here I focus on yet another aspect of employment—technological displacement, or the loss of jobs to machines. The questions are: (1) how are women workers affected by technological change? and (2) what are the implications for sociological theory and research?

In the course of the National Organization for Women's civil rights action for equal employment at American Telephone and Telegraph, we discovered that planned technological change would eliminate more jobs for

248

women than affirmative action would provide. This led me to search sociological literature for explanations of the impact of technological change on women's employment. Conventional literature slights the concept of sex stratification—a hierarchical division of tasks and rewards based on sex—and so explains less than it might. More helpful are new approaches which suggest that the impact of technological change on women's work varies by the political and economic framework of particular technologies, by the stage of development within such frameworks, and by linkages between family and work.

In this paper, I present a case study of technological change in one corporation and the impact of the process on workers. The research arose in response to a stalemate in legislative paths to equal employment opportunity.

Background: Civil Rights Action for Equal Opportunity

AT&T, or the Bell System, is the largest private employer in the United States. It comprises Headquarters, twenty-three operating companies (such as Pacific Northwest Telephone, Illinois Bell, New York Telephone, Long Lines, Bell Laboratories, and Western Electric). (AT&T also manages Sandia, the New Mexico center for nuclear weapons systems research and development.) This research deals with the operating companies and Long Lines, employing some eight hundred thousand people, half of them women.[1]

In 1971, the Equal Employment Opportunity Commission (EEOC), urged by civil rights groups, investigated the many claims of sex and race discrimination at AT&T. It found women and minorities clustered at the lowest levels of both management and nonmanagement categories, the victims of significant discrimination in hiring, promotion, and pay. EEOC called the corporation "the largest discriminator against women in the U.S." (EEOC, 1971) and filed suit under Title VII of the Civil Rights Act.

Judith Long Laws (1976a) testified to the Federal Communications Commission that, within AT&T, "sex discrimination was the primary organizational arrangement: upon this, racial, ethnic and age discrimination were imposed." The two largest departments in each operating company were heavily sex segregated: Traffic (operators and their supervisors) was 96 percent female; Plant (crafts and some clericals) was 94 percent male. Upper-level jobs often required working one's way up through Plant or through an all-male management program.

In 1972, the government required AT&T to produce affirmative action plans, with a three-year timetable of goals for employment of women and minorities at each occupational level. Management programs were to be opened to women; women and minorities were to be hired for positions previously held by white men. The marginals, however, revealed a rather surprising pattern: the plans showed an overall decline in the proportion of women working anywhere in the system after three years of affirmative action. While some women moved up, more moved out. And so we discovered, however belatedly, the process of technological displacement. Affirmative action concerns the equitable distribution of workers among existing jobs. It does not touch the number of jobs available, nor the specific problem of job loss to machines. The plans were legal, despite the projected decrease in the percentage of women workers.

Converging Literature on Technological Change

I explored the literature on technology and workers for information on women's work and especially on the effects of technological change. I found that most of the work was carefully done, generally longitudinal, often based on firms rather than industries. But, with some exceptions, it explained too little. By failing to recognize technology as an intervening variable, it missed the key questions: why certain technologies were selected, by whom, or for what purpose?

Traditional feminist theory and research on employment note the importance of sex stratification in employment, such as the causes and consequences of occupational segregation (*Signs*, 1976). Women function as a flexible source of labor or as a reserve labor army (Ferber and Lowry, 1976a,b). Institutional linkages, especially those between home and workplace, must be analyzed if women's economic condition is to be fully understood (Boulding, 1976a; Safilios-Rothschild, 1976). But Gordon (1976) notes that this literature tends to ignore the role of those who select technology and who organize work. Policy suggestions stemming from even the best of this research rarely deal with the occupational structure or the number of jobs available. Without attention to these problems, affirmative action penalizes white male workers to provide equal opportunity for women and minorities. (We shall see here that this criticism is more myth than reality.)

Marxist literature does deal with who benefits by technological change, and who pays. It explains that profit-oriented firms require a reserve labor army in order to change technologies or move quickly to capture new markets (Baran and Sweezy, 1966), and that women provide this reserve (Christoffel and Kaufer, 1970). Technological change may draw women in when work is being simplified or push them out when simplified work is being automated (Braverman, 1974). Roemer (1978) shows that a Marxist theory of exploitation is valid for a differentially exploited labor force, such as one segregated by sex. Feldberg (1978a), among others, suggests that since women and minorities have been treated differently within the working class, they may be differently affected by capitalist development. Sex or race may have better predictive value than class during certain periods of development within capitalism. A Marxist framework offers explanations for technological displacement—explanations of a high order of abstraction which can be empirically examined—but it subordinates sex to class as an explanatory concept. Sex is important as a divisive factor in the working class at the workplace.

Feminist and radical literatures converge in seeking the material base for patriarchal systems (sex-stratified systems in which men are dominant) of which capitalism is merely a special case. Hartmann (1977) finds capitalism to be only one form of sex/gender-based domination. Her historical analysis of home and work tasks shows how male workers and managers alike derive economic and other benefits from a patriarchal system. Lazonick (1978) notes how the development of capitalism builds on hierarchies of existing patriarchal systems.

Baxandall et al. (1976) and others criticize Braverman's analysis of technology for centering on the work place alone. It is in the family where the consciousness of the worker emerges and is reinforced, where women's unpaid services benefit both management and male workers, and where technological change reshapes homemaking as well (Bose, 1978; Weinbaum and Bridges, 1976).

Articles in *Signs* (1977) address the impact of political/technological development on women in the third world. Some stress sex and culture, while others emphasize class and economic systems, but all point to complex patterns of hierarchies or stratification based on sex, class, and race. One may be more dominant than another as conditions vary. For example, agricultural mechanization sometimes affects the poor, men and women alike, but more often works the greatest hardship on women (see also Boserup, 1970; Leghorn and Roodkowsky, 1977).

The problem of technological displacement of women workers does not appear to be adequately addressed in any of the areas of sociology that should be most relevant. Organizational research pays too little heed to the sex and race of workers. Studies of technological displacement, even when dealing with women's work, too readily accept technology as a given. Feminist studies likewise tend to ignore key questions about who chooses technology. Marxist scholars avoid this pitfall but stumble into another trap by slighting the importance of women's general social role under patriarchal systems of all kinds, and especially the links between family and work. The emergent synthesis of feminist and radical thought promises a more productive approach to the question of women's technological displacement, and other problems as well.

Within this framework, I will discuss employment patterns in a large corporation undergoing rapid technological change. I present data and interpretations in five major sections, each organized around a central question: (1) What was the movement of workers (by sex and race) into and out of various occupations during a time of rapid technological change within AT&T, and how was this movement related to affirmative action legislation? (2) What were the structural relationships between class, race, sex, and organization change? Specifically, what were the best predictors of occupation decline in this period? (3) What is the evidence that corporate planners used women as a temporary and cheaper source of labor in simplified craft work, as this work was readied for automation? (4) What political and economic factors affected AT&T choices and made technology an intervening rather than an independent variable? (5) How did the experiences of women workers—specifically, the interrelationships between their role of worker and that of woman—allow AT&T to make the choices it did?

Findings and Interpretations

Overall Gains and Losses by Sex, Race, and Class,
and Effect of Affirmative Action

Loewenberg (1962) showed the telephone company's shift from female to male labor: from 69.5 percent female in 1946 to 57.9 percent in 1960. He discussed the increasing skill level of workers during this crucial period of postwar technological change:

> While there may have been increased skill requirements in individual jobs, a large part of the overall increase in skill has come from the reduction of people at the lower end of the skill scale. . . . In operating companies, the upward shift has been the result of decreases in lower-rated operating and clerical groups and increases in the generally higher-rated plant crafts, professional workers, and business and sales employees. (1962: 44–45, 47)

Loewenberg's care in phrasing his findings should serve as a model for organizational research addressed to the effects of new technology on the skill level of workers. By showing lesser-skilled work being eliminated and noting the characteristics of those doing that work, he avoids leaving the impression that the process is merely a benign improvement in the skill level of existing workers.

A 1964 study sponsored by the Communications Workers of America noted that all telephone company employment had declined since 1958; women had held most of the 80,000 jobs eliminated in that six-year period (Beirne, 1965). The 1972 affirmative action plans for AT&T and Long Lines showed a continuation of this trend, projecting a three-year decline of women workers from 52.4 percent to 52.0 percent by 1975. This was

Table 1
Occupational Distribution, All Operating Companies Plus Long Lines;
1972 and 1975

Job	Category	# Jobs 1972	# Jobs 1975	Percent Change	Numerical Change
#1	3rd level mgt. and above	15,780	16,610	+ 5.2	+ 830
#2	2nd level	43,168	48,297	+11.9	+ 5,129
#3	1st level	95,492	102,867	+ 7.7	+ 7,375
#4	Administrative positions	32,716	31,181	− 4.7	− 1,535
#5	Sales	5,813	6,541	+12.5	+ 728
#6	Skilled craft, outside	65,107	65,553	+ .7	+ 446
#7	Skilled craft, inside	76,542	78,047	+ 2.0	+ 1,505
#8	Gen. services outside	11,347	13,304	+17.2	+ 1,957
#9	Semiskilled craft, outside	66,104	63,549	− 3.9	− 2,555
#10	Semiskilled craft, inside	18,011	18,012	+ .0	+ 1
#11	Clerical, skilled	82,392	97,336	+18.1	+14,944
#12	Clerical, semiskilled	74,689	70,006	− 6.3	− 4,683
#13	Clerical, entry level	45,140	37,674	−16.5	− 7,466
#14	Operators	148,622	124,431	−16.3	−24,191
#15	Service workers	12,365	11,374	− 8.0	− 991
	Totals	793,288	784,752		

Source: EEOC Date, 1976.

a conservative estimate; in December 1975, women's participation stood at 50.1 percent.

Data from the Iowa Area of Northwestern Bell for the period 1963–73 parallel Loewenberg's historical account, indicating a fairly steady reduction of the share of employment by the female-intensive Traffic Department. Of thirty-eight job titles eliminated from the work force of this Area Office over the same period, thirty-one (primarily clerical) were traditionally female jobs.[2] Company and technical literature indicated that this recent decline in the proportion of female workers is due to new methods of handling and recording calls and of doing clerical work. A Bell Labs engineer reported, for example, that Customer Records and Billing has at times made for "people savings" of up to fifty percent (cf. Thayer, 1968).[3]

These systems reduced the need for operators and lower-level clericals. As these jobs were cut back—a job loss of over 36,000 at AT&T between 1972 and 1975—so were those of lower-level supervisors (level 4). Over 1,500 such positions were eliminated in this time period (Table 1). Women's positions, management and nonmanagement, were being displaced by new technologies.

Table 2 shows that men as a group gained 13,767 jobs over their 1972

Table 2
AT&T Employment Shifts: Operating Companies + Long Lines 1972 vs. 1975 Profile Data

Classification		Grand Total	Total Men	White Men	Minority Men*				Total Women	White Women	Minority Women*			
					Black	SSA	AI	A/O			Black	SSA	AI	A/O
Mgt 1	1	+ 830	+ 423	+ 282	+ 77	+ 35	+ 22	+ 7	+ 407	+ 383	+ 16	+ 5	0	+
Mgt 2	2	+ 5129	+ 2395	+1812	+ 302	+ 186	+ 50	+ 45	+ 2734	+ 2386	+ 246	+ 66	+ 14	+ 2
Mgt 3	3	+ 7375	+ 3547	+1982	+ 847	+ 534	+ 86	+ 98	+ 3828	+ 2229	+1089	+ 335	+ 60	+ 11
Super's	4	- 1535	+ 818	+ 607	+ 111	+ 82	+ 9	+ 9	- 2353	- 3105	+ 480	+ 202	+ 35	+ 3
Sales	5	+ 728	- 161	- 360	+ 133	+ 49	+ 10	+ 7	+ 889	+ 628	+ 207	+ 49	+ 8	+
Sk craft: outside	6	+ 446	- 84	-1830	+ 832	+ 780	+ 65	+ 69	+ 530	+ 441	+ 45	+ 35	+ 8	+
Sk craft: inside	7	+ 1505	- 2409	-3486	+ 537	+ 478	+ 85	- 23	+ 3914	+ 3246	+ 467	+ 151	+ 34	+
General services	8	+ 1957	+ 360	+ 193	+ 50	+ 82	+ 6	+ 29	+ 1597	+ 1149	+ 347	+ 86	+ 6	+
Semisk craft: outside	9	- 2555	- 3735	-3672	- 482	+ 282	+ 93	+ 44	+ 1180	+ 969	+ 136	+ 55	+ 12	+
Semisk craft: inside	10	+ 1	- 2185	-1143	- 722	- 269	- 11	- 40	+ 2186	+ 1575	+ 394	+ 163	+ 17	+ 3
Cler: skilled	11	+14944	+ 4220	+3164	+ 494	+ 427	+ 35	+100	+10724	+ 4514	+4049	+1580	+199	+ 38
Cler: semisk	12	- 4683	+ 3953	+2967	+ 570	+ 304	+ 8	+104	- 8636	-11068	+1611	+ 466	+ 65	+ 29
Cler: entry	13	- 7466	+ 2536	+2119	+ 181	+ 188	+ 9	+ 57	-10002	- 8282	-1623	- 162	+ 11	+ 5
Operat.	14	-24191	+ 4867	+3696	+ 529	+ 539	+ 43	+ 60	-29058	-23058	-6550	+ 306	+121	+ 12
Service workers	15	- 991	- 778	- 103	- 705	+ 22	+ 3	+ 5	- 213	- 204	- 101	+ 79	+ 2	+ 1
Grand Total		- 8506	+13767	+6228	+2754	+3719	+495	+571	-22273	-28197	+ 813	+3416	+592	+110
% CHANGE:			+1.8%			+24.6%				-8.4%			+7.5%		

Source: EEOC, 1976.

*SSA = Spanish American; AI = American Indian; A/O = American Oriental

level, while women lost over 22,000 during the same time. Affirmative action might have been expected to moderate the impact of technological change on women in this case. This was true in middle management. For nonmanagement workers, however, although some women did achieve nontraditional positions, affirmative action placed thousands more men in traditionally women's work than it placed women in traditionally men's work.

These data should counter backlash myths. At AT&T, most white male workers with whom I've talked tell me "a white man can't get a job at AT&T these days," directing job shortage anxiety not toward economic and technological processes but toward affirmative action for women and minorities. The facts are that 16,300 men gained formerly women's work; only 9,400 women gained formerly men's work during these three years of affirmative action.[4] This parallels Carol Jusenius' (1976) reexamination of Fuch's data, showing that where decreasing sex segregation in employment occurs, it is primarily due to men performing traditionally women's work (e.g., public school teaching, nursing, social work) and not to women performing traditionally men's work.

Men taking jobs as operators or clerical workers represent all races. They may form a new underclass, or, as female operators have described them, they may be "young college kids on their way up" or looking for temporary employment. Most likely they needed work, and AT&T could no longer bar them from traditionally women's jobs. This may be a relatively new phenomenon. Milkman (1976) suggests that men did not move into women's work during the Great Depression when the men's own jobs disappeared because of sex stereotyping by male workers. Perhaps management resistance best explains that lack of movement. According to David Copus (1976), EEOC's attorney for the AT&T case, all management had to do to get men into operator and clerical work was lift the proscription and hire them. AT&T management has traditionally preferred women in jobs scheduled for reduction, because women had a higher turnover rate than men (Loewenberg, 1962). In the early 1970s, management still strongly opposed men working as operators. The law insisted; management yielded. Management opposition appears to be fading, as experience reveals that men working as operators have turnover rates three times higher than that of women operators.[5]

The proportion of white women was adversely affected more than that of any other sex/race category during these three years, decreasing by 8 percent, or 28,000 positions held. The proportion of minority women increased 8 percent (with black women showing the lowest increase, at 1 percent). Gains for minority women in skilled clerical and lower-level management, however, may be subject to the next round of automation.[6] Despite some losses, the overall share of minority women's employment has increased during this phase of affirmative action.

White men gained 2 percent over their 1972 level; minority men gained 25 percent. The overall share of employment by minority men, however, is still below their percent in the labor force. (In 1975, the AT&T work-force comprised white men, 45.0%; minority men, 4.9%; white women, 39.3%; minority women, 10.8%.)

White men moved into management and into women's jobs at the bottom of the structure—as operators and clericals. Minority men gained at almost all levels.

In numbers of jobs, men benefited more than women by technological change and by affirmative action. But it is clear that some suffered. Many traditionally male jobs were eliminated, especially at the semiskilled craft levels. At skilled craft levels, there are thousands fewer white male workers than there were, and thousands more minority males in these positions. There are also far fewer men (minority and white, but especially fewer blacks and Chicanos) in semiskilled jobs. Many of these positions are now filled by women.

Men who had aspired to craft jobs cannot be expected to view affirmative action with pleasure, despite gains for their group as a whole in higher-level management or lower-level "women's work." The stage is indeed set for sharp antagonisms by class, race, and sex. White male blue-collar workers are pushed by women and minority men; minority men who might have attained semiskilled craft positions are bumped by women; poor women find even the lowest-level phone company jobs now filling with men; white women see skilled clerical work and low-level management—formally their preserves—taken by minority women and by men. A very small proportion of women and minority men, with higher levels of education or technical skills, are advantaged by the new legislation, which tends to open middle-management positions to them, and some are no doubt advantaged by openings due to newer technologies. But their poorer counterparts—the large majority of each group—have fewer entry-level jobs available to them.

Predicting Structural Change: Class, Race and Sex
Various segments of AT&T's occupational structure appear to be in different phases of technological change at the same time. One can see the automation of women's work and the disappearance of women workers. Simultaneously, one can see the degradation or simplification of men's craft work and the appearance of women clerical workers. Even so, it may be possible to discern some general patterning. Table 1 shows the changes in occupational distribution from 1972 to 1975. Table 3 presents correlations between class, race, and sex characteristics of occupations in 1972 and the planned (columns 1 and 2) and actual (columns 3 and 4) changes in employment at each occupational level. For example, the number and

Table 3

Predicting Occupational Displacement from Sex, Race, and Class:
Sex, Race, and Class Characteristics of Occupations, 1972, by
Predicted and Actual Occupational Change (numerical and
percentage) 1972–1975 (Product Moment Correlations)

Characteristics of Occupational Levels	1972 Predicted Change by 1975		Actual Change by 1975	
	r with % change in jobs available at each occ'l level	r with numerical change in jobs available at each occ'l level	r, % change	r, numerical change
Sex characteristics of each occ'l level:				
number of females at occ'l level	−59†	−22	−40	−53*
% females at occ'l level	−44*	−19	−44*	−34
Race characteristics of each occ'l level:				
number of minorities at occ'l level	−56*	−24	−57†	−72†
% minorities at occl' level	−01	−37	−46*	−38
Class/status characteristics of occ'l level:				
Class (mgt = 0; nonmgt = 1 Point biserial r)	37	08	−21	−26
Status (15 levels, from top mgt. = 1, to service workers = 15)	−10	−13	−56*	−45*

* Sig. at the .05 level.
† Sig. at the .01 level.

percentage of females and minorities at each level are correlated with the change—proportional and numerical—in job opportunities at each level.

In 1972 (columns 1 and 2) the best predictor of *planned* decline in jobs at an occupational level was not class, status,[7] or occupational segregation

Table 4
Predicting Occupational Decline from Sex/Race Characteristics of
Occupations (Product Moment Correlations)

Characteristics of Occupational Levels:	1972 Predicted Change by 1975		Actual Change by 1975	
	r with % change in jobs available at each occ'l level	r with numerical change in jobs available at each occ'l level	r, % change	r, numerical change
Number of white males	04	71†	16	28
% white males	37	25	46*	35
Number of minority males	22	45*	−08	06
% minority males	41	−18	07	07
Number of white females	−59†	−18	−36	−48*
% white females	−42	−16	−38	−28
Number of minority females	−58†	−33	−51*	−69†
% minority females	−44*	−28	−64†	−55*

* Sig. at the .05 level.
† Sig. at the .01 level.

by sex or race (percent female, percent minority)[8] but the number of female ($r = .59$) and minority ($r = .56$) employees at any level.

By 1975 (column 3 and 4), *actual* decline (both proportional and numerical) in an occupational level was most strongly related to the 1972 number of minorities at that occupational level.

We also need to attend to the interaction of sex and race. Minority men, white men, minority women, and white women all have a different set of social experiences and, within AT&T, a different set of occupational experiences. Table 4 examines the ability of these four race/sex categories (numbers and percentages of each within an occupational level) to predict growth or decline during the three-year period of technological change. As before, it appears to be the number rather than the percentage which is the better predictor.

The corporation planned to hold growth or cut back on jobs at occupational levels employing large numbers of females and to increase jobs at levels employing large numbers of white males. In actuality, however, the best predictor of slow growth or decline was both a high number and proportion of minority women employed at that level. Structurally, in this case study, technological displacement is best predicted by a combination of race and sex. Displacement struck most sharply where minority women worked.[9]

How does one reconcile this finding with the fact that white women as a category were most seriously displaced during this time? Occupations such as operator and lower-level clerical suffered most displacement. It is here that minority female employment is greatest (19 to 25 percent). Those levels showing the greatest increase were skilled clerical, general services (e.g., delivery), sales, and upper-level management. Some occupations formerly employing large numbers of white women, such as skilled clerical (81 percent white female) increased, but these are positions into which AT&T moved more minority women than (and as many white men as) white women. Thus, although at this time white women's *employment* suffered most, traditionally minority women's *occupations* were most disparately affected.

Finally, as technological sophistication increased during this three-year period, there was greater differentiation in the workforce. Despite corporate projections, there was an increase in the proportion of management (level 4 and above; 23.6 to 25.4 percent) and a corresponding decrease in size (number of employees). But there was an even greater difference in the proportion of female employees (52.4 to 50.1 percent) than in the proportion of management or nonmanagement during this time. If clerical workers are taken as a whole, there is only minimal change in their proportion of total employment (0.5 percent change). But important transformations are taking place—a sharp (18 percent) increase in skilled but a 6 to 16 percent decrease in lesser-skilled clerical workers.

Planned Technological Change and Division in the Labor Force

A more thought-provoking discovery in the mid-1970s, from Bell journals and reports, was that significant technological changes were also underway in the "male" jobs into which women were being encouraged to move. As women learned to climb poles, AT&T was shifting to microwave and laser (fiberoptic) transmission systems. As women learned to install telephones, "Clip and Take" customer installation and phone stores were markedly reducing the need for installers. Framework is a semiskilled craft job (level 10) in which women have made the strongest inroads into craft work (from 20 percent in 1972 to 32 percent in 1975), often replacing minority men. Framework is slated for total automation. A bell engineer reports that the Electronic Switching System (ESS), first installed on the East Coast in the mid-sixties, can virtually eliminate most switchwork and all framework formerly necessary to change telephone connections. (There are no more wires to disconnect and connect, and computer-stored information can be easily changed.) For example, a manager in the Roxbury plant in Boston, employing many minority men, expected a 60 to 80 percent reduction in the workforce when they changed to ESS in 1976.[10] Furthermore, microwave and laser transmission foretells severe restriction for construction and repair work as well (*Laser Focus*, 1978; Reed, 1971). An international representative for a phone workers' union estimates a 10 percent (80,000) force reduction due to technological change in the near future, particularly in crafts and construction.

AT&T tries to avoid layoffs, letting the humane path of attrition take its toll. Yet attrition is also manipulated by the corporation. A Bureau of Labor Statistics Bulletin (1973) shows that in four Bell companies, AT&T increased the workload and reduced flexibility on the job to help maximize attrition during and after a shift to less labor-intensive telephone technology. These efforts, aided by hiring temporary help, minimized the necessity for layoffs and severance pay. (New York City telephone operators provide earthier descriptions of these processes than "humane attrition" [*Center for United Labor Action Newsletter*, 1972].) More often, however, women tended toward individual explanations, blaming themselves for their lack of advancement.

The question of AT&T's intentional manipulation of social divisions must be addressed directly. In my experience, most people in management were sincere about affirmative action. Those in local offices and operating companies were unaware of the overall displacement of women. Most of them vaguely believed that technological change created more jobs than it eliminated, or at best they reverted to the attrition argument.

At AT&T Headquarters and at Bell Labs, there was less suprise and an unwillingness to share future plans and projections.[11] These incidents and impressions are very soft data. However, Loewenberg's thesis documents intentional displacement of men by women in AT&T's recent past, in readiness for the newer technologies now sweeping through the system.

As early as the 1950s, the company considered moving women into maintenance work in the computerized central offices, as Loewenberg noted. In the case of line assignment:

> Since turnover of males is much lower than that of females, turnover could not play the same part in alleviating displacement following introduction of computers. Management therefore wanted to reduce the number of male assignors before programming their work for computers. (Loewenberg, 1962: III-30)

Data from the New York Telephone Company indicated a planned shift from 69 percent male craft workers and 30 percent female clericals in line assignment in 1957 to 79 percent female clericals in 1965. Similar transformations are reported at New Jersey Telephone Company, for example (V-21). Loewenberg commented prophetically on this reassignment of men's to women's jobs:

> Although women are not used elsewhere in craft work at this time [late fifties], many in the industry believe that the prospective simple skill re-

quirements for regular maintenance in the electronic central office may open the way for more use of women in the plant crafts. It is an open secret that women have been used for general maintenance in the Morris, Illinois, trial of the electronic office. These women, with no previous mechanical experience or special aptitudes, were placed on the job after two weeks' training. If AT&T has assessed the work of these women, it has not made the results of the assessment public; nor has it revealed its plans about staffing other electronic central offices. It is not unlikely, however, that the question of women replacing men in the central office will be one of the future work reassignment problems of implementing change. (III-33)

Loewenberg foresaw little difficulty in this transition; skilled workers would not care for "highly repetitive 'idiot maintenance' work" (IV-14). He concludes:

There are three reasons why work may be reassigned between the sexes, particularly from male to female: 1) preparation for displacement by computer or other mechanized process; 2) simplification of work; and 3) savings in wages. (V-28)

At this point, women's employment has not yet turned upward in the corporation. But, with the help of affirmative action, women are moving into the very craft work Loewenberg described. AT&T top managers quite intentionally used social divisions such as sex to enhance profit and to ease the transition to a new technological base. Whether or not a few actually planned to use affirmative action in this way—aiding the shift from male to female labor, defusing worker hostility toward race and sex issues and toward civil rights legislation—must remain an open question.

Choosing Technology

The picture in the late seventies is that of a vast corporation shifting rapidly to a higher level of process technology. One executive calls it a "giant nationwide computer" (Sutton, 1977). The motive for recent changes derives more from AT&T's desire to compete in the lucrative data transmission market than to improve telephone service. AT&T is not a protected monopoly in data, as it is in voice transmission. That data market (e.g., governmental/military, business, and information) demands more precise digital transmission than does voice, for which analog transmission would suffice. Rate structures are also dependent on the amount of capital investment. The more money tied up in equipment, buildings, and computers, the higher the phone bill can be (Goulden, 1970). The data market is one of the fastest growing in the industry. Its military content may be obscured by new phrases such as "business information processing" (*Fortune,* 1978), and its connection to business *and* military may be obscured by AT&T advertising emphasis on small consumer services such as "conference," "call forward," and "wait" (*Wall Street Journal,* Dec. 26, 1978).

An exploration of AT&T's interorganizational relations suggests that military and economic concerns are paramount in its selection and development of machine technologies such as microwave, satellite, and fiber-optic transmission and computerized switching systems (Cordtz, 1970; Goulden, 1970, 1972; Lambeth, 1967; Shepard, W. G., 1971; Silberman, 1967).[12]

Home and Workplace

Recent criticism of Marxist literature requires that we expand our analysis beyond the narrow economic focus on the workplace, particularly to women's general social role and to the interrelationship of home and work. In this research/action project, I observed these relationships exerting a pervasive influence on the ability of women to organize in their own interests. These efforts were often thwarted by male workers, husbands, and union officials, as well as by management. A few examples may suffice. One set of meetings of women workers ended when the organizer's husband, an AT&T craft worker, felt that his wife took too much time away from the family for these efforts. Another union woman had been active before her marriage, and again after her divorce for similar reasons. In a union local meeting, women's issues on the agenda were postponed for a film on hunting and fishing. In another local, a union representative had worked first for the company, then for the union. She reported more sexism in the union. Women labor officials from three states recalled women workers' difficulties with husbands, male co-workers, and their wives. All of these women are strongly pro-union.

Analysis and practice require attention to ways in which male workers have used unions and the law to keep women in their place (Feldberg, 1978b; Hartmann, 1977), and especially to the fact that child care is still women's work in socialist as well as capitalist societies (Weinbaum, 1977). That the institution of the family has also inhibited men's ability to organize (Christoffel and Kaufer, 1970) clearly speaks to the need for analysis of these interrelationships.

Summary

Taking sex stratification as a major conceptual focus, this case study provides potentially useful insight in several areas of sociological research.

1. Technological displacement was seen to cut across management and nonmanagement categories, affecting most severely white women's employment and traditionally minority women's occupations. Sex and race

were better predictors of structural change and of technological displacement than were traditional categories of management/nonmanagement.

2. Higher levels of skill and responsibility due to technological change reflected the elimination of traditionally women's work.

3. Under affirmative action, men gained more traditionally women's positions than the reverse.

4. Women do serve as a reserve labor army. Here, we can see the conscious manipulation of the push and pull factors, operating at the same time, which affect women workers.

5. Corporations select their technologies. In this case, military and economic interests appear to predominate, with sex and race divisions in the labor force facilitating the change to a more sophisticated telecommunications technology. The corporation was able to shift a large part of its organizational uncertainty to the most disadvantaged groups in society (cf. Noll, 1976).

6. Finally, working men are advantaged to some degree by sex stratification, as Hartmann (1977) suggests. They can and do use unions and the law to keep things that way, and they are directly advantaged by women's subordination in their private as well as public lives. This subordination helps maintain the processes summarized in points 1 to 5 above.

Policy Implications[13]

1. Civil rights groups should become aware of the pitfalls of legal measures to achieve equality in opportunity. But there are creative ways to use affirmative action as it stands. Court decisions such as *Griggs* v. *Duke Power* declare any process illegal which disparately affects disadvantaged groups. Technological change which has such a disparate impact is clearly illegal (Krantz, 1977). However, as Hashimoto's (1974) analysis of two major settlements—AT&T and U.S. Steel—shows, legislation means only paper equality unless there is continual and strongly organized public action insuring enforcement. Otherwise, government agencies such as EEOC are caught between a rock and a hard place. Action and scholarly research can be mutually beneficial. Research can inform efforts to organize into unions or caucuses and efforts to win representation in these groups. Action tends to provide richer insight and data than is usually the case.

2. Backlash myths are fed by the media, which present the AT&T settlement as a landmark victory of women's rights. This is an apt description, perhaps, only for women in middle management. The press could provide

the public with deeper awareness of the effects of technological change and of the realities of affirmative action.[14]

3. In the short run, unions might strengthen requirements for automation clauses, assigning decision making on technology to both management and workers. At present, less than 0.5 percent of the organized U.S. workforce is covered by such clauses (National Center for Productivity and Quality of Working Life, 1977). Loewenberg (1962) remarked that

> . . . perhaps the most notable feature arising from an investigation of contract issues that have occupied the parties since 1946, or almost from the beginning of large-scale bargaining, is the general absence of issues that directly concern (technological) change. (VIII-1)

He saw a major problem in the ability of management to dictate change to the unions. When the company does give information to the union, time is usually too short for the union to explore its implications. The Communication Workers of America did consider an automation clause in a recent contract, requiring six months' notice of new technologies with disemployment implications. Even this modest clause failed to make the contract. In the long run, we should explore models of technological change which do not cause the poorest groups in society to pay for such changes (Nygaard, 1977; *Science for the People,* 1974).

4. Newer models of change which focus only on democratic participation in the workplace, and do not include attention to work performed in the family and community, should remain highly suspect. Analysis and practice directed against patriarchal domination and capitalist exploitation appear the most fruitful for dealing with issues discussed in this research.

Notes

The author owes thanks for help with this research to many people and groups, especially women telephone workers.

1. The action was brought before the Federal Communications Commission, the regulating body for the operating companies and Long Lines, which include about four-fifths of all employees. Most other AT&T components are regulated by the Department of Defense. Hence data are available only for the operating companies and Long Lines. EEOC lawyers note that all operating companies are organized so similarly that the format and much of the text of affirmative action plans were identical from company to company, with blank spaces for the name of a particular company. A finer analysis on a company-by-company basis should, however, reveal some variations in the structure due to different levels of modernization. AT&T began this most recent wave of technological change in highly urban areas, and primarily on the East Coast, some fifteen years ago. Data from more rural areas will not reflect the full impact of new technologies; areas of new construction, e.g., the South, may reflect greater impact.
2. Personal interview with personnel director, 1973.
3. Personal interview, Bell Telephone Laboratories, 1974.

4. *Non-Traditional Male and Female Job Changes.* AT&T Bulletin, 1976.

5. Personal interviews with personnel director, engineer, and president, Iowa Area, North-western Bell, 1973.

6. Table 2 indicates that thousands of black and brown women did lose lower-level jobs; it is unlikely that they were the same women as those gaining jobs at lower levels of management. AT&T prefers women in supervisory positions to have a college degree, according to Loewenberg, to "lessen supervisory aspirations of ordinary operators" (1962: VI-8).

7. Some agree that level 4, lowest-level supervisors, should be included in "management" on objective grounds (such as exclusion from the bargaining unit and supervisory duties) and on subjective grounds (such as title and identification). Traditional research would also place level 4 with management. Others disagree, given objective factors such as relationship to the means of production and wages. These objections, however, refer to all but the top-level executives. In my experience, traditional socialist groups in practice tended to ignore the difficulties of women at this level, some referring to them as "class enemies." In a discussion among socialist sociologists in the early seventies, telephone operators were described as "white collar" or "bourgeoisie" and were excluded from the definition of "proletariat." Engineers and unemployed (declassed) college professors were not. Since these issues are far from settled conceptually, I use the measure of class closest to that in traditional sociological research to indicate the need for attention to sex stratification (management = levels 1–4; nonmanagement = levels 5–15). But, given these difficulties, I also use a continuous measure of status, all fifteen occupational levels.

8. Ferber and Lowry (1976a) show that men in traditionally women's work fare worse than women, e.g., in turnover rate and unemployment. Perhaps this is why the relatively large numbers, rather than the traditional indices of segregation (percents), are the better predictor. One must also note the particular phase of change at AT&T. Skilled clerical, a highly sex-segregated occupation, is expanding as it replaces degraded craft work. However, many thousands of women already work at simplified crafts (e.g., level 10), although their proportion is still relatively small (20 percent in 1972). Relatively large numbers of women, then, work at the least technologically sophisticated, most labor-intensive occupations, both traditional and nontraditional. This will not be re-flected in indices of sex segregation (percents) but will when one uses the number of women employed at any level.

9. Second-order partials in the class, race and sex correlations, above, show that except for management's plans to reduce its own share of employment, neither class nor status predict occupational change, controlling for sex and race. Sex and race, controlling for class or status, still predict change. Multiple regression of the four sex/race categories and class, or the four categories and status, shows again that controlling for all other variables, only the percent and number of minority women significantly predict decline. This analysis, however, is clouded by severe problems of multicollinearity, given that the number of minority women and the number of white women across all levels are corre-lated at $r = 0.95$.

10. MIT Telephony class tour, 1975.

11. As I became more interested in AT&T technology, the two NOW members who first suggested this action to the organization, and who provided much information on em-ployment patterns of women and minorities in the early seventies (and who are highly placed in AT&T's corporate structure), were not as helpful in the mid-seventies in pro-viding information on the planned technological changes underway in the corporation.

12. See Galloway (1972) for the deforming impact of military needs on telecommunications technology. For an analysis of the effects of such needs and technologies on social rela-tions, see B. Hacker (1977). For an account of similar origins—military and economic—

of AT&T's *social* technologies (e.g., job descriptions, personality and aptitude testing, education and training) which then found their way into industry and public schooling, see Noble (1977).

13. The information on displacement has been disseminated to women's, minority, and workers' groups and organizations in different ways: through the NOW AT&T newsletter and correspondence with members of this action committee, composed largely of AT&T workers; through informal and formal meetings with union representatives and other labor organizations; through reports and interviews to women's and workers' newspapers and magazines; through speeches to national meetings of affirmative action officers; and to other civil rights organizations such as the American Civil Liberties Union.

In the early seventies, both NOW and traditional unions were slow to respond to the problem of technological displacement of women, NOW and other civil rights groups were geared heavily toward legal and legislative action. Challenging displacement under the law was and is unpopular because it has such a low probability for success. The movement needed a "success story," such as the millions of dollars in back pay awarded the 1973 Consent Decree or "Settlement" (largely a few hundred dollars apiece to some women and minorities). Also important to long-range goals, NOW began to focus heavily on passage of the ERA.

Unions provided little information, and accepted technological displacement "as a parameter within which we work," in the words of one. Women workers were largely unaware of the overall picture (an exception being the New York-based Coalition of Labor Union Women [CLUW], whose newsletter provided insight into working conditions during periods of technological change). As women move into union management, and as male craft work is simplified, these tendencies are changing.

14. In practice this has been a tricky process, as management in the newspaper industry faces similar issues of technological displacement. In some cities, e.g., Des Moines, NOW members resorted to leafletting as an alternative medium, but one of limited power.

V

Unresolved Questions:
Three Feminist Perspectives

From our examination of women and work, we have learned more about the origins of gender inequalities and about their consequences than about how to end them. Genetic arguments, which imply inevitable inequality, cannot readily explain the wide variations which do occur in women's lives. Theories drawing on personality psychology or on social psychological theories of socialization provide some understanding of how inequalities arise but cannot explain why the differential treatment in the paid labor force is so frequently based on beliefs about the unequal worth of women's contributions. Such theories also are inadequate to explain the different rewards received by women and men for similar work. To explain similarities and variations in the work of men and women, and inequality in the evaluations of and rewards for work done by women, broader theories are necessary.

The feminist and sociological perspectives provided in our preceding chapters all identify interrelated social, cultural, and economic influences on women's work. But their explanations differ considerably, and so do their political implications. There is no agreement on the amount of structural and value change necessary, but there is agreement that the established patterns of work and family are especially damaging to women. And there seems to be little chance to improve women's opportunities without affecting the relationships of men and women and altering the relationships between women and children.

One can identify three schools of feminist thought—liberal, Marxist, and radical (or cultural)—by where they tend to locate the main cause of the discrimination against women. The most radical theories require the most sweeping social changes in our institutions in order to create true gender equality. The least radical theories assume that with some changes in our economic and political structure, women will have the same opportunities as men.

267

Liberal feminists argue that women's exclusion from the paid labor force results from a traditional division of labor within the house, based on the unquestioned assumption that young children require a mother's constant presence. But liberals argue that children have only a limited need for their own mother; other parental surrogates can serve as well. Women can have the right to compete once it is shown that children do not require full-time attention from their own mother. This belief provides the initial accompanying rationale for the view that women are just as capable workers as men in the paid labor force. These feminists also believe that while domestic responsibilities are onerous, they are also rewarding; men are capable of sharing the first and can benefit from the second. In this view, both men and women will profit from the end of our arbitrary division of gender roles.

The liberal feminists try to bring about change by counteracting conventional socialization so that women will not be unwilling or feel unable to enter the market. At the same time, men will not have to assume total responsibility for financial support of the family. Liberal feminists attack the concept of unequal pay for equal work and unequal pay for comparable work, and they lead many political and legal efforts to change our system in accordance with these beliefs. They focus attention on providing more opportunities for choice for both women and men and point to changes that have occurred through such efforts.

For example, advertisers are now eager to help employed women meet their new responsibilities. Commercial products are packaged for women in the labor force as well as for home workers. Women as well as men can buy automobiles, drink expensive Scotch, invest in real estate. This concern for women's buying power—and the popular literature which reflects it—contributes to the picture of women as only modified men. It does not question whether society should be arranged on different principles, or whether demands currently made on women workers are actually unfair or even impossible to meet. Instead, popular magazines stress such issues as how to dress for success, how to get ahead while still maintaining some feminine identity, and how to impress colleagues and superiors with one's efficiency and alacrity at work.

Liberal feminists, in their efforts to help women, do not really question the male values that make these skills seem so advantageous. As Cagan (1978) notes, while women should have the same opportunities as men, in consumption as well as anywhere else, some of the goals of the Women's Movement run counter to the male stress on competition and consumption as indicators of success. From this perspective, women should not be caught by the same pressure that men feel—to earn so that they can spend and to compete whatever the costs to others.

Liberals are also criticized by more radical feminists for accepting a view of change that puts all the burden on women, permitting them to feel inadequate if they are not heroic enough to meet difficult or impossible demands. And the liberals are criticized for trying to gain advantages for only those women sufficiently privileged to compete in a system that permits only some men to achieve. The issue of how to create a society without great disparities between the rich and the poor is left untouched.

Marxist feminists argue that the lack of opportunity or choice for women is a symptom, not a cause. They foresee no real change in the sexual division of labor as long as our economic system remains unchanged. While other values remain secondary to maximizing profit, no real change can be expected, for the traditional sex-role division of labor which arose with industrialization is beneficial to capitalism. Capitalists find men the most reliable because men believe their masculinity is based on the ability to provide for their families while their wives provide necessary services at home. Women, through their responsibility for family consumption and child care, help maintain the current economic system. They guarantee a market for products and train the new generation of disciplined workers. In addition, women serve the economy as a reserve labor force, available when opportunities for paid work exist and willing not to complain when they do not. From this perspective, women's current movement into the paid labor force results from the needs of the capitalist market rather than any efforts by feminists. Such phenomena as the cultural mandate, discussed by Coser and Rokoff, or the belief that women are uncommitted workers are seen by Marxist feminists as part of the ideological system set up to rationalize the unequal and stereotyped treatment of women. These beliefs legitimate the unequal pay women are given for comparable work and obscure the real differences among them. Many women are not dependents or second income earners who can afford to work for a lower wage than men.

Feminists with this Marxist understanding of the causes of the sexual division of labor say that changes must involve the whole economic system. They might examine the history of modern China, for example, to argue that women's position has improved greatly with revolutionary changes in the society even though little attention is paid specifically to women's issues. And with reduction of the distinction between public and private, which developed under industrialization, the community can provide support for weaker members of a family, as now occurs in China (Record and Record, 1976; see also Stacey, 1979, for an incisive discussion of the issue of putting socialism ahead of feminism in China).

The third group of feminists—termed radical or cultural—argue that this Marxist explanation for women's oppression is inadequate because it fails to recognize the fundamentally different interests of men and women. Though both men and women are injured by the demands of capitalism, the roles men are expected to perform bring them more prestige and financial rewards than those women perform. What men do is called "work," while women's work is not perceived as important enough even to merit that term. These feminists argue that the pattern of patriarchy—a system in which men possess superior power and economic privilege over women and children, who are the rightful possessions or subjects of men—varies across societies but are never absent. These patterns existed before the development of capitalism, and the advent of socialism is no guarantee they will disappear (Eisenstein, 1978). This possibility is sometimes forgotten because the interests of men often coincide with the interests of capitalists in contemporary society. Such feminists argue that men benefit from women's location in the home in several ways. Men do not have to face the competition of women in the labor force. Also, they have a monopoly on the valued activity in our society and thus are granted extra power (Gillespie, 1971). One side benefit of this allocation of power is that men may escape the onerous or tedious tasks of day-to-day living, which are managed for them by dependent women. Cultural, or radical, feminists also point to the opportunities available to study the use of male power over women in everyday interactions. For example, West and Zimmerman (1977) found that men exert their power over women in the same way that adults exert power over children: men interrupt women conversationally, just as adults interrupt children. In this view the entire hierarchical relationship between men and women must be altered, even if the only way is for women to live without men. Under such "separatism," the positive characteristics of nurturance behavior can be emphasized, and the noncompetitive relationships common in the organizational patterns of women's groups can be institutionalized. Liberal or Marxist feminists suggest, however, that women have developed these characteristics as tactics useful to the powerless (Hacker, 1951). They question whether women will continue to have these characteristics when they are no longer underdogs.

We have presented this variety of perspectives to show how impossible it is to find easy, readily available answers to the inequalities emphasized in much of this book. Some women will continue to prefer the traditional patterns prescribed in the current division of labor between men and women. They are willing to take the risks such patterns carry, gambling on their ability to be lucky in a protected marriage or to find a benevolent patriarch who will let his wife try to manage both home and outside careers. Others are not so willing— or lucky—as to have the opportunity for a sheltered (or double) existence. Clearly, individual women can help themselves by paying attention to the advice on how to end inequality offered by liberal feminists. Women can refuse to assume the special burdens of child care or demand more assistance from husbands, and they can learn to maximize their opportunities in the paid labor force. These are personal choices. Changing the entire system of discriminatory treatment on the basis of gender is much more difficult. The question always remains: what benefits are worth what costs for ourselves and our children?

Women can recognize, as Marxist feminists suggest, that gender equality will be attained only with the complete alteration of the economic system that makes inequality profitable. But this change may not be so advantageous for everyone. It might mean that upper- and middle-class women, for example, would find they no longer had special privileges in the competition for education and training. Women can recognize, as radical feminists suggest, that real change might mean severing ties to men who are not willing to relinquish their own advantage. We hope that the studies in this collection, and their underlying perspectives, will help students with their own thinking about the work women do.

References

Abbot, Edith
  1906   "The history of industrial employment of women in the United States: An introductory study." Journal of Political Economy 8: 461–501.
  1913   Women in Industry. New York: Appleton.

Abbott, John C.
  1833   The Mother at Home: Or, the Principles of Maternal Duty. Boston.

Abegglen, James
  1958   The Japanese Factory. Glencoe, Illinois: Free Press.
  1973   Management and the Worker, the Japanese Solution. Tokyo: Kodansha International and Sophia University.

Aberle, David and Kaspar Naegele
  1952   "Middle-class fathers' occupational role and attitude towards children." American Journal of Orthopsychiatry 22: 366–378.

Acker, Joan
  1973   "Women and social stratification: A case of intellectual sexism." American Journal of Sociology 78: 936–945.
  1977   "Issues in the sociological study of women's work." Pp. 134–161 in Ann H. Stromberg and Shirley Harkess (eds.), Working Women: Theories and Facts in Perspective. Palo Alto, California: Mayfield.

Acker, Joan and Donald P. Van Houten
  1974   "Differential recruitment and control: The sex structuring of organizations." Administrative Science Quarterly 19: 152–162.

Adams, Francis
  1875   The Free School System of the United States. London: Chapman and Hall.

Alcott, William A.
  1837   The Young Wife, Or Duties of Woman in the Married Relation. Boston.

Aldous, Joan
  1969   "Occupational characteristics and males' role performance in the family." Journal of Marriage and the Family 31: 707–712.

Almquist, Elizabeth
  1977   "Women in the labor force." Signs 2: 843–855.

Anonymous
  1813   The American Lady's Preceptor: A Compilation of Observations, Essays, and Poetical Effusions Designed to Direct the Female Mind in a Course of Pleasing and Instructive Reading. Baltimore.

1856   The Lady's Companion. Edited by a Lady. Philadelphia.

Armytage, W.H.G.
1970   Four Hundred Years of English Education. Cambridge: Cambridge University Press.

Aronowitz, Stanley
1973   False Promises: The Shaping of American Working Class Consciousness. New York: McGraw-Hill.

Association of American Colleges: Project on the Status and Education of Women
1980   On Campus with Women. Washington, D.C. Fall.

Bahr, Stephen
1974   "Effects on power and division of labor in the family." Pp. 167–185 in Lois W. Hoffman and F. Ivan Nye (eds.), Working Mothers. San Francisco: Jossey-Bass.

Bailyn, Bernard
1960   Education in the Forming of American Society. Chapel Hill: University of North Carolina Press.

Baker, Elizabeth Faulkner
1964   (1925) Technology and Women's Work. New York: Columbia University Press. Protective Labor Legislation. New York: Columbia University Press.

Baker, Sally Hillsman
1970   "Entry into the labor market: The preparation and job placement of Negro and white vocational high school graduates." Unpublished doctoral dissertation, Columbia University.

Baker, Sally Hillsman
1975   "Job discrimination—schools as the solution or part of the problem? Some research on the careers of working-class women." Unpublished paper.

Baker, Sally Hillsman and Bernard Levenson
1975   "Earnings prospects of black and white working class women." New York: City University of New York. Unpublished paper.

Balswick, Jack
1974   "Why husbands can't say, 'I love you.'" Woman's Day 37:66, 158, 160.

Balswick, Jack and Charles Peek
1971   "The inexpressive male: A tragedy of American society." The Family Coordinator 20: 363–368.

Bar-Joseph, Rivka
1974   "The meanings of equality and their structural consequences." Paper presented at the annual meeting of the Society for the Study of Social Problems, Montreal, August 24.

Baran, Paul A. and Paul M. Sweezy
1966   Monopoly Capital: An Essay on the American Economy and Social Order. New York: Monthly Review Press.

Bartol, Kathryn M.
1974   "Male versus female leaders: The effect of leader need for dominance on follower satisfaction." Academy of Management Journal 17: 225–
233.
1975   "The effect of male versus female leaders on follower satisfaction
and performance." Journal of Business Research 3: 33–42.

Bartol, Kathryn M. and D. Anthony Butterfield
1974   "Sex effects in evaluating leaders." Working paper #74-10, University of Massachusetts School of Business Administration.

Bass, Bernard M., Judith Krusell and Ralph A. Alexander
1971   "Male managers' attitudes toward working women." American Behavioral Scientist 15: 221–236.

Bayo, Francisco and Milton P. Glanz
1965   "Mortality experiences of workers entitled to old-age benefits under
OASDI 1941–1961." Social Security Administration, Actuarial Study 60.
Washington, D.C.: U.S. Government Printing Office.

Baxandall, Rosalyn, Linda Gordon and Susan Reverby
1976   America's Working Women. New York: Random House.

Beck, E.M. et al.
1980   "Industrial segmentation and labor market discrimination." Social
Problems 28: 113–130.

Becker, Gary S.
1957   The Economics of Discrimination. Chicago: University of Chicago
Press.
1968   "Discrimination, economic." Pp. 208–210 in David Sills (ed.), International Encyclopedia of the Social Sciences 4. New York: Macmillan and
the Free Press.

Beirne, Joseph A.
1965   Automation: Impact and Implications; With a Focus on Developments in the Communications Industry (foreword). A report prepared for
the Communications Workers of America by the Diebold Group, April.

Bell, Carolyn Shaw
1974   "Working women's contributions to family income." Eastern Economic Journal 1: 185–201.

Bellah, Robert
1957   Tokugawa Religion: The Values of Pre-Industrial Japan. Glencoe,
Illinois: Free Press.

Benedict, Ruth
1946   The Chrysanthemum and the Sword. Boston: Houghton Miffllin.

Benét, Mary Kathleen
1972   The Secretarial Ghetto. New York: McGraw-Hill.

Bennett, John
1795   Strictures on Female Education. Worcester, Massachusetts.

Bennetts, Leslie
   1979   New York Times, December 15.

Bennis, Warren G., Norman Berkowitz, Moan Affinito and Mary Malone
   1958a   "Authority, power, and the ability to influence." Human Relations
   11: 143–155.
   1958b   "Reference groups and loyalties in the outpatient department." Administrative Science Quarterly 2: 481–500.

Benston, Margaret
   1969   "The political economy of women's liberation." Monthly Review
   21: 13–27.

Berg, Ivar
   1970   Education and Jobs: The Great Training Robbery. New York: Praeger.

Berger, Michael, Martha Foster and Barbara Strudler Wallston
   1978   "Finding two jobs." Pp. 23–35 in Robert and Rhona Rapoport
   (eds.), Working Couples. New York: Harper & Row.

Berger, Peter and Hansfried Kellner
   1970   "Marriage and the construction of reality." Pp. 50–72 in Hans Peter
   Dreitzel (ed.), Recent Sociology, No. 2. London: Macmillan.

Berger, Peter and Thomas Luckmann
   1967   The Social Construction of Reality. New York: Anchor Books.

Bergmann, Barbara
   1974   "Occupational segregation, wages and profits where employers discriminate by race or sex." Eastern Economic Journal 1: 103–110.

Bergquist, Virginia A.
   1974   "Women's participation in labor organizations." Monthly Labor
   Review 97: 3–9.

Berk, Richard
   1980   "The new home economics: An agenda for sociological research."
   Pp. 113–148 in Sarah Fenstermaker Berk (ed.), Women and Household Labor. Beverly Hills, California: Sage.

Berk, Richard and Sarah Fenstermaker Berk
   1979   Labor and Leisure at Home: Content and Organization of the
   Household Day. Beverly Hills, California: Sage.

Berk, Sara F., Richard Berk and Catherine Berheide
   1976   "The non-division of household labor: A preliminary report." Paper
   presented at the annual meeting of the American Association for the Advancement of Science, Boston.

Bernard, Jessie
   1974   The Future of Motherhood. New York: Dial Press.

Beynon, H. and R.M. Blackburn
   1972   Perceptions of Work. London: Cambridge University Press.

Bibb, Robert and William Form
    1977   "The effects of industrial, occupational, and sex stratification on wages in blue collar markets." Social Forces 55: 974–996.

Bird, Caroline
    1971   Born Female: The High Cost of Keeping Women Down. New York: David McKay.
    1979   The Two-Paycheck Marriage. New York: Rawson, Wade.

Blake, Judith
    1973a   "The teenage birth control dilemma and public opinion." Science 180: 708–712.
    1973b   "Elective opinion and our reluctant citizenry." Pp. 447–467 in Howard J. Osofsky and Joy D. Osofsky (eds.), The Abortion Experience. New York: Harper & Row.

Blau, Francine
    1978   "Women in the labor force." Pp. 29–62 in Ann Stromberg and Shirley Harkess (eds.), Women Working: Theories and Facts in Perspective. Palo Alto, California: Mayfield.

Blau, Peter M.
    1955   Dynamics of Bureaucracy. Chicago: University of Chicago Press.

Blau, Peter M. and O.D. Duncan
    1967   The American Occupational Structure. New York: Wiley.

Blau, Peter M. and W. Richard Scott
    1962   Formal Organizations. San Francisco: Chandler.

Blauner, Robert
    1964   Alienation and Freedom. Chicago: University of Chicago Press.

Blaxall, Martha and Barbara B. Reagan (eds.)
    1976   "Women and the workplace: The implications of occupational segregation." Signs 1 (3, Pt. 2): entire.

Blood, Robert O. and Donald Wolfe
    1960   Husbands and Wives. New York: Free Press.

Blumberg, Rae Lesser
    1976   "The erosion of sexual equality in the kibbutz." Pp. 320–342 in Joan Roberts (ed.), Women Scholars on Women. New York: David McKay.
    1977   "Women and work around the world." Pp. 412–433 in Alice Sargent (ed.), Beyond Sex Roles. St. Paul: West.

Blumer, Herbert
    1969   Symbolic Interaction: Perspective and Method. Englewood Cliffs, New Jersey: Prentice-Hall.

Bonjean, C. W., Grady D. Bruce and Allen J. Williams, Jr.
    1967   "Social mobility and job satisfaction: A replication and extension." Social Forces 46: 492–501.

Bose, Christine
    1978   "Technology and changes in the division of labor in the American

home." Paper presented at the annual meeting of the American Sociological Association, San Francisco.

Boserup, Ester
1970   Women's Role in Economic Development. London: George Allen and Unwin.

Boulding, Elise
1976a   "Familial constraints on women's work roles." Signs 1: 95–118.
1976b   Handbook of International Data on Women. Beverly Hills, California: Sage.
1976c   The Underside of History: A View through Time. Boulder, Colorado: Westview Press.

Bourdieu, Pierre and Jean-Claude Passeron
1977   Reproduction: In Education, Society and Culture. (Trans. Richard Nice; Foreword, Tom Bottomore.) London: Sage.

Bowman, G.W., N.B. Worthy and S.A. Greyser
1965   "Are women executives people?" Harvard Business Review 43: 14–30.

Boyd, Monica
1974   "Equality between the sexes: Results of the Canadian Gallup Polls." Paper presented at the meeting of the Canadian Sociology and Anthropology Association.

Bradley, Mike et al.
1971   Unbecoming Men: A Men's Consciousness-Raising Group Writes on Oppression and Themselves. New York: Changing Times Press.

Brandeis, Elizabeth
1935   "Labor legislation." Pp. 339–697 in Don Lescohier and Elizabeth Brandeis, Volume III of John R. Commons (ed.), History of Labor in the United States, 1896–1932. New York: Macmillan.

Braverman, Harry
1974   Labor and Monopoly Capital: The Degradation of Work in the 20th Century. New York: Monthly Review Press.

Breckinridge, Sophonsiba B.
1906   "Legislative control of women's work." Journal of Political Economy 14: 107–109.

Bridenthal, Renate and Claudia Koonz
1977   Becoming Visible: Women in European History. Boston: Houghton Mifflin.

Broverman, Inge K., Donald M. Broverman, Frank E. Clarkson and Susan R. Vogel
1970   "Sex role stereotypes and clinical judgments of mental health." Journal of Consulting and Clinical Psychology 34: 1–7.

Brown, Judith K.
1970   "A note on the division of labor by sex." The American Anthropologist 72: 1073–1078.

Brown, Linda Keller
1979   "Women and business management." Signs 5: 266–288.

Brown, Richard
1976   "Women as employees: Comments on research in industrial sociology." Pp. 21–46 in Diana L. Barker and Sheila Allen (eds.), Dependence and Exploitation in Work and Marriage. New York: Longman.

Bullough, Bonnie and Vern L. Bullough
1975   "Sex discrimination in helath care." Nursing Outlook 23: 40–45.

Bureau of Labor Statistics
1973   Outlook for Technology and Manpower in Printing and Publishing. Bulletin 1774. U.S. Department of Labor, Washington, D.C.: U.S. Government Printing Office.

Bureau of Vocational Information
1929   Collection deposited in Schlesinger Library, Radcliffe College, Cambridge, Massachusetts.

Burns, Tom
1955   "The reference of conduct in small groups: Cliques and cabals in occupational milieux." Human Relations 8: 467–486.

Butler, M. and W. Paisley
1980   "Coordinated-career couples: Convergence and divergence." Pp. 207–228 in F. Pepitone-Rockwell (ed.), Dual-Career Couples. Beverly Hills, California: Sage.

Cagan, Elizabeth
1978   "The selling of the women's movement." Social Policy 7: 4–12.

Campbell, Margaret A.
1973   Why would a girl go into medicine? Medical Education in the United States: A Guide for Women. Old Westbury, New York: The Feminist Press.

Caplow, Theodore
1954   The Sociology of Work. Minneapolis: University of Minnesota Press.

Carden, Maren Lockwood
1974   The New Feminist Movement. New York: Russell Sage Foundation.

Cattell, Raymond B. and Edwin D. Lawson
1962   "Sex differences in small group performance." Journal of Social Psychology 58: 141–145.

Cecchini, S.
1976   "Women's suicide." Pp. 263–296 in Joyce Lebra et al. (eds.), Women in Changing Japan. Boulder, Colorado: Westview Press.

Celarier, Michele
1981   "The paycheck challenge of the eighties—comparing job worth." MS 9: 38.

Center for United Labor Action Newsletter
1972   167 West 21 Street, New York, New York 10011 (December 4).

Chafe, William H.
    1974   American Woman: Her Changing Social, Economic and Political
            Roles, 1920–1970. New York: Oxford University Press.
    1976   Women and Equality. London and New York: Oxford University
            Press.

Chafetz, Janet
    1974   Masculine/Feminine or Human? Itasca, Illinois: Peacock.

Chicago Sun-Times
    1980   (April 29): 24.

Chicago Tribune
    1978   (January 8): 4.
    1978   (May 8)

Child, Mrs. Lydia
    1831   The Mother's Book. Boston.

Chinoy, Ely
    1955   Automobile Workers and the American Dream. New York: Random
            House.

Chodorow, Nancy
    1971   "Being and doing: A cross-cultural examination of the socialization
            of males and females." Pp. 259–291 in Vivian Gornick and Barbara K.
            Moran (eds.), Women in Sexist Society. New York: New American Library.
    1976   "Oedipal Asymmetries and Heterosexual Knots." Social Problems
            23: 454–468.

Christoffel, Tom and Katherine Kaufer
    1970   "The political economy of male chauvinism." Pp. 310–319 in Tom
            Christoffel, David Finkelhor and Dan Gilbarg (eds.), Up Against the Amer-
            ican Myth. New York: Holt, Rinehart & Winston.

Clark, Alice
    1919   Working Life of Women in the Seventeenth Century. London:
            George Routledge.

Clearing House International Newsletter
    1981   16 N. Wabash Avenue, Chicago, Illinois 60602. Vol. 6, No. 3
            (March).

Clignet, Remi
    1977   "Social change and sexual differentiation in the Cameroun and the
            Ivory Coast." Signs 3: 244–260.

Cohen, Arthur R.
    1958   "Upward communication in experimentally created hierarchies."
            Human Relations 11: 41–53.

Cole, Robert
    1971   Japanese Blue Collar. Berkeley: University of California Press.

Colman, Benjamin
    1716   The Honour and Happiness of the Vertuous Woman. Boston.

Conklin, N.F.
1974   "Toward a feminist analysis of linguistic behavior." The University of Michigan Papers in Women's Studies 1: 51–73.

Coombs, Robert H. and Clark E. Vincent
1971   Psychological Aspects of Medical Training. Springifeld, Illinois: Charles C. Thomas.

Copus, David
1976   Personal communication.

Cordtz, Dan
1970   "The coming shake-up in telecommunications." Fortune (April): 69ff.

Coser, Lewis A.
1968   "Deviant behavior and normative flexibility." American Journal of Sociology 68: 172–181.
1974   Greedy Institutions: Patterns of Undivided Commitment. New York: Free Press.

Coser, Rose Laub
1961   "Insulation from observability and types of social conformity." American Sociological Review 26: 29–39.
1966   "Role distance, sociological ambivalence and transitional status systems." American Journal of Sociology 72: 173–187.

Costantini, Edmond and Kenneth H. Craik
1972   "Women as politicians: The social background, personality, and political careers of female party leaders." Journal of Social Issues 28: 217–236.

Cotgrove, S.
1972   "Alienation and automation." British Journal of Sociology 23: 437–451.

Cott, Nancy F.
1977   The Bonds of Womanhood: "Woman's Sphere" in New England, 1780–1835. New Haven: Yale University Press.
1978   "Passionlessness: An interpretation of Victorian sexual ideology, 1790–1850." Signs 4: 219–236.

Coyle, Grace
1929   "Women in the clerical occupations." The Annals of the American Academy of Political and Social Science 143: 180–187.

Cremin, Lawrence A.
1965   The Wonderful World of Elswood Patterson Cubberley: An Essay in the Historiography of American Education. New York: Teachers College Press of Columbia University.
1970   American Education: The Colonial Experience, 1607–1783. New York: Harper & Row.

Crowley, Joan E., Teresa E. Levitin and Robert P. Quinn
1973   "Seven deadly half-truths about women." Psychology Today 6: 94–96.

Crozier, Michel
    1964   The Bureaucratic Phenomenon. Chicago: University of Chicago Press.
    1971   The World of the Office Worker. (Trans. David Landau.) Chicago: University of Chicago Press.

Cummings, Laurie Davidson
    1977   "Value Stretch in Definitions of Career Among College Women: Horatia Alger as Feminist Model." Social Problems 25: 65–74.

Cussler, Margaret
    1958   The Woman Executive. New York: Harcourt Brace.

Dahlstrom, E. and R. Liljestrom
    1967   "The family and married women at work." Pp. 19–58 in E. Dahlstrom (ed.), The Changing Roles of Men and Women. Boston: Beacon Press.

Dalla Costa, Mariarosa
    1972   "Women and the subversion of community." Radical America 6: 67–102.

Davidson, Lynne R.
    1975   "Sex roles, affect and the woman physician: A study of the impact of latent social identity upon the role of the professional." Unpublished doctoral dissertation, New York University.
    1978   "Medical immunity? Male ideology and the profession of medicine." Women and Health 3:3–10.
    1979   "Choice by constraint: The selection and function of specialties among women physicians-in-training." Journal of Health Politics, Policy and Law 4: 200–220.

Davies, Marjorie
    1974   "Women's place is at the typewriter: The feminization of the clerical labor force." Radical America 8: 1–37.

Davis, James A.
    1965   Undergraduate Career Decisions. Chicago: Aldine.

Davis, Keith
    1967   Human Relations at Work. New York: McGraw-Hill.

Day, D.R. and R.M. Stogdill
    1972   "Leader behavior of male and female supervisors: A comparative study." Personnel Psychology 25: 353–360.

Demos, John
    1970   A Little Commonwealth: Family Life in Plymouth Colony. New York: Oxford.

Deutscher, Irwin
    1973   What We Say/ What We Do: Sentiments and Acts. Glenview, Illinois: Scott, Foresman.

Dittes, J.D. and H.H. Kelley
    1956   "Effects of difference conditions of acceptance upon conformity to group norms." Journal of Abnormal and Social Psychology 53: 100–107.

Dobbs, A. E.
    1969   (1919) Education and Social Movements, 1700–1850. Reprints of
              Economics Classics. New York: August M. Kelley.

Dodge, Norton T.
    1966   Women in the Soviet Economy. Baltimore: Johns Hopkins Univer-
              sity Press.

Dore, P. Ronald
    1973   British Factory and Japanese Factory. Berkeley: University of Cali-
              fornia Press.

Douglas, Mary
    1970   Purity and Danger: An Analysis of Concepts of Pollution and Ta-
              boo. Baltimore: Penguin Books.

Dubin, Robert
    1956   "Industrial workers' worlds." Social Problems 3: 131–142.

Dubin, Robert R., R. Alan Hedley and C. Taveggia
    1976   "Attachment to work." Pp. 281–341 in Robert Dubin (ed.), Hand-
              book of Work, Organization and Society. Chicago: Rand McNally.

Dublin, Thomas
    1975   "Women, work and the family: Female operatives in the Lowell
              mills, 1830–1860." Feminist Studies 3: 30–39.
    1979   Women at Work. New York: Columbia University Press.

Duke, Benjamin C.
    1973   Japan's Militant Teachers: A History of the Left-Wing Teacher's
              Movement. Honolulu: University of Hawaii Press.

Duncan, Beverly and Mark Evers
    1975   "Measuring change in attitudes towards women's work." Pp. 129–
              156 in Kenneth C. Land and Seymour Spilerman (eds.), Social Indicator
              Models. New York: Russell Sage Foundation.

Duncan, Otis D., Howard Schuman and Beverly Duncan
    1974   Social Change in a Metropolitan Community. New York: Russell
              Sage Foundation.

Dyer, William
    1956   "The interlocking of work and family social systems among lower
              occupational families." Social Forcess 34: 230–233.
    1965   "Family reactions to the father's job." Pp. 86–91 in Arthur Shostak
              and William Gomberg (eds.), Blue-Collar World. Englewood Cliffs, New
              Jersey: Prentice-Hall.

Eisenstein, Zillah R. (ed.)
    1978   "Introduction." Pp. 1–39 in Capitalist Patriarchy and the Case for
              Socialist Feminism. New York, Monthly Review Press.

Eisler, Beneta (ed.)
    1977   The Lowell Offering: Writings by New England Mill Women, 1840–
              1845. New York: J. B. Lippincott Company.

Eldridge, Hope T.
    1968   "Population: Population policies." Pp. 380–388 in David Sills (ed.),
    The International Encyclopedia of the Social Sciences 12. New York: Mac-
    millan and the Free Press.

Eninger, Max
    1967   Report on New York State Data from the National Follow-up of
    High School Level Trade and Industrial Vocational Graduates. Pittsburgh,
    Pennsylvania: Educational Systems Research Institute.

Epstein (Easton), Barbara
    1975   "Women, religion, and the family: Revivalism as an indicator of so-
    cial change in early New England." Unpublished doctoral dissertation,
    Berkeley: University of California.

Epstein, Cynthia Fuchs
    1969   "Women lawyers and their profession: Inconsistency of social con-
    trols and their consequences for professional performance." Pp. 669–684 in
    Athena Theodore (ed.), The Professional Woman. Cambridge, Massachu-
    setts: Schenkman.
    1970a   "Encountering the male establishment: Sex-status limits in women's
    careers in the professions." American Journal of Sociology 75: 965–982.
    1970b   Woman's Place: Options and Limits in Professional Careers. Berke-
    ley: University of California Press.

Equal Employment Opportunity Commission
    1971   A Unique Competence: A Study of Equal Employment Opportunity
    in the Bell System. Washington, D.C.: U.S. Government Printing Office.

Ericksen, Julia
    1977   "An analysis of the journey to work for women." Social Problems
    24: 428–435.

Erskine, Hazel Gaudet
    1971   "The polls: Women's role." Public Opinion Quarterly 34: 275–290.
    1972   "The polls: Pollution and its costs." Public Opinion Quarterly 36:
    120–135.

Eyde, Lorraine
    1962   Work Values and Background Factors as Predictors of Women's De-
    sire to Work. Columbus, Ohio: College of Commerce and Administration,
    Ohio State University.
    1968   "Work motivation of women college graduates: 5-year follow-up."
    Journal of Counseling Psychology 15: 109–202.

Facts-On-File Yearbook
    1971   New York: Facts on File, Inc.

Farrell, Warren
    1974   The Liberated Man. New York: Random House.

(FEW) Federally Employed Women, Inc.
    1980   News and Views, vol. 15, no. 2.

Federation of Japanese Teachers' Union
   1975   Educational Journal: Special Focus on Women Teachers. Tokyo: Nikkyoso.

Feinstein, K.W.
   1979   "Directors for day care." Pp. 177–193 in K.W. Feinstein (ed.), Working Women and Families. Beverly Hills, California: Sage.

Feldberg, Roslyn L.
   1978a   Personal communication. Boston University.
   1978b   "Early unions among clerical workers." Paper presented at the annual meeting of the Society for the Study of Social Problems, San Francisco.

Ferber, Marianne A. and Helen Lowry
   1976a   "Women: The new reserve labor army of the unemployed." Signs 1: 213–232.
   1976b   "The sex differential in earnings." Industrial and Labor Relations Review 29: 377–387.

Ferree, Myra Marx
   1974   "A woman for president" Changing responses, 1958–1972." Public Opinion Quarterly 38: 390–399.

Fiedler, Leslie
   1968   The Return of the Vanishing American. New York: Stein and Day.

Figes, Eva
   1970   Patriarchal Attitudes. New York: Stein and Day.

Firestone, Shulamith
   1970   The Dialectic of Sex. New York: Bantam Books.

Flexner, Eleanor
   1968   Century of Struggle: The Woman's Rights Movement in the United States. New York: Atheneum.

Foner, Philip S.
   1980   Women and the American Labor Movement from World War I to the Present. New York: Free Press.

Form, William
   1969   "Occupational and social integration of automobile workers in four countries, a comparative study." International Journal of Comparative Sociology 10: 95–116.
   1973   "The internal stratification of the working class." American Sociological Review 38: 697–711.

Fortune
   1978   "Business communications: The new frontier." (October 9): 40.

Fraiberg, Selma
   1977   Every Child's Birthright: In Defense of Mothering. New York: Basic Books.

Freedman, Marcia
    1969   The Process of Work Establishment. New York: Columbia University Press.

Freeman, Jo
    1975   The Politics of Woman's Liberation. New York: David McKay.

Friedan, Betty
    1963   The Feminine Mystique. New York: Dell.

Friedl, Ernestine
    1975   Women and Men: An Anthropologist's View. New York: Holt, Rinehart & Winston.

Fuller, Raymond
    1944   "Child Labor." Encyclopedia of the Social Sciences 3–4: 412–424. E.R.A. Seligman, ed. New York: Macmillan.

Fundanren (Japan Federation of Women's Groups)
    1975   White Paper on Women. Tokyo: Fundanren.

Gagnon, John H.
    1969   "The woman's revolution." Printed in McCalls under the title: "Is a woman's revolution possible? No." 76: 126–129.

Galloway, Jonathan
    1972   The Politics and Technology of Satellite Communication. Lexington, Massachusetts: Lexington Books.

Gardner, Burleigh B.
    1945   Human Relations in Industry. Chicago: Richard D. Irwin.

Garfinkel, Harold
    1967   Studies in Ethnomethodology. Englewood Cliffs, New Jersey: Prentice-Hall.

Garland, T. Neal
    1972   "The better half? The male in the dual profession family." Pp. 199–215 in Constantina Safilios-Rothschild (ed.), Toward a Sociology of Women. Lexington, Massachusetts: Xerox College Publishing.

Garson, Barbara
    1973   "Women's work." Working Papers I (Fall): 5–14.

Geiger, Kent
    1968   The Family in Soviet Russia. Cambridge, Massachusetts: Harvard University Press.

Giddens, Anthony
    1975   The Class Structure of the Advanced Societies. New York: Harper & Row.

Gillespie, Dair
    1971   "Who has the power? The marital struggle." Journal of Marriage and the Family 33: 445–458.

Gilman, Charlotte Perkins
  1979   (1915) Herland. New York: Pantheon Books. (Originally published as a serial in The Forerunner, a journal published by Gilman.)
Gisborne, Thomas
  1797   An Enquiry into the Duties of the Female Sex. London.
Gissing, George
  1977   (1893) The Odd Women. New York: Norton.
Glazer, Nona
  1976   "Housework (review essay)." Signs 1: 905–922.
  1980   "Overworking the working woman: The double day in a mass magazine." Women's Studies International Quarterly 3: 39–93.
Glazer, Nona, Linda Majka, Joan Acker, and Christine Bose
  1979   "The homemaker, the family, and employment." Pp. 155–169 in Ann Foote Cahn (ed.), Women in the U.S. Labor Force. New York: Praeger.
Glenn, Evelyn N. and Roslyn L. Feldberg
  1977   "Degraded and deskilled: The proletarianization of clerical work." Social Problems 25: 52–64.
Glick, Paul
  1979   "The future of the American family." Current Population Reports, Series P-23, No. 78. Washington, D.C.: U.S. Government Printing Office.
Goffman, Erving
  1959   The Presentation of Self in Everyday Life. New York: Anchor Doubleday.
  1961   "Role distance." Pp. 85–152 in Erving Goffman (ed.), Encounters. Indianapolis, Indiana: Bobbs-Merrill.
Goldberg, Phillip
  1968   "Are women prejudiced against women?" Trans-Action 5: 28–30.
Goldmark Josephine
  1905 "The necessary sequel of child-labor laws." American Journal of Sociology 11: 312–325.
Goode, William J.
  1960   "A theory of role strain." American Sociological Review 25: 483–496.
  1970   World Revolution and Family Patterns. New York: Free Press.
  1971   "Family disorganization." Pp. 467–544 in Robert K. Merton and Robert Nisbet (eds.), Contemporary Social Problems. New York: Harcourt, Brace.
Goodman, Paul
  1964   Compulsory Mis-Education. New York: Horizon Press.
Goodstadt, Barry E. and Larry A. Hjelle
  1973   "Power to the powerless: Focus of control and the use of power." Journal of Personality and Social Psychology 27: 190–196.

Goodstadt, Barry E. and D. Kipnis
    1970   "Situational influences on the use of power." Journal of Applied Psychology 54: 201–207.

Gordon, David M.
    1976   "Comment." Signs 1: 238–244.

Gordon, L.
    1971   "Functions of the family." Pp. 181–188 in L.B. Tanner (ed.), Voices from Women's Liberation. New York: New American Library.

Gorz, Andre
    1973   "Technical intelligence and the capitalist division of labor." Science for the People 5: 6–10, 26–29.

Goulden, Joseph C.
    1970   Monopoly. New York: Pocket Books.
    1972   "A peek at the books." The Nation (January 10): 37–41.

Gouldner, Alvin W.
    1964   Patterns of Industrial Bureaucracy. New York: Free Press.

Greer, Germaine
    1979   The Obstacle Race. New York: Farrar Straus Giroux.

Grimm, James W. and Robert N. Stern
    1974   "Sex roles and internal labor market structures: The 'female' semi-professions," Social Problem 21: 690–705.

Grønseth, Erik
    1970   "The dysfunctionality of the husband provider role in industrialized societies." Paper presented at the VIIth World Congress of Sociology.

    1971   "The husband-provider role: A critical appraisal." Pp. 11–31 in Andree Michel (ed.), Family Issues of Employed Women in Europe and America. Leiden: E.J. Brill.

    1972   "The breadwinner trap." Pp. 175–191 in Louise Kapp Howe (ed.), The Future of the Family. New York: Simon & Schuster.

Gross, Edward
    1968   "Plus ca change . . . : The sexual structure of occupations over time." Social Problems 16: 198–208.

    1970   "Work, organization and stress." Pp. 54–110 in Sol Levine and Norman Scotch (eds.), Social Stress. Chicago: Aldine.

Grunker, William J., Donald D. Cooke and Arthur W. Kirsch
    1970   Climbing the Job Ladder: A Study of Employee Advancement in Eleven Industries. New York: Shelley.

Hacker, Barton
    1977   "Weapons of the West: Military technology and modernization in 19th century China and Japan." Technology and Culture 18: 43–55.

Hacker, Helen Mayer
    1951   "Women as a minority group." Social Forces 30: 60–69.

Hacker, Sally L.
1977   "Farming out the home: Women and agribusiness." Second Wave: A Magazine of the New Feminism (Winter) 5: 38–49.

Hall, Francine S. and Douglas T. Hall
1979   The Two-Career Couple: He Works. She Works. But How Does the Relationship Work? Reading, Massachusetts: Addison-Wesley.

Hall, Richard H.
1975   Occupations and the Social Structure. 2nd ed. Englewood Cliffs, New Jersey: Prentice-Hall.

Halloran, Richard
1972   Japan: Images and Realities. New York: Norton.

Hartmann, Heidi
1976   "Capitalism, patriarchy, and job segregation by sex." Signs 1 (3, pt. 2): 137–170.
1977   "Capitalism, patriarchy and job segregation." Pp. 71–84 in Nona Glazer and Helen Youngelson Waeher (eds.), Women in a Man-Made World: A Socio-Economic Handbook. Chicago: Rand McNally College Publishing.
1981   "The family as the locus of gender, class, and political struggle: The example of housework." Signs 6: 366–394.

Hashimoto, David
1974   "EEOC's use of consent decrees." Unpublished draft of thesis, University of Wisconsin.

Hayghe, Howard
1976   "Families and the rise of working wives: An overview." Monthly Labor Review 99: 12–19.

Hedges, Janice Neipert
1970   "Women workers and manpower demands in the 1970's." Monthly Labor Review 93: 19–29.

Hedges, Janice N. and S. E. Bemis
1974   "Sex stereotyping: Its decline in the skilled trades." Monthly Labor Review 97: 14–22.

Heer, D.
1963   "Dominance and the working wife." Pp. 251–262 in F. Ivan Nye and Lois W. Hoffman (eds.), The Employed Mother in America. Chicago: Rand McNally.

Helfgott, R.B.
1959a   "Puerto Rican integration in the skirt industry in New York City." Pp. 249–279 in A. Antonovsky and L.L. Lorwin (eds.), Discrimination and Low Incomes. New York: New York State Commission Against Discrimination.
1959b   "Women's and children's apparel." Pp. 19–134 in M. Hall (ed.), Made in New York: Case Studies in Metropolitan Manufacturing. Cambridge, Massachusetts: Harvard University Press.

Henderson, L.M. and Talcott Parsons
    1947   Introduction to Max Weber, The Theory of Social and Economic
    Organizations. (Trans. Henderson and Parsons.) New York: The Free Press.

Henley, Nancy M.
    1977   Body Politics: Power, Sex and Nonverbal Communication. Engle-
    wood Cliffs, New Jersey: Prentice-Hall.

Hennig, Margaret
    1970   "Career development for women executives." Unpublished doctoral
    dissertation, Harvard Business School.

Henning, Jenny et al.
    1977   "Women's progress in the corporate world." New York Times,
    Financial Section. June 28: 1–2.

Henshel, Anne-Marie
    1973   Sex Structure. Don Mills, Ontario: Longmans Canada.

Herberg, Will
    1953   "The old-timers and newcomers: Ethnic group relations in a needle
    trades union." Journal of Social Issues 9: 12–19.

Hess, Robert D. and Gerald Handel
    1959   Family Worlds: A Psychosocial Approach to Family Life. Chicago:
    University of Chicago Press.

Hesselbart, Susan
    1978   "Some underemphasized issues about men, women and work." Pa-
    per presented at the annual meeting of the American Sociological Associa-
    tion, San Francisco.

Hetzler, Stanley A.
    1955   "Variations in role-playing patterns among different echelons of bu-
    reaucratic leaders." American Sociological Review 20: 700–706.

Hiestand, Dale L.
    1967   White Collar Employment for Minorities in New York City. Office
    of Research and Reports, Equal Employment Opportunity Commission.
    Washington, D.C.: U.S. Government Printing Office.

Hilaael, Timothy M.
    1975   Job Design in Word Processing/Administrative Support Systems: A
    Research Report on Secretarial Support in the Bell System. Vol. 46, May.

Hill, Herbert
    1963   Congressional Record. January 31: 1569–1572.
    1967   "The racial practices of organized labor." Pp. 365–402. in A.M.
    Ross and Herbert Hill (eds.), Employment, Race, and Poverty. New York:
    Harcourt, Brace and World.
    1973   "Anti-oriental agitation and the rise of working-class racism." Soci-
    ety 10: 43–54.

Hill, Joseph A.
    1929   Women in Gainful Occupations: 1870–1920. Pp. 75–76, Census
    Monograph IX. Washington, D.C.: Government Printing Office.

Himes, Norman E.
    1970   (1936) Medical History of Contraception. New York: Schocken.

Hirshman, Lynette
    1973   "Female-male differences in conversational interaction." Paper presented at the Linguistic Society of America.
    1974   "Analysis of supportive and assertive behavior in conversations." Paper presented at the Linguistic Society of America.

Hochschild, Arlie
    1971   "Inside the clockwork of male careers." Pp. 47–80 in Florence Howe (ed.), Women and the Power to Change. New York: McGraw-Hill.
    1975   "Sociology of feeling and emotion: Selected possibilities." Pp. 280–307 in M. Millman and R. Kanter (eds.), Another Voice: Feminist Perspectives on Social Life and Social Science. New York: Doubleday.

Hoffman, Lois W. and F. Ivan Nye (eds.)
    1974   Working Mothers. San Francisco: Jossey-Bass.

Holcombe, Lee
    1973   Victorian Ladies at Work. Hamden, Connecticut: Shoe String.

Hollander, E.P.
    1958   "Conformity, status and idiosyncracy credit." Psychological Review 65: 17–27.

Holmstrom, Lynda L.
    1972   The Two-Career Family. Cambridge, Massachusetts: Schenkman.

Homall, Geraldine
    1974   "The motivation to be promoted among non-exempt employees: An expectancy theory approach." Unpublished M.S. thesis, Cornell University.

Hoos, Ida R.
    1962   "When the computer takes over the office." Pp. 72–82 in Sigmund Nosow and William Form (eds.), Man, Work and Society. New York: Basic Books.

Horner, Matina S.
    1970   "Femininity and successful achievement: A basic inconsistency." Pp. 45–74 in Judith M. Barwick et al. (eds.), Feminine Personality and Conflict. Belmont, California: Brooks/Cole.
    1972   "Toward an understanding of achievement-related conflicts in women." Journal of Social Issues 28: 157–175.

Howell, Mary
    1973a   "Employed mothers and their families (I)." Pediatrics 52: 252–263.
    1973b   "Effects of maternal employment on the child (II)." Pediatrics 52: 327–343.

Hsu, F.L.K.
    1974   Iemoto: Heart of Japan. Cambridge, Massachusetts: Schenkman.

Hughes, Everett C.
    1945   "Dilemmas and contradictions of status." American Journal of Sociology 50: 353–359.

1959   Men and Their Work. Chicago: University of Chicago Press.
1963   "Professions." Daedalus 92: 655–668.

Humphrey, Heman
1840   Domestic Education. Amherst.

Hunkins, Linda S.
1973   "Status of transit user groups and transportation planning." Unpublished paper, Princeton University.

Hunt, Janet G. and Larry L. Hunt
1977   "Dilemmas and contradictions of status: The case of the dual-career family." Social Problems 24: 407–416.

Hurwitz, Jacob I., Alvin F. Zander and Bernard Hymovich
1968   "Some effects of power on the relations among group members." Pp. 291–297. in D. Cartwright and A. Zander (eds.), Group Dynamics. New York: Harper & Row.

Ichibangasa, Yasuko et al. (eds.)
1973   Problems Faced by Female Teachers. Tokyo: Daiichi Hoki.

Illich, Ivan
1971   Deschooling Society. New York: Harper & Row.

International Labour Review
1960   "Effects of mechanization and automation in offices." Parts I, II, III. International Labour Review 81: (February, March, April). February, pp. 154–173; March, pp. 255–273; April, pp. 350–369.

Israel, J.
1971   Alienation: From Marx to Modern Sociology. Boston: Allyn and Bacon.

Jackall, Robert
1978   Workers in a Labyrinth: Job and Surivival in a Bank Bureaucracy. Montclair, New Jersey: Universe Books.

Japan Census Bureau
1951–1976   Japanese Census. Tokyo: Printing Office

Johnston, Ruth
1975   "Pay and job satisfaction: A survey of some research findings." International Labour Review 3: 441–449.

Jones, Elise and Charles Westoff
1973   "Changes in attitudes towards abortion." Pp. 468–481 in Howard J. Osofsky and Joy D. Osofsky (eds.), The Abortion Experience. New York: Harper & Row.

Jong, Erica
1973   Fear of Flying. New York: New American Library.

Jusenius, Carol L.
1976   "Economics" (review essay). Signs 2: 177–189.

Kamerman, Sheila and Alfred Kahn
1979   "The day-care debate." The Public Interest 54: 79–93.

Kanter, Rosabeth Moss
  1968   "Commitment and social organization: A study of commitment mechanisms in utopian communities." American Sociological Review 33: 499–517.
  1975a   "The problems of tokenism." Working Paper, Center for Research on Women in Higher Education and the Professions, Wellesley College.
  1975b   "Women and the structure of organizations: Explorations in theory and behavior." Pp. 34–74 in M. Millman and R.M. Kanter (eds.), Another Voice: Feminist Perspectives on Social Life and Social Science. New York: Doubleday.
  1976   "Comment VI: Research styles and intervention strategies: An argument for a social structural model." Signs 2: 282–291.
  1977a   "Some effects of proportions on group life: Skewed sex ratios and responses to token women." American Journal of Sociology 82: 965–999.
  1977b   Men and Women of the Corporation. New York: Basic Books.
  1977c   "Women in organizations: Sex roles, group dynamics, and change strategies." Pp. 371–386 in A.G. Sargent (ed.), Beyond Sex Roles. St. Paul, Minnesota: West.
  1977d   Work and Family in America: A Critical Review and Agenda for Research and Policy. Social Science Frontiers Monograph Series. New York: Russell Sage Foundation.

Kato, Tomiko
  1971   Transformation of Female Public Servants—From Office Flowers to Experts. Tokyo: Gakuyo Shobo.

Katz, Michael B. (ed.)
  1971   School Reform: Past and Present. Boston: Little, Brown.

Kaufman, J.J., C.J. Schaefer, M.V. Lewis, D.W. Stevens and E. W. House
  1967   The Role of Secondary Schools in the Preparation of Youth for Employment. University Park, Pennsylvania: Institute for Research on Human Resources, University of Pennsylvania.

Kessler-Harris, Alice
  1973   "Notes on women in advanced capitalism." Social Policy 4: 16–22.
  1981   Women Have Always Worked: A Historical Overview. Old Westbury, New York: Feminist Press.

Kirk, Dudley
  1968   "Population: The field of demography." Pp. 342–349 in David L. Sills (ed.), International Encyclopedia of the Social Sciences 12. New York: Macmillan and the Free Press.

Knudsen, Dean D.
  1969   "The declining status of women: Popular myths and the failure of functionalist thought." Social Forces 48: 183–193.

Kohn, Melvin L.
  1976   "Occupational structure and alienation." American Journal of Sociology 82: 111–130.
  1977   Class and Conformity: A Study in Values, with a Reassessment. Chicago: University of Chicago Press.

Kohn, Melvin L. and Carmi Schooler
    1978   "The reciprocal effects of the substantive complexity of work and intellectual flexibility: A longitudinal assessment." American Journal of Sociology 84: 24–52.

Komarovsky, Mirra
    1946   "Cultural contradictions and sex roles." American Journal of Sociology 52: 184–189.
    1973   "Cultural contradictions and sex roles: The masculine case." American Journal of Sociology 78: 873–885.

Korda, Michael
    1973   Male Chauvinism: How It Works. New York: Random House.

Kornblum, William
    1974   Blue Collar Community. Chicago: University of Chicago Press.

Kornhauser, Arthur
    1965   Mental Health of the Industrial Worker. New York: Wiley.

Kosa, John and Robert Coker, Jr.
    1965   "The female physician in public health: Conflict and reconciliaiton of the sex and professional roles." Sociology and Social Research 49: 294–305.

Kraft, Phil
    1975   "Deskilling work: The case of computer programmers." Paper presented at seminar for Political Economy Colloqium, Department of Sociology, Boston University.

Krantz, Harry
    1977   "The current status of disparate impact." Paper presented at the third annual meeting of the American Association of Affirmative Action. Washington, D.C. (Spring), and personal communication.

Kreps, Juanita
    1971   Sex in the Market Place: American Women at Work. Baltimore: Johns Hopkins University Press.

Laird, Donald A. and Eleanor C. Laird
    1942   The Psychology of Supervising the Working Woman. New York: McGraw-Hill.

Lakoff, Robin
    1975   Language and Woman's Place. New York: Anchor Press.

Lambeth, Edmund B.
    1967   "COMSAT, Ma Bell and ETV." The Nation (January 23): 109–112.

Lamphere, Louise
    1973   "Women's work, alienation and class consciousness." Paper presented at the 72nd annual meeting of the American Anthropological Association, New Orleans.

Land, Kenneth and Fred Pampel
    1980   "Aggregate male and female labor force participation functions: An

analysis of structural differences, 1947–1977." Social Science Research 9: 37–54.

Langer, Elinor
1972   "Inside the New York Telephone Company." Pp. 307–360 in W.L. O'Neill (ed.), Women at Work. New York: Quadrangle.

Langlois, Eleanor and Andrew Collver
1962   "The female labor force in metropolitan areas: An international comparison." Economic Development and Cultural Change 4: 367–385.

Lapidus, Gail Warshofsky
1978   Women in Soviet Society. Berkeley: University of California Press.

LaPiere, Richard T.
1934   "Attitudes vs. actions." Social Forces 13: 230–237.

Lasch, Christopher
1977   Haven in a Heartless World. New York: Basic Books.

Laser Focus
1978   The magazine of lasers and related technologies. Advanced Technology Publications, January.

Laslett, Barbara
1973   "The family as a public and private institution: An historical perspective." Journal of Marriage and the Family 35: 480–494.

Laws, Judith Long
1976a   (1971) "The Bell telephone system: A case study." Pp. 157–178 in Phyllis Wallace (ed.), Equal Employment Opportunity and the AT&T Case. Cambridge, Massachusetts: MIT Press. Original testimony presented in 1971: "Causes and effects of sex discrimination in the Bell system." Expert Witness Testimony, EEOC Exhibit #4, Docket #19143, filed before the Federal Communications Commission. Washington, D.C.: U.S. Government Printing Office.
1976b   "Psychological dimensions of labor force participation of women." Pp. 125–156 in Phyllis Wallace (ed.), Equal Employment Opportunity and the AT&T Case. Cambridge, Massachusetts: MIT Press.
1976c   "Work aspirations of women: False leads and new starts." Signs 1: 33-50.
1978   "Feminism and patriarchy: Competing ways of doing social science." Paper presented at the annual meeting of the American Sociological Association, San Francisco.

Lazonick, William
1978   "Subjection of labor to capital: The rise of the capitalist system." Review of Radical Political Economy 10: 1–31.

Lebra, Joyce et al.
1976   Women in Changing Japan. Boulder, Colorado: Westview Press.

Leghorn, Lisa and Mary Roodkowsky
1977   Who Really Starves? Women and World Hunger. New York: Friendship Press.

Lein, Laura et al.
    1974   "Work and family life." Report to the National Institute of Education, Center for the Study of Public Policy, Cambridge, Massachusetts.

Lemons, J. Stanley
    1973   The Woman Citizen: Social Feminism in the 1920s. Urbana: University of Illinois Press.

Lenski, Gerhard and Jean Lenski
    1973   Human Societies. 2nd ed. New York: McGraw-Hill.

Levenson, Bernard
    1961   "Bureaucratic succession." Pp. 362–375 in A. Etizioni (ed.), Complex Organizations: A Sociological Reader. New York: Holt, Rinehart & Winston.

Levitin, Teresa, Robert P. Quinn and Graham Staines
    1971   "Sex discrimination against the American working woman." American Behavioral Scientist 15: 79–96.

Liebow, Elliot
    1967   Tally's Corner. Boston: Little, Brown.

Lirtzman, Sidney I. and Mahmoud A. Wahba
    1972   "Determinants of coalitional behavior of men and women: Sex roles or situational requirements?" Journal of Applied Psychology 56: 406–411.

Lloyd, Cynthia B. and Beth T. Niemi
    1975   Sex Discrimination and the Division of Labor. New York: Columbia University Press.
    1980   The Economics of Sex Differentials. New York: Columbia University Press.

Lockwood, David
    1958   Black-Coated Workers. London: Unwin University Books, Allen & Unwin.

Loewenberg, Joern J.
    1962   "Effects of change on employee relations in the telephone industry." Unpublished doctoral dissertation, Harvard University.

Long, Clarence D.
    1960   Wages and earnings in the United States, 1860–1890. Princeton, New Jersey: Princeton University Press.

Lopata, Helena Znaniecki
    1971   Occupation: Housewife. New York: Oxford University Press.
    1980   "The Chicago woman: A study of patterns of mobility and transportation." Signs 5(3) (spring), supplement: 161–169.

Lopate, Carole
    1968   Women in Medicine. Baltimore: Johns Hopkins University Press.

Lorber, Judith
    1975   "Beyond equality of the sexes: The question of the children." The Family Coordinator 24: 465–472.

Lublin, Jo Ann S.
1980   The Wall Street Journal (January, 14).

Lydall, Harold
1968   The Structure of Earnings. London: Oxford at the Clarendon Press.

Lynn, David B.
1961   "Sex differences in identification development." Sociometry 24:
372–383.

Maccoby, Eleanor E.
1963   "Women's intellect." Pp. 24–38 in S.M. Farber and R.H.L. Wilson
(eds.), The Potential of Women. New York: McGraw-Hill.

Maccoby, Eleanor E. and Carol N. Jacklin
1974   The Psychology of Sex Differences. Stanford, California: Stanford
University Press.

Madigan, Francis S.J.
1957   "Are sex mortality differentials biologically caused?" Milbank Me-
morial Fund Quarterly 35: 203–223.

Mahoney, T.
1961   "Factors determining the labor force participation of married
women." Industrial and Labor Relations Review 14: 563–577.

Mannes, Marya
1963   "The problems of creative women." Pp. 116–130 in Seymour M.
Farber and Roger H.L. Wilson (ed.), The Potential of Women. New York:
McGraw-Hill.

Manpower Report of the President
1975   Washington, D.C.: U.S. Government Printing Office.

Marcus, Phillip M. and James S. House
1973   "Exchange between superiors and subordinates in large organizations." Administrative Science Quarterly 18: 209–222.

Marglin, Stephen
1974   "What do bosses do? The origins and functions of hierarchy in capitalist production." Review of Radical Political Economics 6: 60–112.

Margolis, Diane Rothbard
1979   "The invisible hands: Sex roles and the division of labor in two local
political parties." Social Problems 26: 524–538.

Marshall, Ray
1974   "The economics of racial discrimination: A survey." Journal of Economic Literature 12: 849–871.

Martin, Walter T. and Dudley L. Poston
1972   "The occupational composition of white females: Sexism, racism,
and occupational differentiation." Social Forces 50: 349–355.

Mason, Karen Oppenheim and Larry Bumpass
1975   "U.S. women's sex-role ideology, 1970." American Journal of Sociology 80: 1212–1219.

Mason, Karen Oppenheim, John Czajka and Sara Arber
1975   "Change in U.S. women's sex-role attitudes, 1964–1974." Unpublished paper.

Matejko, Alexander
1974   Social Change and Stratification in Eastern Europe. New York: Praeger.

Mather, Cotton
1692   Ornaments for the Daughters of Zion. Boston.

Mayer, Kurt B. and Sidney Goldstein
1964   "Manual workers as small businessmen." Pp. 537–550 in A. Shostak and W. Gomberg (eds.), Blue Collar World. Englewood Cliffs, New Jersey: Prentice-Hall.

McLaughlin, Virginia Yans
1971   "Patterns of work and family organization: Buffalo's Italians." Journal of Interdisciplinary History 2: 229–314.

Mead, Margaret
1949   Male and Female. New York: Morrow.

Meissner, Martin
1971   "The long arm of the job: A study of work and leisure." Industrial Relations 10: 239–260.

Meissner, Martin, Elizabeth Humphreys, Scott Meis and William Scheu
1975   "No exit for wives: Sexual division of labor and the cumulation of household demands." Canadian Review of Sociology and Anthropology 12: 424–439.

Melman, Seymour
1951   "The rise of administrative overhead in manufacturing industries of the United States." Oxford Economic Papers (N.S.) 3: 62–112.

Mensel, Herbert
1957   "Public and private conformity under different conditions of acceptance in the group." Journal of Abnormal and Social Psychology 55: 398–402.

Merton, Robert K.
1957   "Introduction." Pp. 105–107 in Robert K. Merton, G. Reader, and P.L. Kendall (eds.), The Student Physician. Cambridge, Massachusetts: Harvard University Press.
1959   "Conformity, deviation and opportunity structures." American Sociological Review 24: 177–188.
1968   (1949) Social Theory and Social Structure. New York: Free Press.
1973   "Social theory and social structure." Pp. 439–459 in Norman W. Storer (ed.), The Sociology of Science. Chicago: University of Chicago Press.

Milkman, Ruth
1976   "Women's work and the economic crisis: Some lessons from the great depression." Review of Radical Political Economy (Summer): 73–97.

1980 "Organizing the sexual division of labor." Socialist Review 10: 95–150.

Miller, Casey and Kate Swift
1976 Words and Women. New York: Anchor Press.

Miller, Daniel R. and Guy E. Swanson
1958 The Changing American Parent. New York: Wiley.

Miller, Margaret and Helene Linker
1974 "Equal rights amendment campaigns." Society 11: 40–53.

Miller, S.M.
1971 "On men: The making of a confused middle-class husband." Social Policy 2: 33–38.
1972 "The making of a confused middle-aged husband." Pp. 245–253 in C. Safilios-Rothschild (ed.), Toward a Sociology of Women. Lexington, Massachusetts: Xerox College Publishing.

Millman, Marcia and Rosabeth Moss Kanter (eds.)
1975 Another Voice: Feminist Perspectives on Social Life and Social Science. New York: Doubleday.

Mills, C. Wright
1956 White Collar. New York: Oxford University Press.
1959 The Sociological Imagination. London: Oxford University Press.

Mincer, Jacob
1962 "Labor force participation of married women." Pp. 63–97 in National Bureau of Economic Research, Aspects of Labor Economics. Princeton, New Jersey: Princeton University Press.

Ministry of Education
1972 Women and Education in Japan. Tokyo: Government Printing Office.

Ministry of Labor
1972 The Status of Female Workers in Japan. Tokyo: Ministry of Labor Printing Office.

Mitchell, John
1973 (1903) Organized Labor. Clifton, New Jersey: Kelley.

Moore, Kristin A. and Isabel V. Sawhill
1978 "Implications of women's employment for home and family life." Pp. 201–225 in Ann H. Stromberg and Shirley Harkess (eds.), Women Working: Theories and Facts in Perspective. Palo Alto, California: Mayfield.

Moore, Wilbert E.
1951 Industrial Relations and the Social Order. Rev. ed. New York: Macmillan.
1964 The Impact of Industry. Englewood Cliffs, New Jersey: Prentice-Hall.

Moore, Wilbert E. and Arnold Feldman (eds.)
1960 Labor Commitment and Social Change in Developing Areas. New York: Social Science Research Council.

Morgan, Edmund S.
1944 The Puritan Family: Religion and Domestic Relations in Seventeenth Century New England. New York: Harper & Row.

Mortimer, Jeylan
1976 "Social class, work and the family: Some implications of the father's occupation for familial relationships and sons' career decisions." Journal of Marriage and the Family 38: 241–256.

Mortimer, Jeylan, Richard Hall and Reuben Hill
1976 "Husbands' occupational attributes as constraints on wives' employment." Paper presented at the annual meeting of the American Sociological Association, New York.

Mouer, Elizabeth Knipe
1976 "Women in teaching." Pp. 157–190 in Joyce Lebra et al. (eds.), Women in Changing Japan. Boulder, Colorado: Westview Press.

Mussen, Paul H.
1969 "Early sex-role development." Pp. 707–729 in David A. Goslin (ed.), Handbook of Socialization Theory and Research. Chicago: Rand McNally.

Myers, George
1964 "Labor force participation of suburban mothers." Journal of Marriage and the Family 26: 306–311.

Nadelson, Carol C. and T. Nadelson
1980 "Dual-career marriages: Benefits and costs." Pp. 91–109 in F. Pepitone-Rockwell (ed.), Dual-Career Couples. Beverly Hills, California: Sage.

Nadelson, Carol and Malka Notman
1974 "Success or failure: Women as medical school applicants." Journal of the American Medical Women's Association 29: 167–172.

Nakane, Chie
1970 Japanese Society. Berkeley: University of California Press.

National Center for Productivity and Quality of Working Life
1977 Productivity and Job Security: Attrition—Benefits and Problems. Washington, D.C.: U.S. Government Printing Office.

National Manpower Council
1957 Womanpower. New York: Columbia University Press.

New York Times
1974 (September 7)
1979 (October 26)
1979 (December 6)
1980 (January 16)
1980 (May 4): 28
1980 (December 25)

Noble, David
1977 America by Design: Science Technology and the Rise of Corporate Capitalism. New York: Knopf.

Noll, Roger
  1976   "Information, decision making procedures and energy policies."
  American Behavioral Scientist 19: 3.

Norbeck, Edward
  1965   Changing Japan. New York: Holt, Rinehart & Winston.

Norton, Mary Beth
  1980   Liberty's Daughters: The Revolutionary Experience of American
  Women, 1750–1800. Boston: Little, Brown.

Nye, F. Ivan and Lois W. Hoffman
  1963   The Employed Mother in America. Chicago: Rand McNally.

Nygaard, Kristen
  1977   "Trade union participation." Lecture given at the Norwegian Com-
  puting Center and University of Oslo, CREST Conference on Management
  Information System, North Staffjordshire Polytechnic, Stafford, England.

Oakley, Ann
  1974   The Sociology of Housework. New York: Pantheon.
  1976   Woman's Work: The Housewife, Past and Present. New York: Vin-
  tage Books.

Odendahl, Teresa J.
  1978   "Women's Employment." Comment: A research action report on
  women. Washington, D.C. Vol. 11.

Office of Prime Minister
  1974   Status of Women in Modern Japan. Tokyo: Government Printing
  Office.

Ollman, Bertell
  1971   Alienation. London and New York: Cambridge University Press.
Oppenheimer, Valerie K.
  1970   The Female Labor Force in the United States: Demographic and
  Economic Factors Governing its Growth and Changing Composition. Population Monograph, Series 5. Berkeley: University of California Press.
  1973   "Demographic influence on female employment and the status of
  women." American Journal of Sociology 78: 184–199.
  1974   "The life-cycle squeeze: The interaction of men's occupational and
  family life cycles." Demography 11: 227–245.

Orzack, L.
  1959   "Work as a 'central life interest' of professionals." Social Problems
  7: 125–132.

Osako, Masako Murakami
  1977   "Technology and social structure in a Japanese automobile factory." Sociology of Work and Occupations 4: 397–427.
  1981   "Social changes and public policy for the aged in Japan: The effects
  of local political process and women's status on welfare programs." Pp. 85–
  97 in Masako M. Osako and Charlotte Nusberg (eds.), Economic Development and Public Policy for the Aged in Asia. Washington, D.C.: International Federation of Aging.

Ossowski, Stanislaw
    1963   Class Structure in the Social Consciousness. New York: Free Press of Glencoe.

Ota, Paula
    1980   "Negotiating motherhood." Unpublished doctoral dissertation, University of Southern California.

Papanek, Hanna
    1973   "Men, women, and work: Reflections on the two-person career." Pp. 90–110 in Joan Huber (ed.), Changing Women in a Changing Society. Chicago: University of Chicago Press.
    1979   "Family status production: The 'work' and 'non-work' of women." Signs 4: 775–781.

Parnes, Herbert, Carol Jusenius and Richard Shortlidge, Jr.
    1975   Dual Careers. Washington, D.C.: U.S. Department of Labor, U.S. Government Printing Office.

Parsons, Talcott
    1937   The Structure of Social Action. New York: The Free Press of Glencoe.
    1942   "Age and sex in the social structure of the United States." American Sociological Review 7: 604–616.
    1949   "The social structure of the family." Pp. 173–201 in Ruth Anshen (ed.), The Family: Its Functions and Destiny. New York: Harper & Row.
    1951   The Social system. Glencoe, Illinois: Free Press.

Parsons, Talcott et al.
    1955   Family: Socialization and Interaction Process. New York: Free Press.

Paulson, Joy
    1976   "Women in media." Pp. 209–232 in Joyce Lebra et al. (eds.), Women in Changing Japan. Boulder, Colorado: Westview Press.

Pavalko, Ronald
    1971   The Sociology of Occupations and Professions. Itasca, Illinois: Peacock.

Pearce, Diana
    1979   "Women, work, and welfare: The feminization of poverty." Pp. 103–124 in Karen Wolk Feinstein (ed.), Working Women and Families. Beverly Hills, California: Sage.

Pearlin, L.I.
    1962   "Alienation from work: A study of nursing personnel." American Sociological Review 27: 314–326.
    1974   Class Context and Family Relations. Boston: Little, Brown.

Pelz, Donald C.
    1952   "Influence: A key to effective leadership in the first-line supervisor." Personnel 29: 3–11.

Pennings, J.M.
    1970   "Work-value systems of white-collar workers." Administrative Science Quarterly 15: 397–405.

Perlman, Nancy D. and Bruce J. Ennis
  1980   "Preliminary memorandum on pay equity: Achieving equal pay for work of comparable value." Center for Women in Government, SUNYA, Draper Hall, Room 302, 1400 Washington Avenue, Albany, New York 12222 (April).

Pidgeon, Mary Elizabeth
  1937   Women in the Economy of the United States of America: A Summary Report. Washington, D.C.: U.S. Government Printing Office.

Pinchbeck, Ivy
  1930   Women Workers in the Industrial Revolution, 1750–1850. New York: G. Routledge.

Piotrokowski, Chaya S.
  1980   Work and the Family System. New York: Free Press.

Plath, David
  1980   Long Engagements: Maturity in Modern Japan. Stanford: Stanford University Press.

Pleck, Joseph H.
  1979   "Men's family work: Three perspectives and some new data." Wellesley, Massachusetts: Wellesley College Center for Research on Women.

Pleck, Joseph H. and Elizabeth H. Pleck
  1980   The American Man. Englewood Cliffs, New Jersey: Prentice-Hall.

Pleck, Joseph and Jack Sawyer
  1974   Men and Masculinity. Englewood Cliffs, New Jersey: Prentice-Hall.

Plumb, J.H.
  1974   "The great change in children." Pp. 338–346 in A. Skolnick and J.H. Skolnick (eds.), Intimacy, Family, and Society. Boston: Little, Brown.

Poloma, Margaret M.
  1972   "Role conflict and the married professional woman." Pp. 187–198 in C. Safilios-Rothschild (ed.), Toward a Sociology of Women. Lexington, Massachusetts: Xerox College Publishing.

Poloma, Margaret M. and Neal Garland
  1971   "The myth of the egalitarian family: Familial roles and the professionally employed wife." Pp. 741–761 in Athena Theodore (ed.), The Professional Woman. Cambridge, Massachusetts: Schenkman.

Prather, Jane
  1971a   "Why can't women be more like men?" American Behavioral Scientist 15: 172–182.
  1971b   "When the girls move in: A sociological analysis of the feminization of the bank teller's job." Journal of Marriage and the Family 33: 777–782.

Preston, Samuel H.
  1975   "Estimating the proportion of American marriages that end in divorce." Sociological Methods and Research 3: 435–459.

Preston, Samuel H. and Alan Thomas Richards
  1975   "The influence of women's work opportunities on marriage rates."
  Demography 12: 209–222.

Psathas, G.
  1968   "Toward a theory of occupational choice for women." Sociology
  and Social Research 52: 253–268.

Purcell, Theodore V.
  1960   Blue Collar Man: Patterns of Dual Allegiance in Industry. Cambridge, Massachusetts: Harvard University Press.

Purnell, R.F. and G.S. Lesser
  1969   Work-Bound and College-Bound Youth: A Study in Stereotypes.
  Cambridge, Massuchusetts: Laboratory of Human Development, Harvard
  University.

Putney, Snell
  1972   The Conquest of Society. Belmont, California: Wadsworth.

Pyun, Chong Soo
  1969   "The monetary value of a housewife: An economic analysis for use
  in litigation." American Journal of Economics and Sociology 28: 271–284.

Quadagno, Jill
  1976   "Occupational sex-typing and internal labor market distributions:
  An assessment of medical specialties." Social Problems 23: 442–453.

Raphael, Edna
  1974   "Working women and their membership in labor unions." Monthly
  Labor Review 97: 27–33.

Rapoport, Rhona and Robert Rapoport
  1969   "The dual-career family: A variant pattern and social change." Human Relations 22: 2–30.
  1971a   "Further considerations on the dual career family." Human Relations 24: 519–533.
  1971b   Dual Career Families. London and Baltimore: Penguin Books.
  1972   "The working woman and the enabling role of the husband." Paper
  presented at the XIIth International Family Research Seminar, International
  Sociological Association, Moscow.
  1976   Dual-Career Families Reexamined: New Integrations of Work and
  Family. New York: Harper & Row.

Rapoport, Robert and Rhona Rapoport
  1965   "Work and family in modern society." American Sociological Review 30: 381–394.

Record, Jane Cassels and Wilson Record
  1976   "Totalist and pluralist views of women's liberation: Some reflections
  on the Chinese and American settings." Social Problems 23: 402–414.

Reed, E.D.
  1971   "Lasers in the Bell System." Bell Labs Record (October): 263–269.

Reich, Michael, David M. Gordon and Richard C. Edwards
    1973   "A theory of labor market segmentation." American Economic Review 63: 359–365.

Reischauer, Edwin O.
    1974   Japan, History of a Nation, rev. ed. New York: Knopf.

Reischauer, Robert
    1977   We, the Japanese. Cambridge, Massachusetts: Harvard University Press.

Reiter, Rayna R.
    1975   Toward an Anthropology of Women. New York: Monthly Review Press.

Richards, F.S.
    1951   The Ready-to-Wear Industry, 1900–1950. New York: Fairchild.

Richardson, Dorothy
    1972   "The long day." Pp. 3–303 in William O'Neill (ed.), Women at Work. New York: Quadrangle Press.

Rico, Leonard
    1967   The Advance against Paperwork. Ann Arbor, University of Michigan: Michigan Graduate School of Business Administration.

Robinson, John
    1980   "Housework technology and household work." Pp. 53–67 in Sarah Fenstermaker Berk (ed.), Women and Household Labor. Beverly Hills, California: Sage.

Robinson, John, Thomas Juster and Frank Stafford
    1976   America's Use of Time. Ann Arbor, Michigan: Institute for Social Research.

Robinson, John, Janet Yerby, Margaret Feiweger and Nancy Sommerick
    1976   "Time use as an indicator of sex role territoriality." Unpublished paper.

Roby, Pamela
    1975   "Sociology and women in working-class jobs." Pp. 203–239 in M. Millman and R.M. Kanter (eds.), Another Voice: Feminist Perspectives on Social Life and Social Science. New York: Doubleday.

Roemer, J.E.
    1978   "Differentially exploited labor: A Marxian theory of exploitation." Review of Radical Political Economy 10: 43–54.

Roethlisberger, F.J. and William J. Dickson
    1939   Management and the Worker. Cambridge, Massachusetts: Harvard University Press.

Rosen, Benson and Thomas H. Jerdee
    1973   "The influence of sex-role stereotypes on evaluations of male and female supervisory behavior." Journal of Applied Psychology 5: 44–48.

Rosenberg, Florence R. and Roberta G. Simmons
1975   "Sex differences in the self-concept in adolescence." Sex Roles 1: 147–160.

Rosenfeld, C. and V.C. Perrella
1965   "Study in mobility." Monthly Labor Review 88: 1077–1082.

Rosenthal, Robert and Lenore Jacobson
1968   Pygmalion in the Classroom: Teacher Expectation and Pupils' Intellectual Development. New York: Holt, Rinehart & Winston.

Ross, Heather L. and Isabel V. Sawhill
1975   Time of Transition: The Growth of Families Headed by Women. Washington, D.C.: Urban Institute.

Rossi, Alice S.
1964   "Equality between the sexes: An immodest proposal." Daedalus 93: 607–652.
1965   "Women in science: Why so few?" Science 148: 1196–1202.
1973   The Feminist Papers. New York: Columbia University Press.

Rossi, Alice S. and Ann Calderwood (eds.)
1973   Academic Women on the Move. New York: Russell Sage Foundation.

Rotella, Elyce
1974   "Occupational segregation and the supply of women to the American clerical labor force, 1870–1930." Paper presented at the Berkshire Conference on the History of Women, Radcliffe College, Cambridge, Massachusetts.

Rousell, Cecile
1974   "Relationship of sex of department head to department climate." Administrative Science Quarterly 19: 211–220.

Rowbotham, Sheila
1972   Women, Revolution and Resistance: A History of Women and Revolution in the Modern World. New York: Pantheon Books.
1974   Hidden from History. New York: Random House.

Rowe, Mary P.
1977   "The Saturn's rings phenomenon: Micro-inequities and unequal opportunity in the American economy." Proceedings of the Conference on Women's Leadership and Authority in the Health Professions. Department of Health, Education and Welfare, Health Resources Administration, Office of Health Resources Opportunity. Washington, D.C.: U.S. Government Printing Office.

Rubin, Lillian
1976   Worlds of Pain: Life in the Working-Class Family. New York: Basic Books.

Rushing, William A.
1967   "The effects of industry size and division of labor on administration." Administrative Science Quarterly 12: 273–295.

Ryan, Mary P.
    1975   Womanhood in America: From Colonial Times to the Present. New York: Franklin Watts.

Ryan, William
    1972   Blaming the Victim. New York: Vintage.

Ryder, Norman B.
    1973   "Two cheers for ZPG." Daedalus 102: 45–62.
    1975   "Notes on stationary populations." Population Index 41: 3–28.

Sacks, Harvey
    1972   "On the analyzability of stories by children." Pp. 325–345 in John Gumperz and Dell Hymes (eds.), Directions in Sociolinguistics: The Ethnography of Communication. New York: Holt, Rinehart & Winston.

Sacks, Harvey, Emmanuel Schegloff and Gail Jefferson
    1974   "A simplest systematics for the organization of turn-taking for conversation." Language 50: 696–735.

Sacks, Michael Paul
    1975   "Unchanging times: A comparison of the everyday life of Soviet working men and women between 1923 and 1966." Paper presented at the annual meeting of the American Sociological Association.
    1976   Women's Work in Soviet Russia. New York: Praeger.

Safilios-Rothschild, Constantina
    1970   "The study of family power structure: A review, 1960–1969." Journal of Marriage and the Family 32: 539–552.
    1974   Women and Social Policy. Englewood Cliffs, New Jersey: Prentice-Hall.
    1976   "Dual linkages between the occupational and family systems: A macrosociological analysis." Signs 1: 51–60.

Sauvy, Alfred
    1961   Fertility and Survival. London: Chatto and Windus.

Sawhill, Isabel V.
    1973   "The economics of discrimination against women: Some new findings." Journal of Human Resources 8: 383–396.

Scanzoni, John
    1965   "Resolution of occupational-conjugal role conflict in clergy marriages." Journal of Marriage and the Family 27: 396–402.
    1970   Opportunity and the Family. New York: Free Press.

Schegloff, Emmanuel
    1972   "Sequencing in conversational openings." Pp. 346–380 in John Gumperz and Dell Hymes (eds.), Directions in Sociolinguistics: The Ethnography of Communication. New York: Holt, Rinehart & Winston.

Schegloff, Emmanuel and Harvey Sacks
    1974   "Opening up closings." Pp. 197–215 in Roy Turner (ed.), Ethnomethodology. Middlesex, England: Penguin Education.

Science for the People
 1974   China: Science Walks on Two Legs. New York: Avon Books.

Scott, Hilda
 1974   Does Socialism Liberate Women? Boston: Beacon.

Scott, Joan and Louise Tilly
 1975   "Women's work and the family in nineteenth century Europe." Comparative Studies in Society and History 17: 36–64.

Seeman, M.
 1967   "On the personal consequences of alienation in work." American Sociological Review 32: 273–285.
 1975   "Alienation studies." Annual Review of Sociology 1: 91–123.

Sennett, Richard and Jonathan Cobb
 1972   The Hidden Injuries of Class. New York: Random House.

Shepard, Jon M.
 1971   Automation and Alienation: A Study of Office and Factory Workers. Cambridge, Massachusetts: MIT Press.
 1973   "Technology, division of labor and alienation." Pacific Sociological Review 16: 61–88.

Shepard, William G.
 1971   "The competitive margin in communications." Pp. 86–122 in William M. Capron (ed.), Technological Change in Regulated Industries. Washington, D.C.: The Brookings Institution.

Sieber, Sam D.
 1974   "Towards a Theory of Role Accumulation." American Sociological Review 39: 567–578.

Siegel, Paul M.
 1965   "On the cost of being a Negro." Sociological Inquiry 35: 41–57.

Signs, A Journal of Women in Culture and Society
 1976   Vol. 1, No. 3, Part 2: "Women and the Workplace."
 1977   Vol. 3, No. 1: "Women and Development."

Sikula, Andrew F.
 1973   "The uniqueness of secretaries as employees." Journal of Business Education 48: 203–205.

Silberman, Charles E.
 1967   "The little bird that casts a big shadow." Fortune (February): 108 ff.

Silverstone, Rosalie and Audrey Ward (eds.)
 1980   Careers of Professional Women. London: Croom Helm.

Simpson, Richard L. and Ida Harper Simpson
 1969   "Women and bureaucracy in the semi-professions." Pp. 196–265 in Amitai Etzioni (ed.), The Semi-Professions and Their Organization. New York: Free Press.

Sklar, Kathryn Kish
    1973   Catharine Beecher: A Study in American Domesticity. New Haven,
    Connecticut: Yale University Press.

Skolnick, Arlene
    1978   The Intimate Environment: Exploring Marriage and the Family.
    Boston: Little, Brown.

Slater, Philip
    1974a   Earthwalk. Garden City, New York: Doubleday Anchor.
    1974b   "Social limitation on libidinal withdrawal." Pp. 111–133 in Rose
    Laub Coser (ed.), The Family, Its Structures and Functions. New York: St.
    Martin's Press.

Smelser, Neil
    1959   Social Change in the Industrial Revolution. Chicago: University of
    Chicago Press.

Smith, Dorothy
    1975–1976   "Women, the family and corporate capitalism." Berkeley
    Journal of Sociology 20: 55–90.

Smith, Ralph E. et al. (eds.)
    1979   The Subtle Revolution: Women at Work. Washington, D.C.: Urban
    Institute.

Smuts, Robert
    1971   (1959) Women and Work in America. New York: Schocken.

Sobol, Marion
    1963   "Commitment to work." Pp. 40–63 in F. Ivan Nye and Louis Hoff-
    man (eds.), The Employed Mother in America. Chicago: Rand McNally.

Soltow, Martha Jane, Carolyn Forché and Murray Massre
    1972   Women in American Labor History, 1825–1935: An Annotated Bib-
    liography. East Lansing, Michigan: Michigan State School of Labor and
    Industrial Relations and Libraries.

Spaeth, Joe L.
    1975   "Differences in the occupational achievement process between male
    and female college graduates." Paper presented at the annual meeting of the
    American Sociological Association.

Spitze, Glenna
    1979   "Work commitment among young women." Unpublished doctoral
    dissertation, University of Illinois at Urbana-Champaign.

Stacey, Judith
    1979   "Toward a theory of family and revolution: Reflections on the
    Chinese case." Social Problems 26: 499–508.

Stein, Barry A.
    1976   "Patterns of managerial promotion." Working Paper, Center for Re-
    search on Women in Higher Education and the Professions, Wellesley Col-
    lege.

Stern, Bernhard J.
    1944   "Women, position in society: Historical." Pp. 442–451 in E.R.A. Seligman (ed.), Encyclopedia of the Social Sciences 15. New York: Macmillan.

Stinchcombe, Arthur
    1965   "Social structure and organizations." Pp. 142–193 in James G. March (ed.), Handbook of Organizations. Chicago: Rand McNally.

Stone, Katherine
    1973   "The origins of job structures in the steel industry." Paper presented at the Conference on Labor Market Segmentation, Harvard University, Cambridge, Massachusetts.

Sullerot, Evelyn
    1971   Woman, Society, and Change. New York: McGraw-Hill.

Suter, Larry and Linda Waite
    1976   "Worker, housewife, mother: Role decisions of young women." Unpublished paper.

Sutton, Edward S.
    1977   "Total human resources development in AT&T." Training and Development Journal 31: 4–5.

Sweet, James
    1973   Women in the Labor Force. New York: Seminar Press.

Syfers, Judith
    1972   "I want a wife." MS (spring) premier issue: 56.

Szalai, Alexander
    1972   The Use of Time. The Hague: Mouton & Co.

Tannenbaum, Arnold S.
    1966   Social Psychology of the Work Organizatin. Belmont, California: Wadsworth.

Tannenbaum, Arnold S. et al.
    1974   Hierarchy in Organizations: An International Comparison. San Francisco: Jossey-Bass.

Tentler, Leslie Woodcock
    1979   Wage Earning Women: Industrial and Family Life in the United States, 1900–1930. New York: Oxford University Press.

Thayer, G.N.
    1968   "BIS in the Bell System." Bell Labs Record (December): 355–361.

Thibaut, John W. and Henry W. Riecken
    1955   "Authoritarianism, status, and the communication of aggression." Human Relations 8: 95–120.

Thorne, Barrie and Nancy M. Henley (eds.)
    1975   Language and Sex: Difference and Dominance. Rowley, Massachusetts: Newbury House.

Thurow, Lester C.
    1972   "Education and economic equality." The Public Interest 28: 66–81.
Thurow, Lester C. and R.E.B. Lucas
    1972   The American Distribution of Income: A Structural Problem. U.S.
            Congress, Joint Economic Committee. 92nd Congress, 2nd Session. Wash-
            ington, D.C.: U.S. Government Printing Office.
Thurston, Donald R.
    1973   Teachers and Politics in Japan. Princeton: Princeton University
            Press.
Tichy, Noel
    1973   "An analysis of clique formation and structure in organizations."
            Administrative Science Quarterly 18: 194–207.
Tietze, Christopher
    1969   "Fertility control." Pp. 382–388 in David Sills (ed.), International
            Encyclopedia of the Social Sciences 5. New York: Macmillan and the Free
            Press.
Tiger, Lionel
    1969   Men in Groups. New York: Random House.
Tilly, Charles
    1978   "Questions and conclusions." Pp. 335–353 in Charles Tilly (ed.),
            Historical Studies of Changing Fertility. Princeton, New Jersey: Princeton
            University Press.
Tilly, Louise
    1975   "Industrialization, the position of women and women's history."
            CRSO Working Paper 118. Ann Arbor: Department of Sociology, Univer-
            sity of Michigan.
Tilly, Louise and Joan W. Scott
    1978   Women, Work and the Family. New York: Holt, Rinehart & Win-
            ston.
Tilly, Louise, Joan W. Scott and Miriam Cohen
    1976   "Women's work and European fertility patterns." Journal of Inter-
            disciplinary History 4: 447–476.
Tolles, Arnold
    1968   "Wages: Wage and hour legislation." Pp. 418–424 in David Sills
            (ed.), International Encyclopedia of the Social Sciences 16. New York: Mac-
            millan and the Free Press.
Tryon, Rolla Milton
    1917   Household Manufactures in the United States, 1640–1860. Chicago:
            University of Chicago Press.
Tsuchigane, Robert and Norton Dodge
    1974   Economic Discrimination Against Women in the United States. Lex-
            ington, Massachusetts: Lexington Books.

Tuchman, Gaye
  1975   "Women and the creation of culture." Pp. 171–202 in M. Millman
          and R.M. Kanter (eds.), Another Voice: Feminist Perspectives in Social Life
          and Social Science. New York: Doubleday.

Uesugi, Thomas K. and W. Edgar Vinacke
  1963   "Strategy in a feminine game." Sociometry 26: 35–88.

United Nations
  1973   The Determinants and Consequences of Population Trends 1. Pop-
          ulation Studies No. 50. New York: Department of Economic and Social
          Affairs.

Urban and Rural Systems Associates/Women's Action Program (HEW)
  1976   An Exploratory Study of Women in the Health Professions Schools.
          Department of Health, Education and Welfare, Office of Special Concerns,
          Women's Action Program, September. Washington, D.C., U.S. Government
          Printing Office.

U.S. Bureau of the Budget, Office of Statistical Standards, Technical Committee on
Industrial Classification
  1957   Standard Industrial Classification Manual. Washington, D.C.: U.S.
          Government Printing Office.

U.S. Bureau of the Census
  1973   "Earnings by occupation and education." Census of Population:
          1970 Subject Reports, Final Reports PC (2)-8B. Washington, D.C.: U.S.
          Government Printing Office.
  1979   "Divorce, child custody, and child support." Current Population Re-
          ports, Series P-23, No. 84. Washington, D.C.: U.S. Government Printing
          Office.

U.S. Civil Service Commission, President's Commission on the Status of Women
  1963   "Report of the Committee on Federal Employment" Appendix F.
          Washington, D.C.: Government Printing Office.

U.S. Department of Labor
  1928   Summary: The Effects of Labor Legislation on the Employment Op-
          portunities of Women. Women's Bureau Bulletin No. 68. Washington,
          D.C.: U.S. Government Printing Office.
  1969   Handbook of Women Workers. Washington, D.C.: U.S. Govern-
          ment Printing Office.
  1974a   "Twenty facts on women workers." Washington, D.C.: U.S. Gov-
          ernment Printing Office.
  1974b   Why Women Work. Women's Bureau, 2. Washington, D.C.: U.S.
          Government Printing Office.

Vanek, Joann
  1974   "Time spent in housework." Scientific American 231: 116–120.
  1980   "Household work, wage work and sexual equality." Pp. 275–291 in
          Sarah Fensternmaker Berk (ed.), Household Labor. Beverly Hills, Calif-
          ornia: Sage Publications.

Vickery, Claire
    1979   "Women's economic contribution to the family." Pp. 159–200 in
            Ralph E. Smith et al. (eds.), The Subtle Revolution: Women at Work.
            Washington, D.C.: Urban Institute.

Vinacke, W. Edgar
    1959   "Sex-roles in a three-person game." Sociometry 22: 343–360.

Vogel, Ezra
    1963   Japan's New Middle Class. Berkeley: University of California Press.
    1971   Japanese Organizations. Berkeley: University of California Press.
    1977   Examination Hell. Berkeley: University of California Press.

Wadsworth, Benjamin
    1712   The Well-Ordered Family. Boston.

Wagatsuma, Hiroshi
    1977   "Some aspects of the contemporary Japanese family: Once Confu-
            cian, now fatherless?" Daedalus 106: 181–210.

Wagley, Charles and Marvin Harris
    1964   Minorities in the New World. New York: Columbia University
            Press.

Waldman, Eleanor and Barbara McEaddy
    1974   "Where women work: An analysis by industry and occupation."
            Monthly Labor Review 95: 3–13.

Walker, Kathryn E.
    1969   "Time spent in household work by homemakers." Family Econom-
            ics Review 3: 5–6.
    1970a   "Time-use patterns for household work related to homemaker's
            employment." Paper presented at the 1970 National Agricultural Outlook
            Conference. Washington, D.C., February 18.
    1970b   "Time spent by husbands in household work." Family Economics
            Review 4: 8–11.
    1974   Unpublished data.

Walker, Kathryn E. and Margaret Woods
    1976   Time Use: A Measure of Household Production of Family Goods
            and Services. Washington, D.C.: American Home Economics Association.

Wall Street Journal
    1978   (December 26)

Wallace, Phyllis (ed.)
    1976   Equal Employment Opportunity and the AT&T Case. Cambridge,
            Massachusetts: MIT Press.

Walshok, Mary L. and Marco G. Walshok
    1978   "The personal and social benefits of paid employment for urban
            women in skilled and semi-skilled occupations." Paper presented at the
            Ninth World Congress of Sociology, Uppsala, Sweden.

Watanabe, Kei
1973   A Woman Reporter's Struggle for Survival. Tokyo: Shufunoto Sei-katsu Sha.

Waters, L.K. and Carrie Wherry Waters
1969   "Correlates of job satisfaction and job dissatisfaction among female clerical workers." Journal of Applied Psychology 53: 388–391.

Weber, Max
1930   (1907) The Protestant Ethic and the Spirit of Capitalism. New York: Scribner.
1969   The Theory of Social and Economic Organization. New York: Free Press.

Weinbaum, Batya
1977   "Redefining the question of revolution." Review of Radical Political Economy 9: 54–78.

Weinbaum, Batya and Amy Bridges
1976   "The other side of the paycheck: Monopoly capital and the structure of consumption." Monthly Review 28: 88–103.

Weiss, Robert
1979   Going It Alone. New York: Basic Books.

Weitzman, Lenore
1975   "Socialization." Pp. 105–144 in Jo Freeman (ed.), Women: A Feminist Perspective. Palo Alto, California: Mayfield.
1979a Biased Textbooks: A Research Perspective. Washington, D.C.: National Foundation for the Improvement of Education.
1979b Sex Role Socialization: A Focus on Women. Palo Alto, California: Mayfield.

Wertheimer, Barbara Mayer
1977   We Were There: The Story of Working Women in America. New York: Pantheon.

West, Candace
1977a "Some interactional issues concerning women's place in the health professions." Proceedings of the Conference on Women's Leadership and Authority in the Health Professions. Washington, D.C.: Department of Health, Education and Welfare, Health Resources Administration, Office of Health Resources Administration, Office of Health Resources Opportunity. Washington, D.C.: U.S. Government Printing Office.
1977b "Against our will: Negotiating interruption in male-female conversation." Paper presented at the New York Academy of Science meeting of Anthropology, Psychology and Linguistic Sections, New York, October 22.

West, Candace and Don H. Zimmerman
1977   "Women's place in everyday talk: Reflections on parent-child interaction." Social Problems 24: 521–529.

Westoff, Charles
1978   "Marriage and fertility in the developed countries." Scientific American: 51–57.

Whiting, Beatrice and Carolyn Pope Edwards
    1973   "A cross-cultural analysis of sex differences in the behavior of chil-
    dren aged three through eleven." Journal of Social Psychology 91: 171–
    188.

Wikler, Norma
    1976   "Sexism in the classroom." Paper presented at the annual meeting
    of the American Sociological Association, New York.

Wild, Ray
    1969   "Job needs, job satisfaction, and job behavior of women manual
    workers." Journal of Applied Psychology 54: 157–162.

Wilensky, Harold L.
    1964   "The professionalization of everyone?" American Journal of Sociol-
    ogy 70: 142–156.
    1968   "Women's work: Economic growth, ideology, structure." Industrial
    Relations 7: 235–248.

Williams, Gregory J.
    1975   "A research note on trends in occupational differentiation by sex."
    Social Problems 22: 543–547.

Williamson, T. and E. Karras
    1970   "Job satisfaction variables among white female clerical workers."
    Journal of Applied Psychology 54: 343–346.

Women's Bureau, City of Tokyo
    1974   The Conditions of Tokyo Women. Tokyo: City of Tokyo, Depart-
    ment of Welfare.

Wood, Ann Douglas
    1973   "The fashionable diseases, women's complaints and their treatment
    in nineteenth century America." Journal of Interdisciplinary History 1: 25–
    52.

Woody, Thomas
    1929   A History of Women's Education in the United States 1. New York:
    Science Press.

Work in America
    1973   A Report of a Special Task Force to the Secretary of Health, Edu-
    cation and Welfare. Washington, D.C. Government Printing Office.

Wrong, Dennis
    1961   "The oversocialized conception of man in modern society." Ameri-
    can Sociological Review 26: 183–193.

Yankelovich, Daniel
    1974   "The meaning of work." Pp. 19–48 in J.M. Rosow (ed.), The
    Worker and the Job. Englewood Cliffs, New Jersey: Prentice-Hall.

Young, Michael and Peter Willmott
    1973   The Symmetrical Family. New York: Pantheon.

Youssef, Nadia Haggag
    1974   Women and Work in Developing Societies. Berkeley: University of California Press.

Zeitlin, Irving M.
    1973   Rethinking Sociology: A Critique of Contemporary Theory. Englewood Cliffs, New Jersey: Prentice-Hall. Pp. 103–138.

Zimmer, Troy
    1975   "Sexism in higher education: A cross-national analysis." Pacific Sociological Review 18: 55–67.

Zimmerman, Don and Candace West
    1975   "Sex roles, interruptions and silences in conversation." Pp. 105–129 in Barrie Thorne and Nancy M. Henley (eds.), Language and Sex: Difference and Dominance. Rowley, Massachusetts: Newbury House.

Acknowledgments

The readings in this book are edited versions of these articles and are used with the permission of the Society for the Study of Social Problems:

Patricia Gerald Bourne and Norma Juliet Wikler, "Commitment and the Cultural Mandate: Women in Medicine," *Social Problems* 25, No. 4 (April, 1978), 430–440.

Rose Laub Coser, "Stay Home Little Sheba: On Placement, Displacement, and Social Change," *Social Problems* 22, No. 4 (April, 1975), 470–479.

Rose Laub Coser and Gerald Rokoff, "Women in the Occupational World: Social Disruption and Conflict," *Social Problems* 18, No. 4 (Spring, 1971), 535–554.

Barbara Epstein, "Industrialization and Femininity: A Case Study of Nineteenth-Century New England," *Social Problems* 23, No. 4 (April, 1976), 389–401.

Roslyn L. Feldberg and Evelyn Nakano Glenn, "Job Versus Gender Models in the Sociology of Work," *Social Problems* 26, No. 5 (June, 1979), 524–538.

Pamela M. Fishman, "Interaction: The Work Women Do," *Social Problems* 25, No. 4 (April, 1978), 397–406.

Evelyn Nakano Glenn and Roslyn L. Feldberg, "Degraded and Deskilled: The Proletarianization of Clerical Work," *Social Problems* 25, No. 1 (October, 1977), 52–64.

Sally L. Hacker, "Sex Stratification, Technology and Organizational Change: A Longitudinal Study of AT&T," *Social Problems* 26, No. 5 (June, 1979), 539–557.

Sally T. Hillsman and Bernard Levenson, "Job Opportunities of Black and White Working-Class Women," *Social Problems* 22, No. 4 (April, 1975), 510–532.

Joan Huber, "Toward a Sociotechnological Theory of the Women's Movement," *Social Problems* 23, No. 4 (April, 1976), 371–388.

Janet G. Hunt and Larry L. Hunt, "Dilemmas and Contradictions of Status: The Case of the Dual-Career Family," *Social Problems* 24, No. 4 (April, 1977), 407–416.

Rosabeth Moss Kanter, "The Impact of Hierarchical Structures on the Work Behavior of Women and Men," *Social Problems* 23, No. 4 (April, 1976), 415–430.

Richard M. Levinson, "Sex Discrimination and Employment Practices: An Experiment with Unconventional Job Inquiries," *Social Problems* 22, No. 4 (April, 1975), 533–542.

Masako Murakami Osako, "Dilemmas of Japanese Professional Women," *Social Problems* 26, No. 1 (October, 1978), 15–25.

Joseph H. Pleck, "The Work-Family Role System," *Social Problems* 24, No. 4 (April, 1977), 417–427.

Norman B. Ryder, "The Future of American Fertility," *Social Problems* 26, No. 3 (February, 1979), 359–370.

Jack W. Sattel, "The Inexpressive Male: Tragedy or Sexual Politics?" *Social Problems* 23, No. 4 (April, 1976), 469–477.

Index